DATE			
JUL 2 1985			
	REFERENCE		

HOCKEY'S 100

HOCKEY'S 100

A Personal Ranking of the Best Players in Hockey History

Stan Fischler
Research Editor: George Hall

BEAUFORT BOOKS, INC.
New York/Toronto

Library of Congress Cataloging in Publication Data

Fischler, Stan.
  Hockey's 100

  1. Hockey players—Rating of. 2. Hockey—Records.
I. Title. II. Title: Hockey's one hundred.
GV848.5.A1F495   1984   796.96′2′0922 [B]   84-11130
ISBN 0-8253-0245-5

Published in the United States by
Beaufort Books, Inc., New York
Published simultaneously in Canada by
General Publishing Co. Limited

Printed in the U.S.A.   First Edition

10 9 8 7 6 5 4 3 2 1

To Munson Campbell, who for four decades has been to off-the-ice hockey greatness what Gordie Howe was to on-the-ice immortality.

"I'll Take Hockey Anytime!"
by John Kieran

I'm a fairly peaceful man, and an old-time baseball fan,
You can hear me yell when Heilman hits the ball;
And I howl when Ty Cobb stabs one, and I growl
   when Speaker grabs one,
And I roar when Babe Ruth's homer clears the wall.
But the diamond sport is quiet to that reeling rousing riot,
To a splashing game of hockey at its prime;
It's a shindig wild and gay; it's a battle served frappé;
Give me hockey, I'll take hockey any time!

Once, while crazy with the heat, I coughed up to buy a seat,
Just to watch a pair of robbers grab a purse.
It was clinch and stall and shove and "Please excuse my glove,"
Till I blessed them with a healthy Irish curse.
But for fighting, fast and free, grab your hat and come with me,
Sure the thing they call boxing is a crime,
And for ground and lofty whacking and enthusiastic smacking,
Give me hockey, I'll take hockey any time!

I've an ever-ready ear for a rousing football cheer,
And I love to see a halfback tackle low.
It's a really gorgeous sight when the boys begin to fight
With a touchdown only half a yard to go.
But take all the most exciting parts of football, baseball, fighting,
And then mix them up to make a game sublime,
Serve it up with lots of ice, you don't have to ask me twice,
Give me hockey, I'll take hockey any time!

Yes, for speed and pep and action, there is only one attraction,
You'll see the knockouts, they're a dozen for a dime,
When the bright steel blades are ringing and the
   shiny sticks are swinging,
Give me hockey, I'll take hockey any time!

Contents

Preface

Writing this book was like walking down the street, knowing I was being followed. I constantly felt as if I should be looking over my shoulder, ducking into an alleyway to avoid those who would *get* me. My metaphorical pursuers, of course, are those critics who would take issue with my selection of *Hockey's 100*.

I would imagine, without getting hysterical about it, that the legion of those who would disagree with my choices far outnumber people who believe that I selected correctly and with a high degree of fairness.

Shortly before the manuscript was completed, I discussed some of my choices with Joe Fitzgerald, an old friend who is sports columnist with the Boston *Herald-American*. "You gotta be kidding," he snapped, "picking Bobby Orr as low as number thirteen."

No, I wasn't kidding. There is a good reason for Orr being listed as thirteen, just as there are a number of criteria which Wayne Gretzky must fulfill before he can obtain a higher ranking. I did not make these selections casually or with any sense of frivolity. A strict set of standards were established up front: These included longevity—Howe, for example, played thirty-two years while Orr lasted but twelve years in the majors—and championship teams. But they also featured impact on the game, character, numbers of awards, the quality of the hockey at that point in time, not to mention the quality of the team on which the man played.

Since the list includes goaltenders, defensemen and forwards, I arbitrarily decided to place one goalie in every group of ten where feasible and to maintain a balance between scorers and defenders, although this was not possible throughout the volume.

In most cases my opinions are based on personal experience. I began watching hockey in person in 1939 and have been a student of the game ever since I became a season ticket-holder at Madison Square Garden in 1946. I watched Maurice Richard, Gordie Howe, Bobby Hull and Bobby Orr come and go, but I never saw Hobey Baker, Howie Morenz or Georges Vezina.

To obtain a correct line on the greats of the past, I relied, as much as possible, on the word of those who were there and, in other cases, the printed word. Only an octogenarian would have had the opportunity to see Hobey Baker in his prime and there are, unfortunately, precious few of them left.

Comparing the various eras of professional hockey was a difficult yet fascinating task. Obviously, the game has changed dramatically from the days when it was played on natural ice in unheated arenas.

In some ways the game is worse than it was in the Roarin' Twenties when the intensity of body contact was infinitely greater than today, but in many ways the spectacle is better. With improved equipment, players skate faster, shoot harder and, thanks to the technology of television, are able to examine the game more expertly.

What hasn't changed is the fun of arguing who is better. When I was a kid the question was: who would you take, Maurice Richard or Gordie Howe? Now the question is: Wayne Gretzky or Bryan Trottier?

The problem when comparing forwards of different eras is the value of a goal. In baseball the barometer is the .300 average. As Maury Allen pointed out, ''The .300 average is as significant a mark of excellence today as it was fifty years ago.'' The same yardstick cannot be applied in hockey. The quality of a goal has cheapened with inflation.

In the 1940s, for example, a forward was regarded as a ''.300 hitter'' if he scored 20 goals in a season. Nowadays, a shooter would have to score twice that many to be regarded as a .300 hitter. Until 1961 only one player had scored 50 goals in a season throughout all of big-league hockey's history. Nowadays it is almost commonplace for a hot shooter to reach the plateau of 50 goals.

All of the factors inherent in hockey's revolution were taken into account when producing the ratings, but there were intangibles as well. Since this is a *personal* ranking, a number of the choices were made because of the player's particular impact on yours truly. In some situations a great deal of self-control was necessary to keep from inserting a player who once had been a personal favorite but who lacked the qualifications for the exalted list.

Needless to say, a number of readers will react in the Joe Fitzgerald manner and take umbrage with my picks. I hope that they do so in the same spirit of amusement that Fitz has done and not take the matter too seriously. I, for one, will be the first to admit that my selections may be flawed and may be totally in error. I'll buy that as long as you understand that I did my best to produce an acceptable—if controversial—*Hockey's 100*.

Stan Fischler

Acknowledgments

This book was conceived almost accidentally over lunch because a lovely editor named Ruth Pollack instantly detected a passionate desire on the author's part to write a book about the best 100 hockey players of all time. I am eternally grateful to Ruth for perceiving my passion and, more important, helping me translate it into a manuscript. Without Ruth passing me the puck, I couldn't have drilled it into the net.

Not to be overlooked is Maury Allen of *The New York Post*. It was Maury who launched the series with his splendid *Baseball's 100*. It was Maury's work which provided direction and, ultimately, inspiration for the hockey version.

Production of the volume would not have been possible without the nitty-gritty research work of George Hall, who was a superb aide from beginning to end. Others who contributed nobly to the effort include Shirley Fischler, Kelly Lynn, Kenny Kaplan, Janet Wilson, Sharon Kopitnikoff, Rich Friedman, Paul Fichtenbaum, Michael Berger, Grace Nevins, Ralph Russo, Lenny Hochberg, Debby Klein, Phil Davis, Donna Hughes, Doreen Hughes, Sara Kass, Phil Czochanski, John Giaccio, and Doug Sutherland.

To come to the various conclusions the excellent works of a number of authors provided invaluable assistance. These include Trent Frayne, Eric Whitehead and Claude Larochelle.

Finally, the book could not have been written without the inspiration of my top line—Shirley, Ben and Simon.

Photo Acknowledgments

The author owes a debt of gratitude to several hockey sources who provided much-needed assistance in the gathering of photos for this book. Janet and John Halligan, who so superbly orchestrate the New York Rangers public relations department, and their able lieutenants, Dave Freed and John Totaro, unearthed a number of splendid pictures. Lefty Reid, curator of the Hockey Hall of Fame in Toronto, came through in the clutch as did Bill Galloway, who mans the National Archives of Canada in Ottawa. NHL vice president Steve Ryan was a vital catalyst, and the public relations directors of the NHL teams came through admirably. Warm thanks are extended to all.

Introduction

The willingness of Stan Fischler to lay his hockey reputation on the line for all addicts of the game to dissect and analyze has produced a book that is stocked full of hockey lore, and at the same time as controversial as it is comprehensive. It is the hockey fanatic's history book and, as such, unlocks a wealth of heretofore little-known hockey facts and faces. The anecdotes, vignettes and treasured memories of hockey wars past give us all a taste of the action through the game's formative eras—the pre-NHL years, the prewar years, the war years, preexpansion, postexpansion and the WHA—right up to the game as it stands today.

From the perspective of a former Detroit Red Wings fan, I found nostalgia such as the recreation of Rocket Richard's playoff goals against the Wings to be particularly painful. The mental pictures and emotional strains evoked by Stan's description of such moments brought upon me the same empty feeling that I had as a fan when it actually happened. I would not be surprised if my fellow readers experienced similar flashes of *déjà-vu* in reading about a special moment in their own hockey lives. And, like myself, I am sure all readers will enjoy learning about some players and episodes of which we have never heard before.

But, above all, I believe that my fellow readers will derive the most enjoyment from this book in disagreeing with the rankings. For example, how could Bobby Orr not be rated in the top three? And how, incredibly, can Alex Delvecchio not be included in the top ten? And can any of us hockey loyalists ever forgive Mr. Fischler for placing The Great Gretzky only tenth? And so on, and so forth.

Stan, I am sure that with this work you have provided fuel for the Hot Stove League arguments for years to come. From one hockey fan to another, thanks for the hard work that produced just what we addicts needed: a volume chock-full of colorful stories about out past and present ice heroes.

And, to your many readers, I pose one final question: When you prepare your own top 100, will you be as well researched as Mr. Fischler was in his listing? Whatever your reply, enjoy the road to your conclusions.

Thank you, Stan, for the honor of introducing this thoroughly delightful book.

Sincerely,
John A. Ziegler, Jr.
President
National Hockey League

1 Gordie Howe
(1946–1980)

When the pseudonym "Mister Hockey" was coined one did not require Sherlock Holmesian logic to deduce that there was one—and only one—performer who qualified for that distinction. Gordie Howe did it all.

The slope-shouldered native of Floral, Saskatchewan, was a star virtually from the moment he stepped onto a major league rink at the age of six. Miraculously, Howe remained a first-liner in the bigs forty-five years later.

In a moment of understated drollery, Aldo Guidolin, an opponent of Howe, once remarked: "Gordie plays the funny kind of game; he doesn't let anyone else touch the puck!"

A right wing possessed of extraordinary strength in a body measuring 6' 1", 200 pounds, Howe's armament was the most formidable the game has known. "His shot was uncanny," said goalie Glenn Hall, a Hall of Famer, "because it would come at the net in so many different ways."

Unique among superstars, Howe was an ambidextrous stickhandler who would deliver a remarkably accurate shot with so fluid a motion that goalies frequently failed to see the puck leave Gordie's stick.

Howe's credentials said it all. He won the Hart Trophy as the NHL's most valuable player in 1952, 1953, 1957, 1958, 1960 and 1963. "He was not only the greatest hockey player I've ever seen," said defenseman Bill Gadsby, a Hall of Famer, "but also the greatest athlete."

Skating for the Detroit Red Wings, with whom he spent most of his professional career (1946–71), Gordie led the NHL in scoring in 1951, 1952, 1953, 1954, 1957 and 1963.

It has been said that hockey is a game of mistakes. And when one considers that players employ artificial feet (skates), artificial arms (sticks) and maneuver on an artificial surface (ice) it is not surprising that errors are part of the game's fabric. Yet, Howe was a flawless performer in a flawed and often brutal pastime.

Two episodes define the essential Howe. The first, which occurred on a night in March 1950, nearly ended his life at the age of twenty-two. The Red Wings had taken on their bitter rivals, the Toronto Maple Leafs, in the opening round of the Stanley Cup playoffs.

Ted (Teeder) Kennedy, the Leafs' captain and center, was carrying the puck toward the Wings' zone when Howe swerved diagonally across the ice to intercept his foe. A split second before Gordie connected, Kennedy pulled up and, according to the Red Wings, fouled Howe with his stick. Gordie was catapulted into the wooden sideboards and crumpled to the ice with a fractured skull. Removed to a hospital, Gordie was considered a goner. His parents were summoned from distant Saskatchewan and, at best, it was presumed that if he did manage to survive, Howe never would play professional hockey again. A year later he was the league's scoring leader.

The second incident took place during a regular season game between the Wings and the New York Rangers. Howe had learned from the Kennedy affair that it was essential for survival in the ice jungle to hit first, keep the elbows high and ask questions later. "Gordie," explained Islanders general manager Bill Torrey, "would simply psych out his enemies."

Rangers coach Phil Watson had assigned his behemoth left wing Eddie Shack the dubious task of checking Howe. At one point the foes collided behind the Rangers' net whereupon Shack's teammate, Lou Fontinato, then regarded as the NHL's best fighter, pushed in and began flailing at Gordie. It was the worst move in Fontinato's career.

Referee Art Skov, who was a yard away from the battlers, describing the ensuing blows: "Howe began smashing him with lefts and rights and then fired an uppercut that smashed Lou's nose. I just stood back and said, 'No way I'm going to break up this one.' Big George Hayes was the other linesman in the game and he told me to stay out of it. Howe cleaned Fontinato like you've never seen."

It was a measure of Howe's absolute superiority over all challengers that he not only outperformed but outlasted the aces with whom he was most frequently compared. In the early 1950s the standard argument was: "Who's better, Gordie Howe or Maurice Richard?" Yet, upon his retirement in 1960, Richard was the first to allow that Howe was the best of them all. "Gordie," said Richard, "could do *everything*."

Howe had already been an NHL star when Bobby Orr was born in 1948 and Gordie was still in the majors when Orr retired as an NHL defenseman in 1979. Neither Richard nor Orr, nor any other skater for that matter, could compare with Howe when it came to surviving the test of time.

Ironically, Gordie suffered severe doubts about his ability to make a career out of hockey, although from the moment of his NHL debut he had winner written all over him. Even after he led all scorers in the 1949 playoffs, Gordie wondered how he rated against the Richards and Kennedys. "I still wasn't so sure I was a star," Howe explained. "When I went home to Saskatchewan that summer, I started playing baseball again. One day, a kid came up for my autograph and while I signed it, he said, 'Mister Howe, what do you do in the winter?' "

In 1971 Gordie played his last game for the Red Wings and accepted what he later, sadly, discovered was an innocuous front office job. After two years of inactivity, Gordie executed one of the most astonishing comebacks in sports history. At age forty-five, he signed with the Houston Aeros of the World Hockey Association. His teammates were sons Mark and Marty. Slower perhaps but no less superb, Gordie orchestrated the Aeros the way Leonard Bernstein conducts the New York Philharmonic. Houston won the AVCO World Cup and the WHA title. That done, Gordie was selected to play for Team Canada against the Soviet All-Star team. Having shown the Russians the tricks of his trade, Howe returned to Houston and led the Aeros to another AVCO Cup in 1975.

Gordon Howe was born March 31, 1928, in Floral, Saskatchewan, near the city of Saskatoon. Gordie was the fourth of nine children of Catherine and Albert Howe. The Howes were a loving family, but, like so many others living through the Great Depression, they were poor.

"The only equipment I had was skates," Howe remembered, "and a stick. I took magazines and mail order catalogues, stuck 'em in my socks, and had shin pads. I tied 'em together with rubber bands made from inner tubes. We played with tennis balls instead of a puck. The ball would get so hard from the cold (often thirty to forty degrees below zero, Fahrenheit) we'd have to get new ones all the time. A woman next door used to warm them up in an oven for us.''

Despite the hardship, Gordie recalled his youthful hockey years with affection. Long after he had established himself as the game's greatest star, he acknowledged that his most fervent wish was to skate on a line with his eldest sons, Mark and Marty. That wish came true on February 17, 1971.

''It was,'' said Howe, ''the game I'll never forget.''

It was an exhibition charity match—the Detroit Red Wings against the Junior A Red Wings. Gordie skated alongside his kids, who then played for the Junior club. It was then that Gordie perceived what other hockey scouts later would realize— that Mark Howe had many of the same ice gifts possessed by his dad.

No matter where Howe skated, his trademark—effortless excellence—made an impression on critics. ''Gordie had the ability and the knack for making the difficult plays look easy, routine,'' said Chicago Black Hawks vice-president Tommy Ivan.

He was no less appreciated in Hartford, where he emigrated with his two boys in 1977 to play for the Whalers. When Hartford was admitted to the NHL in 1979 Gordie returned to his former hunting grounds and drew capacity crowds. They wanted to see whether the fifty-year-old grandfather could skate with young Turks like Bryan Trottier, Marcel Dionne and Wayne Gretzky.

''Gordie proved that he could,'' said Whalers president Howard Baldwin. ''In our first year in the NHL we were the only former WHA team to make the playoffs. We can thank Gordie for that.''

A year later Howe retired at age fifty-one. But Howe, nevertheless, remains with the Whalers as a special assistant. He also has been helpful to the NHL promoting the Emery Edge and Milestone awards. The Whalers have not made the playoffs since he hung up his skates.

Over a period of thirty-two years, Gordie scored 975 goals, 1,383 assists and 2,358 points. Most of these were obtained when the value of a goal in a defense-oriented game was considerably more than it is now. He was the most gifted forward, an accomplished defensive player, revered as a team man and the only player to have dominated three different eras—postwar NHL, the Golden Era of the 1960s and the Expansion Era.

''Hockey,'' Gordie liked to say, ''is a man's game.''

In that game Gordie Howe was *the* man.

2 Eddie Shore (1926–1940)

When the then all-Canadian National Hockey League decided to expand and embrace American cities in 1924 there was considerable doubt that spectators in New York, Boston, Detroit and Chicago would accept the ice sport from north of the border.

"In order to succeed," said Frank Boucher, who starred for and later became manager of the New York Rangers, "the league needed a superstar of extraordinary dimensions."

Eddie Shore, alias, "The Edmonton Express," was the ace who, more than any, put professional hockey on the American map. Charismatic to a fault, Shore was a product of the Canadian frontier and carried the imprint of that upbringing to the NHL.

Absurdly fearless, totally talented and dedicated to his profession like nobody before or since, Shore was a defenseman who was so extraordinary a skater that he instinctively became an intrepid puck-carrier and thus added a new dimension to the game—defender-on-the-attack—decades before another Boston skater, Bobby Orr, would copy his style.

During an era when hockey featured more woodchopping than the Canadian northwoods, Shore was virtually indestructible. Opponents understood that if they could neutralize the Boston Bruins' defenseman the game would be theirs. A game involving the Montreal Maroons exemplified the brand of assaults inflicted upon Shore.

One of the Maroons tore open Eddie's cheek with his stick blade, and another sliced his chin. One after another, the Maroons belabored Shore. Late in the game Shore was clobbered in the mouth. He fell to the ice minus several teeth and remained inert for fourteen minutes while doctors worked him over. When he was finally removed to the dressing room, medics discovered that he had suffered a broken nose, three broken teeth, two black eyes, a gashed cheekbone and a two-inch cut over the left eye. The assortment of wounds would have been sufficient to sideline lesser athletes for more than a month. Shore donned a Bruins uniform for the very next game.

During the early 1920s Shore's reputation carried across western Canada. He starred in the Pacific Coast League alternately playing for Regina, Edmonton and Victoria, and, soon, his reputation for consummate defensive play carried to the East where the NHL was undertaking its most ambitious period of expansion.

Boston, already a center of amateur hockey, was selected as the first American NHL franchise. The Bruins' owner, millionaire grocery magnate Charles F. Adams, spent liberally to develop a winner but the Bruins were militantly inadequate until the Pacific Coast League folded in 1926 and a number of superior players became available on the open market.

Adams opened his wallet and obtained a seven-man package including Shore, Frank Boucher and Duke Keats—all future Hall of Famers. The tab was $50,000 for all seven, which made it one of the best bargains in sport. (By today's fiscal standards, the seven would have been worth $5,000,000.)

Shore arrived in Boston with suitable fuss and fanfare and on November 16, 1926, made his debut in a Bruins uniform. The Boston *Transcript* commented: "Eddie Shore caught the fancy of the fans. The new defenseman is tall, yet sturdily built. His speed is exceptional and he handles his body and stick well."

Within two years Shore had guided the Bruins to their first Stanley Cup championship and had firmly established professional hockey as a major sport in Beantown. Fans who had never before seen a game were captivated by the iron-muscled defenseman who, at once, seemed to be blunting an enemy attack, wheeling with the puck and then launching a counterattack against the opponent's goal.

"Shore's abnormally long stride built up a momentum that carried him down the ice with frightening speed," said writer-editor Ed Fitzgerald. "His chilling disregard for personal safety enabled him to maintain the peak speed to a point well beyond the limit dared by lesser men. The result was that he came up consistently with plays that other stars were lucky to duplicate once in a lifetime."

From time to time other enterprising NHL owners cast covetous eyes at Shore and hoped to lure him away from the Bruins but, of course, neither Adams nor manager Art Ross would part with his meal ticket. By far the most absurd offer for Shore was generated by the New York Rangers.

Colonel John Hammond, president of Madison Square Garden, suggested to Lester Patrick, the Rangers' manager, that it would be to the Rangers' advantage if they obtained Shore. Patrick realized that Hammond was naive about hockey, but had no choice except to listen to his boss. Colonel Hammond demanded that Patrick offer Myles Lane, a young, modestly talented defenseman, to the Bruins for Shore.

Patrick obliged and, reluctantly, telegraphed the bid to Ross: Myles Lane for Eddie Shore. A day later Ross cabled back what has become a legendary squelch. The Bruins cable read:

"LESTER: YOU ARE SO MANY MYLES FROM SHORE YOU NEED A LIFE PRESERVER."

Teamed with such stalwarts as Lionel Hitchman, Dit Clapper and Cooney Weiland, Shore was named the NHL's most valuable player in 1933, 1935, 1936 and 1938. Not surprisingly, Eddie was voted to the First All-Star Team in 1931, 1932, 1933, 1935, 1936, 1938 and 1939.

Shore was no less galvanic nor capable at age thirty-seven when the 1938–39 edition of the Bruins finished first with 36 wins, 10 losses and 2 ties—16 points ahead of the runner-up Rangers. The Broadway Blueshirts tested the Bruins to the limit in a best-of-seven series that ranks among the classics. During one interlude Shore rammed Rangers pesky center Phil Watson into the boards with such vigor that Watson's teammate Muzz Patrick felt obliged to come to the rescue. The robust Patrick, who once had been amateur heavyweight champion of Canada, walloped Shore so hard that Eddie absorbed a broken nose and a black eye.

Significantly, though Patrick had won the battle, Shore helped win the war. Eddie had his wounds patched and then replied by steering his mates to a four-games-to-three win over the Rangers.

The Bruins next were challenged by the Toronto Maple Leafs who were powered by Harvey (Busher) Jackson, a future Hall of Famer. In the pivotal third game of the series, Shore defused Jackson with a crunching bodycheck that dislocated the Toronto player's shoulder. The Bruins won the series, four games to one, and annexed the Stanley Cup.

Edward William Shore was born November 25, 1902, in Fort Qu'Appelle, Saskatchewan, and spent his early years working on the family farm. His youthful passion was breaking wild horses and his interest in farming inspired him to enter the Manitoba Agricultural College in Winnipeg.

Shore's interest in hockey was tangential at best, and might never have been cultivated had it not been for his brother Aubrey, who challenged Eddie to try out for the school team. Eddie accepted the challenge, and he mastered every aspect of the sport. When the Shore family suffered financial hardship, he quit college and began his professional hockey career. He had been steeled by the harsh Saskatchewan winter and imbued with the work ethic by his parents. Armed with these assets, Eddie was to continually startle the world with his extraordinary exploits. But none better said it about Shore than an incident which took place on the night of January 2, 1929.

En route to meet his teammates who were boarding a train that would take them to Montreal and a game with the Maroons, Shore got stuck in a traffic jam and missed the express train by a few moments. In those days there was no airline service to Montreal and no further trains that night.

But Shore knew that the Bruins already had a defenseman on the injured list and his presence was needed. He was determined to reach Montreal. Unfortunately, a mid-winter blizzard was reaching its peak and only the most hardy would even venture out into the streets of Boston.

Eddie contacted a wealthy friend, explained his predicament and persuaded his pal to supply him with an automobile and a chauffeur. But after five miles of plowing through the storm, the driver told Eddie he would not continue at the wheel. Shore took over and headed for the Green Mountains and the perilous route to Canada. When snow gathered on the windshield, Eddie opened the top half of the glass and bore the brunt of the icy wind and storm. By the time they had reached the halfway point to Montreal the car had slid off the road four times.

The auto reached the Quebec border at three in the afternoon, but soon fell into a deep ditch. Shore hiked a mile to a farmhouse and persuaded the farmer to hitch a team of horses to his car and put it back on the road. That done, Eddie resumed the drive, arriving at the team's quarters, the Windsor Hotel, at 6:00 p.m. Manager Art Ross was there when Shore arrived and recalled the sight of him:

"His eyes were bloodshot, his face was frostbitten, his fingers bent and set like claws after relentlessly gripping the steering wheel so long and his unsteady gait showed that his leg was almost paralyzed from tramping on the foot brake."

Ross was reluctant to allow Shore to play that night, but Eddie would not be stopped. Except for a two-minute penalty he was assessed early in the game, *Shore played the entire sixty minutes*. He played one of the greatest games of anyone's career.

"On defense," Ross recalled, "he smacked the hard-driving Maroons left and center and the Bruins finally won the gruelling game by a score of 1–0. I might add that Shore also found the energy to score that one goal!"

It is quite possible that had Shore entered the NHL at an earlier age—he was twenty-four when he joined the Bruins, he would have won even greater acclaim.

Nevertheless, he eminently qualifies for the number two position. The Midnight Ride to Montreal was only one of a hundred reasons why.

3 Red Kelly
(1947–1977)

As a long-time admirer of Leonard Patrick (Red) Kelly once noted: "Red's problem was that he never had a good press agent!"

One can only imagine how different Kelly's station in the hockey firmament might have been if there had been a tub-thumper to beat the drums for this most versatile of hockey players.

More than Gordie Howe, more than Eddie Shore, more than Bobby Orr, Red Kelly mastered every aspect of positional hockey except goaltending. While Howe earned his spurs as a right wing and Shore and Orr were defensemen par excellence, Kelly was one of the best defensemen of all time *and* a truly superb center.

Curiously, the first half of Red's career was spent on defense for the Detroit Red Wings. Like Shore, Kelly was equally proficient at defending as well as rushing the puck. It was Kelly who was the first of the modern backliners to carry the rubber deep into the enemy zone. Kelly was every bit as smooth a rushing defenseman as Orr and a much better defensive defenseman. What better proof than the fact that Red skated for eight championship squads and four Stanley Cup winners in Detroit. (By contrast, Orr played for only four first-place teams and two Cup winners.) He won the Lady Byng Trophy for competence combined with gentlemanly play four times and was a First All-Star six times.

In 1959 the Red Wings high command estimated that Kelly was washed up and dealt him to the Toronto Maple Leafs, who were being rejuvenated by general manager George (Punch) Imlach.

The turnabout, not to mention the events preceding it, proved to be most unusual for both Kelly and the NHL high command.

During the 1959–60 season, Red was approaching his thirteenth season as a Detroit defenseman and appeared a fixture in the Motor City because of his unwavering competence and devotion to the team. But Jack Adams, the Red Wings' aging and crusty manager, had become angry at Red because of a contract dispute they had had the previous summer.

Adams stewed over the dispute and midway in the season completed a trade with the Rangers. He dealt Kelly and forward Billy McNeill to New York for defenseman Bill Gadsby and forward Eddie Shack. "When I heard about the trade," said Kelly, "it didn't take me long to make up my mind about what I was going to do. I decided to retire rather than go to New York. So did McNeill."

Kelly didn't know it at the time but his stance was the predecessor of free agentry. The NHL was rocked by his decision, and the Rangers, not surprisingly, cried foul. Adams had no choice but to call off the deal while Gadsby and Shack returned to the Rangers.

NHL President Clarence Campbell advised Kelly that he had five days to report back to Detroit or go on the retirement list. "If I went on the retirement list," said Kelly, "I couldn't become active again if even one NHL club objected."

Kelly returned home and mulled over the matter for three days. He finally decided—reluctantly—to quit the game and concentrate on his bowling alley and tobacco farm. Two days remained before Campbell's deadline took force when King Clancy, assistant coach of the Maple Leafs, phoned. "Punch (Imlach) wants you on his hockey club," snapped Clancy. "Come to Toronto and the three of us will talk about it."

Unlike most of his contemporaries, Imlach believed that older, experienced hockey players were more useful in building a championship team than youngsters. He pointed out to Kelly how important he would be to the Maple Leafs' future even though he had turned thirty-two. Kelly was persuaded and agreed to play in Toronto providing that a deal could be worked out with Adams. Imlach phoned Detroit and offered Marc Reaume, a younger defenseman who was believed to be a potential ace.

Adams approved the trade but there was still the league to contend with; particularly Rangers general manager Muzz Patrick, who was furious over Kelly's snub of New York. The deal was ultimately approved, but not before Kelly phoned his nemesis Adams. "I had to tell him I was reporting back to the Wings," said Red, "so he could reinstate me and trade me to the Leafs."

Had the trade not been consummated and Kelly retired as threatened, Red would have been remembered for what he was: one of the game's premier defensemen. But the night of February 10, 1960, proved to be a milestone in Red's life and in the life of the Maple Leafs. He donned the royal blue and white Toronto jersey and was presented with the same number four jersey as he wore in Detroit.

Imlach, the innovator, was not certain precisely how he would exploit Kelly's talents, but he knew for sure that he would at least experiment with him at center although Red had been a defenseman all his life. The Leafs' opponents that night were the Montreal Canadiens, already winners of four straight Stanley Cups and, perhaps, the greatest team of all time.

"I want you to go up against (Jean) Beliveau," said Imlach. The tall, majestic Beliveau was merely the best center in the league. Kelly skated to center ice, lined up opposite Beliveau and waited for the referee to drop the puck for the opening face-off. "I was as nervous as a rookie," said Kelly. "I won the draw and sent the puck straight into the Montreal zone. The Canadiens' goalie, Jacques Plante, darted out to intercept the puck before I got there. I came right down like a shot and somehow got tangled up and went head over heels—into the net!"

Although the Leafs lost the game, 4–2, Imlach understood that his instincts were accurate; that Red would be more valuable to him as a center than as a defenseman. Never has the game known a more brilliant brainstorm. The next question was, with whom should Kelly play?

Imlach had a huge, brooding young left wing named Frank (The Big M) Mahovlich, who could skate like a zephyr and fired the puck with the fury of a howitzer. Somehow, The Big M's power had not yet been harnessed, no doubt for want of a competent center. The Leafs also possessed Bob Nevin, an unobtrusive right wing but one who excelled at all of a forward's basic skills. Imlach decided to unite Kelly with Mahovlich and Nevin.

From that point on the Maple Leafs' troubles were over. With Kelly ladling the passes to The Big M and Nevin, the Maple Leafs won four Stanley Cups in the seven-and-a-half years Red performed in Toronto. (Bill Gadsby, for whom Kelly was traded, played twenty years in the NHL and never skated for a Stanley Cup champion.)

Even more astonishing is the fact that Kelly was able to maintain his standard of playing excellence in Toronto while serving a term as a member of Canada's Parliament.

Leonard Patrick Kelly was born July 9, 1927, in Simcoe, Ontario, and like so many youngsters determined to become professional hockey players, he enrolled at Toronto's St. Michael's College (a private high school by American standards), where he teamed with such future NHLers as Ted Lindsay and Jim Thomson.

"When I was ready to turn pro," Kelly recalled, "the scouts took a good look at me. The Leafs didn't want me because their scout said I wasn't good enough to last twenty games in the NHL. Detroit didn't see it that way, so the Red Wings signed me." Red was only seventeen when he launched his major league career in Detroit.

Low-key throughout his hockey and political careers, Kelly to this day remains the most underrated superstar to come down the pike, yet his dossier cannot be disputed. He was the balance wheel of champions as a defenseman in Detroit, and as a center, the most decisive factor in creating a dynasty in Toronto more than a decade later.

No other hockey player can make that statement, which is why Red Kelly deserves to be number three in *Hockey's 100*.

4 Frank Boucher
(1921–1944)

If a blue-ribbon panel of purists had ever been convened to select the one player who best epitomized clean, textbook hockey, the choice would have to be Frank Boucher.

The game never has known a center who parlayed style, selflessness and sense of fair play like this native of Ottawa, Ontario. "I always recognized that hockey was a tough sport," said Boucher, "a rough one and one that can be played fairly. I was always a stickler on that. I got an exhilaration out of being able to avoid the checks in a violent game and tried to play it cleanly."

That was an understatement. Boucher won the Lady Byng Trophy exemplifying competence and clean play in 1928, 1929, 1930, 1931, 1933, 1934 and 1935—seven times in an eight-year stretch. At this point Walter Gilhooly, a sportswriter for the Ottawa *Journal,* wrote an open letter in his column urging Lady Byng to give Boucher the trophy outright; and she did!

Boucher was more than a super-clean stickhandler. He was a creative genius who steered the New York Rangers to two division titles, three second place finishes, four appearances in the Stanley Cup finals and two Stanley Cups. Finally, he was the balance wheel on what many observers regard as *the* most proficient line in NHL history—Boucher pivoting for Bill Cook on right wing and Bunny Cook on the left.

Among other plays, Boucher and the Cooks invented the drop-pass. Bill would steer a puck-carrier to Boucher, who would hook the puck away. Bun raced down his wing and Frank flipped the puck to him. "As soon as he crossed the other team's blue line," said Boucher, "he faked a shot, drawing a defenseman to him. Then he left the puck for me coming in fast behind him."

Frank and the Cooks were a part of the original Rangers team which made its NHL debut in 1926. Previously, he had played professionally with the Ottawa Senators and the Vancouver Maroons. When Madison Square Garden decided to add its own team to its original hockey tenant, the New York Americans, Conn Smythe, a Toronto sportsman, was asked to select the talent. Smythe spoke to Bill Cook, who, in turn, recommended Boucher to Smythe.

Boucher only weighed 134 pounds when he met Smythe prior to training camp. Smythe anxiously eyed the seemingly frail athlete and then asked Frank how much he weighed. Boucher allowed that it was about 135 pounds.

"I paid fifteen thousand dollars for *you,*" Smythe groaned. "Bill Cook must be crazy."

Smythe eventually signed Boucher to a contract, but he had a falling out with the Garden brass prior to training camp and was replaced as Rangers' boss by the courtly and insightful Lester Patrick. When the new club convened for training camp at Toronto's old Ravina Gardens, Patrick called Boucher to him and said, "I'm going to try you at center between Bill and Bunny Cook."

Patrick never had cause to change his mind. The unit remained intact in Rangers

uniforms for ten years. Unlike today's units who take the ice for three-minute stretches and then are replaced, Boucher and the Cooks worked almost the entire game.

Frank Boucher was born October 7, 1901, in Ottawa, Ontario. He and his brothers George, Carroll, Billy, Joe and Bobby learned to skate and play hockey on the snow-bordered Rideau River. "We played from dawn until dark," Frank recalled, "and in all kinds of weather, even forty degrees *below* zero. It was best after your toes froze; they turned numb and didn't bother you anymore—until later."

It was no accident that Boucher developed a meticulously clean style of play. His idol as a kid was Frank Nighbor, a star with the Ottawa Senators. "Nighbor," said Boucher, "was every young lad's hero in Ottawa in those days. He was a magnificent center who rarely lost his temper, who could hookcheck and pokecheck like nobody else. Nighbor's influence must have found its reflection in the years that followed."

Playing at a time when hockey was infinitely more rugged than today's game, Boucher engaged in only one fight in his ten-year NHL career and that in his very first game at Madison Square Garden against the Maroons. He had been singled out by Bill Phillips, a square-set, rugged player who flattened Frank early in the game. In the third period Phillips tangled again.

"I had simply had too much of him," said Boucher. "We threw aside our sticks and our gloves and went at each other. The crowd was standing a-roaring, and he knocked me down, and I got up and knocked him down and he got up and we grabbed each other and swung wearily. When the referee separated us he sent us off with major penalties, five minutes each. It was as rough as any I ever played.

"My philosophy always had been that fighting never solved anything—provided you didn't back down if you had to stand up. I was the one who swung on Phillips. I was the first Ranger ever to get a major penalty. Still, it was my last fight, too."

Boucher continued playing until 1938 when he accepted Lester Patrick's suggestion that he turn to coaching. Patrick gave him control of the New York Rovers, the Rangers farm club in the Eastern Hockey League. Frank was an instant success as a coach after seventeen years as a player, four with the Vancouver Maroons, one with the Ottawa Senators and twelve with the Rangers. He had led the New Yorkers in scoring in five seasons and was named to the NHL All-Star team three times.

After a year steering the Rovers to a spectacularly successful campaign, Boucher was named coach of the Rangers, succeeding Patrick, who concentrated on managing the club. "The team Lester gave me," said Boucher, "was the best hockey team I ever saw."

In March 1940, Frank's rookie year as coach, the Rangers won their third Stanley Cup. It was the last time they annexed hockey's foremost prize.

Boucher's awesome Rangers' club was decimated by World War II and plunged to the bottom of the league. During the 1943–44 season at age forty-two, Frank brought himself out of retirement and played fifteen games. His legs obviously didn't have it, but the creative mind still functioned on the ice and he managed to produce four goals and ten assists in fifteen games. Although he hadn't played a game in five years, Frank outscored *nineteen* other players the Rangers had tried that season.

It is unfortunate that only the genuine oldtimers had the good fortune to enjoy the skill of Boucher. One who did was Foster Hewitt, the dean of hockey announcers. Once during the Team Canada–Soviet All-Stars series of 1972, Hewitt was asked if he ever had seen anything to match the dazzling Russian skaters.

"There aren't many people around to remember," Hewitt told Canadian columnist Trent Frayne, "but the way the Russians play reminds me of the old Rangers, especially the line of Boucher and the Cooks. They were even better than the Russians. When Frank, Bill and Bunny were on the ice, it always seemed to me they had the puck on a string."

Frank Boucher, who died in 1977, was the most completely beautiful hockey player ever to grace an arena and eminently qualifies for fourth place among the hundred best.

5 Maurice Richard
(1942–1960)

Frankie (Mister Zero) Brimsek, a Hall of Famer and one of the best goalies ever to don the pads, watched the galvanic Maurice (Rocket) Richard terrorize his ilk for almost a decade and finally concluded that no one in the hockey world could fire the puck like the Montreal Canadiens' right wing.

"He can shoot from any angle," said Brimsek. "You can play him for a shot to the upper corner and the Rocket wheels around and fires a backhander to the near, lower part of the net."

Brimsek's teammate, defenseman Murray Henderson, described what it was like trying to defuse the Rocket at the blue line. "When Richard breaks on one defenseman there's no telling what he'll do. If he gets his body between you and the puck, you just can't get at it. He cradles the puck on the blade of his stick, steers it with one hand, and wards off his check with the other. Strong? That guy is like an ox, but he sure doesn't look it."

Or the word of Canadian author and television personality, Peter Gzowski. "Richard was the most exciting athlete I have ever seen. So much has been written about Richard that for me to offer a flood of new praise would be roughly equivalent to a Ph.D. candidate announcing he is going to prove *Hamlet* is an interesting play."

Mention "The Rocket" to anyone who played with or against him, or had the good fortune to watch him in the 1940s or 1950s, and a special glow instantly crosses the face. There was nobody quite like him before or since, nobody who generated such intensity, so much élan. If he had been a soldier, Richard would have been the ultimate *poilu*.

Richard was the penultimate scorer. He burned with an intensity that put fear in the hearts of goaltenders because they could actually see the desire on Maurice's face. "When he skated in on the net," said Hall of Fame goalie Glenn Hall, "The Rocket's eyes would shine like a pair of searchlights. It was awesome to see him coming at you."

The Rocket not only was a potent scorer but a clutch player of the highest order. His sudden-death overtime goals became legends and his leadership and passion for the game helped make Les Canadiens the most revered dynasty in the NHL.

In March 1944, when The Flying Frenchmen won their first Stanley Cup with Richard on right wing, the Toronto Maple Leafs assigned Bob Davidson, a rugged and intelligent left wing, to stymie Richard. The Rocket was held scoreless in the opener but in the second game, on March 23, 1944, Maurice scored three goals in the second period, breaking a scoreless tie, and added two more in the third period. The final score was *Richard* 5, Toronto 1! The last time a player had scored five or more goals in a Stanley Cup match was in 1917 when Bernie Morris scored six against Les Canadiens for Seattle.

After disposing of Toronto, the Canadiens challenged Chicago and, once again, Richard dominated an entire game. The Montrealers defeated Chicago, 3–1, on

April 6 in the second game of the final round and Richard scored *all three goals!* Just to prove it was no fluke, Maurice practically single-handedly saved Montreal in the fourth and last game of the series after Chicago had mounted a 4–1 lead after two periods. The Rocket's second goal of the game tied the match, 4–4, sending it into sudden-death overtime. Then his pass to Toe Blake set up the winning goal.

Every night that Richard took the ice during the 1944–45 season it became apparent that he could not be stopped. Like nobody in the modern game, Richard blazed into the home stretch of the season maintaining a goal-a-game pace. In those days the NHL played a fifty-game season. In Richard's forty-eighth game—on March 15—he scored his 49th goal. In the next-to-last game, against the Black Hawks on Forum ice, Les Canadiens triumphed, but somehow Maurice was blanked. That left him with only one more match to make it 50 in fifty. The final game of the season was against the Bruins in Boston Garden. This time The Rocket came through in a 4–2 win and he finished the season with 50 goals in fifty games, a modern hockey average that had not been equalled until 1980 when Mike Bossy of the New York Islanders matched Richard's mark.

Another who tried to torment Richard was (Terrible) Ted Lindsay, the truculent Detroit Red Wings left wing. During the 1950–51 season Detroit manager Jack Adams dispatched Lindsay to unnerve Richard. The Rocket wound up with a five-minute major penalty and Detroit rapidly scored two goals. "Perturbed by the turn of events," wrote author Vince Lunny, "rivers of anger scalded The Rocket's brain. When he served his time he leaped from the bench like all hell breaking loose."

The Rocket pounced on the puck and drove it past the Detroit goaltender. He remained on the ice and seconds later, took a pass from his center, Elmer Lach, rounded the defense, and fired one of his patented backhanders into the twine. By now Montreal coach Dick Irvin figured The Rocket was ready for a respite and called him to the bench. "Never mind," countered Richard, "I had my rest in the penalty box."

Lach won the next face-off and passed the puck to a teammate who relayed it to Richard. He skated straight into Lindsay, bowling him over, and then raced in for another goal. Montreal won the game, 3–2.

Maurice Richard was born August 4, 1921, in Montreal's Bordeaux section. "Nearly everybody who lived there was French-Canadian," The Rocket remembered. "English was never spoken in our house."

Whenever he got a chance, young Maurice put on the skates. "Besides skating to school all the time," he remembered, "I used to skate on the frozen Back River near our house, or sometimes on our makeshift backyard rink or on the public rink run by the city."

In time he gained a reputation as a quality amateur player and in the fall of 1942 was invited to the Canadiens' training camp. The Habitants were a mixture of French- and English-Canadian players who played harmoniously. Young Richard, however, could only say "yes" and "no" in English when he joined the team as a rookie. "I was deathly afraid to even try to say anything in English for fear of making a mistake and looking foolish. I'd just sit there silently."

Despite his promise as a scorer, Richard was also viewed as a brittle skater, prone to injury. He brooded about his seemingly endless series of wounds and doubted whether he would be kept on the Canadiens. "Fortunately," Richard recalled, "Dick Irvin wouldn't give up on me and I was invited back to training camp for the 1943–44 season."

From that point on until his retirement in 1960, The Rocket's red goal glare was rarely snuffed out and he emerged as the NHL's most exciting, if not complete, player. It has been said—with justification—that Richard was not as all-inclusive a player as Gordie Howe. The Rocket's specialty was taking a pass from Lach—and later his brother, Henri—at or near the blue line and steaming relentlessly to the net for his shot on goal.

During a playoff game against the Bruins, The Rocket was viciously blindsided by Leo Labine, knocked unconscious and carried from the ice, apparently finished for the series. Refusing to be hospitalized, Richard eventually returned to the bench as the teams battled to score the go-ahead goal in a bitterly played tie match.

Late in the game Richard took the ice, charging along his right wing when the pass came his way. Bruins' defenseman Bill Quackenbush guarded The Rocket closely and appeared to have him boxed into the corner when, somehow, releasing his special quantity of pent-up energy, The Rocket whirled around Quackenbush and stuffed the puck behind goalie (Sugar) Jim Henry.

The 1951 playoff semi-finals against Detroit was a vintage Richardian showcase. The first game of the series ended in a 2–2 tie after regulation time. Two sudden-death periods were played without a score. After midnight the third overtime session began. At 1:10 a.m. Richard snared a loose puck like a leopard spotting an antelope. "He sped past the Detroit defense," said the *Canadian Press,* "with a blazing burst of speed. Alone in front of the net, he paused before lining a ten-footer past goalie Terry Sawchuk."

The second game of the series was a duplicate of the first, only this time it ended in a 0–0 tie after three periods. Again the teams struggled through two scoreless sudden-death periods. Early in the third overtime Billy Reay of the Canadiens saw Richard zooming in from the left and slid him the puck. Richard's shot was so hard it nearly tore a hole in the goal mesh. "He is as great an opportunist as the game has ever known," said Baz O'Meara, sports editor of the Montreal *Star.*

Detroit rebounded to win the next two games but it was The Rocket again in the fifth game scoring the winning goal in the third period as the Canadiens prevailed, 5–2. In the sixth and final game of the series the game was tied 2–2 but The Rocket took over again, scored and the Canadiens won the series.

In all, Richard played for eight Stanley Cup winners and eight first-place teams. He was a First All-Star eight times and six times a Second All-Star. More than that, Rocket Richard was the Babe Ruth of hockey.

Maurice Richard's name is synonymous with exciting hockey. Detroit *Times* columnist Bob Murphy said it best: "The Rocket was made to watch and write about."

6 Howie Morenz (1923–1937)

One of the major selling points of professional hockey is speed. It is called the "fastest game on earth." The essential pace of the game is what captured the hearts and minds of American fans when the NHL planted franchises in Boston, New York, Chicago and Detroit, and one skater, more than any other, epitomized the dynamic quality of the game—Howie Morenz.

Dubbed "The Stratford Streak," Morenz seemed to be charged with lightning every time he took the ice for his beloved Montreal Canadiens. "He would challenge the opposing defenses by dazzling dash and deception rather than by shooting from longer range and following up for a rebound," said Montreal journalist Andy O'Brien, who covered Les Canadiens during the Morenz era.

Like Maurice Richard, who followed him, Morenz possessed the rare knack of producing the dramatic goal, the *chef d'oeuvre*. One such score won the 1931 Stanley Cup for the Canadiens. It was the fifth and last game of the best-of-five finals against the Chicago Black Hawks and Morenz took the ice with his linemate Aurel Joliat.

As Joliat recalled, Morenz executed a near-impossible turnaround to deliver the goal. "Howie," said Joliat, "had rushed away from us with the puck down center and was checked at the Chicago defense. A Black Hawks forward picked up the loose puck at the gallop but I checked him at mid-ice. I had taken only two strides when I heard 'Joliat!' screamed at me from right wing.

"It was incredible; even with the play going at top speed Morenz raced back on my left wing, whirled around behind me and had again picked up full speed down right wing. To catch him before he was offside at the blue line I had to fire a shot rather than a pass. Howie picked up the puck as if he was using a lacrosse stick and without losing a stride.

"He was by the Chicago defense in a flash and in on goalie Chuck Gardiner before anybody really recognized the menace. His shot, fired with every last ounce from an exhausted body, hit an upper corner of the net. The Forum crowd gasped, then raised the roof in one earsplitting wave of cheering thunder."

From the moment he made his debut with the Montrealers, Morenz dazzled the enemy with his footwork. "The rookie Morenz was the fastest man on the ice," commented Toronto writers after Howie skated against the Toronto St. Pats in the fall of 1923. Morenz never stopped. He paced Les Canadiens to their first Stanley Cup in the seven-year history of the NHL. In a two-game total-goals Eastern playoff against Ottawa, Montreal won, 5–2. Howie scored three and assisted on a fourth goal.

Although Morenz was of Swiss descent and Maurice Richard was a French-Canadian, the two had many traits in common, especially their seething hatred of defeat. Elmer Ferguson, who was sports editor of the Montreal *Herald* during Morenz's halcyon years, remembered an episode from the 1928–29 season. The Canadiens visited Boston and dropped a pair of gripping 1–0 games to an excellent Bruins club. As usual, Morenz played a capable game.

"I was sleeping soundly when at six o'clock in the morning after the second game, there was a knock on my door," said Ferguson. "It was Morenz, face still drawn from the toll of fierce, close conflict the night before. He was dressed for the street. But he wasn't going out. He had just come in. He had tramped the winding, crooked streets of Boston all night, his mind still in a raging torrent of turmoil and conflict, through which the episodes of the battle were still running. 'I couldn't sleep,' he apologized, 'now I want to talk.'

"And so we talked, far towards noon. Play after play he ran through, analyzed, putting a finger on the spot where a different stride, another shift, might have meant the whole tide of battle . . . Other players had long since dismissed defeat and the game from their minds and were sleeping peacefully, but not Morenz. He blamed only himself for the team's defeats."

During an era when low-scoring games were the norm and goals were hard to come by, Morenz totaled 270 in 546 regular season games but his game was more comprehensive than most.

Howarth William (Howie) Morenz was born September 21, 1902, in Mitchell, Ontario, but moved with his parents to Stratford. By the time he had reached his early teens he had created something of a sensation within his community but somehow failed to excite the Toronto St. Pats, the closest major league team.

Lou Marsh, sports editor of the Toronto *Daily Star,* who doubled as an NHL referee, went out of his way to catch a glimpse of Morenz. Marsh was so impressed he contacted Leo Dandurand, boss of the Canadiens, and urged him to sign the fleet forward. Dandurand dispatched his emissary Cecil Hart to the Morenz household. Hart spread $850 on the table and Howie signed with the Habitants.

It was one of the biggest bargains in sport. Morenz won the Hart Trophy as the NHL's most valuable player three times, thrice was a First All-Star and twice won the league scoring championship. Still, it was less Howie's statistics and more his style that counted.

For years Morenz owned Montreal and then, almost as quickly, his legs began to go and the fans who once revered number seven now reviled him. At thirty-two years, Morenz still had plenty of good hockey in him and when the Black Hawks made an offer, Dandurand shipped Howie to the Windy City.

Howie couldn't summon his enthusiasm in foreign Chicago, and in the middle of the 1935–36 season he was dealt to the Rangers for Glenn Brydson. "HERE COMES HOWIE!" shouted a headline in *The New York Times.* His arrival was hailed as a major event in the city's sporting history but, once again, Morenz was a shadow of his former starry self.

During the summer of 1936 Cecil Hart was offered the job as coach of the Canadiens. He agreed, with one condition—that the Canadiens "bring back Morenz to where he belongs."

A trade was agreed upon and Howie once again donned the *bleu* (blue), *blanc* (white) *et rouge* (red) uniform of the Canadiens. The Forum fans took him to their hearts and during several moments he looked like the Morenz of old although he was thirty-four years old.

On the night of January 28, 1937, the Black Hawks came to town and Howie was playing a splendid game. At one point in the contest he grabbed the puck and went one-on-one with crack defenseman Earl Seibert.

As Morenz executed his end run, Seibert crouched and managed to hurl Howie off balance with a clean check. Before he could regain his equilibrium, Morenz flew, legs first, into the boards. "The point of one skate imbedded itself in the wood," said Andy O'Brien, "as the rest of Howie rolled over."

Witnesses instantly understood that this was an extraordinary accident. Linemates Joliat and Gagnon rushed to Howie's side as did members of the Black Hawks. Writhing in pain, Morenz had suffered a double fracture of his leg.

Under normal conditions, Morenz should have gradually recovered from the mishap but conditions were not normal at Hopital Saint-Luc. Morenz received many visitors, but those who knew him best estimated that beneath the facade, Morenz was brooding over his declining career. On March 8, 1937, he died of cardiac failure.

Morenz's body lay in state at mid-ice in the Forum where thousands paid their last respects to "The Stratford Streak." During the funeral service 15,000 fans sat in complete silence with heads bowed while 200,000 Montrealers lined the streets as the cortege rolled on to Mount Royal Cemetery.

"Howie Morenz," Andy O'Brien concluded, "will be recalled as the *beau sabreur* of hockey—*sans peur, sans reproche.*"

It was a brilliant career; not quite as long as Howe's, Richard's or Kelly's but certainly worthy of sixth on the honor roll.

7 Jean Beliveau
(1951–1971)

In French-speaking Quebec City, where Jean Beliveau originally carved a niche in hockey's annals, they called him *"Le Gros Bill"* (Big Bill). As the majestic center progressed through senior ranks and finally the National Hockey League, his stature as a player grew to Bunyanesque proportions.

Articulate, diffident and the supreme team player, Beliveau was captain and balance wheel of a Montreal Canadiens dynasty that annexed ten Stanley Cups during his extraordinary reign. He was twice voted the Hart Trophy as the NHL's most valuable player, was a First All-Star in 1955, 1956, 1957, 1959, 1960 and 1961.

Versatile in the extreme, Beliveau's passing was matched only by his radar-accurate shot. He was NHL scoring champion in 1956 and won the Conn Smythe Trophy as the most valuable playoff performer in 1965.

One hard-bitten hockey journalist who had covered the game for over three decades remarked that Beliveau was the only superstar to span twenty years of active performing "literally above criticism."

Beliveau's teammates shared that view. "It's hard to put into words how we felt about Jean," said Ralph Backstrom, who teamed with Beliveau on several championship clubs. "It's just that . . . well, we were so damned proud to have him as our captain."

Although he made his mark as an offensive threat, Beliveau could play a sound defensive game and, when necessary, could play a rough—if not dirty—brand of hockey although it was not his nature to trespass beyond the realm of fair play.

"It's practically impossible for anyone who knows him well to have any ill feelings toward Jean," said Toronto Maple Leafs manager Punch Imlach, who coached Beliveau as a junior. "He would go on the ice, play one heckuva game, change and leave without saying much. He was one player all the fellows liked."

Playing alongside such boisterous performers as Bernie Geoffrion and Maurice Richard, Beliveau might have been rendered obscure were it not for his stylish efforts on the ice. To put Jean in a baseball perspective, he was to Rocket Richard what Lou Gehrig was to Babe Ruth.

"It was his quiet dignity," said ex-teammate Dick Duff. "He was so unassuming for a guy of his stature. He had great moves—that great range—and anybody playing on a line with him was certain to wind up with a lot of goals. If you got there, the puck would be there."

At the height of his career, in the late 1950s and through the 1960s, Beliveau was the toast of Canadian sport. The late Leonard Shecter, one of America's most perceptive journalists, made this observation: "Jean Beliveau is like Mickey Mantle and Joe DiMaggio in the United States. When Beliveau walks down the street in Quebec the women smile, the men shake his hand, and the little boys follow him."

With Beliveau wearing the captain's "C" on his jersey, the Canadiens domi-

nated hockey through the 1960s and, in the fans' eyes, Big Jean could do no wrong —even when he suffered through a horrendous slump.

During the 1966–67 season he went through the first fourteen games with nary a goal. The municipality of Montreal shared the Canadiens' depression and by the time the Habitants were scheduled to play the Chicago Black Hawks on December 3, 1966, Beliveau wondered whether he'd ever see the red goal light go on again.

Jean did virtually nothing in the first period. During the subsequent intermission Beliveau made a television appearance with the Canadian Prime Minister, Lester Pearson, himself a hockey fan. The two exchanged pleasantries and then Pearson asked about Beliveau's scoring drought. "I have a feeling" said the PM, "that you'll score tonight." Jean said he would do his best to oblige.

In the second period Beliveau powered his way through the Chicago defense and fired a wrist shot at Black Hawks goalie Denis DeJordy. The initial drive was blocked but DeJordy gave up a rebound and Beliveau lifted the puck over the fallen netminder.

The exultant crowd toasted Jean with a four-minute ovation and littered the ice with everything from overshoes to fedoras. Teammates hugged him and Beliveau blushed as the tribute continued. Later, Beliveau would say, "That goal was my biggest thrill—imagine the fans sticking with me like they did."

Jean Marc Beliveau was born August 31, 1931, in *Trois Rivieres* (Three Rivers), Quebec. He began capturing headlines during the 1947–48 season when he made his debut as an amateur with a team in Victoriaville, Quebec. By 1949–50 he had moved up to the strong Quebec Citadelles in the Quebec Junior League. Big Jean so thoroughly dominated the Junior circuit that a new and larger rink was needed to handle the hordes of fans who wanted to see him play. Thus, *Le Colisée* (The Coliseum) was erected and colloquially called "Chateau Beliveau."

In those days an amateur player was allowed to play five "trial" games with the professionals without losing his amateur status. So, while Beliveau was still nineteen, Les Canadiens invited him for a couple of NHL games. After watching *Le Gros Bill* in one turn on the ice coach Dick Irvin of the Canadiens compared Beliveau to the legendary Lester Patrick, which was tantamount to linking the kid with God.

The Canadiens dearly wanted Beliveau to sign with them but he was deeply attached to the fans of Quebec City and snubbed Montreal in favor of a contract with the Quebec Aces, a professional team in the fast Quebec Senior League. Crowds who had filled *Le Colisée* to watch him star with the Citadelles now became aficionados of the Aces.

"The NHL must certainly know by now that my boy rates only with Gordie Howe and Rocket Richard in their league," chirped Aces coach Punch Imlach.

Needless to say, the Canadiens' manager, Frank Selke, was more determined than ever to wrest Beliveau from the Aces, but it would not be easy. Big Jean was being well paid in Quebec and he savored the ambiance of the quaint city where he had so many friends.

But several factors worked in the Canadiens' favor. Although the Aces paid him well, the Canadiens were willing to open their vault for him. In addition there was a matter of professional pride. In the Quebec Senior League, Jean was a big fish in a small pond. Professional pride demanded that he ultimately show how well he could play in the bigs. His advisor, Emile Couture, also influenced Beliveau's decision to sign with Montreal.

"I told Jean," said Couture, "that if he really loved to play hockey, there was only one league in which to play and one team with which to play. Again, his idol had always been Rocket Richard and the thought of being a teammate intrigued Jean."

By the time Beliveau signed with Montreal in 1953 he had become the most widely acclaimed young player ever to step on to an NHL rink. Not surprisingly, Beliveau succumbed to the pressure and won less than total raves in his rookie season in the NHL.

His gentlemanly play invited every low-salaried skater from New York to Chicago to get a piece of *Le Gros Bill* and many of them did. He suffered a cracked fibula after being heavily checked in Chicago and was sidelined a total of twenty-six games.

A year later Beliveau began asserting himself and his tormentors began to disappear. From that point on there was no stopping him. "The playing of Beliveau," commented Canadian novelist Hugh MacLennan, "is poetry in action."

Skating side by side with The Rocket, Beliveau propelled the Canadiens to new heights of excellence and, naturally, prompted comparisons between his style and that of the inimitable Richard. "Big Jean," said coach Toe Blake, "doesn't have the desire to score that Maurice has."

It was a perceptive comment. With his abundance of skills, Beliveau nevertheless seemed too mechanical in a sport that relies more than most on human fire.

"The difference between the two best players in the game today is simply this: Beliveau is a perfectionist, Richard, on the other hand, is an opportunist," said another expert.

Richard and Beliveau comprised two-fifths of the most devastating power play in hockey. Doug Harvey and Bernie Geoffrion were stationed at the left and right points near the blue line. Beliveau, Richard and tenacious left wing Bert Olmstead played up front. The Habs' power play became so overwhelming that the NHL had to legislate against it. At the time a penalized player was compelled to serve the full two minutes of a minor penalty. When that happened the Canadiens would often score as many as three goals. The NHL decreed that the player could return to the ice if a goal was scored during a power play.

Long after Richard retired, Beliveau maintained his high standard of excellence. He scored one of the most spectacular goals of his career during the 1971 playoff upset of Bobby Orr and the Big Bad Bruins, and then decided to call it a career. His timing, as always, was exquisite. He packed it in and became an executive with the Canadiens, still remaining very visible and very likeable.

Yet, it is a fact of life that Beliveau never obtained the intensity of acclaim accorded Gordie Howe, Rocket Richard and Eddie Shore. He simply could not fulfill the enormous buildup he received as a junior and senior player in Quebec.

"People would come to the rinks," Beliveau concluded, "and want to see me score two, three or four goals in a game. If I would score only once the people would be unhappy."

Nevertheless, *Le Gros Bill* created an enormous number of happy moments for Canadiens' fans and is well-suited for the number seven position.

8 Cyclone Taylor (1908–1923)

Fred Taylor was professional hockey's original superstar and, as such, a legend grew around him. It has been said, by several who swore they were witnesses, that Taylor once scored a goal by skating backwards along a good portion of the rink.

Whether or not the story is apocryphal is less relevant than the fact that Taylor was the titan of his time, a zephyr on skates whose style instantly earned him nicknames wherever he played. In Manitoba he was labelled "The Tornado." When he played in the International League, he was dubbed "Whirlwind."

The handle that finally stuck with Taylor for the rest of his life was coined by Malcolm Bryce, sports editor of the Ottawa *Free Press*. After watching Taylor score five goals *as a defenseman* for Ottawa against the Stanley Cup champion Montreal Wanderers, Bryce decided that a new nickname was in order. He devoted an entire page of his newspaper to the game and Taylor's exploits and concluded: "Based on his performance last night I am re-christening him 'Cyclone' Taylor."

The tale of Cyclone's backward skating goal grew out of an intense rivalry between the Ottawa Senators and the Renfrew Millionaires. Organized by wealthy businessmen, the Renfrew sextet lured Taylor to the new team in 1910 after he helped Ottawa win the Stanley Cup in 1909. Because of his defection, Taylor was reviled in Canada's capital city and revered in Renfrew, a boom town in northern Ontario.

Taylor became increasingly peevish over the taunts emanating from Ottawa and in an imprudent moment wagered that when next Renfrew and Ottawa played he would skate backwards through the entire Senators' team and score a goal.

The long-awaited match finally did take place and Ottawa triumphed, but Cyclone did score his goal. It is apparent that Taylor skated backwards—"about five yards"—before firing a sizzling backhand shot into the Ottawa net.

Taylor, who received an estimated $4,000 bonus to jump from Ottawa to Renfrew, spent two years with the Millionaires until the franchise folded.

At this time the Patrick Brothers—Lester and Frank—had decided to gamble and launch hockey in British Columbia where it had not existed before because of the relatively temperate climate. They built arenas in Vancouver and Victoria and made a major sport of the game while raiding scores of skaters from the eastern leagues.

"Frank went out and found twenty-five of the best hockey players from around Montreal, Toronto and Quebec," said Taylor. "I was one of them and signed with Vancouver. In Renfrew, I was getting $5,260, the most ever paid a hockey player up to that time. And if I had been smart I could just as easily have gotten $10,000 because they wanted me very badly. So did Vancouver, when the Patricks got their league organized, and I had no trouble accepting their offer and moving out west."

Taylor remained with Vancouver until he reached the age of thirty-six and once

and for all retired. "I was playing a full sixty-minute game at the time," he recalled, "and for a guy my age that was a lot of hockey."

Fred Taylor was born in Tara, Ontario, on June 23, 1883. He began impressing railbirds at the turn of the century while playing for a team from Listowel, Ontario, in the provincial junior championships.

The final game was between Listowel Juniors and the Kingston Frontenacs and was played at the Mutual Street Rink in Toronto. Enthusiasm for the match was so high that some 700 fans came by special train from Listowel alone (almost the entire population).

By mid-point in the match, Kingston had built a 4–1 lead. Then, young Fred Taylor went into action. "He skated down the ice like a veritable streak of lightning," remembered Captain James Sutherland, one of the early hockey historians. "Taylor passed all the would-be checks with ease and with his shot cut the score down to 4–2."

With a pair of "shadows" guarding him Taylor continued to excel. "We were watching," said Captain Sutherland, "a fellow who would become one of the greatest hockey stars that Canada has produced."

Cyclone's talents were all-inclusive even in those early years when he roamed the Ontario circuit, playing most of his games on outdoor rinks. "I didn't actually come into my own until I was nineteen," said Taylor, "and people started to really notice my style."

Taylor turned pro with Ottawa, starting as a rover but then moving back to defense. In the opening game at the capital's new arena the Governor General of Canada, His Honor, Earl Grey, was in attendance along with 7,000 other fans.

"It was the first time I played defense," said Cyclone. "We beat Montreal 8–5 and I got five goals, all of them on solo rushes up the ice. Some sixty years later Bobby Orr came up to the National Hockey League and began rushing the puck from defense and everybody made a big fuss about it. Heck, I was way ahead of him."

Taylor starred during an era of iron men when it bordered on unthinkable to take leave of a game for anything less than amputation.

Compared with contemporary standards, equipment in Cyclone's day was primitive, particularly the skates. Yet, Taylor, who avidly watched NHL games well into the 1970s, insisted that he skated as fast as any of the moderns. "Today's game just *looks* faster," he explained, "because of the longer passes. We'd held on to the puck until we could give it to a teammate or until the puck was taken away from us.

"Shooting a puck was a little different then, too. We didn't have anything like today's slapshot. Ours was a wrist shot, pretty damaging and ten times more accurate than the slapshot. But in my day 90 percent of the game was skating and 2 percent stickhandling; the rest was courage and condition."

Taylor was an exceptional player wherever he performed. When Ottawa won the Stanley Cup in 1909 and Cyclone was the toast of the town, he had scored 17 goals in twenty-one games, a marvelous accomplishment at the time.

"My skating was such," he added, "that once I passed an opponent I didn't have to worry about him anymore. I made no attempt to be rough or dirty. I'd have been foolish to try that because I didn't have any enemies and I didn't want to make any.

"It was easy to get into trouble, considering that we were on the ice for sixty out of sixty minutes and we were getting hit after hit. The physical aspect would grow on you. Today players hit each other one minute, but they're pulled off the ice the next and they cool down.''

Unlike many retired aces who become distant from the game and embittered because of their treatment, Cyclone remained a keen follower of hockey. In his eighties he was still active as honorary president of the British Columbia Amateur League.

Cyclone Taylor was a man of his word. He lived an active life in Vancouver until his death in 1979 at the age of 93, just two weeks short of his 94th birthday.

When he was eighty, the critics were comparing Gordie Howe, Bobby Hull and Bobby Orr to Cyclone Taylor because he was the original great one and certainly earned eighth ranking on *Hockey's 100.*

9 Doug Harvey
(1947–1969)

If ever there was a hockey player whose style could be described as eminently laconic it was that of Doug Harvey, who appeared never to panic in more than two decades of defense play that, modestly speaking, was marvelous to behold.

Others were more emphatic about the crew-cut Montrealer who always seemed to wear a whimsical grin. "Doug Harvey was the greatest defenseman who ever played hockey—bar none," said Toe Blake, who coached Harvey and the Canadiens for six years. "Usually, a defenseman specializes in one thing and builds a reputation on that, but Doug could do everything well."

When Harvey played out his career during the 1968–69 season, Bobby Orr had emerged as the new defensive phenom and, in years to come, inexperienced journalists, who did not have the good fortune to view Harvey in his prime, labelled Orr the best ever.

Orr, clearly, was not and, unlike Harvey, never did stand the test of time. Harvey, even in his declining years, was a better defensive defenseman than Orr.

The Harvey dossier is filled with superlatives. He won the Norris Trophy as the NHL's best defenseman (remember it wasn't awarded until 1953, six years after Harvey became a Canadien) in 1955, 1956, 1957, 1958, 1960, 1961 and 1962. Doug was a First All-Star in 1952, 1953, 1954, 1955, 1956, 1957, 1958, 1960, 1961 and 1962.

Thanks to Harvey's uncannily accurate passes, the Canadiens were able to create a style all their own called "Firewagon Hockey." Always, the Montrealers appeared to be in a grand rush to get the puck out of their zone and into enemy territory with Harvey orchestrating the attack.

Harvey often betrayed a touch of the Harpo Marx spirit which was a vital ingredient in the Canadiens' makeup. "Doug," recalled the often somber Maurice Richard, "had a terrific sense of humor and he'd relax us with a gag whenever we were tense."

Doug was not all laughs. Although he was neither as consummately tough nor as hard-hitting as Eddie Shore (an important distinction between the two), Harvey's nice-guy facade could be penetrated by an enemy's indiscretion. He played the game clean, but woe to the foe who played him dirty.

Harvey-watchers agree that Doug's aplomb was lost in the extreme during a game against the Rangers in November 1956. It had been Harvey's contention that a wiry New York center, never lauded for his lily-white play, had developed an obnoxious, not to mention dangerous, habit of "kicking skates." When Harvey and Red Sullivan would pursue the puck into a corner of the rink, Red would kick Harvey's skates out from under him, making it very easy for Doug to fall on his head.

Several warnings failed to impress Sullivan so Harvey decided to escalate the war. During the fateful game in question Harvey and Sullivan once again appeared to be on a collision course when Harvey planted the pointed blade of his stick in

Sullivan's gut. The Rangers' center was taken to the hospital with a ruptured spleen.

For a time Sullivan's condition was so grave he was given the last rites of the Catholic Church. Fortunately, Sullivan recovered and resumed his playing career. When Harvey was traded by the Canadiens to the Rangers in 1961, Doug immediately became player-coach and one of his centers was none other than Sullivan. They maintained a reasonably amicable relationship, at least superficially, but insiders believed that the mutual loathing remained.

At the time that Harvey was dealt to New York the Broadway sextet had been in the slough of despond. Few critics expected Harvey to turn them around—especially in his dual role. He fooled them, not only turning the Rangers into a playoff club but winning the Norris Trophy and a nomination to the First All-Stars to boot.

The Rangers relationship didn't last long, mostly because of Doug's desire to remain one of the boys and not a martinet coach. "When I was coach," he explained, "I couldn't be one of the boys. This way, if I want a beer with 'em, I get a beer."

Harvey hooked on briefly with the Detroit Red Wings but when the NHL expanded from six to twelve teams in 1967 he was signed by Lynn Patrick, manager of the St. Louis Blues. For Doug it was like old times. His buddy from Canadiens days, Dickie Moore, was making a comeback in St. Louis and another old crony, Jacques Plante, soon would arrive.

Harvey's excellence surfaced during the 1968 divisional playoffs when the Blues met the favored Philadelphia Flyers. St. Louis won the series in seven games and made it to the Stanley Cup finals in the club's first year of existence.

Douglas Norman Harvey was born December 19, 1924, in Montreal, and like many of his future teammates such as Dickie Moore and Rocket Richard perfected his game on the city's outdoor rinks.

Those who remember the young Harvey believe that he could have become a major league baseball star. He played two summers in the Border Baseball League at Ottawa, once leading all hitters with an average of .351. When the Boston Braves (then in the National League) tried to persuade him to forsake hockey for baseball he refused and concentrated on the ice game.

Doug's apprenticeship was served with the Montreal Royals of the high-grade Quebec Senior Hockey League. In 1947 he was promoted once and for all to Les Canadiens. During his blue line stewardship the Montreal sextet finished first five times and won the Stanley Cup a remarkable six times.

Based on his performance, Harvey deserved to be inducted into the Hockey Hall of Fame shortly after his retirement in 1969, but four years went by before the NHL nabobs got around to inducting Doug. The reason—to anyone familiar with Harvey's habits—was obvious. He always had been an antimanagement maverick who liked nothing better than twitting the establishment. By letting Harvey twist in the wind before they got around to installing him in the Hall, the hockey barons got their revenge.

But Doug got the last laugh. When the rival World Hockey Association made its professional debut in 1972, a bitter scramble for talent ensued. One of the prize prospects was Mark Howe, son of the immortal Gordie Howe. The NHL bosses expected that Mark would sign with one of their teams, either Boston or more appropriately Detroit.

Harvey, who had been named assistant manager of the WHA's Houston Aeros, persuaded the Texas-based hockey club to sign both Mark and his older brother, Marty. The Aeros agreed and included Gordie in the package, thereby completing one of the most astonishing coups in sports.

Unfortunately, Harvey's liaison with hockey was less pleasant after that. The affiliation with the Aeros was short-lived and, according to friends, Doug fell upon less pleasant times.

Those who felt a kinship with Doug preferred recalling his golden years with the Canadiens, especially when he was the linchpin of their power play, the defenseman at the point when they won an unparalleled five Stanley Cups in succession and finished in first place in six out of seven years.

Thanks, in large part, to Doug Harvey. As the ultimate defenseman, he was surpassed only by Shore, who could deliver the more robust bodychecks. Doug earned his way into the select circle.

10 Wayne Gretzky
(1978–   )

There has never been anything quite like *The Kid*.

At age nine he was commanding headlines across Canada. No one had ever scored goals with the ease and frequency of thimblelike Wayne Gretzky.

He was, of course, no one to be taken seriously. By the time he reached his teens he would discover cars, girls and beer. Hockey would be forgotten as it was with so many other high-scoring tykes before him.

But at age sixteen Gretzky, who by now was built along the dimensions of a giant needle, was scoring at such a profligate pace he was being pursued by every major league scout on the continent.

Still, few believed that he could ever cut it with the pros. He was too skinny, relatively slow and with no disposition to bodycheck. Nevertheless, defying all odds, at age seventeen Gretzky signed a professional contract with Indianapolis of the World Hockey Association.

People in the know said he would last a month—if that long—under the bombardment of hockey's most notorious headhunters. Instead, he was an instant star and got better by the month. When the Racers of Indianapolis suffered an assortment of financial traumas, Gretzky was dealt to the Edmonton Oilers and continued his relentless improvement. And when the Oilers were admitted to the National Hockey League in 1979 a substantial number of doubters remained.

The WHA was easy, they scoffed. The NHL was the real thing. Gretzky, it was suggested, would wilt under the incessant pressure.

At age eighteen, *The Kid* made his NHL debut. The results were mind-boggling, to say the least. He finished tied for first in total scoring points with 51 goals in seventy-nine games, not to mention a league-leading 86 assists and a total of 137 points. He additionally won the Hart Trophy as the league's most valuable player, was picked to the Second All-Star Team and surely would have been designated the rookie of the year had he not been disqualified on a technicality (he had previously played in the WHA and therefore was deemed ineligible for the Calder Memorial Trophy). And he captured the Lady Byng Trophy for sportsmanship and excellence. "Right from the start," said St. Louis Blues coach Red Berenson, "he just tore the league apart. It's scary to think what he might do before he's done."

Just as Berenson suggested, Gretzky increased his scoring dynamics with each passing year. As a sophomore in the NHL, *The Kid*—now nineteen years old—alternated between devastating and terrifying. This time he led the NHL in scoring (55 goals, 109 assists, 164 points), won the Hart Trophy, made the First All-Star Team and set NHL records for assists and points in a regular season.

"He has the greatest moves I've ever seen," said Henri Richard, a Hall of Famer who, as a center like Gretzky, was acclaimed for *his* moves.

Richard watched from a seat in Montreal's hallowed Forum in April 1981 as Gretzky choreographed one of the most uncanny upsets in Stanley Cup playoff annals. The Oilers, not merely underdogs but 200–1 longshots, routed the Cana-

diens in three straight games of the best-of-five series as *The Kid* mesmerized the foe.

Gordie Howe, who played against Gretzky and watched Wayne develop from his WHA debut on to NHL maturity, perceived *The Kid* another way: ''Wayne's the only guy I've ever known who plays 70 percent of the game from the neck up.''

By the time the 1981–82 season—Gretzky's third in the NHL—had begun it had become evident that all previous adjectives would be inadequate to describe his performance. From the very first drop of the puck he sprinted far ahead of his closest pursuers and then an irony developed; Wayne had principally been renowned for his stickhandling and playmaking rather than his shot, but now he was popping goals at a breathtaking pace.

Only two players in NHL history had been able to score 50 goals in fifty games. Maurice Richard did it in 1944 and Mike Bossy equalled the mark in 1980–81. As stoppable as a runaway spaceship, *Gretzky scored his 50th goal in only his thirty-ninth game* and finished the 1981–82 campaign leaving the record book in shambles. He totalled 92 goals, exceeding the all-time record (76) previously set by Phil Esposito, collected 120 assists, topping his own mark, and amassed 212 points.

During the 1981 Stanley Cup quarterfinals between the Oilers and defending Stanley Cup champion Islanders, Gretzky very nearly developed an even more monumental upset than the previous one over the Canadiens. Although the Islanders eventually prevailed, they were defeated twice and even their respected general manager, Bill Torrey, was moved to verse to put Gretzky in perspective. Torrey sent the following poem to his pal, Lou Nanne, general manager of the Minnesota North Stars:

> *This epistle will be rather short*
> *and sweet*
> *I need time to figure a way to*
> *keep number 99 off the score*
> *sheet.*
> *It's scary to think disaster lurks*
> *due to some 20-year-old,*
> *But after looking at the tapes,*
> *Gretzky is something to behold.*

Gretzky was shut out by the Islanders in the 1983 Stanley Cup finals, but he got revenge a year later scoring pivotal break away goals against New York goalie Bill Smith in the finals. Gretzky, the Oilers captain, thus carried the Stanley Cup over his head for the first time. Gretzky's other accomplishments were no less arresting. In 1984 and for the fifth consecutive time, he was voted the Hart Trophy as the league's most valuable player, which he claimed was ''the best because it goes well beside the Stanley Cup.'' A first-team All-Star center for the fourth consecutive season, he won the Art Ross Trophy as the NHL's leading scorer, also for the fourth successive time. Playing in 74 games, he scored 82 goals and 118 assists for 205 points, just seven short of his own record of 212 set in the 1981–82 season. In addition, he set records for scoring the most consecutive points (51 games), most consecutive assists (17 games) and the most shorthanded goals (12). To top it all, for the third year in a row he was voted the Seagram's Seven Crowns of Sports

Award, an objective computer analysis of all pertinent statistical data upon which athletic achievement is based.

Wayne Gretzky was born January 26, 1961, in Brantford, Ontario. Almost from the moment his father, Walter, handed him a stick, Wayne was able to perform magic with the rubber. "He never had to skate well," his father pointed out, "because as a kid he could stay in the same place and beat a player three or four times."

He was seventeen-years-old and weighed only 161 pounds when he signed a four-year, $875,000 contract with the Indianapolis Racers. When the Racers tripped, Oilers' owner Peter Pocklington bought Gretzky's contract for $850,000 and moved him to Edmonton. It proved to be one of the most sagacious moves in the chronicles of any sport. From the moment he set skate in Edmonton's Northlands Coliseum, Gretzky guaranteed that all 17,300 seats would be filled—and they were. By January 1982 Gretzky had become so outstanding an attraction that scalpers were demanding $200-a-ticket for a regular Oilers-Maple Leafs game in Toronto because the fans wanted so desperately to see *The Kid*. "The NHL needs someone to hang its hat on, and Gretzky looks like a hat tree," said Gordie Howe.

Because of his virtuosity as a goal-scorer, playmaker, leader and ruler of offensive hockey in the 1980s, Gretzky must qualify for the inner circle of *Hockey's 100* —the top ten players of all time—and for several meaningful reasons, but most of all for his extraordinary arithmetic.

In 1982–83 for example, Gretzky led the league in goals (71) and assists (125) for 196 points. It marked the second consecutive season in which he was the top goal, assists *and* point producer. Not surprisingly, he also was named to the first All-Star team for the third year in a row. All legitimate barometers of talent—such as the Seagram's Seven Crown of Sports award—rated him at the head of the class. Despite his excellence, Gretzky nevertheless was subject to an occasional barb.

In fairness to Wayne's critics it is important to note some minority views about him. To begin with, Gretzky has not even come close to passing the vital test of time. While his goal and assist largesse is staggering to behold, he cannot be listed ahead of titans such as Gordie Howe, Eddie Shore, Red Kelly, Frank Boucher and Maurice Richard, each of whom survived more than a decade in an NHL which was infinitely tougher than it is today.

Hall of Famer Toe Blake once very accurately suggested that a "ten-year-rule" be enforced before a player could legitimately be called "great." Blake believed that a major leaguer had to demonstrate that he could excel over a decade before he could be lumped with the immortals. When asked about Gretzky during the 1981–82 season, Blake asserted: "Gretzky is the best player *this* year. Bobby Orr was the best over ten years. Maurice Richard was the best over fifteen years. Jean Beliveau was the best over twenty years and Gordie Howe was the best over twenty-five."

Other critics have perceptively noted that Gretzky, for all his records, is basically a one-way player. "You can't deny his offensive virtues," said NHL scout Aldo Guidolin, "but there is a center named Bryan Trottier of the New York Islanders, who can score, set up plays *and also* play equally as well defensively. Gretzky is not as versatile when you take into consideration the bodychecking and backchecking that a Trottier does."

In an informal poll of professional hockey people conducted in *The Hockey News* during the 1981–82 season, coaches, managers and scouts were asked which player they would prefer in their lineup *to win one game,* Trottier or Gretzky. The answer was unanimously in Trottier's favor because of his defensive skills, bodychecking ability and overall versatility.

Others in the anti-Gretzky claque have noticed that, under pressure, he has been prone to become petulant, "like a spoiled child," as one reporter noted. "He's always complaining to officials," said Richard Brodeur, the Vancouver Canucks goaltender. "Guy Lafleur and Bryan Trottier take as much (bleep) as Gretzky does but you don't see them squawking. Wayne is a nice guy away from the rink, but on the ice he's arrogant."

Some opponents suggest that Gretzky could not maintain his peerless pace were it not for the presence of hulking Dave Semenko on the Oilers' bench. Semenko, one of the largest and toughest players in the NHL, has often portrayed the "enforcer" when a foe threatened Gretzky.

"It reached a point during the 1981–82 season," said Ron Smith, assistant coach of the Canucks, "that if someone just brushed Gretzky, Wayne would wink over to Semenko, telling him to get that man."

When Semenko was slapped with a six-game suspension midway in the 1981–82 season, it was considered pertinent that Gretzky's—and the Oilers'—performance dipped conspicuously.

Whatever Gretzky's debits, his assets cannot be disputed. "Not since Bobby Orr came into the NHL in 1966 as an eighteen-year-old has anyone captured the imagination of hockey fans the way Gretzky has," wrote E. M. Swift in *Sports Illustrated.* "And no one has appealed to the general public like Gretzky since Bobby Hull appeared on the cover of *Time* in 1968."

It is quite possible that ten years from now Gretzky will emerge as the greatest hockey player of all time. At the moment he is the best in his class—a worthy member of *Hockey's 100*—but until he survives Blake's "ten-year-rule," he will have to remain no better than tenth.

Finally, it should be noted that Gretzky has not played for a Stanley Cup-winner and not scored a single goal in the 1983 playoff finals when his Oilers were shellacked in four straight games by the New York Islanders.

11 Glenn Hall
(1952–1971)

When Chuck Rayner played goal for an embattled New York Rangers team during the late 1940s, somebody asked him what he would do if his son announced he was going to enter the goaltending profession. Rayner wasted little time telling the other that he'd grab the goalie stick out of his hand and hit him over the head with it. Goaltending was the toughest job in sports, according to Rayner, particularly in those primitive days when goalies never dreamed of wearing a mask to protect their oft-stitched faces. Any goaltender who could survive 100 straight games without missing a contest was considered extraordinary. How, then, can one describe Glenn Henry Hall, who tenaciously guarded the twine for 552 straight games without a mask and with an artistry rarely matched for his position? They can simply call him "Mr. Goalie," the monicker he earned for nineteen seasons in the NHL as the epitome of the professional goaltender.

Hall broke in with the Detroit Red Wings in 1955, displacing the great Terry Sawchuk as the Wings' regular goalie. He wasted no time making his mark in the NHL, skating off with the Calder Trophy as the league's rookie of the year. After two campaigns in Detroit, Hall was traded to Chicago where he captured the Vezina Trophy in 1963 and 1967 (shared with Denis DeJordy). In 1961, Hall led the Black Hawks to their first Stanley Cup since 1938, performing spectacularly as Chicago eliminated, ironically, the Red Wings in the final round. With the coming of expansion, Hall was drafted by the St. Louis Blues with whom he won his third Vezina in 1969 (shared with Jacques Plante), and the Conn Smythe Trophy in 1968. Hall also was an eleven-time All-Star; his seven First-Team berths a record for NHL goaltenders.

More indicative, however, of the intensity of Hall's play than any number of awards could ever be is an incident that occurred during a game between the Red Wings and Boston Bruins in the semifinal round of the 1957 playoffs. Minding the net for Detroit, all of a sudden Hall found himself the only Red Wing around and, as such, the target of a straight-on rush by Boston's Vic Stasiuk. Stasiuk roared in on the young goalie and shot a bullet that caught Hall on his unprotected face. He dropped to the ice cold, blood flowing from his mouth. The crowd buzzed and one writer noted that Hall, lying in a heap in his goal crease, "looked dead."

Taken from the ice on a stretcher, Hall regained consciousness in the trainer's room. Hardly impressed by the severity of his injury, Hall's first words upon awakening were, "C'mon, doc, let's get this thing over with." The physician then proceeded to weave twenty-three stitches into Hall's upper lip and mouth, which the puck had ripped open.

A half-hour later, Hall emerged, skating onto the ice, his eyes black, his face swollen and covered with bandages. As he took up his position in front of the goal, a Bruins player remarked, "I don't believe it. How do you stop this guy?" By that time the answer was clear: you didn't.

Resistant to change in his refusal to don a protective mask until late in his career,

Hall was an innovator nonetheless. He is credited with being the forerunner in the development of the "butterfly" style of goaltending, the fanning out of the pads toward the goalposts while dropping to the knees to block shots. Hall's technique, originally scoffed at as a perversion of the traditional stand-up goaltending style, eventually became the standard for goalkeepers from the late 1960s to the present.

Glenn Hall, a native of Humboldt, Saskatchewan, was born in 1931, the son of a railroad engineer. As a boy he played center and captained his public school hockey team. When he was ten, the club's goalie quit. "I picked someone to replace him but he refused," Hall said. "So did the next ten guys. As captain, I had no choice but to put on the pads myself. After a few years I actually got to like it."

So treacherous did Hall find his work that he became unique in his pregame preparations. "Before every game, and sometimes between periods, I'd get sick to my stomach; I'd have to throw up. Sometimes it happened during a game and I'd have to fight it off until the whistle blew. I tried drinking tea between periods and that seemed to help. But I didn't worry about it. Nervousness is part of the game. It helps keep me sharp." It was Hall's love-hate relationship with his profession which made his iron-man streak that much more remarkable.

Far from the madding sounds of the hockey rink, Hall now spends most of his time on his farm, although he once was a goaltending coach for the late Colorado Rockies. The old master of puck-stopping is hardly impressed with the direction of today's game and harks back to the good old days when defense was not yet against the law. "We're seeing darn little defense and I don't particularly like what I'm seeing," Mr. Goalie remarked.

From the beginning of his career Glenn Hall was a defensive gem amidst a conglomerate of offensive specialists such as Howe and Delvecchio in Detroit and Hull and Mikita in Chicago. Nonetheless, Hall retired with a shining 2.51 GA average to go with 84 shutouts in 906 career contests. He was inducted into the Hall of Fame in 1975.

Coiled in readiness in front of his cage, Hall's hair-trigger reflexes consistently kept him ahead of the most dangerous shooters in the NHL for close to two decades. For valiant service under fire with a steadiness unmatched by any other puck-stopper, Glenn Hall is hereby awarded his distinguished place among *Hockey's 100*.

12 Syl Apps (1936–1948)

With all deference to Frank Boucher and Howie Morenz, there never has been a hockey player who filled the role of a Frank Merriwether on ice better than Syl Apps. When his lilting style began gracing NHL rinks in 1936 he was hailed as the All-Canadian boy. And for good reason.

To begin with, his virtues were beyond reproach. He played the game with infinite finesse, yet with a courage and vigor that inspired every hockey-loving father to tell his son that *that* was the way he wanted his kid to do it.

Most youngsters didn't have to be told. The Toronto Maple Leafs' center was tall, handsome, lithe and lively. "He is," said Canadian author Vincent Lunny, "a Rembrandt on the ice, a Nijinsky at the goal mouth. He plays with such grace and precision you get the impression that every move is the execution of a mental image conceived long before he goes through the motions."

Apps inspired the Maple Leafs to the single most astonishing comeback hockey —and maybe all professional sport—has known when Toronto lost the first three games of the 1942 Stanley Cup finals and then regrouped and took the next four straight and the Cup.

After serving in the Canadian Army, Apps returned to the NHL and captained the Maple Leafs to two consecutive Stanley Cups in 1947 and 1948. He was thirty-three years old at the time and seemed capable, thanks to his fluid skating and superb condition, of at least two to five more years of superlative play. But he shocked the hockey world with the announcement of his retirement.

Apps won the Calder Trophy as NHL rookie of the year in 1937 and the Lady Byng Trophy in 1942. He was First All-Star center in 1939 and 1942 although there were other times when he was unaccountably overlooked by the voters.

Jack Adams, the irascible Detroit Red Wings' manager who considered the Maple Leafs his most loathed enemies, could not ignore the quality of Apps' play. "Apps," said Adams, "is the greatest center I have ever seen."

Although Apps produced many a melodramatic moment, many of his fans consider his exploits in the homestretch of the 1947–48 season his finest hour. It was a magnificent race, with Toronto neck-and-neck with Detroit in the run for first place while Apps was shooting for his 200th goal, at the time a remarkable achievement. When the final buzzer had sounded Apps had completed a three-goal "hat trick" and finished the season with 201 goals.

As dramatic as Apps' goal-scoring was, his adherence to a special code of honor won him even more applause. "He was the cleanest athlete I've ever known," said his coach Hap Day. "I used to figure I came pretty close to that myself. I didn't drink and didn't smoke but I used to do my share of swearing. That's where Apps had me beaten. He didn't smoke. He never bent his elbow except to twist his stick over an opponent's wrist. The strongest language he ever used was 'By Hum' and 'Jiminy Christmas'."

Apps' code of honor was so comprehensive that he once suggested to his boss,

Conn Smythe, that he was being overpaid. "It was the only time that ever happened to me," Smythe recalled. "Syl had crashed into a goal post, shattered his leg, and missed half the games of the 1942–43 season.

"I was paying him $6,000 that year and he came to me and said: 'Conn, I'm making more money than I deserve. I want to give you this check for $1,000.' When I heard that I almost died of heart failure. I refused the check. I figured anyone who thought in such terms was bound to square off what he thought was a debt the next season."

Joseph Sylvanus Apps was born in Paris, Ontario, on January 18, 1915, and by the time he had become a teenager exhibited superior ability in both team and individual sports. At the age of seventeen he entered McMaster University in Hamilton, Ontario, and turned out for the track team. His specialty was pole-vaulting and he became so adept at it that in 1934 he was invited to represent Canada at the British Empire Games in London, England. He later became captain of the McMaster football team and played for the college hockey squad as well.

While playing hockey for the collegians he was discovered by Smythe's friend, Bill Marsden. Smythe actually refused to scout Apps but, quite by accident, watched him play a magnificent game of football for McMaster as halfback, which changed Smythe's mind. He signed with the Maple Leafs but only after appearing in the 1936 Olympiad where before 100,000 spectators he vaulted to a sixth-place tie for Canada.

In his rookie NHL season Apps finished second in scoring to Dave "Sweeney" Schriner of the New York Americans and polled 79 out of a possible 81 points for the Calder (best rookie) Trophy.

Apps quickly established that he would brook no nonsense from the bullies. His most persuasive performance occurred when Bill (Flash) Hollett, a persnickety Boston Bruins defenseman, jammed his stick in Apps' mouth, removing two teeth.

"By hum!" snapped Apps. "This has gone far enough." He then belabored Hollett with a series of jabs and hooks that reminded onlookers of heavyweight champion Joe Louis. It was a lesson that Syl would be obliged to repeat from time to time; that he could handle his dukes as well as he could deliver goals, or help create them for a teammate.

"Syl was a terrific skater," a critic once observed, "stickhandler, and had speed to burn at all times on the ice. He possessed the faculty of breaking fast from a standing stop, which left his opposition flatfooted. He took great pride in having one of his linemates score from a play set up by him. In fact, I think that he enjoyed that better than if he had bulged the twine himself. Every time Apps touched the puck, the crowds would let out a deafening roar, because they sensed something spectacular, and in most cases he did not disappoint them."

Watching Apps in action was a wonderful experience right down to the final games of his career. In the spring of 1948, after the Leafs finished first, the Toronto sextet met the Boston Bruins in the opening playoff round.

Underdogs though they were, the Bruins led the Maple Leafs 4–2 with only eight minutes remaining in the opening game. But Syl rallied his club, scored a goal and Jim Thomson followed to tie the count, whereupon the Leafs won in overtime. They eliminated the Bruins in five games and then swept the Red Wings in four straight to retain the Cup.

When the triumphant champions stepped off the train from Detroit they were hailed by tens of thousands of Toronto fans. At city hall another 10,000 fans cheered as captain Apps was introduced. It was the last time Syl would be seen as a Maple Leaf, although his teammates urged him to reconsider.

"If Syl would only come back for one more season," said center Max Bentley, "we would be a cinch to repeat next year."

Apps, as always, was a man of his word. He retired—prematurely of course—but as a champion, just as he was when he entered the NHL.

The All-Canadian Boy had become the All-Canadian Man. His comprehensive excellence guaranteed him an exalted position among *Hockey's 100*.

13 Bobby Orr (1966–1979)

Had Bobby Orr been blessed with a pair of unassailably healthy knees his ranking most certainly would have been at least five levels higher than this position. Threatened with wobbly wheels almost from his National Hockey League debut, Orr managed to play only eight full seasons and, in the end, failed to pass the test of time, even though he was at his prime during the diluted expansion era.

A physically fit Orr would still have been playing through the early 1980s. He was an effortless skater (when the knees were right) and an intuitively brilliant tactician who was so idolized by friend and foe alike that he rarely was challenged by the NHL's woodchoppers. He was second to Eddie Shore as the ultimate Boston Bruin.

In his prime Orr was evaluated as the "Perfect Hockey Player." He played defense well enough to have won the Norris Trophy in 1968, 1969, 1970, 1971, 1972, 1973, 1974 and 1975. Offensively, Orr was no less awesome and although he was, technically, listed as a backliner he won the Art Ross Trophy for the league scoring championship in 1970 and 1975.

Orr's legion of admirers would cite chapter and verse to underline his position among hockey's definitive leaders. Harry Sinden, who coached Orr when the Bruins won the Stanley Cup in 1970, perceived aspects of Orr's play that were superior to those of Gordie Howe.

"Howe could do everything but not at top speed," said Sinden. "Hull went at top speed but couldn't do everything. Orr would do everything, and do it at top speed."

That was true only during those precious few years when Orr was not under the knife or recuperating from knee surgery. After two NHL seasons he underwent two operations.

By the time Orr retired in 1979, he had amassed an impressive collection of silverwear. Apart from the Norris and Ross trophies, he had won the Calder Trophy as rookie of the year in 1967; the Hart Trophy as the NHL's most valuable player in 1970, 1971 and 1972 and the Conn Smythe Trophy as the most valuable player in the Stanley Cup playoffs in 1970 and 1972.

Still, there were several chinks in Orr's armor. He betrayed numerous defensive weaknesses and rarely threw a damaging bodycheck. He won the Norris Trophy not because of defensive ability but rather because he amassed points on offense. Additionally, Orr, for all his abilities, played on only two Stanley Cup-winning teams—in 1970 and 1972. (By contrast, Doug Harvey skated for six Cup-winners.) And in some ways Orr was a selfish hockey player. During the 1974 Stanley Cup finals in which the Philadelphia Flyers upset the Bruins, the Bruins were defeated because Orr insisted on carrying the puck rather than pass off to teammates.

Yet, Orr possessed a quality that only a few have brought to the game: charisma. His blond hair flowing in the breeze he created by skating upwards of twenty-seven miles per hour gave the illusion of a Mercury on skates. Orr was a dashing figure and seemingly capable of coming up with the big play at the appropriate time.

Robert Gordon Orr was born in Parry Sound, Ontario on March 20, 1948. His all-inclusive talents were detected by big-league scouts before he reached his teens, but it was the Boston Bruins who made the decisive move in gaining a lock on his services after watching him as a twelve-year-old playing in Gananoque, Ontario. In those days a professional team could gain control of a twelve-year-old simply by putting his name on a protected list. That done, the Bruins patiently waited for Orr to mature.

His ripening as a hockey star was faster than anyone could imagine. By the time he was sixteen he had become the talk of Canada, and the Bruins, then a last-place club, began the unusual ritual of touting a teenager who had never played a professional game as the eventual Messiah who would save the franchise.

The NHL establishment then became shaken by the kid from Parry Sound because he did what neither Gordie Howe nor Rocket Richard had done when they were invited to the bigs: Bobby brought an agent with him. His representative, Toronto attorney R. Alan Eagleson, stunned Bruins' manager Hap Emms with the declaration that Orr would not come to Boston unless he was rewarded with a contract commensurate with his ability. At the time, it was an outrageous demand, particularly in view of the fact that Orr had yet to play a single game as a professional. Emms objected to Eagleson's presence but Orr replied, in effect, no Eagleson, no Orr.

The result was a two-year $150,000 contract that caused reverberations throughout the league. Although nobody knew it at the time, Orr was helping to organize and perpetuate an NHL Players' Association with Eagleson at the helm.

Orr's salary ballooned as his value increased. When he became a Bruin they were at the bottom of the league. Within three years they were at the top and Orr became the biggest drawing card in the game. "Bobby," said Eagleson, "is the only player capable of filling every rink in the NHL."

The "Orr Effect," as his style came to be known to analysts, had, and continues to have, a profound impact on the manner in which hockey is played. Before Bobby donned a Bruin's uniform, defensemen, as a rule, concentrated on defense. While there were rushing backliners of note in the past—Eddie Shore and Red Kelly being the most prominent—none of them influenced a major change in the mode of play. But Orr did.

Bobby's idea of playing defense was to poke the puck away from the foe and then carry it the length of the rink for either a shot on goal or a pass to a teammate, usually center Phil Esposito. In no time at all every Canadian kid wanted to be another Bobby Orr.

In a sense the NHL became too dependent on Orr. When his knees began crumbling in the late 1970s so, too, did the NHL. It lost a network television contract and suffered at the gate. There simply was no successor to the golden boy —at least none who could sell the game so effectively.

Yet, Orr's rainbow evaporated almost as quickly as it appeared on the hockey horizon. After Boston's 1972 Stanley Cup win, Bobby was never the same, literally, figuratively and physically. He betrayed his weaknesses during the 1973 playoffs when, without his teammate Esposito, who had been injured, he could not lift the Bruins past the opening round and they were upset by the Rangers. Again, in 1974, he was stymied by Fred Shero and the Flyers. He never again played on a Cup-winner and soon became embroiled in an intense and prolonged contract dispute with the Bruins' owners.

If the NHL had become too dependent upon Orr, so, too, did Bobby become too dependent upon Eagleson. Had Orr been left to his own devices it is likely that he would have remained a Bruin until he was compelled to hang up his skates. But Eagleson was calling the shots and Bobby did what nobody familiar with the NHL scene had ever believed possible: he left the Bruins and wound up signing with the Chicago Black Hawks in 1976.

In some ways the declining days of Orr were reminiscent of those of Babe Ruth, who will always be associated with the New York Yankees. Ruth's final season was spent playing for the Boston Braves. Orr did his thing in the Windy City. For both it was terribly anticlimactic.

On the few occasions when the knees were not causing him excruciating pain, Orr displayed signs of the glorious past. But the flashes of finesse were insufficient for the Black Hawks, the fans and, most of all, Bobby himself.

He announced his retirement in 1979 and, like Ruth, seemed out of place on the sidelines. His long-term friendship with Eagleson ended abruptly and bitterly for both sides.

In 1979, amid much pomp and circumstance, Orr was named a special assistant to NHL President John Ziegler but, again, the marriage was not binding. Less than two years later Orr, complaining that he was not much more than a figurehead, said he would no longer work with the league.

Returning to his beloved Boston, Orr maintained his income by doing endorsements and, in 1981, he became the unofficial advisor (agent) to Bobby Carpenter, the teen-aged wonder from Massachusetts who was selected first in the NHL draft by the Washington Capitals. He has since become a successful businessman while remaining active in hockey as a consultant.

He was a delightful athlete who at one point could claim that the sky was his limit. In truth, one can only say that Orr's career can be summed up by what might have been.

He was a great one but, because of his limbs, not the greatest.

14 Bobby Hull
(1957–1980)

It is not symbolic that Bobby Hull, the Golden Jet of the ice lanes, should be selected for fourteenth position in *Hockey's 100*. Despite the lustre that characterized his career, it ended amid a tragic divorce scenario, followed by a new romance and a horrible automobile accident. Thirteen should have been the number.

These unfortunate events seemed patently unfair to a glamorous performer who brought nothing but guts, goals and glamour to his profession. He did so as a member of a colorful Chicago Black Hawks team in the late 1950s and 1960s, and then did it again with the Winnipeg Jets of the World Hockey Association.

Adulation for Hull was generated by veteran journalists such as Jim Proudfoot of The Toronto *Star* as well as newcomers to the game like Dwight Chapin of the *Los Angeles Times*. Chapin watched the Golden Jet and offered the following critique: "Hull did everything. He scored twice. He added two assists. He was in on power plays. He killed penalties. He talked to his team, and argued moderately with officials."

Hull's impact on the contemporary game was manifold. He popularized the slapshot to such an extent that players who never before had tried the golf-type blast were adding it to their repertoire. He was easily the most magnetic player of the early 1960s and, more than any other player, popularized the game and inspired the NHL to expand from six to twelve teams in 1967.

In terms of his impact on the course of hockey history, Hull was pivotal in the creation of the World Hockey Association and the fact that the upstart league was able to survive and challenge the NHL for six years.

"One reason for that," commented Proudfoot, "was that Bobby was a pro. And he always had plenty of time for the fans."

Like Gordie Howe, Hull was an utterly courageous athlete. Once, during a playoff game against the Red Wings, Hull's nose was smashed by the stick of Detroit's Bruce MacGregor. Doctors said it was futile for Hull to dress again for the series. But a few hours before the match Hull left the hospital, dashed to the airport and caught a plane to Detroit. Although his face was covered almost completely by a plaster mask and he could hardly breathe, the Golden Jet scored a hat trick.

Hull won the Art Ross Trophy as the NHL's leading scorer in 1960, 1962 and 1966 and the Lady Byng Trophy for skill and gentlemanly play in 1966. He was a First Team All-Star left wing in 1960, 1962, 1964, 1965, 1966, 1967, 1968, 1969 and 1972. Hull was voted into the Hockey Hall of Fame in 1983.

Perhaps the most meaningful goal in Hull's career was scored on March 12, 1966, against the New York Rangers. The Golden Jet had scored his 50th goal earlier, tying the mark set by Maurice Richard, Bernie Geoffrion and himself. But no one ever had levitated above the 50-goal level during the regular season.

Earlier in the 1965–66 campaign Hull had missed five games because of torn knee ligaments but he managed to regain his form and scored his 50th goal in his fifty-seventh game. Now the entire hockey world had its eyes on Hull.

He failed to flash the red goal light in game fifty-eight, game fifty-nine and game sixty. The site of game sixty-one was cavernous Chicago Stadium, which was overflowing with 21,000 spectators—4,000 above the listed seating capacity.

The Rangers scored twice in the second period to take a 2–0 lead while Hull was manacled by the New York checking corps. Early in the third period, Bobby broke free and skimmed a pass to teammate Chico Maki, who converted it for the Black Hawks' first score. Shortly thereafter New York defenseman Harry Howell was tagged with a two-minute slashing penalty.

Black Hawks coach Billy Reay fingered Hull to take the ice as point man on the Chicago power play. For more than a minute the Rangers defused the Black Hawks' attack but Hull and teammates Eric Nesterenko, Lou Angotti and Bill Hay regrouped for another assault. Angotti headmanned the rubber to Hull, who loped across the New York blue line. He had decelerated to three-quarter time as his mates moved into position. Nesterenko swerved in front of the Rangers' net where stringbean goalie Cesare Maniago had his eyes riveted on Hull's stick.

Instead of relying on his potent slapshot Hull flicked his mighty wrists and the puck blurred its way toward Maniago. The Rangers' goalie prepared for the blast, was momentarily distracted as Angotti tipped the goalie's stick and continued across the goal mouth. Before Maniago could regain his composure the puck plopped into the twine and Chicago Stadium turned into a cacophony of screaming, hoarse voices. The Golden Jet had scored his 51st goal at 5:34 of the third period. As the decibel count rose, Bobby skated to the section where his wife was sitting and whispered to her through the protective glass, "Well, I did it."

He finished the season with a total of 54 goals. During the 1968–69 season he scored 58 goals and in 1971–72, his last NHL year before his remarkable "jump" to the WHA, he reached 50 goals once more.

Hull's contract was up for renewal and his popularity had reached an all-time high in the Windy City. Few doubted that he would wear the Indian-crested Black Hawks jersey when the 1972–73 season began. But the WHA had arrived, promising bundles of cash to NHL superstars who would dare leave the established league for the uncharted future of the new circuit.

When it was learned that Hull was having difficulty agreeing on a new pact with the tightwad Black Hawks, the WHA zeroed in on him and began what would become a long romance. The Winnipeg Jets, owned by rotund Ben Hatskin, had drawn Hull's name in a draft of NHL flesh. Hatskin offered Hull a then astronomical $1,000,000 for five years.

When Hull balked the WHA raised the ante to $2,000,000. Meanwhile, the Black Hawks' high command failed to impress Hull with their salary offerings or their sincerity. On June 27, 1972, Hull rode a Rolls-Royce through St. Paul, Minnesota, to autograph the WHA portion of his contract. Then the motorcade headed for the airport where a chartered airliner waited to take Hull and family, Hatskin, and their entourage to Winnipeg, where he signed the Jets contract.

Robert Marvin Hull was born January 3, 1939, in Point Anne, Ontario. When he was a fourteen-year-old skating for a Woodstock, Ontario, Junior B team, Black Hawks coach Bob Wilson discovered Bobby and lined him up for a future contract much in the manner that the Bruins landed Bobby Orr.

Bobby made his NHL debut in 1957–58 and despite his powerful strides and Promethean strength he was less than prolific. The turnabout for Hull, oddly enough, was a postseason European junket involving the Black Hawks and the Rangers. "Bobby got a lot of ice time," said Muzz Patrick, then manager of the Rangers, "and he seemed to gain confidence with each shift. He was a different player after that."

Within three seasons Hull had traumatized goalies with what was officially regarded as the hardest shot ever to be hurled netward. Its speed was variously estimated at between 110 and 120 miles per hour. "When the puck left his stick," recalled former Pittsburgh Penguins goalie Les Binkley, "it looked like a sweet pea. Then, as it picked up speed it looked smaller and smaller. Then, you didn't see it anymore."

Bobby led the league in goals (39) and points (81) in 1959–60 and repeated two years later with 50 goals and 84 points. In 1961 he figured prominently in the Black Hawks' first Stanley Cup triumph since 1938 and only one since then.

Hull's shot was only one feature of his armament. His mighty legs and equally powerful arms enabled Bobby to withstand bodychecks that would have demoralized lesser players. With such raw power at his disposal Hull could have been a menacing player but—to his everlasting credit—he chose to play clean hockey. Hull suffered as a result and was goaded into numerous embroglios by "shadows" like Bryan Watson and John Ferguson. One evening Ferguson broke Hull's jaw. A few weeks later Bobby returned to combat wearing a massive guard around his injured mouth. Before the night was up, Ferguson had provoked Hull into another fight, completely oblivious to the Golden Jet's wound.

Hull's positive attitude toward the WHA, its fans and its administrators did much to perpetuate the league's existence long after its projected life expectancy. He was a First Team All-Star left wing in 1974 and 1975. During the 1974–75 season he scored 77 goals in seventy-eight games although the opposition was not up to NHL standards. Nevertheless, in his advanced years Hull seemed like a colt, skating on a line with two creative Swedes, Anders Hedberg and Ulf Nilsson.

When Hedberg and Nilsson jumped to the NHL's New York Rangers it marked the beginning of the end for Hull. Family problems began to affect his play and Hull "retired" until the NHL and WHA finally merged. The Golden Jet had hoped that Winnipeg would swing a deal with the Black Hawks so that he could complete his career in Chicago. But neither Jets general manager John Ferguson nor his Black Hawks counterpart, Bob Pulford, could agree on a deal, so Hull unwillingly returned to Winnipeg and played eighteen games for the Jets as an NHLer once more.

In February 1980 he was traded to Hartford, where he teamed with Gordie Howe, another distinguished senior citizen. Hull had played nine games when his lady friend was involved in a near-fatal automobile accident. Rather than continue playing, Hull visited the hospital as often as possible and decided against finishing the season.

And that, sadly, is how Bobby Hull ended his hockey career. It was an anticlimactic last act to an otherwise glorious pair of decades and does not in any way detract from Hull's accomplishments on and off the ice. He merited 14th position in every way.

15 Joe Malone
(1909–1922)

When all is said and done the essence of hockey is goal-scoring, and for the first fifty years of the game's existence nobody did it better than Joe Malone.

During the 1917–18 season Malone scored 44 goals in twenty games, a pace that never has been matched in major league hockey. In terms of a single red light outburst Malone also stands alone, having scored seven goals in a game on the night of January 20, 1920. Three of the goals were scored during two minutes of the third period.

Many respected observers regard Malone—more than Maurice Richard or Mike Bossy—as the greatest all-around scorer who ever trod the NHL lanes. "Joe might have been the most prolific scorer of all time if they had played more games in those days," said Frank J. Selke, the former Montreal Canadiens managing director who remembered Malone as a young professional.

Normally a center, Malone also showed to advantage on left wing. The handsome native of Quebec City played his early hockey for teams in Ontario before being signed by the Quebec Bulldogs.

"Quite often," Malone remembered, "I played fifty or fifty-five minutes of a sixty-minute game. In those days they didn't bother too much about changing lines, only individuals. There were only about nine or ten players on each team."

One might wonder why Malone never attained the prominence of a Richard, Howe or Bossy. Mostly it was because of the nature of professional hockey in the years immediately before, during and after World War I when Joe was in his prime. The NHL, and its predecessors, were all-Canadian leagues that lacked the advantage of American media coverage, and so little was known in the United States of Malone or his uncanny scoring gifts.

Unlike contemporary scorers who frequently play against second- and third-rate goaltenders, Malone regularly faced the best including the revered Georges Vezina after whom the Vezina Trophy is named.

Malone's impact on the game transcended his goal-scoring. Like Bobby Hull, Joe had a profound effect on both a specific team (Montreal Canadiens) as well as the National Hockey League itself. Born on November 22, 1917, the NHL launched its premiere season with four teams—Les Canadiens, Ottawa, Montreal Wanderers and the Toronto Arenas. Before the season had ended the Wanderers folded and the Canadiens were ailing as well but the addition of Malone, who had been acquired from Quebec, was just the tonic the Canadiens required.

Had Malone been a player in the 1980s he would have commanded a salary in the $200,000–$300,000 range. But during the tenuous days of the NHL's youth, players like Malone were so poorly paid they often were compelled to find outside work to supplement their income. During the 1918–19 season Joe played only in the Canadiens' home games so that he could keep his other source of employment.

"I had hooked on to a good job in Quebec City which promised a secure future," Malone explained, "something hockey in those days couldn't."

When the Quebec Bulldogs were revived for the 1919–20 season Joe was returned to his old team and devoted his energies full time to hockey.

He was virtually irresistible and never more so than on his record-breaking seven-goal night in 1920. Unfortunately, the game was played during an evening when the temperature hovered between twenty and twenty-five below zero and only a handful of spectators turned up at the rink.

Even when Joe set his 44-goal record, he received a minimum of attention, a remarkable contrast to the furor over Maurice Richard's 50 goals in fifty games and Mike Bossy's similar accomplishment, not to mention Wayne Gretzky's 50 goals in thirty-nine games.

"The funny thing," said Malone, "is that there was more publicity about my record when Maurice Richard broke it than there was when I set it, and all the years afterward."

Maurice Joseph Malone was born February 28, 1890, in Quebec City and enjoyed his first glow of glory in his hometown, beginning in 1909 when he signed with the Quebec Bulldogs of the National Hockey Association, the predecessor of the NHL. Within two years he had become the architect of a champion. Quebec won the Stanley Cup in 1912 after a splendidly pulsating regular season race.

In time a splendid rivalry—not unlike the Joe DiMaggio-Ted Williams match-up —developed between Malone and Frank Nighbor, Ottawa's gifted center. During the 1916–17 season the pair were running neck-and-neck for the scoring championship. After nineteen games Malone had 41 goals while Nighbor had 36 in the same number of contests.

On March 3, 1917, Ottawa and Quebec met in the final game of the twenty-game schedule. "This game," said Malone, "would, more than any, prove to me that you can be a hero one day or one year and a bum the next."

The game would decide whether Ottawa or Quebec would face Montreal in a playoff for the championship of eastern Canada. It was a game that Malone wanted badly, not only for his team but for the fact that he would win the goal-scoring championship for the third time if he could maintain his lead over Nighbor.

Before the opening faceoff, several of the Ottawa players warned Malone that they would do everything in their power to insure that Nighbor regain the league scoring lead.

"Ottawa had two players covering and shadowing me all night," Malone remembered. "I finally lost my temper and, as a result, gave my most ineffective performance of the season, perhaps of my entire career. I didn't score a single goal."

Nighbor was at the top of his game but only managed one goal after two periods. Malone had the impression that he would hold his scoring lead. "But Nighbor showed me something in the third period," Malone said. "He scored four times and tied me for the lead. Each score was a picture effort." Because of Nighbor's comeback the names of Malone and Nighbor are bracketed in the record book for the 1916–17 season.

Malone completed his career with the Canadiens in 1924 and has remained to this day one of the game's least heralded superstars. "Joe," said Canadian journalist Bill Roche, "liked to talk freely about the hockey feats of others, but seldom about his own."

Sad to say, Joe's modesty was reflected in his contracts. Judging by his production, he must have been one of the most underpaid aces in the history of professional sport.

"My salary," Joe recalled, "was about one thousand dollars a year with the Canadiens and then went up to two thousand when I joined Hamilton in 1921. We could make another three or four hundred by playing with a Stanley Cup-winner and maybe a few dollars by endorsing hockey equipment. But there were no trophies or additional money for being leading scorer and things like that."

There is, however, no disputing Malone's extraordinary scoring ability and his sportsmanship. As prolific as Gretzky, Hull and Bossy have been, none could claim to have averaged two goals a game. Only Joe Malone could make that statement.

16 Bill Cook
(1926–1937)

Before Maurice Richard, Gordie Howe and Andy Bathgate redefined the role of a right-winger there was Bill Cook, the original New York Ranger who combined lyricism with true grit. Since Cook's era spanned the 1920s and 1930s, preceding the time of the high-speed game, it is not quite fair to compare him with the moderns. But some who played with and against Cook and who watched the moderns insist that Bill was in his own class.

"He's my choice as the best right-winger hockey ever knew," said Frank Boucher, who opposed Cook and later teamed with him in New York. "He was better than The Rocket (Richard) and, in my estimation, better than Gordie Howe as well."

Well-proportioned, the glint-eyed Cook took the game every bit as seriously as Richard and fought his foe as grimly as Howe. "He was," said Boucher, "the finest all-around player in Ranger history."

The pity of it all is that Cook did not make his National Hockey League debut until the age of thirty, at a time when other players were retiring. He won the NHL scoring championship in his rookie year and repeated again in 1933 at the age of thirty-seven!

A series of unavoidable circumstances delayed Cook's ascent to the NHL clouds. A farm boy from Kingston, Ontario, his hockey skills were sufficient to earn him a professional invitation by the time he was twenty, but duty came first. With the outbreak of World War I Bill enlisted in the Canadian army and was assigned to a field artillery unit overseas.

His reward, upon returning home, was a soldier's allotment of land in Saskatchewan. But the life of an agriculturalist was not stimulating enough for him so Cook resumed his hockey career in 1922 with Saskatoon of the Western League. It was fast company—Eddie Shore and Frank Boucher were among other top-flight opponents—and Cook established himself among the best. When Madison Square Garden moguls decided to organize the Rangers and asked Conn Smythe to do the recruiting, Bill and his brother, Bun Cook, were the first choices.

Cook wasted no time establishing his credentials. Skating against the champion Montreal Maroons, the Rangers held them to a scoreless tie until Bill and Bunny broke away against Clint Benedict, the Montreal goalie. Bun took the first shot but Benedict made the save but he retrieved the rebound and tapped the puck to Bill, who flicked the rubber over the fallen goalie.

As the red light glowed, Benedict crumpled to the ice momentarily stunned by his crash into the goalpost. A short delay was necessary for the netminder to be repaired. "During this lull," Boucher remembered, "the crowd stayed on its feet, cheering and clapping for the Cooks and refusing to sit until Benedict returned to finish the period."

Bill had scored the winning goal in a match that tickled the fancy of New York hockey fans and instantly gave the Rangers credibility along with their rivals, the

New York Americans. The Rangers had one advantage and that was the Cooks-Boucher line which combined like perfectly meshed gears.

Although Boucher and Bunny were critical to the line's success, Bill had the commanding personality and gave the unit a Pattonesque leadership.

"When the three of us got together to discuss strategy," said Boucher, "Bill would give the orders. Once, he said, 'When I want that puck I'll yell for it, and you get that damn puck to me when I yell.' On the ice, Bill's cry was the most amazing half-grunt, half-moan, half-yell that I ever heard. He'd let this weird sound out of him, meaning that he was in the clear."

Cook, who was a superior player to brother Bunny, was named to the NHL First All-Star Team in 1931, 1932 and 1933. In any debating over the best forward line in hockey history, the Cooks-Boucher line at the very worst would rank among the top three and certainly would obtain innumerable votes as *the* best. Both Bunny and Boucher were good shooters but Bill's shot was more potent than his line-mates.'

"Bill didn't have a bullet shot," Boucher explained, "or at least not a *long* bullet shot like the golf-style slapshot Bobby Hull perfected. But he had a very hard wrist shot from close in and could score equally well backhand or forehand."

Over eleven seasons—at a time when the NHL played a short schedule—Bill scored 229 goals and was a conspicuous contributor to the Rangers' Stanley Cup wins in 1928 and 1933. The most striking similarity between Cook's play and Gordie Howe's was in their aggressive play. Some journalists referred to the right wing as "Bad Bill" and had enough episodes to support the nickname.

By far the most sinister episode involved Cook and Nels Crutchfield, a Montreal Canadiens rookie who had made the jump from McGill University to the NHL. Their fateful collision took place during a playoff game in 1935 after Crutchfield—according to Cook—had committed several fouls without being penalized.

"Crutchfield was interfering with me throughout the game and the referee wouldn't do anything about it," said Cook. "So I finally caught Crutchfield with the butt end of my stick. Then he hit me right on the bean with his stick. The next thing I saw was a million stars."

Cook might have been killed by the two blows delivered by Crutchfield but he avoided catastrophe by instinctively deflecting each clout with his arm. "When I finally came around," said Bill, "all I saw was the stockings of the players who were scrapping. I never saw so many people getting belted on the ice."

What Bill didn't see was his brother, Bunny, leading the charge of Rangers over the boards. Bun carried his stick over his shoulder racing toward Crutchfield, who didn't see him coming. Boucher sensed that Bunny wanted to murder Crutchfield and rather subtly stuck his skate out and tripped Bun a few feet short of his intended victim. "Frank told me," said Bill, "that he had to stop my brother or he would have killed Crutchfield."

After eight stitches had been embroidered in Bill's wounds he returned to the bench. "I was kind of groggy," he admitted, "but I wanted to finish the game."

The Rangers' doctor outfitted him with a makeshift helmet and Bill finally took his position on the right side of Boucher. Late in the game he gained control of the puck and bobbed and weaved his way through the Canadiens' defense to score the game-winning goal. Bill maintained that it ranked among his two greatest thrills in hockey—the other being the winning goal he scored against Toronto in 1933 to provide the Rangers with their second Stanley Cup title.

The Cooks and Boucher had become popular heroes alongside Babe Ruth and Lou Gehrig in the well-publicized New York sports fraternity. Writing in the New York *Sun*, journalist Harold C. Burr composed this ditty.

> *Old adages live because they are true;*
> *If they weren't they wouldn't survive.*
> *But once in a while there are a few*
> *That shouldn't be kept alive.*
> *In hockey, where speed and grit hold forth,*
> *Some sayings sound awfully funny.*
> *'Too many cooks spoil the broth.'*
> *Did you ever meet Bill and Bunny?*

William Osser Cook was born October 9, 1896, in Brantford, Ontario, and learned the essential hockey skills on the frozen outdoor rinks near the family home. The rugged farm life helped steel him for the ice wars ahead and accounted, in part, for Cook's longevity as a professional. He played regularly for the Rangers until 1937 when he was forty-one and was named player-assistant to Lester Patrick.

When a coaching job became available with the Cleveland Barons of the American Hockey League Bill left the Rangers. In 1951 his old pal, Boucher, who had become Rangers manager, asked Bill to coach the slumping New York sextet. Rangers president General John Reed Kilpatrick hoped that Bill could revive the Rangers, but he couldn't. He was fired in 1953, on Kilpatrick's orders. Bill blamed Boucher and for three years they wouldn't talk until they met one night at a banquet. Bill threw his arms around Boucher's shoulders and said: "What the hell, Frankie, it's been too many years. Let's forget the whole thing."

Nobody should forget that Bill Cook was one of the definitive NHL right wings.

17 Max Bentley
(1940–1954)

I saw my first hockey game in 1939 and have watched thousands since then every-where from Pittsburgh to Prague. If I had to pick one player above all whom I'd like to view in action just once—or maybe a hundred times—more, there is no hesitation on my part in coming up with an answer.

Max Bentley.

It isn't even close. Maurice Richard was electrifying and Wayne Gretzky is disarmingly smooth. Bobby Orr offered supersonic dimensions and Bobby Hull's speed with both skates and shots was irresistible to the eye.

But Max Bentley delivered something more to this viewer. Even at a time when the National Hockey League was not peopled by behemoths, Bentley looked frag-ile. He measured 5'8½", 150 pounds which made him susceptible to the crunching bodycheck. But as many a defenseman noted, you can't hit what you can't see.

What set Max apart from other artists was the manner in which he combined his amalgam of talents. For starters, he was the best and fastest stickhandler I have ever seen. It wasn't simply a matter of keeping the puck from the foe, which Howe did to perfection, but rather the magical series of jiggling maneuvers (all without ever having his eyes on the puck) in front of him, to the sides and, sometimes, behind his back.

Jean Beliveau executed many of these tricks with a liquid motion that was im-pressive but not exciting. Bentley's motions had something more deliciously fren-zied. He was aptly described by one writer as skating like a scared jackrabbit.

Max's stickhandling was complemented by his rapid acceleration and decelera-tion. His movements were reminiscent of the crazy electric bumping cars at amuse-ment parks. If Max were one of the cars he would have zigzagged through the maze without being bumped. Finally, there was the wrist shot; again the speediest, most accurate in my memory.

As a center, Max could deliver a pass as deftly as he could fire a puck, and for many years the recipient of his passes was his older brother, Doug, who was built along the same lighthorse dimensions as Max. It was mistakenly believed by some skeptics that Max could not excel without Doug on his wing, but this theory was obliterated in the second half of his career when Max wrote himself into the records as a one-of-a-kind center who helped create several Stanley Cup champions.

Bentley twice (1946 and 1947) led the NHL in scoring; won the Hart Trophy as the league's most valuable player in 1946 and the Lady Byng Trophy for excellence and clean play in 1943. He was voted First All-Star center in 1946 and skated for three Stanley Cup winners.

Apart from his obvious skills, Max had something likeable about him. There never was any doubt in the minds of spectators or opponents that this man was interested, above all, in playing the game—not in maiming or taunting or intimidat-ing.

Max remained in the bigs for fourteen years and in that time one vignette said

more about Bentley, his style and his clutch ability, than any other—and it wasn't a goal he scored either.

It was the fifth game of the 1951 Stanley Cup finals between Bentley's Toronto Maple Leafs and the Montreal Canadiens paced by Maurice Richard. Toronto led the series three games to one but the Canadiens were coming on strong. They led 2–1 with little more than a half-minute to play and appeared strong enough to take the game and eventually tie the series.

Leafs' coach Joe Primeau removed his goalie Al Rollins and dispatched Bentley to the right point as the sixth skater along with Ted Kennedy, Sid Smith, Tod Sloan, Harry Watson and Gus Mortson. Kennedy won the face-off deep in the Canadiens' zone and sent the puck back to Bentley.

Ed Fitkin, who was the Maple Leafs' publicist at the time, remembered Max's moves: "In a thrilling and artistic display of stickhandling, Bentley fought his way across the front of the Montreal net and then fired. The puck hit a defender's leg and bounced out to Smith. He shot and hit the goalpost but the rebound fell at Sloan's feet and Tod promptly blazed it home."

The Leafs won the game and the Cup in sudden-death overtime. "That game," said Bentley, "was one of my greatest thrills."

Maxwell Herbert Lloyd Bentley was born March 1, 1920, in Delisle, Saskatchewan. His grandfather came from Yorkshire, England, and originally settled in Pembina, North Dakota. His father had a livery barn there and would have remained an American were it not for Prohibition in North Dakota in the 1880s.

Bill and Mathilda Bentley had thirteen children including seven daughters who, in their own right, were remarkable hockey players, but Doug was the first Bentley to reach the top. He broke in with the Chicago Black Hawks in 1939 and kept telling management that he had a kid brother playing in Saskatoon who was even better.

There was no disputing Max's ability but his health was questionable. In 1938 he was told by physicians to quit hockey because of a serious heart condition, but Max returned to the ice with no ill effects and in 1940 joined Doug on the Black Hawks. By the 1941–42 season the Bentleys had become the sensations of State Street. Although they looked like they would crumble on contact, each possessed a damaging shot. Then right wing Bill Mosienko, another lightweight, was welcomed to the Black Hawks, and "The Pony Line" of Mosienko and the Bentleys was formed.

Along with "The Punch Line," "The Kid Line" and "The Production Line," the Bentleys-Mosienko unit proved one of the most fetching trios the game has known. The pity of it all was that they had little substance behind them and the Black Hawks rarely were contenders.

At the end of World War II most of the NHL teams were bolstered by the return of prewar stars who had been in the armed forces, but the Black Hawks remained inept except for "The Pony Line." The club's most marketable player was Max Bentley, who was at the top of his game. Rumors that Max would be traded surfaced for several weeks during the start of the 1947–48 season but there were a number of considerations raised. Could Max retain his edge without Doug? What would the Black Hawks demand in return? How would Chicago fans handle the departure of Max?

On November 4, 1947, the biggest trade in hockey history was consummated. The Maple Leafs sent an entire first team (less a goaltender) to the Black Hawks for Max. Included in the package was a complete (and rather good) forward line called "The Flying Forts" comprising Gaye Stewart, Bud Poile and Gus Bodnar, as well as a pair of defensemen, Bob Goldham and Ernie Dickens.

Max was heartbroken at the news for it meant splitting with Doug. "It makes me feel," said Max, "like I lost my right arm."

For a time it seemed that Maple Leafs' mogul Conn Smythe had goofed in making the trade. Max went ten straight games without a goal while coach Hap Day sought appropriate linemates for him. He finally settled on Nick Metz and Joe Klukay and, soon, Bentley regained his form. When Metz retired Ray Timgren was added to the line and Max was better than ever.

Max, Ted Kennedy and Syl Apps were centers on that 1947–48 club which finished first and won the Stanley Cup. No hockey team ever boasted more awesome strength down the middle. When Apps retired in 1948 more pressure was applied to Bentley to take up the slack and, again, he proved his worth. The Leafs won the Stanley Cup again and almost repeated in 1950 when the Detroit Red Wings edged them in a seven-game series. A year later Toronto regained the championship and Max was the most popular Maple Leaf.

Throughout his career Max was notorious as the NHL's foremost hypochondriac. But once he passed the thirty-year milestone he was assailed by both real and imagined injuries. Rather than embarrass himself before the Toronto fans he advised Smythe that he would retire and did so in 1953. He decided to return to Saskatchewan and play hockey with Doug, who had become player-coach of the Saskatoon Quakers, a New York Rangers farm team. It was then that Rangers manager Frank Boucher got a brainstorm; why not reunite the Bentleys on a line with his club? He obtained permission from the Maple Leafs and Black Hawks to negotiate with them and Max finally agreed to sign.

Doug was hesitant and ultimately chose to start the season in Saskatoon. Boucher employed Max as point man on the Rangers' power play and in spot duty. A bit slower, perhaps, Bentley still had the touch of the poet and made Boucher look good. Early in January 1954 the Rangers' manager convinced Doug to sign with the Rangers. This time he agreed and on January 21, 1954, one of hockey's most magnificent moments took place as the Bentleys were reunited.

Moving, as one reporter described them, "like a pair of black-haired waterbugs on the ice, darting, gliding, driving," the Bentleys worked with another oldtimer, Edgar Laprade, and they bewitched the Boston Bruins to the tune of 8–3. The 13,463 fans gave them a standing ovation at game's end and in the dressing room Max openly wept.

"He's crying for happiness," said Doug. "He's tickled because we finally played together again . . . and so am I."

It was a uniquely magnificent moment that caused many in the crowd to shed a tear because they knew they would never see anything like it again. "We recognized," said Boucher, "that we had sat in on something very rare, not to be turned on like a recording or an instant replay."

The charm and skill of Max Bentley has never been duplicated and, I am certain, never will, because he was the only one of his kind. He died in 1984 after living in semiretirement with his wife, Betty, in Saskatoon.

18 Georges Vezina (1917–1926)

"*The* Vezina!"

How often we have heard the equation with goaltending excellence. The Vezina Trophy, since 1927, has been awarded to the netminders who have delivered the lowest goals against average each season. In 1982 it simply was given to the NHL's "outstanding goalie."

More than any other National Hockey League prize, this one has the deepest meaning because Georges Vezina, after whom the trophy is named, was a nonpareil athlete whose ability was matched only by his infinite sportsmanship.

A gangling six-footer, Vezina guarded the Montreal Canadiens' nets when the team played in the National Hockey Association and later for the Habitants when the National Hockey League was organized.

In each milieu he excelled. The Canadiens won the NHA championship twice with Vezina between the pipes and won three NHL championships and two Stanley Cups. He played a total of 373 consecutive games for Les Canadiens in an era when goaltenders masks were unheard of, and was nicknamed "The Chicoutimi Cucumber" for his birthplace and his cool under fire.

Vezina starred for the Canadiens for fifteen years, from 1910 to 1925, and no doubt would have remained the master of his trade for several more seasons had he not been fatally stricken with tuberculosis. A quiet man, Vezina continued to play although he was aware that his life was doomed.

On November 28, 1925, his body wracked with pain, Vezina skated out onto the ice of Mount Royal Arena to face the visiting Pittsburgh sextet. "No one knew," wrote author Ron McAllister, "that the great goaltender had struggled to the arena despite a temperature of 105 degrees.

"A deathlike chill settled over him; but with Pittsburgh forcing the play from the face-off Vezina functioned throughout the first period with his usual dextrous ease, deflecting shot after shot. In the dressing room he suffered a severe arterial hemorrhage, but the opening of the second period found him at his accustomed place in goal."

Fighting desperately against the fatigue and fever that completely throttled his body, the great Vezina could no longer see the puck as it skimmed from one side of the rink to the other. Suddenly a collective gasp engulfed the arena. Vezina had collapsed in the goal crease. "In the stricken arena," said one observer, "all was silent as the limp form of the greatest of goalies was carried slowly from the ice."

It was the end of the trail for Georges and he knew it. At his request he was taken home to his native Chicoutimi where doctors diagnosed his case as advanced tuberculosis. On March 24, 1926, he passed away. An enormous funeral, held in the old cathedral at Chicoutimi, saw players and fans from all parts of the country deliver their final tribute to the gallant goaltender. A year later the Canadiens' owners donated a trophy in his honor.

Georges Vezina was born January 1887 in Chicoutimi, Quebec, a city which sits on the edge of the dark Saguenay River and flows into the blue St. Lawrence at historic Tadoussac.

Although young Vezina established himself as a class-A goalie even as a youth in Chicoutimi he had developed a habit of playing without skates. For some peculiar reason he found the idea of wearing skates a bother, and it wasn't until two years before he graduated to Les Canadiens that he actually learned to wear skates while tending goal.

Conceivably, the Montrealers would never have discovered Vezina were it not for a chance exhibition game between the Canadiens and the local Chicoutimi club on February 23, 1910. The match between the awesome professionals from Montreal and the patchwork amateur outfit figured to be so one-sided that only a handful of fans turned out for it.

Chicoutimi hardly looked like a formidable foe except for the six-foot goalie, wearing a red-and-white *Habitant toque* on his head. Leaning against the goalpost, the tall, lanky Vezina appeared almost too bored for words. But once the overpowering Canadiens sliced through the fragile Chicoutimi defense, Vezina suddenly responded with a peripatetic style that thoroughly dumbfounded the pros. Try as they might, the Canadiens could not score. Chicoutimi won the game, 2–0.

That was all the Canadiens' high command had to know. They invited Vezina to Montreal and he made his debut on December 31, 1910. Curiously, Georges never signed a contract with the Montrealers. He preferred a gentleman's handshake with his managers, first Joe Cattarinich and later Leo Dandurand.

The father of twenty-two children, Vezina was virtually impregnable once he took his position in the goal crease. Once, during a game at Hamilton, Bert Corbeau smashed into him with such force that the goaltender's head was cut open and his nose broken. Vezina continued playing despite the wounds, his ability undiminished by pain.

According to hockey historians, Vezina was the author of several hockey classics including the 1916 Stanley Cup final between Les Canadiens and the Pacific Coast Hockey Association's Portland Rosebuds. The best-of-five series went the limit, the final game being played on March 30, 1916. With the score tied, 1–1, Vezina defused the most explosive Portland offensives until Goldie Prodgers scored the winner for Montreal. Vezina and each of his Stanley Cup-winning teammates received $238 for taking the championship.

In the Roaring Twenties Vezina was better than ever. During the 1923–24 season he allowed only 48 goals in twenty-four games, including three shutouts for a 2.00 goals against average. He than blanked Ottawa, 1–0, in the NHL playoff opener and sparkled as Montreal swept the series. Montreal went on to rout Calgary and Vancouver for the Stanley Cup. Vezina's Stanley Cup record was six goals in six games—an even 1.00 average.

By this time Vezina's body was afflicted with the early symptoms of tuberculosis. "Beads of perspiration formed on his forehead for no apparent reason," said Ron McAllister. "An expression of pain flitted momentarily across his face, but the Great Vezina invariably settled down to the business at hand, turning in his usual matchless performance."

During the 1924–25 season, despite the ailment, he came up with a 1.9 goals against average, easily the best in the league. But when he arrived at the Canadiens' training camp in the fall of 1925 he seemed unusually fatigued.

It has been said that not even those in his own family realized that Vezina was fighting for his life as he prepared for the 1925–26 season. This would be a particularly fascinating year for the worldly Vezina. The NHL was expanding into the United States more than ever. It had embraced a Boston franchise a year earlier and now New York and Pittsburgh had been added, as well as a second Montreal team, the Maroons, who would provide an English-speaking team as natural rivals for the Canadiens. Needless to say, the outstanding attraction in the American cities among Montreal players was the redoubtable Vezina.

Sadly, "The Chicoutimi Cucumber" donned the *blue, blanc et rouge* uniform for the last time in the season opener of the 1925–26 season. There were 6,000 spectators in the stands on that rainy night who had come to see the Great Vezina.

Few realized that, as he left the ice after a scoreless first period, that he was bleeding from the mouth. But they began to perceive his pain in the second period when he fell to the ice for the last time.

Georges Vezina was the personification of courage and capability. When someone in hockey says "The Vezina," he need say no more.

19 King Clancy (1921–1937)

In the final game of the 1923 Stanley Cup series between Ottawa and Edmonton, a goal by Punch Broadbent of Ottawa won the game, 1–0, and the championship for the skaters from Canada's capital city.

Yet it was neither Broadbent's score nor the triumph by the Senators that proved so extraordinary. On that night manager Tommy Gorman of Ottawa had five stars sidelined with injuries and was able to dress only eight skaters for the climactic game. What was so astonishing was that one of those eight stalwarts, defenseman King Clancy, came to Gorman's rescue and *played every position on the team, including goal.*

"He had taken turns on defense, at center and had filled in on both wings," Gorman recalled. "In the last ten minutes of the game our goalie, Clint Benedict, drew a penalty. In those days, a goalie actually had to serve his sentence in the penalty box, himself, and any substitution occurred in the net, and not in the box.

"Clancy volunteered to take over Benedict's goaling job and I let him do it. Not only did he stop Edmonton but he almost scored on them while he was playing goal. King had made a save and saw a loose puck in front of his cage. He dashed out, got his stick on the puck, wiggled past an Edmonton attacker and started to rush down the rink."

Gorman kept yelling at Clancy to get back in his net but the King paid his boss no heed and moved in on the enemy defense. "He pulled one of Edmonton's defensemen out of position," said Gorman, "and then fired a shot. Then, grinning happily, he scooted back to his own end of the rink to resume business as a goalie."

Such was the manner of Clancy, a man of infinite humor, ability and guts. At a time when defensemen such as Eddie Shore and other Goliaths of the rink would as soon carve their initials in an opponent's brow as score a goal, the lilliputian Clancy backed away from no one and also emerged as the definitive backliner who was twice a First All-Star and played on three Stanley Cup winners.

More than Shore, Doug Harvey, Red Kelly or Bobby Orr, Clancy offered an exuberance to the game that had a more positive touch than Maurice Richard's almost sinister pursuit of the almighty goal. There was an "I love life—I love hockey" aura about the King that was infectious on any team that had Clancy playing defense.

Perhaps it was imperative that King adopt such a philosophy. When he tried out for Gorman's Ottawa Senators in 1921 *he weighed in at 125 pounds.* And this was a defenseman. Gorman was appropriately flabbergasted but figured he'd go along with the gag so he invited young Clancy to lace on the skates and have his audition with the big-leaguers. "If you make the team," said Gorman, "I'll sign you for three years at $800 per season."

Gorman, whose team were Stanley Cup champions in two of the past two seasons, did not expect Clancy to come close to making it; not when aces such as Frank Nighbor, Eddie Gerard and Sprague Cleghorn were on the team. Clancy

was militantly unimpressed by his surroundings. "Everyone who watched his debut marvelled at the confidence of the Irish lad as he sailed into the Stanley Cuppers as though they were all kids together playing shinny on a local rink," commented one reporter.

Gorman had no choice but to sign the lad, although the manager suffered doubts about Clancy's size. "We'll put fifty pounds of rock salt in your shirt," said Gorman, "to weigh you down."

Clancy played on four Stanley Cup winners in Ottawa and appeared to be a fixture in the capital city. Then the Great Depression cast a black cloud over the continent and the Senators' attendance dropped at an alarming rate. The team needed money to survive and a decision was made to sell the Senators' most marketable player. Thus, King Clancy became the centerpiece in professional hockey's biggest trade up until that time.

The Toronto Maple Leafs, operated by the flamboyant Conn Smythe, wanted Clancy, as did the New York Rangers and Chicago Black Hawks. Both the Rangers and Hawks seemed to have the edge because of their bigger bankrolls. But Smythe had a colt named Rare Jewel entered at Toronto's Woodbine Racetrack. The odds were 100–1 against Rare Jewel but Smythe put his money on the colt. It obliged by coming in first and filling its owner's pockets with enough cash to bid for Clancy. He offered Ottawa $35,000 cash as well as two players—Art Smith and Eric Pettinger—worth a total of $15,000. Clancy cost Smythe $50,000 (today $500,000 would be a low figure) and was worth every penny of it.

Clancy realized early on that he was not going to prevail on his strength, so he compensated in other ways. Toronto *Telegram* sports columnist Ted Reeve observed Clancy as a rookie with Ottawa in 1921 to his final game with the Maple Leafs in 1937 and had this to say about King's style:

"His main forte was his ability to break fast, to come leaping off the blue line as though it were a springboard, with the loose puck tossed out in front. He could pass on the dead tear, though not a graceful skater (he was almost running on his blades at times), and he had a wicked shot.

"It was that indefinable something—the competitive spirit—that made Clancy so valuable to the Leafs. And the God-given gift of fun in him that would bring them out of the doldrums with a whoop and a holler. That high-pitched sort of husky voice, his piping exclamations and infectious grin."

Francis Michael Clancy was born February 25, 1903, in Ottawa, Ontario. His father, Thomas Clancy, pushed his son into sports despite the lad's size. Tom Clancy was the original "King" in the family. An accomplished football player, he was known as "the King of Heelers" because of his ability to get the ball into play from scrimmage in the manner of that day.

The second King developed into an even better athlete than the original. Teaming up with the likes of Hap Day, Charlie Conacher, Harold Cotton and Ace Bailey, Clancy revelled in his role with what became The Gashouse Gang of hockey. "We didn't win the Cup every year," said Clancy, "but winter after winter we won the world's championship for assorted pranks and jokes in Pullman cars and hotels."

What is so remarkable about Clancy's career is that it just seemed to begin after he finally began losing his edge with the Leafs. On November 24, 1936, he realized that it was time to pack it in. He walked into the dressing room and addressed his buddies. "Fellows," said King, "I just want to say a few words . . ." Tears welled in his eyes and he lifted a hand in farewell. The Clancy era had ended in Toronto.

When Clancy retired, NHL president Frank Calder came through and made Clancy a referee. He was to become one of the most beloved referees in the game. For the most part Clancy employed the laissez-faire philosophy of officiating. And he had a rather unusual manner of giving penalties for offenses that he didn't see. "If Clancy caught a player swiping at another with his stick," said one NHLer of the Clancy refereeing era, "he'd give 'em *both* two minutes. He figured that the other guy must have started it; and, usually, King was right."

Clancy refereed from 1937 to 1949. From 1953 to 1956 he coached the Maple Leafs, again employing the same easygoing style that succeeded as a player and referee. Although he didn't win any Stanley Cups, Clancy was able to get more out of his players than most coaches. He later became an invaluable aide-de-camp to Maple Leafs general manager-coach Punch Imlach and club president Harold Ballard.

The ubiquitous Clancy rarely missed a Maple Leafs road game with Ballard at his side well into the 1980s and he seemed to have lost none of the enthusiasm that he brought to the Ottawa training camp in 1921.

When Conn Smythe stepped down as boss of the Maple Leafs, he turned to Clancy and said, "You're the biggest name of any we've got."

He was one of the biggest—and most uplifting—names hockey ever had. Frank Clancy's nickname was more than apt; he was truly a King.

20 Nels Stewart (1925–1940)

There was a time in the 1950s when the only names on the minds of hockey fans were Nels Stewart and Maurice Richard.

Nicknamed "Ole Poison" for his inevitable sting around the enemy net, Stewart reigned for more than a decade as the National Hockey League's all-time goal scoring titlist. Stewart's career record of 324 was pursued and finally surpassed by Richard but not until the race finally focused attention on the oft-overlooked and occasionally maligned center with the radar stick.

One reason why Stewart got a bum rap was his mobility, or rather, lack of it. He displayed none of the dash of a Howie Morenz or fluidity of an Eddie Shore.

"Nels was slow," said Myles Lane, a New York Rangers defenseman when Stewart skated for the Montreal Maroons. "But he made up for his lack of speed with his stick. He was tremendous around the net."

Husky and handsome with a wide grin, Stewart broke in with the Maroons during the 1925–26 season, playing both center and defense. He won the scoring championship with 34 goals and also annexed the Hart Trophy as the NHL's most valuable player.

Stewart's scoring ability inspired the Maroon's high command to play him exclusively at center where he pivotted The Big S Line with Babe Siebert and Hooley Smith. The line was less than discreet in handling the opposition and earned notoriety as the roughest trio in the league.

It was not uncommon for Stewart to chew a wad of tobacco, produce juice and then spit it unerringly in the eyes of a goalie as he shot the puck.

Cooper Smeaton, who refereed when Stewart was in his heyday, regarded Ole Poison as a vastly underrated talent. "In today's game," said Smeaton, "Nels would have scored 100 goals. He was terrific in front of the net, a big strong fellow who had moves like a cat. Stewart never seemed to be paying any attention to where the puck was and, if you were checking him, he'd even hold little conversations with you; but the minute he'd see the puck coming his way he'd bump you, take the puck, and go off and score."

In his rookie season Stewart spearheaded the Maroons to the NHL playoff championship, qualifying them to meet Victoria for the Stanley Cup. Ole Poison scored six goals in four games for the Maroons as they carried the Cup back to the Montreal Forum.

Stewart's laser shot often caused serious damage to members of the Goaltenders' Union. The most devastating injury from Ole Poison's shot was inflicted upon Rangers goalie Lorne Chabot during the 1928 playoffs.

"The shot," recalled Rangers center Frank Boucher, "struck Chabot squarely on the left eyeball, causing a hemorrhage. Lorne didn't play again for the rest of the series."

In 1930, when he finished second in scoring in the NHL's Canadian Division

with three fewer points than the leader Hec Kilrea, Stewart nevertheless was voted the Hart Trophy for the second time.

Such accomplishments failed to still his detractors, one of whom was referee Bobby Hewitson, who doubled as sports editor of the Toronto *Telegram*.

"I always felt that Stewart had an exaggerated reputation," said Hewitson. "I never thought he was such a great player. Nels was big and tall but awfully lazy. He wouldn't backcheck and he'd just stand around the net waiting for the centering pass, then flip the puck in. That much he could do. We used to say that Nels stood in one spot all the time."

Similar charges have, from time to time, been levelled against other superstars. Stewart was deceptive, not lazy. Nobody who scored 324 goals during an era when red lights were at a premium could legitimately be labelled lazy. In fact, Ole Poison was an ardent competitor who, like Gordie Howe in a later period, would resort to any technique for victory.

Stewart gave the Maroons seven solid years of service before being traded to the Boston Bruins where he centered a line with Dit Clapper and Red Beattie. Just as effective, Nels scored his 200th career goal as a Bruin and remained a boisterous attacker. In 1935, after he had been suspended for fighting, Stewart was traded to the New York Americans with whom he played until his retirement in 1938.

The truculent scoring champion from Montreal, Quebec, was born December 29, 1902, so it was rather natural for him to eventually sign up with the Maroons in his home town. A true professional, Stewart played as efficiently in Boston and New York as he did in Montreal.

Stewart saved one of his finest performances for the 1938 playoffs. The Americans, who had played second fiddle to the Rangers for more than a decade, finished second in the Canadian Division while the Rangers were runner-up in the American Division. The rivals, who shared Madison Square Garden, met in a best-of-three playoff round.

Coached by Red Dutton, who had once been a Montreal Maroons teammate of Stewart, the Americans won the opener 2–1, lost the second game 4–3, and appeared doomed in the finale.

A capacity crowd of 16,340 watched the Rangers jump into a 2–0 lead but Lorne Carr scored for the Americans as the game bristled with tension. It was then that Ole Poison came through with the tying goal, sending the match into sudden-death overtime. After three extra periods the Americans scored and moved into the next round against the Chicago Black Hawks.

By this time Stewart was showing the effects of his age and his labored skating style. He was thirty-six years old and too often to suit him, the Black Hawks were tying up his wings. In the second game, with the Americans leading one game to none, the score tied 1–1 in the third period, Ole Poison tried one of his patented plays.

"Nels shouldered his way between a couple of players who were scrapping for possession of the puck," recalled Clarence Campbell, who refereed the game. "He nabbed it and passed it back to Tommy Anderson, his wing, who was just inside the Chicago blue line. Then, as fast as he could, Nels ambled over to a side edge of the goal crease—home sweet home to him."

Instead of passing, Anderson took a shot. At that moment Stewart whacked Chicago goalie Mike Karakas over the shins so hard that the goalie fell to the ice.

Meanwhile, the puck sailed into the net for what could have been the game-winner for the Americans.

"I disallowed the goal for interference," said Campbell.

A bitter argument ensued between the Americans, led by Stewart, and referee Campbell. Stewart and cohorts were finally becalmed and the game continued in a deadlock until Chicago won it in overtime to tie the series. The Black Hawks also won the decisive third game and eliminated the Americans.

Stewart remained one of Dutton's stalwarts until he retired in 1940. A few critics have been tough on Ole Poison but none can take away his Hart Trophies, the fact that he led the league in scoring, played on a Stanley Cup winner and in 1962 was deservedly inducted into the Hockey Hall of Fame.

If you want to know how good Nels Stewart was, ask anyone who scored 324 goals. Maurice Richard would be delighted to tell you.

21 Lester Patrick (1905–1928)

If anyone did more to advance the game of hockey than Lester Patrick he must be hiding somewhere. And that is precisely why "The Silver Fox" and his contributions as a player have been overlooked by many talent appraisers.

Lester and his brother, Frank, were responsible for more innovations, more positive rule changes and more miscellaneous improvements in the game than any other personalities. Most of these alterations were accomplished while Lester was either a coach, manager or club owner and thereby overshadowed his role as a player of note.

Most relevant is the fact that Lester was the very first defenseman ever to make a practice of lugging the puck out of his zone and deep into enemy territory. It happened in 1902 when Patrick played for a team in Brandon, Manitoba. Lester could never comprehend why forwards and only forwards were the puck-carriers and, conversely, why defensemen did nothing but engage the enemy attackers.

"Instinct and temperament proved too strong for Lester," said Elmer Ferguson of the Montreal *Herald*. "He felt that a defenseman should do more than defend, so he rushed the puck as well."

When his coach demanded an explanation, Lester replied: "Why not let defensemen rush if it works—and if the fans like it?" His logic was impeccable and reinforced when he scored a goal.

That was just the first of innumerable Patrick innovations. He thought it rather foolish for defensemen to stand in front of each other like the point and cover-point players in lacrosse. "That doesn't make sense," said Patrick. "It would be wiser to have the defensemen line up abreast." And once again the Patrick imprint was indelibly etched in hockey strategy.

Lester graduated from Brandon to the powerful Montreal Wanderers in 1903. It was a time when organized hockey was dominated by the Ottawa Silver Seven, a club that captured the Stanley Cup in 1903, 1904 and 1905.

The Wanderers finally dethroned the Silver Seven in the 1906 two-game total-goal series, 12–10. Patrick scored the eleventh and twelfth goals for Montreal.

Imperial-looking—many fans said he reminded them of the distinguished actor John Barrymore—Patrick stood six-feet tall, was slim but solidly built, with a crown of thick curly hair. (When the mane grew gray, he was dubbed "The Silver Fox.") Lester had an inimitable knack of striking dramatic poses, tossing his head back and staring archly.

He was, actually, one of the first of the high-priced athletes because he knew the value of a buck and, more important, the value of Lester Patrick.

While Lester was starring for the Wanderers a wealthy group of businessmen in Renfrew, Ontario, decided to organize a major league team and pursued Lester. He eventually signed with them for what, at the time, was regarded as an absurdly high fee for a hockey player—$3,000 for twelve games.

It was a honey of a deal but Patrick only stayed a season and then abruptly

moved west to British Columbia with his family when his father established a lumber business in the Canadian northwest. While logging the giant trees of the Fraser Valley, Lester and Frank came up with an ambitious plan to run their own hockey league along the Pacific coast. The only problem was that there was no natural ice and no rinks.

Undaunted, Lester borrowed $300,000 from his father and with Frank's assistance built a chain of rinks that gave birth to the Pacific Hockey League, including Victoria, Vancouver, Seattle, Edmonton, Calgary, Regina and Saskatoon. Lester operated the Victoria team while Frank operated Vancouver.

"The Patricks," said Ferguson, "took hockey into an area where no hockey existed, built magnificent rinks and made a major sport of it. They were the greatest personal factors in twentieth-century hockey."

Lester never gave up his skates for the executive suite. He was a one-man gang, who owned, managed, coached and played for his club. Patrick did wonders for the Cougars but never more than in 1925 when Victoria met the Montreal Canadiens in the Stanley Cup finals.

"All the sportswriters had conceded the series to Montreal," said Frank Frederickson, a Hall of Famer who played for Victoria. "But they didn't bargain for Lester's analytical mind and we wound up beating the Canadiens."

The triumph added another ribbon on Patrick's uniform but it soon was dwarfed by his unexpected performance in the 1928 playoffs when he was forty-four years old and had retired as an active defenseman. It was then that Lester startled the hockey world by actually going into the nets and *playing goal* for the New York Rangers against the Montreal Maroons.

"This dramatic moment," wrote Toronto *Sun* columnist Trent Frayne, "has become a part of the lore of sport, as legendary in hockey as the World Series home run Babe Ruth hit off Charley Root of the Chicago Cubs when he pointed to the distant center field bleachers and then laced the ball there."

Patrick was manager of the Rangers at the time and his regular goalie, Lorne Chabot, was nearly blinded by a shot from the stick of Montreal Maroons ace Nels Stewart. The Rangers had no spare goaltender so Lester agreed to put on the pads.

John Barrymore couldn't have played the part better had the playoff been staged by Hollywood. "Lester struck poses in the net," one of his players recalled. "He would shout to us, 'Let them shoot!' He was an inspiration to the rest of us."

Patrick had a shutout going—the Rangers scored once—until late in the third period when Nels Stewart finally beat him. The game went into overtime and Lester foiled the Maroons until Frank Boucher scored the winner for New York. At that moment Lester Patrick became immortalized.

He was half-dragged, half-carried off the ice by his players while he received a tumultuous ovation from the crowd. It was Lester's final curtain as a player.

Lester Patrick was born December 30, 1883, in Drummondville, Quebec, not far from Montreal. Although hockey was his forte, Lester was equally gifted at rugby, lacrosse and cricket. He enrolled in McGill University when he was seventeen but quit after a year to devote his energies to hockey. His first raves were received in Brandon where he led the Manitoba sextet to the provincial championship and then to the Stanley Cup round where they almost beat the mighty Ottawa Silver Seven. When he became captain of the Montreal Wanderers they won the Stanley Cup in 1906 and 1907.

"Lester was a classical player in every phase of the game," said Cyclone Taylor, who teamed with Patrick on the Renfrew Millionaires.

It is fascinating to note that a number of Patrick's most glorious moments as a player occurred at a time when most observers figured him for washed-up. He had decided to retire and concentrate on front office duties in Victoria in 1921 but a year later two defensemen on his Cougars club were seriously injured so Lester retrieved his skates and took his position on right defense.

"From the start," one of his opponents commented, "he was a sensation."

The Cougars, who had not won a game in seven starts, went 19–5 and Patrick was never better. He personally won two games, scoring a goal to win an overtime game against the Saskatoon Sheiks and scored the only goal in a 1–0 win over the Vancouver Maroons.

Patrick's facile mind already had wrought permanent changes in the game. After watching a soccer game in England, Lester and Frank introduced the penalty shot to hockey. To this day it remains one of the most exciting aspects of the game. Lester and Frank were the first to put numbers on the players' jerseys. "It was a Patrick innovation," said Elmer Ferguson, "pure and simple. And has been universally adopted by all major sports."

The Patricks were the first to adopt forward passing and to legalize puck-kicking in certain areas as a means to sustain play. They invented the assist in hockey and they broadened the rules governing goalies. Under the older rules, the goalie could not legally make a stop while in any other position but a vertical one. The Patricks said a goalie could fall to the ice. Today, that's all they ever seem to do when blocking the rubber.

"The Patricks," said Ferguson, "legislated hockey into modernism."

More than that, Lester and his brother brought the professional hockey establishment to its knees. They fought the National League, raided it, took a whole champion team away on one of their forays, and forced the National League to terms. They organized, reorganized and then broke up a whole league on the Pacific coast. When it became obvious that the Pacific League could no longer compete with the NHL he sold his Victoria team to a Detroit group for a quarter-million dollars.

Lester became manager and coach of the Rangers at the start of the 1926–27 season. He continued to display his tactical brilliance. With the inception of All-Star Teams in 1930–31, Lester dominated the voting as outstanding coach in seven of the first eight seasons, from 1930 through 1938. He missed only the 1936–37 season.

The Rangers won three Stanley Cups in their 56 years of existence, all of them with Lester Patrick as manager. "Lester," said Babe Pratt, who starred on defense for him as a Ranger, "was to hockey what John McGraw was to baseball."

That is true. But one can interchange the names of Babe Ruth, Connie Mack and Christy Mathewson for McGraw and still not be doing enough justice to The Silver Fox of Hockey.

22 Marcel Pronovost
(1950–1970)

When Marcel Pronovost was a lad of seven years, he experienced a common childhood accident: he fell off his bicycle. But where other kids might fall and scrape their knee or bruise their elbow, Marcel broke his nose. Although not obvious at the time, that particular mishap was an omen of things to come for Pronovost during his NHL career in which he stood as one of the premier defensemen in the league for the better part of two decades. Pronovost, through his days with the Detroit Red Wings and Toronto Maple Leafs, accumulated his fair share of awards and recognition for his on-ice accomplishments. But the one title to which he holds sole possession was not awarded by the NHL and doubtless never will be: Marcel Pronovost—The Most Injured Man In Hockey.

Pronovost's dubious distinction makes his career accomplishments that much more remarkable. It is a rare athlete indeed who can suffer just about every injury in the medical dictionary and overcome each one and return to perform at his previous level of excellence. But Marcel Pronovost took all that in stride.

Pronovost first laced up and donned a Red Wings sweater in 1950 when an injury to Gordie Howe forced the Wings to move defenseman Red Kelly to the forward line and bring up the youngster from the Omaha Knights to fill the gap on the backline. With the nineteen-year-old Pronovost playing the brand of hockey that earned him the U.S. League's Rookie of the Year, the Wings captured their first Cup since 1943, defeating the Rangers in a hotly contested final series. Pronovost, with less than a season of NHL experience behind him, played with the composure of a hardened veteran and became one of the youngest players to have his name inscribed on the Stanley Cup. He went on to play on seven championship teams in Detroit including Cup-winning teams in 1952 and 1954.

When Marcel arrived in training camp in 1951, he fully expected to crash the Detroit varsity. Instead, he was blasted right out of the NHL. On a patented Pronovost rush, he tried bisecting the defense of ironmen Leo Reise and Bob Goldham. When the three fell to the ice, Goldham's stick creased Marcel's face. His noble charge cost him a fractured cheekbone and a ticket to Indianapolis. But after thirty-four injury-free games in the minors he was recalled and from that time on he became a fixture on the Detroit blue line.

Stitches, bruises, fractures and separations have all spent time in one spot or another on Pronovost's 6'1", 175-pound body, but none were able to penetrate the determination which was his armor. No injury, it seemed, could discourage Pronovost from playing his position with nothing short of reckless abandon.

Dancing with danger never fazed Pronovost and he dismissed the perils of the rink as just another fact of life. "Making a dangerous play on the ice didn't make me any more nervous than crossing the street might make someone else. He doesn't worry about getting hit by a car and I don't worry about getting hurt on the ice. If I did, I'd probably go crazy."

Pronovost's kamikaze approach to the game may not have taken its toll on his

nerves but it had a significant effect upon him physically. As a young horse in his early NHL days Pronovost was known as one of the finer rushing defensemen of his time, sometimes compared to the likes of Ken Reardon before him and Bobby Orr after him. But those rink-long dashes were not only glorious but gruelling as well. As the injuries mounted, Marcel mellowed into a graceful puck-carrier and a solid two-way defenseman.

Overshadowed by the brighter stars of the powerful Red Wing teams of the 1950s, Pronovost emerged as a bona fide star himself when Red Kelly was traded from Detroit to Toronto in 1959. Along with recognition by his team as the anchor of its blue line corps, Pronovost began to gain more notoriety league-wide and was thusly named to the First Team All-Stars in 1960 and 1961.

René Marcel Pronovost was born June 15, 1930, in Lac la Tortue, Quebec. At the age of fifteen Marcel was "stolen" out of the French-Canadian province by Detroit scout Marcel Cote, who first eyed the youngster in action playing juvenile hockey in Shawinigan Falls.

During his NHL career, which ran from 1950 to 1970, Marcel Pronovost played 1,206 games, netting 88 goals and adding 257 assists. He also was engaged in 134 playoff contests, scoring 8 goals and 23 assists, and 11 All-Star games. His personal high for offensive production was 34 points for the 1954–55 season.

Pronovost worked for the Detroit club for fifteen seasons until, at the age of thirty-four, he was traded to Toronto as part of an eight-player swap. Prior to the trade, Pronovost was second only to Gordie Howe in length of service with the Red Wings. With the Maple Leafs, Pronovost played five more seasons and drank from the Stanley Cup one more time, in 1967, before retiring in 1970.

When hockey historians grasp for comparisons to measure Marcel Pronovost against, they will be hard pressed to find any. To add a new twist to an old cliché, it could be said that if they hadn't broken the mold after they made him, he probably would have broken it himself. He did, after all, manage to break everything else.

In the contemporary game, where players are motivated by incentive clauses, the likes of Pronovost's pure dedication to the game are simply nonexistent. One scenario, which took place during the 1961 Stanley Cup finals, fully illustrates the intensity that typified Marcel Pronovost. With the Red Wings matched against the Chicago Black Hawks, Pronovost played four games on a badly cracked ankle. He would arrive at the arena on crutches, play the game, and then put his leg back in a cast. A teammate who watched him suffer through each tortuous turn on the ice put it simply: "He played on guts alone, nothing else." He played for two decades, always underrated, but one of the most versatile defensemen of all time.

23 Toe Blake (1934–1948)

In any discussion of the outstanding five forward units of professional hockey the Montreal Canadiens' "Punch Line" of Maurice Richard, Hector (Toe) Blake and Elmer Lach invariably is included.

Reaching their apex during the mid-1940s, The Punch Line featured Richard, the inimitable Rocket, at right wing, Elmer Lach at center and Blake on the port side. "It was," said Canadian hockey historian William Roche, "one of the best-balanced arrays seen in hockey in many a day."

Because of his élan and flamboyant goal-scoring, Richard inevitably obtained the most attention but, as Roche has noted, Blake made the line tick. "He was the line's sparkplug," said Roche, "and anchor. The line suffered an irreparable loss when Blake broke a leg and retired in the 1947–48 season."

What is, perhaps, most surprising—if not ironic—about Blake's career is that despite his truculence and affinity for rough play, he won the Lady Byng Trophy for good sportsmanship combined with ability in 1946.

From the moment he entered the bigs as a rookie with the now defunct Montreal Maroons in 1935, "reckless, truculent and boisterous," were some of the terms employed to describe Blake, the rookie. At the time he often appeared too busy fighting his own battles to be effective to the Maroons.

The Maroons, in what proved to be a classic blunder of a dying franchise, failed to realize Blake's potential and soon traded him to the Canadiens. No less impudent, Blake proceeded to get himself into a mess of trouble.

Playing against the Detroit Red Wings, he attempted to hit Detroit's Ebbie Goodfellow with his stick. Before the blow could be struck, Toe's stick was deflected by another Detroit player. Several Red Wings immediately jumped Blake and pummelled him on the ice. "They really went amok," remembered Jack Adams, who was Red Wings coach at the time. "But Blake never backed away from any of them. He was a helluva competitor."

His zeal for combat was matched only by his ability to score goals and by the start of the 1940s Blake had been nicknamed "The Old Lamplighter," as in red goal lamp. In thirteen years of NHL play he scored 235 goals and 292 assists, skating for three Stanley Cup-winning teams, and five first-place clubs.

In 1939 Blake was voted Canada's outstanding athlete and had become, as one observer put it, "as gentlemanly as a hockey player can afford to be." The metamorphosis from pugnacious brawler to mature hockey player added to Blake's effectiveness and, according to *Sports Illustrated,* contributed to the devastating success of the Canadiens from 1943 to 1947.

At the start of the 1940s, Toe was used on a unit with Johnny Quilty and Joe Benoit, a pair of effective but unspectacular linemates. During the summer of 1943 Montreal's astute coach Dick Irvin realized that his young right wing, Maurice Richard, was capable of spectacular production if aligned with the proper linemates.

Irvin had theorized that hard-nosed Elmer Lach was the ideal center for Richard but he wasn't so sure about left wing. He finally decided that Blake would be worthy of an experiment on the unit and in no time the line was made—for keeps.

Originally nicknamed "The Mad Dog Line," Blake's trio was more appropriately renamed "The Punch Line" as they dominated the NHL during its most offense-minded era. The trio finished one-two-three (Lach, Blake, Richard) in scoring on the team.

"Being on a line with Toe," said Richard, "was probably the greatest thrill I had experienced up until then."

Richard and Blake were kindred spirits and soon developed what would become a lifelong affection for each other. Professionally speaking, it would work to the advantage of both of them, particularly for Blake when he turned coach of the Canadiens and Richard continued to excel as a player. As captain, Blake inspired the Montrealers to first place and the Stanley Cup in 1944 and another Stanley Cup in 1946.

Hector Blake was born August 21, 1912, in Victoria Mines, a smelting and mining community in northern Ontario. Unlike many Hall of Famers, Blake was discouraged from playing hockey by his mother. Her goal for her son was a "nice and steady" job in the mines.

At the age of twelve Blake was hired by a milk company to hitch the horses before they embarked on their day's journey. Until then Toe had been a goaltender —without skates. With his newly acquired wealth he bought a pair of skates and passionately involved himself with hockey and more hockey.

His diligent pursuit of the puck eventually won him starting assignments with an assortment of amateur teams in Canada. Ultimately, he made his way to a club in Sudbury, Ontario, which happened to be scrutinized by some major league scouts. Sudbury's best prospect was a lad named Nakina Smith. Sam Rothschild, who was scouting for the NHL Maroons, watched the Sudbury sextet and then wired Maroons coach Eddie Gerard: "FORGET SMITH. BLAKE'S THE ONE."

And he was. Smith had an undistinguished big-league career whereas Blake became the cornerstone of the Canadiens rebuilding program at the start of the 1940s.

Blake certainly would have gone much farther as a scorer had he not suffered a shattered ankle as a result of a bodycheck on the night of January 10, 1948. The blow was to end Toe's playing career but it was to launch one of the most successful coaching experiences in all of sports.

Before the 1948–49 season had ended Frank Selke, Sr., managing director of the Canadiens, signed Blake as coach of the Houston club in the old United States Hockey League. When Houston promptly won the league championship Toe was promoted to coach of the Buffalo sextet in the still faster American Hockey League. A disagreement—"They said I was too easygoing," said Blake—with the front office forced Toe to quit but then he signed on as coach of the Valleyfield Braves on the Quebec Senior Hockey League.

When an opening as coach of the Canadiens developed in the spring of 1955 a number of promising candidates bid for the job but Selke sided with Blake who proceeded to coach the Canadiens to eight Stanley Cup championships, including an unprecedented five in a row. His teams finished first nine times.

Blake retired from coaching after his club had won the Cup in 1968 but he was retained by the Canadiens in a number of advisory capacities after that.

As magnificent as Blake was as a player, his coaching proved so extraordinary that many critics revere him more as a coach than a player although he was one of the most severe taskmasters in the business. "It's the way I am," Blake would say by way of explanation. "It's the only way I know how to get there."

He *got* there; both on the ice and behind the bench. Few have made more meaningful contributions to the game than the man from Victoria Mines.

Best Wishes
Bernie Geoff

24 Bernie Geoffrion (1950–1968)

He was nicknamed "Boom Boom" and there was more than a metaphor in that. Bernie Geoffrion caused reverberations throughout the hockey world from the moment he stepped on to a National Hockey League rink in 1950 to the day of his retirement eighteen years later.

His galvanic personality was a match for his dynamic shot, one that set a new standard for offense in the professional ranks. It was The Boomer, as he was often called, working the right point on the Montreal Canadiens power play, who popularized the fearsome slapshot that soon would be copied by Andy Bathgate of the New York Rangers and Bobby Hull of the Chicago Black Hawks.

Zooming at speeds of upwards of 100 miles per hour, the Geoffrion slapper put fear in the hearts of enemy goaltenders as never before. The Boomer's shot, blended with his effervescent play and unquenchable desire to win, enabled him to win the Calder Trophy as rookie of the year in 1952 and the Hart Trophy as the NHL's most valuable player in 1961. He twice led the league in scoring (1955 and 1961) and was named to the First All-Star Team in 1961 and the Second Team in 1955 and 1960.

Geoffrion played on six Canadiens' Stanley Cup-winning teams and no fewer than seven first-place clubs. His contributions in both cases were substantial. Yet for a very good reason Geoffrion never attained the accolades that should have come his way. It was The Boomer's misfortune to be a right wing during an era when both Gordie Howe and Maurice Richard dominated that position.

At the time of his retirement The Boomer had totalled 393 goals which then placed him fifth on the NHL's all-time goal-scoring list behind Gordie Howe, Maurice Richard, Bobby Hull and Jean Beliveau.

He teamed with Richard and Beliveau, often working on a line with the masterful Beliveau at center and tenacious Bert Olmstead on left wing. It was one of the best-balanced units the game has known.

Nicknamed "Boom Boom" because of the reverberation of his stick hitting the puck and the puck hitting the end boards (although it often went directly into the net), Geoffrion had many of the incendiary qualities of Richard.

But the Geoffrion character had one ingredient that was missing in the Richard psyche, a flamboyant sense of humor. He began delighting teammates late in the 1950–51 season after scoring 103 goals in fifty-seven Montreal Junior League games. Geoffrion was under great pressure to turn pro with Les Canadiens and he resisted until there were only eighteen games remaining in the 1950–51 schedule. He realized that the Calder Trophy for rookie of the year was given to players who had skated in twenty or more games. By waiting until there were fewer than twenty games in the 1950–51 schedule he thus became eligible to win it the following season.

When approached by Selke, Geoffrion laid the facts on the line: "I'll lose my chance for the Calder. It's too late in the season to catch up with the other guys."

The Boomer was no fool. He opened the 1951–52 season with two goals, including the winner, against Chicago in a 4–2 Montreal victory and immediately established himself as the newest Canadiens' hero. For Geoffrion it was relatively easy. Not only was he an excellent young prospect but he had recently married Marlene Morenz, the attractive blonde daughter of the late Howie Morenz.

Not long after Geoffrion's opening scoring burst, Les Canadiens visited New York and Geoffrion was interviewed by New York *Daily News* sports columnist Jimmy Powers. The writer observed that the NHL had a prize crop of rookies and wondered just who the Boomer thought would win the prize.

"Me," said Geoffrion, in as candid a reply as Powers could hope for.

As he had so candidly predicted, Geoffrion had become the foremost rookie-of-the-year candidate but it was more the manner in which he was scoring that was meaningful than merely the fact that he was scoring at an amazing clip. Geoffrion, although he may not have realized it at the time, had become a hockey revolutionary. Instead of using the traditional forehand wrist shot or the backhand shot for his tries at the goal, Geoffrion would draw his stick back like a golfer and slap the puck. The result was the "slapshot" that would eventually be adopted by most of the leading scorers in the NHL and would dramatically change the face of the game.

Bernard Geoffrion was born in Montreal on February 14, 1931, and learned his hockey on the many neighborhood outdoor rinks sprinkled throughout the city. He originally made his mark with the St. Francis Xavier school team and then moved up the teenaged ranks until he was discovered by ex-Canadiens defenseman Sylvio Mantha. The Boomer played Junior "A" hockey for Mantha on Montreal Nationales and continually improved his shot with endless workouts.

By the mid-1950s Geoffrion was regarded as one of the most magnetic personalities in the game and a major cog in the dynastic Canadiens' machine.

Yet, as glittering as the Boomer's career may have seemed on the surface, it nevertheless concealed the fact that for most of those seasons he skated with a double burden: he was the son-in-law of the Canadiens' superstar Howie Morenz and he was manacled by a succession of injuries that would certainly have defeated a less persevering individual. Geoffrion's ability to ignore pain during hockey crises was one of the primary reasons why he was a cut above the normal star and no episode illustrates this better than one which occurred during the 1961 championship round between the Canadiens and Black Hawks.

Bernard Boom Boom Geoffrion sat brooding in his compartment as the train sped the Montreal Canadiens to Chicago for the sixth game of the Stanley Cup playoffs. Although Boom Boom had won the NHL scoring championship, tied Maurice Richard's 50-goal record, and led the Canadiens to first place, the breaks once again were going against him.

He studied the heavy plaster cast imprisoning his injured knee, then called captain Doug Harvey. "Look, Doug," he said in his deep, rich voice, "one more loss and we're out. Let's cut the cast."

Harvey borrowed a knife and they slipped into the washroom where they delicately removed the hard plaster. Geoffrion's knee was blotched with red. "It hurt so much I couldn't sleep," the Boomer recalled. "But I wanted to play. Next morning I asked coach Toe Blake to let me take a turn."

At game time Boom Boom's leg was frozen with pain-killer. On his first turn, Bobby Hull and Reg Fleming of Chicago crashed him into the ice; he tried to get up but collapsed as if his knee were stuffed with cardboard. Later he attempted again to play but the knee was useless. Without Geoffrion Montreal lost the game and missed the Stanley Cup finals for the first time in eleven years.

After his retirement from the Canadiens in 1964, Geoffrion began coaching but returned to the NHL as a player with the Rangers in 1966 and remained active until 1968. In the Rangers' second game of the opening playoff round against the Black Hawks, Geoffrion set up a goal by Harry Howell. It was The Boomer's 822nd—and last—NHL point.

Geoffrion tried his hand at coaching several times—with the Atlanta Flames, New York Rangers and Montreal Canadiens—but each attempt ended disastrously. After the Flames left Georgia for Calgary, Geoffrion stayed in Atlanta, still a favorite although the hockey team was gone.

It was an unfortunate denouement but could in no way dim the lustre of a superbly exciting career.

25 Newsy Lalonde (1910–1922)

For the first fifty years of organized hockey's existence the standard for toughness and ability, combined in equal parts, was spelled out N-E-W-S-Y L-A-L-O-N-D-E.

"Newsy," said hockey historian Bill Roche, "was the greatest French-Canadian athlete of all time."

While the assertion is, at the very least, debatable, there never has been any question about Lalonde's relevance to professional hockey. He was the Montreal Canadiens first superstar, playing forward or defense. He scored 441 goals in 365 pro games—one of the most astonishing percentages in the game—and was five times leading scorer in various leagues.

As any opponent will attest, Newsy could fight as well as score. "We were a different breed, those of us who were born in the nineteenth century," said Lalonde, "because life was a lot tougher than it is now."

So was hockey infinitely more brutal than the contemporary game. Some of the goriest battles involved Lalonde and (Bad) Joe Hall, who played for the Quebec Bulldogs when Lalonde skated for Les Canadiens.

Newsy didn't reserve his venom for Hall. On December 22, 1912, the Canadiens played their hometown rivals, the Wanderers, in an exhibition game. Midway in the game Lalonde dispatched Odie Cleghorn of the Wanderers into the boards with such force that Odie's brother, Sprague, charged across the rink and smashed Newsy across the forehead with his stick. The blow just barely missed Lalonde's eye and he required twelve stitches to close the gaping wound.

Lalonde's distillation of fury and finesse had a very beneficial effect on the Canadiens from the very beginning. "Newsy not only had class," said Elmer Ferguson, one of the most distinguished Canadian sports columnists, "but he oozed color. Once, he scored nine goals in a game his team won with an eleven-goal performance."

In his first season as a Canadien, 1910–11, Newsy emerged the scoring champion with 38 goals in eleven games but an asterisk must be inserted here. In those footloose days of pro hockey, players were not tied down to the teams that had contracted them. Newsy's Canadiens were destined to last place in the seven-team National Hockey Association but the Renfrew Millionaires were taking aim at the top. As the teams reached the homestretch, Newsy suddenly was seen wearing Renfrew's colors. As one reporter noted: "It was easy to arrange because J. Ambrose O'Brien owned the Canadiens and he also owned the Renfrew club."

The Canadiens retrieved Newsy for their second season and climbed to second place. Lalonde seemed right at home with the Canadiens and destined for a long and happy career in Montreal when, on December 7, 1911, the NHA suffered its own day of infamy—the Pacific Coast Hockey Association was organized in Vancouver and immediately began raiding the eastern teams.

Vancouver made an offer Newsy could not refuse and he bade the Canadiens *au revoir* and took the train west. "They offered me $6,000 for twelve games," Newsy recalled. "In 1912 that was pretty good money. I was getting eight dollars a minute."

Newsy repaid Vancouver by winning the PCHA scoring championship, which whetted the Canadiens' appetite for him even more. The Montrealers finally swung a deal with Vancouver and Newsy returned to Les Canadiens. He was never better than in 1917 when the Canadiens beat Ottawa for the right to compete for the Stanley Cup against the Seattle Metropolitans. The Pacific Coast representatives took the series but Montreal challenged Seattle again in 1919 after defeating Ottawa.

Lalonde's career spanned twenty-one seasons, divided between 1905 and 1927 among teams representing Cornwall, Toronto, Renfrew, Montreal, Vancouver, Saskatoon and New York.

Edouard Lalonde was born October 31, 1887, in Cornwall, Ontario, and was nicknamed "Newsy" after a brief job in a newsprint plant. "I got my first pair of skates in 1902 when I was fifteen. We played wherever there was ice—the street, a pond, whatever."

By the time Lalonde was eighteen he was good enough to sign up with a team from Sault Ste. Marie, Ontario. Hockey was big stuff in the area of the Sault and northern Michigan and Lalonde quickly learned how tough his new profession could be.

Newsy's final days with the Canadiens were filled with misery. During the 1921–22 season Lalonde received more heat from the Montreal brass and on January 10, 1922, Newsy abruptly announced his "retirement."

Lalonde bolting Les Canadiens was tantamount to Babe Ruth walking out on the Yankees. It was a national catastrophe and compelled National Hockey League president Frank Calder to intervene and mediate the dispute. After missing four games, Newsy returned to the Habitants' lineup.

Newsy was never the same player after that. Later in the season the Montreal fans began razzing him and soon he was handed the supreme insult: he was demoted to a substitute's role and eventually traded to the Saskatoon Sheiks of the Western Canada League for young Aurel Joliat.

Even as a coach in Saskatoon, Newsy had strong ties to his alma mater in Montreal. When his young goaltender, George Hainsworth, displayed the moves of a future star, Lalonde wrote a letter to the Canadiens' brass advising them to keep Hainsworth in mind. They did, and when Montreal's ace goalie Georges Vezina died Hainsworth moved right into the Canadiens' net.

Lalonde finally donned the Canadiens' tricolor in 1932—only this time as coach. Although he was blessed with the likes of Howie Morenz, Aurel Joliat and Johnny (Black Cat) Gagnon, Lalonde presided over a crumbling dynasty. Some of the players, including Gagnon, later charged that they couldn't get along with the tough-talking coach.

Lalonde's coaching career lasted until 1934 when he received his walking papers. He remained in Montreal and was a loyal follower of Les Canadiens even in his later years.

On the night of November 8, 1952, Newsy was sitting in a Montreal Forum box when Maurice Richard scored his 325th goal in regular season play and broke Nels Stewart's long-standing record of 324.

Newsy cheered The Rocket and The Forum faithful cheered Newsy. Well they might. Lalonde was the original Canadiens ace and paid his dues to the game in spades. As Newsy himself so modestly put it when asked to review his career, "I have no complaints."

He well deserves being high on *Hockey's 100.*

26 Henri Richard (1955–1975)

When Henri Richard turned up at the Montreal Canadiens' training camp in September 1955 his appearance was interpreted by the media as a publicity stunt. Henri was nineteen at the time and, as all the experts surmised, there was no room on the talent-laden Canadiens for a kid with no professional experience.

But he *was* the brother of Maurice (The Rocket) Richard and therein was the essence of the gimmick. It was assumed that Henri would be placed on Maurice's line, photos would be taken, the customary interviews would be held following the workout and then the kid brother would be dispatched to a suitable minor league team for his year or two years apprenticeship.

Henri obviously didn't read the script. Centering a line with Maurice and galvanic left wing Dickie Moore, the kid brother orchestrated play from the moment he obtained the puck to the moment a line change was made. He did it again and again until it became clear that here was a very special young man. More than that, his appearance proved a tonic to thirty-five-year-old Maurice while Moore complemented the line with his tough checking and superb shooting.

Clearly, Henri's appearance was no stunt. Nicknamed "The Pocket Rocket," he would not be dropped from the varsity. "He's a little small yet," said coach Toe Blake, "but with his speed we keep telling him not to try to go through the big opposition defensemen, just go around them."

Henri accepted the advice and ripened into one of the NHL's most creative centers during his two decades of major league play. He was voted to the First All-Star Team in 1958 and the Second Team in 1959, 1961 and 1963. More important, The Pocket Rocket provided essential ingredients—leadership, goal-scoring, playmaking—of the highest quality for no less than eleven Stanley Cup championship teams.

Vintage Henri was an episode in the sixth and what proved to be final game of the 1966 Stanley Cup finals between the Canadiens and Detroit Red Wings. Montreal led the series three games to two and had held the Red Wings to a 2–2 tie in regulation time of game six. But now it was sudden-death overtime and a goal for the Canadiens would mean the Stanley Cup.

With a little more than two minutes gone in the overtime the Canadiens launched a counterattack against the Red Wings' defense. Montreal defenseman Jean-Guy Talbot skimmed the puck to left wing Dave Balon, who, in turn, lifted a pass over Red Wings defenseman Gary Bergman. At that moment The Pocket Rocket, skating at more than twenty miles per hour, lunged to deflect the puck just as defenseman Gary Bergman threw his body at Richard.

As the foes collided Richard slid headfirst toward goalie Roger Crozier. The puck nestled just under the upper portion of Richard's right arm. The momentum carried the stomach-down Richard just past the left goal post while the puck slid into the far left corner of the net. The rubber had been deflected into the net by Henri's body, giving Montreal another world's championship.

Henri Richard surmounted the most challenging demand of all: playing in the

shadow of his uniquely gifted brother, Maurice, and then maintaining his stardom after The Rocket retired in 1960.

There was some question about the long-term durability of the Dickie Moore-Richards line, especially because Maurice was en route to his thirty-sixth birthday. Despite The Rocket's age he managed to keep pace with his younger cronies, although one afternoon he nearly regretted it. The Canadiens were in the midst of a workout when Henri rounded the net at full speed from one side and Maurice approached on the same track from the other direction. They collided violently and both fell to the ice unconscious. When they were finally revived, both were escorted to the first-aid room where Maurice needed twelve stitches to close his wound and his kid brother, six stitches.

Then, in a masterful understatement, Maurice intoned: "You'd better watch yourself, Henri. You might get hurt."

Henri and Maurice Richard began drifting apart as the kid brother came into his own around the league. The Rocket was like the maternal lioness, watching over her cub at first but leaving it to fight for its place in the world once it reached maturity. For Henri, maturity came fast. He fought on even terms with his tormentors. He would not be run out of the league and he would be a very accomplished hockey player although never the electrifying personality that the Rocket was.

By contrast, The Pocket was determined but not explosive, strong but not overpowering. If The Rocket was the home-run hitter, The Pocket was more the base stealer and opposite-field hitter. He also had The Rocket's touch of the brooder in him.

The Pocket Rocket was an essential cog in managing director Frank Selke's rebuilding plan, and he was an asset to Pollock, too, in Sam's first years in Montreal. Les Canadiens finished first in 1965–66, breezed past Toronto in the first round of the playoffs with four straight wins, and appeared capable of disposing of the Detroit Red Wings at will in the Cup finals, especially since the series opened with two games at the Forum. But Detroit's hot hand, goalie Roger Crozier, was sizzling, and the Red Wings upset Les Canadiens in the first two games.

It was then that The Pocket Rocket rallied the troops and capped the adventure by scoring the Cup-winning goal in the sixth game on enemy ice.

But no matter how many major goals he scored Henri could never fulfill the demands of fans who wanted him to be a clone of his tempestuous brother, Maurice. Exasperated to the core, Henri once complained: "What do they expect from me? I am *me,* not my brother. Maurice is the best hockey player of all time. I do not try to imitate him. I just try to do my best. All I can say is that I try to play my best."

To the purist, Maurice never was the best in such skills as stickhandling and playmaking but others believed that Henri came close to perfection. "The Pocket," said Canadiens coach Toe Blake, "became a better *all-around* player than Rocket was. But it's asking an awful lot of any man to be the scorer that Rocket was. He was the greatest scorer under pressure that I've ever seen."

Henri had exceptional powers of self-insight. He perceived that he never could be the athlete that Maurice had been. "My brother's biggest thrills," said Henri, "came when he scored many goals. I am most satisfied when I play in a close game and do not have any goals scored against me. Sometimes people have asked me whether it helped or hurt having Maurice as an older brother.

''It was not easy, because many people expected me to be as spectacular as Maurice. But I believe it also helped me as well as hurt me. Don't forget, Maurice was a great scorer, and he could get goals that many other players could not get. That helped my passing because I knew that he would always be near the net waiting for a shot. But Maurice never gave me any advice. I never asked him for it and he never offered it.''

The Pocket Rocket finally packed it in following the 1974–75 campaign and concentrated on his *brasserie* which he had opened in Montreal. His twenty NHL years were consistently superior and memorable. They would have been even more so had he not been Maurice Richard's kid brother.

27 Dickie Moore
(1951–1968)

"Dickie Moore is one of the kids making the customers forget Maurice Richard."
—Jim Vipond, *The Toronto Globe and Mail*.

Such a testimonial is roughly equivalent to suggesting that a promising playwright is capable of making literary critics forget William Shakespeare.

But such was the promise of Montreal-bred Moore that only the most lavish praise was adequate for his contribution to the Canadiens. Dickie played left wing for a dozen years in Montreal, won two scoring championships, was twice the First All-Star, played for six Stanley Cup winners and six first-place teams.

It was a measure of Moore, the competitor, that he limited his battles to the tougher members of the opposition. He was absolutely unsparing in the manner in which he sacrificed his body for the cause of victory, and, eventually, such grit would take its toll on his body.

During the 1958–59 season Moore set a standard for courage that rarely has been matched in professional sport. His left wrist, which had been broken two years earlier, had not mended properly and required regular reinforcement. His right wrist had suffered a chipped bone and, by all rights, Dickie should have been recuperating in a hospital. But he would not miss a game.

"Sure, my wrist hurts when I shoot," Moore said, "but the only time I'll stop playing is when it breaks off."

He was true to his word. Although the wrist is the essential transmission behind a hockey shot, Moore endured the agony and when the season had ended he had scored 96 points (41 goals and 55 assists) to break the NHL scoring record during the six-team league.

Moore blended his scoring prowess with a special brand of truculence and constantly was embroiled in one fight or another. One of the first feuds was with Ted Lindsay, who was then with the Detroit Red Wings and later of the Chicago Black Hawks. Picking on the Lindsay of that era was like walking unarmed into a den of tigers.

Lindsay soon discovered that Moore was tough too. Threats couldn't stop Dickie, but a string of crippling injuries did; they almost forced him to retire. First, he suffered three shoulder separations. Then he had recurring knee trouble, after that, broken right knuckles. All required operations.

Hobbled by injuries, Moore remained a disappointment until the 1955–56 season, when he scored 50 points. More importantly, he played a full seventy-game schedule for the first time, which seemed to be just the psychological tonic he needed. From then on he zoomed off like a space missile and hit his own personal moon when he won the scoring title in 1958.

Typically, Dickie had to clear some cumbersome hurdles to win that title. Moore, Andy Bathgate of the Rangers, and Montreal's Henri Richard were locked in a tight race for the scoring lead with three months left. Then, Dickie broke his left wrist. The Canadiens' management feared he would be lost for the season, but Moore had other ideas. "How about putting a cast on my arm?" he suggested. "Let me take care of the rest."

Sure enough, when the Canadiens faced-off in their next game, there was Moore on the ice, handcuffed with a bulky plaster cast on his left arm. Gone was the freedom to stickhandle and the possibility of flicking a wrist shot, but nothing dampened Dickie's spirit. He played in every game and scored 36 goals—tops in the league—with 48 assists, a total of 84 points. And Dickie had spent most of the season playing right wing—an unfamiliar position for him.

In the 1958–59 season, without any consequential injuries, Moore, now back at left wing, won his second scoring title, beating Gordie Howe's 1952–53 scoring record of 95 by 1 point.

Dickie's talent was all-inclusive. He shot hard and accurately, stickhandled and passed well, played right or left wing, worked easily with all players, and, at 5′11″, 170 pounds, played rugged and smart defense.

While there were a few egomaniacs on the championship Canadiens clubs, Moore conspicuously was not one of them. He was unselfish to a fault. In 1958–59, for instance, when Geoffrion jumped into an early scoring lead, Moore said honestly, "I'd like to see the Boomer win it and I'd like to finish second." Later Geoffrion was sidelined and Moore and Jean Beliveau outraced Andy Bathgate to finish first and second, respectively, in scoring.

Richard Winston Moore was born January 6, 1931, in Montreal and grew up in an intensely hockey-oriented environment. Dickie played for the Canadiens Juniors and Montreal Royals before being called up to the Canadiens. He alternated the next two seasons among Buffalo, the Montreal Royals and the Canadiens. He came up to stay in 1954–55 and scored 36 points in sixty-seven games, while playing with a trick shoulder that popped out of place almost every third game. The condition was bad enough for Frank Selke to put Moore on the trading block. Failing to make a deal, the Canadiens decided to see how Dickie would respond to an operation. It was successful and so too was Moore from then on.

Although Moore's wrists plagued him during the apex of his career it would be his gimpy legs which would prove to be his undoing in later years. His final season as a Canadien was 1962–63. Dickie decided to hang up his skates and went into business, but the lure of the rinks proved too much and when he was invited to make a comeback by general manager Punch Imlach of the Toronto Maple Leafs in 1964, he accepted. The comeback lasted for a season and, again, Dickie returned to the business world, seemingly for keeps.

When the NHL expanded from six to twelve teams in the 1967–68 season the St. Louis Blues made a policy of signing over-the-hill veterans who had starred elsewhere. Dickie and his old pal, Doug Harvey, provided the leadership the Blues required and took them to an upset victory over the Philadelphia Flyers in the seven-game opening round of the playoffs. Moore played spectacularly as the Blues reached the final round against the Canadiens before being eliminated in four games. Dickie's totals were 7 goals and 7 assists for 14 points in eighteen games. He missed tying for the scoring lead by a point.

Cut from the same cloth as Rocket Richard and Howie Morenz, Moore desperately wanted to continue—and the Blues would have welcomed him again—but this time his legs delivered an emphatic rejection of still another season in the bigs.

Dickie Moore never did make the customers forget Maurice Richard but he did make a very large name for himself on a team filled with giants such as Richard, Jean Beliveau, Doug Harvey, and Jacques Plante.

After retirement, Moore became as successful in business as he had been on the rink. He may not have possessed Richard's goal-scoring flare but he was a big winner and as courageous a player as the ice game has ever known.

28 Joe Primeau (1928–1936)

The career of Joe Primeau has been so thoroughly intertwined with that of his partners on the Toronto Maple Leafs' "Kid Line"—Busher Jackson and Charlie Conacher—that his virtuoso performances as a center have been ignored by too many hockey critics.

Yet, there was little that the skater known as "Gentleman Joe" could do about his position as centerpiece on one of the National Hockey League's most accomplished trios. When respected hockey people such as Frank Selke, Sr., discuss the mighty Maple Leafs of the early 1930s Primeau invariably is lumped together with his linemates.

Although Primeau's trophy collection is less bountiful than some of his contemporaries', it was only because he was the quintessential team player who thought of his own accomplishments as secondary to those of the club. Primeau did, however, play on three first-place teams and one Stanley Cup winner. And in 1932 he won the Lady Byng Trophy for his impeccably clean play combined with a high level of proficiency.

Joe's instincts and insights into the game were well above average. An example was the manner in which The Kid Line profited by a rule change permitting forward passing in the enemy's zone. Primeau mastered the new form by skating over the opposition blue line and luring the defensemen toward him while Conacher and Jackson outflanked the foe. At the last possible second Primeau would skim a pass to one of his mates, who would have an unimpeded shot on goal.

The Kid Line jelled to perfection in 1932 when the Maple Leafs won the Stanley Cup although they had originally been melded as a unit during the 1928–29 season.

Whether Primeau would have been accorded more attention had he been a flamboyant sort like many of his teammates is a moot point. He was never once picked as the First All-Star center. Twice he finished second in the scoring race, trailing Jackson the first time and Conacher the second. He was voted to the Second All-Star Team for the 1933–34 season.

There is no mention of it in the NHL record book but Primeau was the only player ever to have scored a goal at each end of the rink on successive plays. It happened in a game against the Boston Bruins. Joe happened to be near the Maple Leafs' goal when a Boston player took a hard shot at his goalie, George Hainsworth. As Joe tried to deflect the shot, the puck caromed off his stick and sailed into the Toronto net.

Primeau was so angry—and determined—that on the ensuing face-off he captured the puck, sped straight toward the Bruins' goal, faked a pass that fooled the Boston defense, skated in on goalie Tiny Thompson, faked *him* and slid the rubber into the open net.

Joe's admirers often have cited a match with the Montreal Maroons during the 1932–33 season as one of his most arresting performances. The Montreal club was leading 2–0 after the first period when Maple Leafs manager Conn Smythe roared into the dressing room in a fit of pique. "He walked around the room," said Primeau, "and told each of us personally just what he thought of us. We went out of that room fighting mad. Everyone felt like showing that so-and-so Smythe what we could do. I just happened to get lucky."

Primeau scored a goal in the second period and another early in the third to tie the score. Then, Toronto moved ahead, 3–2, but the Maroons kept threatening to knot the count again. Suddenly, Primeau stole the puck from Montreal's ace defender Lionel Conacher, raced in to score his third goal and clinched the decision.

Joseph Primeau was born in Lindsay, Ontario, January 29, 1906. His relatively fragile-looking physique seemed to militate against his professional hockey aspirations but young Primeau excelled wherever he played.

But Frank Selke, Sr., who had managed an amateur club on which Primeau played, told Conn Smythe that Joe was a comer. Smythe took the advice and Gentleman Joe never looked back.

Perhaps the most startling aspect of Primeau's career was his decision to retire at the end of the 1936 season. He was only thirty years old at the time and believed to be good for several more good years. But Joe had made up his mind.

Joe's departure from the Maple Leafs marked the beginning of the end of a marvelously colorful era in Toronto hockey. Along with Jackson, Conacher, and such amusing teammates as Hap Day, Hal Cotton and King Clancy, the Maple Leafs of that era were to hockey what the St. Louis Cardinals were to baseball.

Upon his retirement from the Maple Leafs, Primeau became a successful businessman in Toronto. But he never could resist the lure of the rinks and soon returned to coaching where he achieved a "first." Joe became the only coach ever to lead a team to the Memorial Cup, emblematic of junior hockey supremacy; the Allan Cup, senior hockey's major trophy; and the Stanley Cup.

Gentleman Joe was a superior professional on the ice and behind the bench. He qualifies for a high rank in *Hockey's 100*.

29 Frank Mahovlich
(1956–1974)

There was a time, a little more than two decades ago when the most pursued target in hockey was Maurice (Rocket) Richard's accomplishment of 50 goals in a regular season.

The Rocket set his mark during the 1944–45 season and while many, such as Gordie Howe of the Detroit Red Wings, came close to reaching the Richardian plateau the 50-goal mark remained inviolate through the 1950s.

It was during the 1960–61 campaign that the most serious threat to The Rocket's hallowed "50" was delivered. Frank Mahovlich, a Toronto Maple Leafs left wing with mighty strides and a dynamite shot to match them, was beating enemy goaltenders at better than a goal-a-game pace by the middle of the 1960–61 season.

Skating on a line with the veteran center Red Kelly and workmanlike right wing Bob Nevin, the diffident Mahovlich emerged as the most exciting shooter of his day and was assailed by newsmen in the manner of Roger Maris at the time that the New York Yankees outfielder was challenging Babe Ruth's 60-home-run record.

Unlike Maris, Mahovlich never did break the record, although he ultimately did quite well by himself and his assorted teams. He won the Calder Trophy as rookie of the year in 1958 and was a First All-Star left wing in 1961, 1963 and 1973. He made the Second Team in 1962, 1964, 1965, 1966, 1969 and 1970. Frank played on no fewer than five Stanley Cup champions, four with the Maple Leafs and one with the Montreal Canadiens.

The statistics suggest that Mahovlich luxuriated through a lengthy career sprinkled with laughs and coated with dollars. In fact Mahovlich was plagued with trauma and tribulation ever since 1960–61.

"Life was never the same after that," Frank smiled. "I wound up with 48 goals that year, so everybody figured that next year I would do better. And the season after that would be greater than the other two."

Mahovlich can afford to laugh now. He has been knighted by hockey's Hall of Fame, owns a travel agency in Toronto and is graced by a charming wife, Marie, and devoted kids.

But the scars remain.

Like Hall of Famer Jean Beliveau before him, Mahovlich was truly superb; but never superb enough.

"They expected too much from me," he says. "The year of the 48 goals I had scored 38 in thirty-five games. I was on a roll, heading for The Rocket's record but that was expecting too much.

"We didn't have depth on that club. All of a sudden four of our guys got injured and our balance was gone. So, the opposition began zeroing in on me and I was neutralized."

Unfortunately for Frank, neither the Toronto Maple Leafs nor general manager-coach Punch Imlach was neutralized.

The abrasive Punch had his own way with hockey players and he nettled The Big M. He mispronounced his name, calling him Mahallovich, and he often would treat Frank—and others—as if they were invisible.

One of the favorite tortures in the Imlach concentration camp was inflicted after a losing weekend of hockey for the Leafs. They would often play at home on Saturday night and travel as far as Chicago or Boston for a Sunday night game. Explained Mahovlich:

"We'd catch a plane back to Toronto on Monday morning, and then he would take us directly from the airport to the rink for a practice. If that were the case, why didn't he practice us on the ice right after the game?

"After a while I began to wonder how long I could take this kind of thing. A day off from hockey does a man a lot of good, but we never seemed to get a day off with Imlach."

Then there were the demands from the supposedly sophisticated Toronto fans. If Frank had scored 48 goals when he was twenty-three years old, they reasoned, he should score at least 50 goals a year later. On top of that Chicago owner Jim Norris allegedly had offered $1 million for Mahovlich, but the Leafs had turned him down. When Frank slipped to 33 goals in 1961–1962, a few local purists in Maple Leaf Gardens began what was to be a chronic chorus of boos whenever The Big M played a mediocre game. Soon the hoots began grating on his nerves, not to mention those of other stars around the league.

Mahovlich couldn't conceal his anxiety. He became introverted and distant. "I played with Frank for eleven years," said teammate Bob Baun, "and didn't say twenty-two words to the guy."

In Toronto, hockey is by far the most popular sport. The city has three English-speaking dailies that carry by-lined stories about the Leafs every day from September through the end of the playoffs in April. Mahovlich began to feel hounded by some of the reporters, and he burrowed even deeper into his shell.

Mahovlich succumbed to his first breakdown on November 12, 1964. He was suffering from what doctors later described as "deep depression and tension," but the exact diagnosis wasn't made public at the time.

While Torontonians indulged in the usual wild speculation about The Big M's condition, Frank remained in seclusion for a couple of weeks before returning to the Leaf lineup. He remained secretive about his ailment, and he became exceptionally confidential about his interviews with reporters.

Once, a season later, Paul Rimstead asked to talk with him. "Okay," said Frank, "but not on the team bus. I'll see you later sometime."

They eventually held their rendezvous at a Montreal hotel, where Mahovlich allowed that his relationship with Imlach was worsening. The Big M pointed out that his doctor advised him to ignore Punch whenever possible. "He told me to pull an imaginary curtain around myself whenever Punch was around," Frank said. "I've been doing it, and feel a lot better."

But the boos from the crowds became more frequent and more annoying. In the middle of the 1967–68 season Mahovlich played superbly and the Leafs routed the Montreal Canadiens 5–0 at Maple Leaf Gardens. Frank scored a goal and two important assists. Even his archcritic, Imlach, described Frank's game as "outstanding."

Mahovlich was named the second of three stars picked after every home game by broadcaster Foster Hewitt. Normally a "star" is greeted with cheers or, at worst, mild applause when he skates out on the ice to acknowledge the selection. When Frank planted his blades on the ice, he heard some applause, but there was no mistaking the boos that were uttered by some spectators.

Mahovlich completed the home-game ritual and returned to the dressing room. He showered and changed into street clothes and later headed for the team's sleeping car, which would carry the Leafs to Detroit for their next game. The Big M boarded the sleeper and prepared to go to bed, but somehow he couldn't shake the memory of the catcalls, and he couldn't get to sleep.

Torn by his anxiety, Mahovlich finally walked off the sleeper at about 4:00 a.m. He contacted a club doctor and was escorted to a hospital. This time his ailment was no secret. Dr. Hugh Smythe disclosed that The Big M was suffering from "deep depression and tension" and was in the care of Dr. Allen Walters, a psychiatrist.

The Maple Leafs' brass had begun thinking about dealing Frank to another team, but they couldn't make a move until he returned to the lineup and proved to the satisfaction of prospective buyers that he was capable of playing big-league hockey again. The sabbatical proved beneficial to both Mahovlich and the Leafs, and he once again rejoined the club after a few weeks rest.

Early in March 1968, Imlach finally concluded a deal with Detroit. The Leafs would receive Norm Ullman, Floyd Smith and Paul Henderson in return for Mahovlich, Pete Stemkowski, and Garry Unger, all forwards.

In addition the Leafs would receive the right to obtain ace defenseman Carl Brewer, who had quit pro hockey but who might be induced to return.

The deal was one of the most spectacular trades ever negotiated in the NHL. Mahovlich, of course, was delighted to be free of Imlach's shackles. For years the Red Wings were renowned as a relaxed team with an obvious joie de vivre. During playoff time, manager Sid Abel would take his men to the racetrack rather than seclude them in some distant hideaway. Frank was aware of this, but he wasn't quite sure how the Detroit players would react to him.

The Big M was restored to life in Detroit and played with similar enthusiasm after being traded to the Montreal Canadiens. At last he seemed to have been rewarded with the happiness and relaxation that had eluded him during the halcyon days in Toronto.

Francis William Mahovlich was born January 10, 1938, in Timmins, Ontario. The son of a Croatian immigrant, Frank was scouted as a teenager by the Maple Leafs and several other NHL clubs. His father was persuaded by Leafs scout Bob Davidson to send Frank to a Catholic high school in Toronto from where he could eventually graduate to the pro ranks.

The Big M's all-time NHL totals were 533 goals, 570 assists for 1,103 points in 1,182 games. He ended his career in the World Hockey Association and then retired to devote time to his travel agency in Toronto. When he was inducted into hockey's Hall of Fame in 1981 someone asked Frank if he missed the limelight. No, he insisted, he didn't miss it a bit. "You see," smiled Frank, "I'm content and happy. I don't have to play hockey anymore!"

30 Milt Schmidt
(1937–1955)

A case could be made for Milt Schmidt as the greatest center in National Hockey League history. It is made by those who have played against the hard-bitten Boston Bruin and not by those who live by statistics and awards alone. They swear by his creativity, his endurance, his strength, but most of all, by a soldierly fearlessness that somehow enabled him to accomplish more in the heat of battle than his contemporaries.

Not that Schmidt was a slouch when it came to production. He led the NHL in scoring in 1940, was picked to the First All-Star Team three times and was voted the Hart Trophy as the league's most valuable player in 1951, all as a member of the Bruins.

Schmidt's career, unfortunately, was shortened by World War II. Milt, along with his "Kraut Line" buddies, Woody Dumart and Bobby Bauer, enlisted in the Royal Canadian Air Force at the very height of his career and, thus, "lost" the best three years of playing time. Nevertheless, he played for four first-place teams and two Stanley Cup winners.

Apart from his own personal achievements, Schmidt was pivot on a remarkable forward line whose roots could be traced to the city of Kitchener, Ontario. Milt and his boyhood pals, Bobby Bauer and Woody Dumart, originally gained recognition on a local team known as The Greenshirts.

Dumart and Bauer, the oldest of the trio, were signed by the Bruins and assigned to their farm team, the Boston Cubs. When Bauer and Dumart arrived at Boston Garden they immediately made an appointment with Bruins general manager Art Ross. They insisted that their center, Schmidt, was as good if not better than they were as professional prospects.

Ross did not want a seventeen-year-old in Boston and rebuffed the lads but they persisted and Ross finally mailed a letter to Kitchener inviting Schmidt to the Bruins' training camp in the autumn of 1936.

A week later Ross received a letter from Schmidt, accepting the invitation and promising that he "would work all summer to save the money needed to report in Boston and would pay his train fare and board."

Schmidt made his NHL debut late in the 1936–37 season and even though he scored two goals he nurtured doubts about his future. He mailed his first paycheck home to his mother with a note saying, "Better bank this for me, mom; it may be the last I'll get."

Once the trio got the feel of big-league hockey they became a dominant factor for the Bruins and a hit with the fans. They were alternately known as The Kraut Line, The Sauerkraut Line and The Kitchener Kids.

The Krauts not only played together, travelled together and relaxed together but they also presented a united front when it came to contract-signing time. "We felt if we went in together, asked for exactly the same salary for each, and took a stand in our dealings we'd be better off," said Schmidt.

So close were The Krauts that when Schmidt married Marie Peterson in 1946 Dumart and Bauer had to toss a coin to decide which one would be best man. When Bauer married, Schmidt and Dumart had also tossed. When, in January 1948, Schmidt became the father of a daughter, Nancy, he announced that Dumart and Bauer were *both* godfathers!

This closeness was often reflected in the scoring statistics. During the 1939–40 season, when the Bruins finished first, Schmidt led the league in scoring with 52 points while his linemates were tied for second with 43 points apiece.

Not surprisingly, The Kraut Line enlisted as a unit in the Royal Canadian Air Force and played from time to time against other service teams. While stationed in England, where Schmidt played as often as possible when not performing his duties as a Flying Officer, he was as popular as ever.

Milton Conrad Schmidt was born March 5, 1918, in Kitchener, Ontario, a German-Canadian community which had originally been named Berlin until the outbreak of World War I. The youngest in a family of six, Milt attended King Edward Public School and began playing hockey almost as soon as he was able to walk.

It was young Schmidt's good fortune to meet Montreal Canadiens goalie George Hainsworth, who had grown up in Kitchener, at a trophy presentation in King Edward School. Hainsworth gave the dark-haired Schmidt words of encouragement which remained with him through his lengthy career.

The hallmark of Milt's play, both as a youth and later as an NHL star, was a muted ruggedness. "Schmidt," said one longtime admirer, "was a gentleman's hockey player—until someone started pushing his teammates around."

It had been feared that Schmidt, like so many other NHL stars returned from the war, would have lost his touch but Milt regained his form and in 1946–47 enjoyed the best productivity—27 goals, 35 assists, 62 points—of his entire career. Even the retirement of Bobby Bauer failed to put the brakes on Schmidt and in 1950–51, still teaming with Dumart, he produced 22 goals and 39 assists for 61 points. It was enough to win him the Hart Trophy.

On March 18, 1952, the Bruins held a "Schmidt-Dumart Night" and talked Bobby Bauer out of retirement for that one game. After elaborate pregame ceremonies The Krauts got down to the business of winning a hockey game against the Chicago Black Hawks. Boston won the game, 4–0, clinching a playoff berth in the process, and Bauer went back into retirement.

Schmidt remained an active player until 1955 when he was given the coaching reins of a struggling Boston hockey club. He stayed on until 1962–63 when Phil Watson was called in to take charge. But Watson could not rejuvenate the Bruins and Schmidt took over again in the middle of the 1962–63 season. He remained at the helm of the Bruins as general manager from 1966 until 1973 and enjoyed two Stanley Cup triumphs, in 1970 and 1972, with the help of trades he had engineered.

Easily the greatest accomplishment of Schmidt, the manager, was a deal he made with the Chicago Black Hawks. He sent goalie Jack Norris, defenseman Gilles Marotte and center Pit Martin to Chicago in return for forwards Phil Esposito, Fred Stanfield and Ken Hodge.

In the view of some experts it was the most one-sided deal in NHL annals, and was directly responsible for the Cup victories in 1970 and 1972.

Milt left Boston in 1974 to become the first general manager of the new Washington Capitals franchise but it was a move that generated nothing but woe. The Caps, under his administration, never became competitive and Schmidt eventually left the disaster scene, returning to Boston where he went to work for the Bruins in the ticket-selling department.

He was embittered by the Washington experience and lamented the fact that none of the other twenty-one NHL teams saw fit to utilize his talent and experience.

Nevertheless, the debacle with the Caps couldn't obscure Schmidt's handsome playing career nor his exceptional victories as a manager. That is enough to qualify him for a finish in the top thirty of *Hockey's 100*.

31 Ted Kennedy
(1942–1956)

"I was dumbfounded by his mature observations on the game as it progressed. I remember telling sportswriter Ed Fitkin that I thought we might have acquired a superstar."

The speaker was Frank Selke, Sr., acting manager of the Toronto Maple Leafs. The subject was Ted (Teeder) Kennedy, the seventeen-year-old Maple Leafs center who had been injured and was sitting next to Selke during the 1943 Stanley Cup playoffs.

Selke's radar, in this case, was extraordinarily accurate. Kennedy would be orchestrating a Stanley Cup championship for the Maple Leafs before he was even twenty years old and ultimately would skate for no fewer than five Cup winners of which he captained two.

Perhaps most difficult of all, from a personal standpoint, was Kennedy's ascendency to the Maple Leafs' captaincy. From the start of the 1940s through the spring of 1948 Syl Apps had been the captain and acknowledged leader of the Leafs. More than that, Apps had been the most revered athlete in Canada during his time, which meant that when Apps retired at the end of the 1947–48 season his successor, Kennedy, would be in a position roughly equivalent to Mickey Mantle following Joe DiMaggio in center field at Yankee Stadium.

At a city hall ceremony honoring the Stanley Cup champions in April 1948 it was felt by many of the thousands of spectators that they were witnessing the swan song of the Maple Leaf hockey club. Apps officially announced his resignation and Kennedy, at age twenty-three, accepted the captaincy.

Apps' heir apparent did not—at least superficially—suggest a dominating hockey player. Whereas Syl had been an exceptionally strong and fluid skater, young Ted seemed to agonize through every stride. But despite his plodding style, he managed to get from point A to point B as well as any and better than most.

From the moment he skated out on the ice wearing the "C" on his royal blue and white jersey Kennedy demonstrated that he was no less a leader than Apps and, in some ways, even more forceful. The Maple Leafs, in the first three years of Kennedy's leadership, won two Stanley Cups.

The captain himself never was dazzling enough nor productive enough to win scoring prizes. He was twice voted to the Second All-Star Team and in 1955 captured the Hart Trophy as the NHL's most valuable player.

At Maple Leaf Gardens, Kennedy became a folk hero in the same mold as Apps. John Arnott, a service station operator, especially deified Kennedy with a periodic yell during a lull in the action that soon became a trademark of every Toronto game in which Kennedy played.

Several years earlier Arnott had delivered a regular cheer for Peter Langelle, a Toronto hero who went off to the wars and never played again for the Leafs. The cheer was a penetrating "C'monnnnn PETER!" Now it was altered.

Just as a face-off was about to take place, a booming voice could be heard across Maple Leaf Gardens. "C'monnnn, TEEDER!" Somehow it sounded just as good as the cheer for the retired Langelle.

Although Kennedy had been well-schooled in hockey basics by his mentor, Nels Stewart, Teeder was weak in one department: skating. His strides were labored, almost painful to watch, and he often seemed to be moving like an express train with one set of brakes locked into its wheels. He finished his freshman season with 26 goals and 23 assists for 49 points in a year in which inept goaltending made high scoring relatively simple.

It was, of course, no fluke. Kennedy would emerge as a consistently productive pointmaker, much in the style of a solid .300 hitter who invariably comes through in the clutch. During the 1946–47 season, in which he scored 28 goals and 32 assists in sixty games, Teeder was placed at center between two equally eager youngsters, Howie Meeker on right wing and Vic Lynn on the left.

The trio was christened "The New Kid Line," a reference to the Maple Leafs' original Kid Line of the 1930s featuring Charlie Conacher, Joe Primeau and Busher Jackson.

Once again an ideal blend had been devised. In the 1947 Stanley Cup finals between the Maple Leafs and Canadiens, the Montrealers were heavily favored but the effervescent Kid Line defused Montreal's big guns and the Maple Leafs won the Stanley Cup in six games.

Maple Leafs president Conn Smythe regarded Kennedy as one of the most valuable acquisitions the team had ever made and Teeder received acclaim throughout the NHL—except for the city of Detroit, where he was permanently painted as a villain. To this day there is a question whether or not Kennedy was the culprit in one of the most controversial episodes in hockey history: the accident which nearly killed the Red Wings' young ace, Gordie Howe.

The incident took place during the first game of the Stanley Cup semifinal round between Detroit and Toronto on March 28, 1950, at Olympia Stadium. By the middle of the third period Toronto had a 4–0 lead in what already had become a bitter series.

The Toronto-Detroit rivalry was extraordinarily bitter so it was not surprising that the tempers remained taut in the dying minutes of the game as the Leafs' captain launched a counterattack for the visitors.

Kennedy was six feet from the left boards as he reached center ice. Behind him in hot pursuit was Wings defenseman Jack Stewart. Sweeping in from the right side was Howe, who attempted to crash Kennedy amidships. Howe was skating a trifle too slow to hit Kennedy with full force, and it appeared that the best he might do would be to graze the Leaf and throw him off balance. But he missed even that opportunity, and as Kennedy stopped short and then pressed forward, Howe tumbled, face first, into the thick wooden sideboards. Seconds later he was lying unconscious on the ice, his face covered with blood. As 13,659 fans sat horror-struck, Gordie Howe, the young favorite, was carried off the ice on a stretcher and removed to Harper Hospital.

For several hours there was some doubt that he would survive. A call was put through to Saskatoon, Saskatchewan, to urge Gordie's mother to take the first plane to Detroit so that she could be at her son's bedside.

Gordie pulled through. But as far as Detroit's press and public were concerned, Gordie had been lethally assaulted and somebody would have to pay for it. Toronto naturally denied responsibility, and the argument raged like a forest fire with sportswriters, coaches and fans from both sides pouring verbal gasoline on it to keep it going.

Detroit's theory was that Teeder Kennedy had deliberately speared Howe. Kennedy offered to take an oath that he had not caused the injury. "I saw Howe lying on the ice with his face covered with blood," said the Leaf captain, "and I couldn't help thinking what a great player he was and how I hoped he wasn't badly hurt. Then Detroit players started saying I did it with my stick. I knew I hadn't, and as I've always regarded Coach Tommy Ivan as a sensible, levelheaded man, I went over to the Detroit bench and told him I was sorry Howe was hurt but that I wasn't responsible."

Leaf defenseman Garth Boesch suggested that Howe was hurt accidentally by his own teammate Jack Stewart, an opinion that was shared by other members of the team. Al Nickleson, who covered the game for *The Globe and Mail,* wrote: "It appeared to this observer that Kennedy, in stopping short, had raised his elbow as a protective gesture and that Howe had struck it, before smashing into the boards with his face as he fell."

Sportswriter Red Burnett, of the Toronto *Daily Star,* added: "Referee George Gravel saw the mishap to Howe, didn't call a penalty, and that proves, as far as we are concerned, that Kennedy did not hit Howe."

But Paul Chandler, who covered the Red Wings for the Detroit *News,* was not to be soothed by such unheated reporting. "The *Telegram,*" he wrote, "has made Kennedy a martyr, an innocent man put to torture by a cruel conspiracy between the Detroit sportswriters and the Detroit Red Wings. 'Kennedy Cleared,' screamed the *Telegram* on page one of its news section the day after Howe was injured. Cleared of what?"

It didn't take long for the antagonists to find a common enemy in NHL President Clarence Campbell, whom they blamed for his failure to prevent the brutality and violence that both preceded and followed Howe's injury.

Despite the charge of vacillation Campbell quickly took a stand on the Howe case and exonerated Kennedy. "Kennedy," said Campbell, "as a right-handed player, had the butt part of his stick tight to the fence as he was going up the ice. He was being checked from his right. The injuries to Howe were on the right side of the head. Kennedy had stopped to avoid the check, and Howe went in front of him."

The Toronto player was further exonerated when the referee Gravel submitted a report. It read: "Jack Stewart carried the puck in the Toronto end and was checked by Kennedy, who carried the puck into the center zone right close to the fence on the players' bench side. I turned to follow the play, and Stewart was trying to check Kennedy and was right close to him. Just as Kennedy crossed the Toronto blue line, I saw Howe cut across toward Kennedy, skating very fast. Just before Howe got to Kennedy, Kennedy passed backhanded and stopped suddenly. Howe just brushed him slightly and crashed into the fence and fell to the ice. Stewart fell on top of him. Play carried on for a few seconds as Toronto had possession."

Even the mayor of Toronto, the Honorable Hiram McCallum, squeezed into the act and dispatched a message to Kennedy: "The people of Toronto know that absolutely no blame in any way can be attached to you for the accident to Gordie Howe. They are 100 percent behind you all the way and know you will go on and continue to play wonderful hockey and lead the team to the Cup. We regret very much the injury to Howe as he is a great player, but at the same time we know that he was the aggressor in attempting to crash you on the boards.''

Although Kennedy was ultimately exonerated in all quarters but Detroit, the Red Wings never forgave him and pinpointed Teeder for all manner of vicious assault in the remainder of the playoffs and for years to come.

Theodore Kennedy was born December 12, 1925, in Humberstone, Ontario. Once Ted had shown he had special hockey talents he caught the attention of Hall of Famer Nels (Old Poison) Stewart who took the lad under his wing. ''I've been around the NHL for fourteen years,'' counselled Stewart. ''You'll do all right. Just take this advice: keep your head up when you're near the goal. Just take your time —and pick that corner!''

Early in 1942 Stewart conferred with coach Hap Day of the Maple Leafs. ''If I were in your shoes,'' said Stewart, ''I'd trade away twelve players to get young Kennedy.''

The Maple Leafs' high command took Stewart's advice—although not literally —and signed Kennedy to a contract late in the 1942–43 season. Teeder scored 55 goals in his first two full seasons in the NHL, underlining the faith Stewart had in the young man.

He remained a Maple Leaf until his retirement after the 1955–56 season. Although he was only thirty years old at the time, his legs were gone and there was little that his enormous heart could do to keep him in the bigs.

Kennedy was equally successful and respected off the ice. He became an official of the Ontario racing association and still is a familiar figure at the annual Hockey Hall of Fame banquet in Toronto. He paid his dues to get into *Hockey's 100*.

32 Charlie Conacher (1929–1941)

"The trouble with Big Charlie," a friend once said, "is that he thinks he's a truck, so he takes on the other team in a personal, hand-to-hand battle!"

Most of the time Charlie Conacher came out on top, whether he was challenging an enemy defenseman or shooting at the opposition goaltender.

During an era when the wrist shot prevailed and such high-velocity scorers as Babe Dye, Cooney Weiland and Nels Stewart dominated the game, Conacher's shot was regarded as the hardest of all. The overpowering right wing could crack a two-inch plank with the fury of his shot.

Although Conacher skated for an assortment of NHL clubs including the Detroit Red Wings and New York Americans, his niche as a superstar was carved during his seven-year tenure on the Toronto Maple Leafs' renowned "Kid Line" along with Busher Jackson and Joe Primeau.

In the seven years they were together from the 1929–30 season until Primeau retired at the end of the 1935–36 season, the unit amassed a total of 792 points in regular league play and an additional 71 points in playoff competition for a grand total of 863 points. Significantly, that was 20 points more than New York's famed line of Frank Boucher and Bill and Bun Cook collected during the same seven-year span.

Conacher's importance to The Kid Line was reflected in the stats. Over the seven-year era he scored 204 goals and 122 assists for 326 points. Jackson collected 153 goals and 119 assists for 272 points while Primeau's mark was 71 goals and 194 assists for 265 points.

Charlie won the scoring championship in 1934 and 1935, was a First Team All-Star in 1934, 1935 and 1936 and made the Second Team in 1932 and 1933.

Among Conacher's finest hours was a game in April 1936, when the Maple Leafs were fighting elimination in the second game of a two-game total goal series against the Boston Bruins. The Bruins had taken the first game on their home ice, 3–0, and scored another goal in the second game to lead the round, 4–0.

With his team still down 0–4 in the second period, Conacher rallied his troops. First, he set up King Clancy with Toronto's first goal. Then, Charlie scored to make it 2–4. Red Horner scored for Toronto, reducing the deficit to one whereupon Conacher scored his second goal of the night, tying the count. Next, Charlie set up Jackson, who put Toronto ahead, 5–4 and Buzz Boll made it 6–4 for the Leafs. Conacher then capped the glorious evening with his third goal of the game, thereby eliminating the Bruins.

"The grateful crowd," noted one report of the game, "waited in pouring rain on Carlton Street and cheered the Big Bomber to the echo."

Charles William Conacher was born December 10, 1909, in Toronto, within shouting distance of a hockey rink, and it was inevitable that the gifted youngster would be discovered by professional birddogs.

Scouting Conacher was easy. Charlie learned his hockey on Toronto's venerated

Jesse Ketchum Public School rink, and he learned all other sports from his older brother, Lionel, who was to be voted Canada's athlete of the half-century. Charlie broke in as a hockey player guarding the goal, but soon he moved to the front line.

Conacher eventually became captain of Frank Selke's Marlboros in 1926, a club that won the Memorial Cup for Canada's Junior championship. Conacher's booming shot was his forte, but his skating still left something to be desired. Thus, when Smythe announced that Charlie had made the team for 1929–1930, straight out of juniors, there was considerable surprise.

Charlie made his NHL debut on November 14, 1929, at Mutual Street Arena. Chicago's Black Hawks, with the redoubtable Charlie Gardiner in goal, were the opponents, and the fans filling the old Toronto ice palace were frankly skeptical of Conacher's ability to skate and shoot with the pros, especially since he had never had basic hockey training in the minor leagues.

The game was close, but Charlie was never out of place. At one point the puck came to him as he skated over the blue line. Conacher caught it on the blade of his stick and in the same motion flung the rubber in Gardiner's direction. Before the Chicago goalie could move, the red light had flashed, and Charlie Conacher was a Leaf to stay.

At first Smythe used Conacher on a line with Primeau at center and Harold Cotton on left wing; but despite Conacher's instant success, Primeau still failed to click. Just before Christmas, 1929, Smythe made the move that would alter hockey history. He pulled Cotton off the line and inserted Busher Jackson in his place on right wing. Hockey's first and most renowned "Kid Line" was born. Success was as dramatic as a volcanic eruption. Toronto defeated the Black Hawks, the Canadiens, and the Maroons right after Christmas and went undefeated until January 23 of the new year.

Off the ice, Conacher was something else. Like other members of the Maple Leafs, hockey's Gashouse Gang, Conacher was an inveterate prankster.

A legendary Toronto gag involved Conacher and his teammates King Clancy and Hap Day. It occurred after an earlier prank at New York's Hotel Lincoln. The Leafs had moved on to Boston for a game against the Bruins, and Clancy and Day were rooming together. On such trips the players usually convened for their pregame meal in the afternoon and then retired to their rooms to rest.

In those days Bruins games started at 8:30 p.m., so it was customary for Clancy to get up about 6:30 p.m., enabling him to get to the rink about an hour before game time. Conacher and Day huddled after the pregame meal and agreed that it was time for another joke on Clancy.

When King and Hap retired to their room, Clancy set his alarm and soon fell into a deep sleep. Day remained awake, and when he saw that Clancy was well into slumberland, Hap tiptoed out of the room, met Conacher in the hall, and the two of them took the elevator to the lobby. With the secrecy of an espionage plot the pair persuaded the room clerk to ring Clancy's room in a few minutes. The hotel employee was advised to inform Clancy that he was working for Boston Garden, it was game time, and the two teams were on the ice ready for the opening face-off.

The culprits returned to their floor and huddled outside Clancy's room. They listened as the phone rang and King screamed in horror. A moment later Clancy ran out the door, dashed downstairs, and sprinted for the nearest taxicab. He found one and advised the astonished driver that he was King Clancy of the Maple Leafs and was late for his hockey game. The driver happened to be a hockey fan and knew very well that the Bruins match wouldn't start for more than two hours. He asked what Clancy's rush was all about since the time was only 6:00 p.m.

The truth dawned on King, and he ordered the cab stopped. He slowly climbed out and walked back to the hotel, where Day and Conacher were waiting for him in the lobby. There is no official record of what Clancy said to them, but it probably could not be printed here anyway.

When The Gashouse Gang began to disintegrate in the late 1930s Conn Smythe decided to reshape the Maple Leafs as a younger team. Conacher was dealt to the Detroit Red Wings in 1938 and then to the New York Americans in 1939. He finished his career on Broadway in 1941.

Charlie stayed close to the hockey scene and in 1948 was named coach of the Chicago Black Hawks. At the time the Windy City sextet was a shambles and Charlie did little to restore the club to life. He had an unfortunate run-in with Detroit *Times* sportswriter Lew Walter and gave up coaching in 1950.

Beloved by Torontonians, Charlie remained a hero in his birthplace. He died on December 30, 1967, but his name remains one of the most venerated in the sport.

33 Denis Potvin
(1973–   )

It was Denis Potvin's misfortune, even before he set foot in the National Hockey League, to be labelled "the next Bobby Orr." At the time the comparison was made, in the early 1970s, Orr was the king of hockey and believed by many to have been the greatest defenseman of all time.

"I didn't like being compared with Orr," said Potvin, "because we were different personalities with different playing styles, skating for different teams. The only thing we had in common was that we both played defense. What these statements about me and Orr do is make my job that much harder; but I accept it as part of the business."

Remarkably, Potvin then proceeded to justify the lofty comparisons. He emerged as one of the brightest young players on the hockey horizon, winning the Calder Trophy as rookie of the year in 1974. He was named to the First All-Star Team in 1975, 1976, 1978, 1979 and 1981 and to the Second Team in 1977 and 1984. In addition he was voted the Norris Trophy winner as the NHL's best defenseman in 1976, 1978 and 1979.

There was some question as to whether age would corrode Potvin's glittering talents. During the 1982–83 season he amassed 12 goals and 54 assists for 66 points and was among the Islanders' leaders in the significant plus-minus category.

Potvin could score and create attacking opportunities in the Orr manner but he added a dimension to his game that never was part of the Orr repertoire; he could deliver crushing bodychecks behind the blue line—and often did.

Potvin was the cornerstone of a New York Islanders team which won Stanley Cup championships in 1980, 1981, 1982 and 1983. But, perhaps even more important, it was Potvin who helped establish the Islanders, at a time when they were struggling at birth, into one of the league's most robust franchises. During the 1983–1984 season, the Islanders' captain tallied 85 points with 22 goals and 63 assists. And during the Stanley Cup round he set an NHL record for most career playoff assists (99).

The arrival of Denis on Long Island in 1973 meant the club had its first legitimate superstar. The Isles' graph, which had been at a solemnly low point, began a relentless upward climb, culminating with captain Potvin hoisting Stanley Cups three straight years—a record for an American team.

Planting Denis' skates at Nassau Coliseum was more than a difficult chore for Isles president-general manager Bill Torrey. In the spring of 1973, when Potvin graduated from junior hockey, the World Hockey Association was making strenuous efforts to lure young players away from the NHL. This was a major problem for Torrey.

Three WHA teams, the New York Raiders, the Chicago Cougars and the Ottawa Nationals, had contacted Potvin's representative with offers. This was not surprising considering the impact Denis already had made on Canadien amateur hockey.

Once, when Denis and his Ottawa 67s played a game against the Toronto Marlboros at Maple Leaf Gardens an unofficial record number of scouts were in attendance. "There were more elbowing infractions (among the scouts) around the coffee urn than there were out on the rink," wrote Jim Proudfoot of the Toronto *Star*. They were there, of course, to scout Potvin.

Another time, an All-Star Team from the Ontario Hockey Association (all teenagers) played a powerful touring squad from the Soviet Union. Potvin scored a goal in the 6–3 upset of the Russians. Once again, Denis got rave reviews.

"The poise and skill which Potvin displayed impressed the large number of NHL scouts on hand," wrote Frank Orr of the Toronto *Star*. "They knew he could go against boys, but wanted to see him against men. He didn't disappoint them."

Bill Torrey was acutely aware of the notices and equally certain that Potvin would be a winner on the Island—that is, if Torrey could land him.

D (for draft) Day took place in June 1973 at The Queen Elizabeth Hotel in Montreal. Although the WHA teams still were flexing their wallets, Denis had decided once and for all that the *real* challenge would be in the NHL. He arrived at The Queen Elizabeth in a conservative business suit ("I wanted to look like anything but a hockey player," said Potvin) to witness firsthand the decision on his fate.

It was rumored before the draft had even begun that the Montreal Canadiens had offered the Islanders four good players in exchange for Potvin.

Torrey, whose club had finished last the previous season, enjoyed first pick. But before NHL President Clarence Campbell signalled the Islanders' leader for his choice, Sam Pollock, the boss of the Canadiens, requested a time-out. Pollock walked over to Torrey and the two began whispering. It appeared as if Pollock was making an eleventh hour attempt to obtain Potvin.

When the secret conference had ended the audience waited breathlessly as Campbell ordered Torrey to at last make his move. "The New York Islanders," said Torrey, "wish to draft as their first choice—DENIS POTVIN!"

Denis, who privately told friends that he did not want to play for Montreal, was the most relieved person in the building. "It was," Potvin said, "a marvelous moment for me."

It was to be the harbinger of many marvelous moments for the Islanders.

Decorated with a Fu Manchu mustache, Denis arrived at the Islanders' training camp in September 1973 determined to fulfill his advance notices, which were considerable.

From the very start in the NHL, Denis was "tested" by his foes. In Pittsburgh, long-time needler Bryan (Bugsy) Watson lured him into a fight. Potvin took the decision, opening cuts above and below Watson's left eye. "He's a strong kid," Bugsy allowed.

He was strong on defense as well as offense. From the opening face-off it was evident that Denis Potvin was a winner.

It was also evident that Denis had a special quality which pleased coach Al Arbour.

On February 14, 1974, Denis cracked a bone on his left ankle in a game at St. Louis. Other athletes would have begged off but Denis continued playing. He wore a plastic cast on the ankle which severely limited his skating but he played nonetheless.

Playing against the Canucks in Vancouver he escaped serious injury when a blazing shot by defenseman Jocelyn Guevremont smashed into his helmet above the right eye.

Denis bounced back from all of the hits, bumps, pokes and other annoyances with commendable resiliency. He was nominated to play in the 1974 All-Star game at Chicago Stadium. Skating with *la crème de la crème* of the NHL, he scored a goal and was toasted by coach Scotty Bowman.

Potvin's excellence was apparent right down to the homestretch and in the final game of the season, against the Minnesota North Stars at Nassau Coliseum, Potvin demonstrated that the future could only be bright for the home club.

He assisted on Billy Harris' three goals and then personally sewed up the contest by scoring the tie-breaker with only five minutes left in the game.

And when the final arithmetic was completed the leading scorer on the Islanders was a defenseman, Denis Potvin.

That spring of 1974 Denis was awarded the Calder Trophy as rookie of the year. Those who remembered what had happened a year earlier then realized that Torrey was so right in rejecting the Canadiens' offer.

With Denis Potvin on defense, the sky was the limit for the Islanders. And after helping the Islanders to a fourth consecutive Stanley Cup championship in 1983 Potvin was fast approaching that pinnacle.

34 Bryan Trottier (1975–   )

At a time when Wayne Gretzky was breaking all available National Hockey League scoring records there remained a significant group of players, coaches and general managers who publicly asserted that the one man they would prefer having on their team in a crunch was *not* Gretzky but rather Bryan Trottier, the New York Islanders' center.

Unlike Gretzky, who is obsessed with scoring, Trottier has ripened into the most effective total forward since Gordie Howe.

While Gretzky limits his play to the offensive half of the ice, Trottier is equally concerned with offense and defense. He will take his regular turn at center, work the power play, kill penalties and take all key face-offs in his defensive zone.

''Trottier,'' says Vancouver Canucks general manager Harry Neale, ''has another edge over Gretzky. Bryan has been a champion four times. When that happens to Wayne, then we can take another look at them.''

Leading scorer in the 1980 Stanley Cup playoffs, Trottier paced the Islanders to Stanley Cup triumphs in 1980, 1981, 1982 and again in 1983. His last cup win was most amazing since he played through three of the four playoff rounds despite an injured knee. He won the Calder Trophy as the NHL's rookie of the year in 1976, twice was First All-Star center, won the Hart Trophy as the league's most valuable player in 1979, the same year that he led the NHL in scoring, and in 1980 was voted the Conn Smythe Trophy as the most valuable player in the playoffs. Trottier played in 68 regular season games during the 1983–84 season and collected 111 points on 40 goals and 71 assists.

By no small coincidence, the Islanders' production as a team also slipped. If nothing else, it demonstrated his intrinsic value to the club.

Many hockey historians have tried to compare the rugged Trottier to superforwards of other years. His body-checking ability has caused some to liken his play to that of Hall of Famer, Milt Schmidt, who starred for the Boston Bruins during the late 1930s and through the early 1950s.

There is a fluidity about his play that suggests Gordie Howe. ''He's rugged like Howe,'' explained former teammate Eddie Westfall. ''Gordie liked to play a physical game and so does Bryan.''

At times Trottier appears more concerned with bodychecking than scoring although his statistics indicate otherwise. Beginning in 1978 he scored more than 100 points in a season five years running and was as responsible as anyone for turning the Islanders into the powerhouse of the early 1980s.

Watching Trottier in action, one senses that the game is fun for him. ''I'd think nothing of playing twice in one day, if I could,'' said Trottier. ''That's how much I love this game.''

Trottier not only has made hockey fun for himself but has been an intrinsic factor in the development of teammate Mike Bossy's scoring prowess. A right wing, Bossy has played alongside Trottier since 1977 and, together, they have been two of the most productive linemates in history. ''It's instinct,'' said Bossy. ''There aren't any little signals. The thing between us is the communication we have. We're not afraid to tell each other that we should have done this, or we should have done that. As much as Bryan helps me, I've helped him.''

Unselfish to a fault, Trottier cruises around the rink seemingly unemotional and unaware of the abrupt changes in the ebb and flow of play. Yet, he invariably is the first one where the puck happens to be and, though he masks his feelings, plays with an intensity rare among his colleagues or foes.

Trottier's shot is not especially hard nor is he as fast as a Lafleur. "Bryan doesn't stand out in any one area," said Bruins general manager Harry Sinden. "He's deceptive. When he's in close, he can find an opening and he has tremendous patience and poise. He is able to control the puck and keep it away from the opposition until he's good and ready to shoot."

If there was one shortcoming to Trottier's game it was his playoff failings in his earlier years in the NHL. He had scored but five goals in his first forty-two playoff games before he finally exploded in the 1980 Stanley Cup rounds. "When I was holding the Cup," Bryan recalled of his first Stanley Cup triumph, "I could feel all the names. My senses peaked. I could hear everyone. The crowd was incredible, one continuous roar."

Bryan John Trottier was born July 17, 1956, in Val Marie, Saskatchewan, in the heart of Canada's wheat country. By the time Bryan was in his mid-teens he had been more than casually scouted by several NHL teams. Bill Torrey, architect of the Islanders' juggernaut, was in Swift Current, Saskatchewan, to watch the teen-aged Trottier in action. "One night," said Torrey, "it was so cold the wind-chill factor was about eighty-three degrees below. Trottier got two or three goals, two or three assists, and he had the puck the whole night. The first thing you noticed was instinct. Things happened."

Torrey and coach Al Arbour remembered and when draft time came and there was a choice between Trottier and Tiger Williams, Bryan's teammate at Swift Current, the question was settled when Arbour asked which one was the better player. That's how Trottier became an Islander.

When the solidly built baby-faced kid turned up at the Islanders' training camp in September 1975 there were those who believed he was at least two or three years away from making it in the NHL. But each time a training camp roster cut was made Trottier survived and he was in the lineup when the Islanders opened their home season at Nassau Coliseum. He responded with three goals and two assists, tying a team record with five points.

"Bryan is a tremendous skater who controls the puck extremely well," said Clark Gillies, who has played on a line with Trottier on and off since Bryan's rookie season. "His main strength is that he's always coming up with the puck in the corners. He's also good at causing the other team to make a mistake. He anticipates so well that he's often able to intercept passes. But he rarely makes mistakes himself."

It is the totality of Trottier's game that marks him as superior and it is conceivable that, in time, he may eventually be ranked among the top three or four centers of all time. "He has flashes of moves that put him with any player," added Resch.

That includes Jean Beliveau, Syl Apps, Marcel Dionne and, of course, Wayne Gretzky.

Bryan's coach, Al Arbour, has said that he would never trade Trottier for Gretzky. Many other experts have said that Trottier adds a special dimension to his game that Gretzky lacks and even Wayne admits it. "Bryan is more aggressive than I am," Gretzky allowed. During the 1981–82 season Trottier scored 50 goals, 79 assists and 129 points in helping the Islanders to first place in total points and another Stanley Cup. He was voted to the Second All-Star Team behind Gretzky but as any hockey expert would agree that's plenty to be proud of and right now Trottier's cup of pride is overflowing.

35 Bobby Clarke (1969–   )

What Pete Rose has meant to any baseball team with which he has been affiliated, Bobby Clarke has been to the Philadelphia Flyers. From 1969 when he made his National Hockey League debut, until his retirement in 1984 the gap-toothed center was the Charlie Hustle of hockey.

"Clarke," said Dave Schultz, who teamed with him on the 1974 and 1975 Stanley Cup-winning Flyers teams, "was the heart and soul of our club."

Like Rose, Clarke displayed a fervor for his pastime that never diminished with age. In 1982, at the age of 32, he was clawing for position with greater zeal than rookies fourteen years his junior. During his final season, 1983–1984, he still managed 60 points on 17 goals and 43 assists in 73 games.

Bobby's contributions were duly recorded. He was voted the Hart Trophy as the NHL's most valuable player in 1973, 1975 and 1976. He was First All-Star center in 1975 and 1976 and Second Team All-Star in 1973 and 1974. He starred for Team Canada in the eight-game series against the Soviet All-Stars in 1972 and played for the NHL All-Stars against the Soviet selects in the 1979 Challenge Cup.

Perhaps the most emphatic testimonial to Clarke's excellence was his ability to successfully stand the test of time. For example, during the 1982–83 season he led the Philadelphia Flyers in scoring, although he was one of the team's senior citizens at age 33.

It always has been less than easy for Clarke. A diabetic, he lacked the smooth skating skills of a Bobby Orr or Guy Lafleur. His shot was never particularly potent but he made the most of what he had. "Guts is what he has," said ex-Flyer Larry Zeidel. "Not everybody saw his qualities at first but, after a while, they realized that he was a winner."

If anyone suggested to Philadelphia Flyers' boss Ed Snider that the seventeenth player claimed in the 1969 amateur draft would, in May 1973, be selected for the Hart Trophy as the NHL player adjudged the most valuable to his team, it is quite possible that Snider would have tumbled from his chair laughing.

Yet, in September 1969, while the Flyers's first-year men were working out at Le Colisée in Quebec City, someone detected that rare quality of utter superiority in just such a man.

"Within three years," said Bud Poile, then general manager of the Flyers, "that twenty-year-old boy will be the best in the league. And if he's not the best I'll guarantee you that he will be in the top three."

Poile was talking to his heir apparent, Keith Allen, about a rather awkward center named Bobby Clarke. Precisely what it was about Clarke that inspired Poile's raves was somewhat of a mystery. But as the 1972–73 season wound down to a playoff conclusion, it was evident that Poile either knew what he was talking about or had made an awfully good guess.

By the time the Flyers went up against the Montreal Canadiens in April 1973, Bobby had irrevocably become Mister Hockey in Philadelphia. Such veterans as

Ed Van Impe, an original Flyer, knew it as well as the man in the street. Players such as forward Terry Crisp, who was new to the team, sensed it immediately.

Robert Earle Clarke was born August 13, 1949, in the mining town of Flin Flon in northern Manitoba. Bobby played for the local junior team, the Flin Flon Bombers, in a frontier atmosphere that was rife with brawling and intimidation.

He survived the battles and seemed destined for professional hockey when word of his diabetic condition circulated through the NHL scouting grapevine. Fortunately for Clarke, his coach, Paddy Ginnell, was determined to see that his crack center got a fair chance to reach the top.

Ginnell arranged for Clarke to visit the famed Mayo Clinic in Rochester, Minnesota. His coach personally escorted him before the 1968–69 season. Following a battery of tests, the doctors agreed that there was absolutely no reason why Bobby could not play pro hockey, provided he took good care of himself. What's more, the doctors put it in writing.

"That was all I needed," Ginnell said. "We went home and when the scouts came around the following season I showed them the letter. I wanted everyone from any NHL team who came to Flin Flon to know about Bobby exactly what the doctors at Mayo Clinic knew."

Skeptical though they were, the Flyers gambled on Clarke, picking him seventeenth overall in the 1969 amateur draft. He made the team on his first try and by the 1972–73 season had exceeded the 100-point mark.

His modesty notwithstanding, Clarke could not deny his accomplishments, which were immense during the 1972–73 season. For example, during a game against the Montreal Canadiens at the Forum, Philadelphia came away with a 7–6 victory. Bobby scored a hat trick, the winning goal achieved with only 3:39 remaining in the game. Even partisan Montrealers agreed that the kid from Flin Flon was Hart Trophy (most valuable player) material and Flyers manager Keith Allen was not disinclined to agree.

"In Philadelphia," Allen observed, "there's nobody but Clarke to consider. Rick MacLeish has had a remarkable year, but I'd hate to think where the Flyers would be without Clarke." Together with his diabetes, Bobby also has a little difficulty with his eyesight, which is 200–100 myopic. "That means," he explains, "trouble seeing far away. I never wore lenses in junior hockey. If I'm on top of the play, I'm okay. It's when the puck is in the air that I have trouble judging it."

Yet Clarke would still be the All-Canadian Boy, except for one factor: the company he was keeping. By the middle of the 1972–73 season the Broad Street Bullies had established themselves as the riotous swashbucklers of the NHL. Their scorn for the rule book was notorious from Flin Flon to Toronto and a cause for alarm at NHL headquarters in Montreal.

Inevitably Clarke would be affected by the brawlers around him. For like Gordie Howe, who once defended hockey violence by asserting that "It is a man's game," Clarke too is aware.

By playoff time, 1973, Bobby Clarke had fulfilled the promise of his September press clippings when he surprised everyone in the Team Canada camp. He finished second in the scoring race behind perennial leader Phil Esposito with 37 goals and 67 assists for 104 points in seventy-eight games.

In 1974–75 and 1975–76 he led the NHL in assists with 89 each time. He also led in playoff assists in both years with 12 and 14, respectively. But by the late 1970s, the wear and tear was taking its toll, and Bobby's point production began a downward spiral—90, 89, 73, 69 and 65 in the 1980–81 season.

The Flyers attempted to relieve him by making Clarke an assistant coach and limiting his playing time, but his will to play was overwhelming, and in 1981–82 he helped regenerate the Flyers' rebuilding process with a gallant show of energy.

It seemed perfectly natural for the man who had done so much for the Flyers on the ice to become a factor in their front office. Few were surprised when Bobby Clarke, at 35, retired and became the Flyers' general manager. But when all is said and done, on courage alone, Clarke rates a pass into *Hockey's 100*.

36 Jacques Plante
(1952–1975)

That Jacques Plante was the third-best goalie of all time is an assertion that few could challenge. That Plante was the best goalie ever is a statement that could be supported in some quarters although not this one. However, Plante's eminence in his field is certainly without question. He may not have been the iron man that Glenn Hall was with the Chicago Black Hawks or the implacably perfect puck-stopper that Georges Vezina had been during an earlier era with the Montreal Canadiens but Plante *was* stupendous in his own right.

He was a winner. He was expert. He was creative and he was durable. He won the Hart Trophy as the National Hockey League's most valuable player in 1962 and won the Vezina Trophy as the top goalie from 1956 through 1960 and again in 1962 and finally, sharing it with Glenn Hall, in 1969. He was named to the First All-Star Team in 1956, 1959 and 1962 and to the Second Team in 1957, 1958, 1960 and 1971.

Unlike Terry Sawchuk, whose skills eroded with time, Plante was in mint condition at the age of forty when he starred for the St. Louis Blues. Plante played for six Stanley Cup-winning teams and eight clubs that finished in first place. And, more than Sawchuk, Plante was the most innovative of the modern goaltenders. In fact it would be safe to say that Jacques did more to revolutionize the modus operandi of puck-stopping than anyone in the past thirty years. On top of that Plante, plainly and simply, was a very interesting character.

In his spare time, Plante, alias "Jake the Snake," had a hobby of knitting toques, the French-Canadian wool caps worn by his ancestors. He was confident to the point of being cocky and betrayed a bizarre goaltending style that would soon be copied by other netminders around the league. It was Plante's idea that he would be aiding his defensemen by roaming out of his cage, formerly a strict taboo, and behind the net when the pucks were caromed off the boards and skidded behind his cage. By so doing, Plante was able to control the puck and pass it off to a teammate, while scrambling back to his goal crease before any shots were taken. This style was introduced when the Canadiens, coached by Dick Irvin, were engaged in a thrilling semifinal playoff against the Chicago Black Hawks in 1953.

All this was well and good and terribly fascinating, but for the adventurous and unconventional Plante to experiment with the Canadiens in the playoffs and on the brink of elimination was something else! But Irvin had made a commitment, and Plante was his goalie. Jacques the Roamer immediately went into the cage and stopped the Black Hawks cold. He foiled a breakaway early in the fifth game, and with that impetus Les Canadiens won two straight games and captured the first round. Plante won himself a job and helped the Canadiens to the Stanley Cup. By the late 1950s, Montreal had the most formidable club of the decade—if not all time —with the defense of Doug Harvey and Tom Johnson available to thwart attackers. Toe Blake had replaced Irvin as coach and a coolness eventually developed between the explosive coach and his enigmatic goalkeeper.

Still the best in the league, Jake the Snake occasionally enraged spectators with his scrambles behind the net for the puck. Once, the play backfired on him. He missed the disk; an opponent retrieved it and shoved the rubber into the yawning cage before Plante could return to guard it. In November 1958, Plante's goals against average began climbing, matched by Blake's temper.

The Blake-Plante repartee was, perhaps, even more ominous than it sounded. Severe to a fault, the coach was down on his goaltender and was to become more and more disenchanted with Plante's behavior as the seasons progressed.

It was ironic that the Plante-Blake rift widened at the precise point when Jacques executed one of his most courageous acts. The date was November 2, 1959. Plante was in the Canadiens' net facing the Rangers at Madison Square Garden. Right wing Andy Bathgate of the Rangers, one of the league's hardest shooters, released a quick shot that struck Plante squarely in the nose and sent him bloodied to the ice. His face looking like a mashed potato laden with ketchup, Plante was helped to the dressing room where seven stitches were taken in his pulverized proboscis.

Until then, Plante had been experimenting during practice sessions with a mask that was molded to his facial contours. Blake, an old school hardliner, was irrevocably opposed to Jacques' using the face piece in a regular game but, this time, the Canadiens had no spare goalie and Plante would not go back onto the ice without a mask. Blake had no choice but to oblige and, on that night, history was made. Plante wore the mask, won the game and vowed to continue wearing the device as long as he played. Blake was not the least enamoured of the idea although he publicly asserted that, as long as it helped Plante keep the pucks out of the net it would be all right. For 1959–60 the mask proved effective enough to enable Plante to win the Vezina Trophy.

But Blake was a hard man and his grievances against Plante—anger that transcended the mask issue—simmered within him and, often, without. The breaking point came in 1963 when he was dealt to the Rangers. Blake would have preferred it if Plante had displayed an uncompromising attitude toward the game, the kind that marked other Canadiens, most notably Maurice Richard. This, however, was not Plante's way. He pursued his unorthodoxy with the Rangers, then the St. Louis Blues, Toronto Maple Leafs and Boston Bruins.

Jacques Plante was born January 17, 1929, in Shawinigan Falls, Quebec, and like many a French-Canadian youngster, played his hockey on the outdoor rinks of *La Belle Province*. His goaltending excellence was unquestioned in the early 1950s yet he was not given a serious thought as a potential goalie for the Canadiens because they had a relatively young and quite efficient Gerry McNeil guarding the twines for them. But Dick Irvin took a dramatic gamble in 1953 and Plante rewarded him with a memorable clutch effort.

Plante concluded his NHL career with the Boston Bruins in April 1973, then became general manager-coach of the Quebec Nordiques in the World Hockey Association. It was another case of a superstar being unable to orchestrate from the sidelines as well as he had on the ice. A season later, at the age of forty-five, he returned to the nets, this time with the WHA's Edmonton Oilers. He played commendably for the Oilers but finally retired for good at the conclusion of the campaign and became a part-time goaltending coach for the Philadelphia Flyers, a position he retained through the early 1980s when he became a netminding advisor to the Montreal Canadiens.

Through the years Plante rubbed several people the wrong way and many have never forgotten what they interpreted as his abrasive manner. But no follower with a sense of hockey history will ever forget the comprehensive contributions made by Plante or his consummate skill at blocking a puck.

There was nobody like him before and there will not be anyone like him again. An original. A craftsman.

37 Aurel Joliat
(1922–1938)

They called him "The Little Giant." Aurel Joliat weighed in at 140 pounds (on a heavy day) and appeared only slightly taller than a fireplug. But size was no more a debit to the French-Canadian left wing than it was to the likes of King Clancy and Frank Boucher.

"Aurel was as slippery as Howie Morenz was swift," said Boucher.

Despite his size Joliat played sixteen seasons in the NHL, all with the Montreal Canadiens. He scored 270 goals—the same number as Morenz—and was voted the Hart Trophy as the league's most valuable player in 1934. He made the First All-Star Team in 1931 and the Second Team in 1932, 1934 and 1935. Joliat played on three Stanley Cup championship teams.

Both teammates and foe were intrigued and often amused by Joliat and his idiosyncracies. "Aurel always wore a black cap," Boucher recalled. "He wore it on the ice whenever he played. It was a baseball cap and he positively would not chase the puck if it were knocked from his head."

Joliat's forte was stickhandling. He could pass with the best of them and many oldtimers insist that he was similar in style with Gil Perreault, the clever Buffalo Sabres center.

One of the Canadiens' finest lines comprised Joliat, Howie Morenz and Johnny (Black Cat) Gagnon. "Aurel always used to get the puck and pass it to me," Gagnon remembered, "and then I'd pass it to him. We had pretty much the same stickhandling style and I always knew what kind of moves he'd make. For instance as soon as he'd hit the blue line he'd throw me a pass behind his back. Morenz wasn't as good a playmaker so I'd play more with Aurel."

The Joliat-Gagnon connection was primarily responsible for the Canadiens' Stanley Cup victory over the Chicago Black Hawks in the 1931 finals. The series was tied at two games apiece in a best-of-five round. In the final match Joliat dispatched a perfect pass to put Gagnon in the clear, giving Montreal a 1–0 lead. Gagnon scored again late in the game and Montreal triumphed 2–0.

"Morenz may have been 'the Babe Ruth of Hockey' but Joliat was more of an artist, a stickhandler," said Gagnon. "Aurel always made beautiful passes. He wasn't as fast as Morenz but he could move when he wanted to."

Joliat was paid almost $10,000 in his prime and returned the favor by leading the Canadiens in scoring in 1933 and 1934. It was to be the apex of his career not because his abilities diminished but because of the decline and fall of Morenz and, therefore, the Joliat-Morenz-Gagnon line.

Morenz was traded to Chicago during the 1934–35 season but his replacements on the Joliat-Gagnon line proved inadequate and the Canadiens slipped to last place in the 1935–36 campaign.

Joliat yearned for his old pal, Howie, and then in a surprise move, the Canadiens reobtained Morenz for the 1936–37 season. The line was reunited and while it

lacked the élan of earlier years it still provided the old thrill for Montreal fans. But the leg fracture suffered by Morenz on January 28, 1937, ruined the line, broke Joliat's spirits and, of course, spelled finis for the great Morenz.

Writing about Joliat in his book, *Hockey's Hall of Fame,* author Tim Moriarty noted that Morenz's death had a debilitating effect on Joliat's career. "The fierce spark in Joliat seemed to die, too," wrote Moriarty. "Age and injuries were catching up to the tiny French-Canadian. He was thirty-six and had suffered six shoulder separations, three broken ribs, five nose fractures, plus an assortment of routine injuries."

Joliat played two more seasons, scoring 17 goals and 6, respectively, before retiring after the 1937–38 season. "He was," noted Moriarty, "one of hockey's greatest left wingers."

Aurel Joliat was born August 29, 1901, in Ottawa and, like Hall of Famers King Clancy and Frank Boucher, learned to play the game on the frozen Rideau Canal. Joliat and Boucher were the same age and enjoyed the *joie de vivre* of kids hockey in the crisp outdoors.

Joliat and Boucher grew up together on the rinks and fields of Ottawa but took different routes to the NHL. A superb football player, Aurel went west to play professionally in Regina, Saskatchewan. He suffered a broken ankle but stayed in Saskatchewan. When his injury mended he signed on as a left wing with the Saskatoon Sheiks hockey club.

Frank Boucher's brother, Billy, also a chum of Joliat's, watched Joliat mature with the Sheiks and urged Canadiens' owner Leo Dandurand to obtain Aurel for Les Canadiens. Dandurand obliged by unloading his aging ace Newsy Lalonde for the young left wing.

Aurel weighed 140 pounds, at his heaviest, but his size never bothered him. It apparently motivated him to compensate with a vast repertoire of stickhandling maneuvers and pirouettes.

Joliat teamed up with Morenz in the 1923–24 season. The pair jelled perfectly right from the start, although Aurel was to prove that season that he could excel with or without Morenz at his side. The Canadiens had gone up against Calgary in the playoffs and Morenz's shoulder was broken after he intercepted an enemy pass and circled his own net to gain momentum.

Joliat was a constant source of annoyance to his larger opponents. Once, after Aurel had thoroughly confounded Toronto's huge Baby Dye with a series of fakes, the distressed Dye skated over to Dandurand and said: "I'm tired of chasing that shadow of yours, that Frenchman, Joliat. Move him to center, Leo, hold a mirror to each side of him, and you'll have the fastest line in hockey." Later, Howie Morenz told a reporter, "If it wasn't for Joliat, you wouldn't be writing about me so much."

Goal-wise, Joliat's best season was 1924–25 when he produced 29 red lights in twenty-four games. Morenz had 27 and Billy Boucher, who now was his teammate, had 18. When the Canadiens finished first in 1927–28 Joliat and Morenz were the talk of the hockey world and were partly responsible for propagating the game in American cities such as New York, Chicago, Detroit and Boston.

The boundless energy that was a hallmark of Joliat's play remained an essential part of his makeup long after he retired, and little Aurel was frequently welcomed at hockey functions both in Canada and the United States.

One of his most memorable appearances took place at the old Madison Square

Garden in New York at ceremonies prior to the final hockey game played there in 1968 before the opening of the new Garden.

The host New York Rangers invited every living member of hockey's Hall of Fame including the boyhood pals, Joliat and Frank Boucher. The well-orchestrated program featured individual introductions of each Hall of Famer whereupon the personality would skate on the ice in his original team jersey.

Maurice Richard, Eddie Shore, Babe Pratt, Bill Cook and Ching Johnson were among the luminaries who were toasted by the crowd as they modestly made their appearance, and sometimes immodestly as in Richard's case.

Tim Moriarty, who reported the game for his newspaper, Long Island *Newsday*, remembered the Joliat appearance. "Aurel stole the show. Wearing the same tiny peaked cap that was his trademark as a player, Joliat skated the entire length of the ice, turned, and then cut several figure-eights on the way back. As the crowd roared its approval, Joliat did a series of pirouettes, bowed and tipped his cap. It was a remarkable performance."

Especially remarkable, considering that Joliat was sixty-seven years old.

Joliat made his home in Ottawa where he held a job as a railway passenger ticket agent and later enjoyed a quiet retirement. He enjoyed life—especially his life on ice—to the hilt and leaves a legacy of spectacular plays and heroism for a little man that may never be matched. "The Little Giant" is a big man in *Hockey's 100*.

38 Sprague Cleghorn (1919–1928)

There are still some octogenarians around who will tell you that hockey *really* was a tougher game forty years ago and when it comes time to citing chapter and verse the name Sprague Cleghorn instantly enters the conversation.

Sprague and his brother, Odie, were maturing professionals at a time when hockey still was a sport played with a backwoods spirit. For them it was not uncommon to wield the stick as a sabre and pity the poor enemy who crossed either of the Cleghorn brothers.

Sadly, it was Sprague's reputation as a hyperaggressive defenseman that beclouded the fact that he was one of the foremost backliners in an era when professional hockey was burgeoning on both sides of the border.

A member of two Stanley Cup-winning teams, Cleghorn was at his best playing for the Ottawa Senators in 1920 and the Montreal Canadiens in 1924.

It is significant that Cleghorn was signed as the centerpiece of what was to be the beginning of a Montreal Canadiens dynasty when Leo Dandurand took over as manager-coach in 1921 and began rebuilding the Habitants.

Dandurand obtained Cleghorn from Hamilton in a three-for-two trade. The Canadiens' boss was aware that Cleghorn had finished up the previous season with Ottawa by drawing four penalties (the last one a match penalty) in the Stanley Cup final at Vancouver.

In many ways it was only fitting that Sprague skate for Les Canadiens. He was a native of Montreal and his brother, Odie, already was a member of the Habs.

When it came to spicy hockey, Sprague Cleghorn never let them down. He joined a team with teammates who would become legends in their time—Georges Vezina, Didre Pitre, Bert Corbeau and Billy Boucher, to name a few.

Almost immediately, Sprague Cleghorn became the Canadiens' leader. When Newsy Lalonde briefly walked out on the team Dandurand appointed Cleghorn as a sort of "ice general." Sprague's idea of generalship was to move up to the front lines and knock the enemy flying. It was an extraordinarily rough brand of hockey which would be immediately condemned today.

Nobody was more vigorous than Cleghorn. A report of a game against Ottawa says it all: "Sprague and Odie Cleghorn made a shambles of the opposition. Three Ottawa stars, Eddie Gerard, Frank Nighbor and Cy Denneny were knocked out of action for the next two games. Referee Lou Marsh publicly classed the Cleghorns 'a disgrace to hockey'."

In a direct appeal to NHL President Frank Calder, the Ottawa team demanded that Sprague Cleghorn be expelled from the league but the request was denied. For the most part hockey officials preferred to give Cleghorn the benefit of the doubt. Bobby Hewitson, who was an NHL referee, sports editor and later curator of the Hockey Hall of Fame, said of Cleghorn: "He was a product of a rough neighborhood where everything you got you had to fight for. And he played hockey the same way. You could be sure that Sprague was well fitted for it."

Sprague Cleghorn was born in Montreal in 1890, and after achieving success on his hometown rinks he was invited—along with several other Montreal skaters including his brother, Odie, and Cooper Smeaton—to play for the New York Crescents and the New York Wanderers in 1909 and 1910. In addition to playing hockey in New York, the visitors were given jobs. Sprague worked for the telephone company, Odie with a stock brokerage concern and Smeaton with Spalding Sporting Goods Company.

Curiously, the various companies for whom the players worked also paid their hockey salaries. They played in a little rink near Central Park, an old riding academy that had skating facilities on the second floor.

Cleghorn returned to Canada in 1911 playing for the Renfrew Millionaires and then moved to the Montreal Wanderers.

On December 12, 1912, the Wanderers, fortified with Sprague and Odie Cleghorn, played an exhibition game in Toronto against the Montreal Canadiens. Never were the Cleghorn boys more brutal.

Midway in the game Newsy Lalonde of the Canadiens dispatched Odie into the boards with such force that Sprague charged across the rink and smashed Newsy across the forehead with his stick. The blow just barely missed Lalonde's eye and he required twelve stitches to close the gaping wound.

The episode didn't go unnoticed officially and a constable served a summons on Cleghorn. Sprague turned up in a Toronto court and was fined fifty dollars for his efforts, not to mention an additional fifty-dollar fine slapped on him by the National Hockey Association President Emmett Quinn. Cleghorn was also suspended for four weeks but such was the laissez-faire atmosphere of pro hockey at the time that Sprague absented himself from only one game and then promptly returned to the Wanderers' lineup with impunity.

Interestingly, Cleghorn launched his professional hockey career in the United States and finished it in the States. His three last NHL seasons were spent in a Boston Bruins uniform. He retired after the 1927–28 season and went out a winner. The Bruins finished first that year.

His fights notwithstanding, Cleghorn accumulated 154 goals in 296 games, a substantial amount for a defenseman in an era when they concentrated on defense and not scoring. He was a champion, albeit a rough and blemished one. But his scraps should not detract from his overall superiority at his position. Sprague Cleghorn deserved membership in the Hall of Fame and certainly earned his place on *Hockey's 100*.

39 Terry Sawchuk
(1950–1970)

No less an authority than Emile Francis, a professional goaltender for more than twenty years, regards Terry Sawchuk as the greatest goalie of all time.

Were it not for a series of debilitating injuries and some erratic behavior rooted in personal problems, Sawchuk could be regarded as number one. But he lacked Glenn Hall's extraordinary durability, strength and even temper. At times Sawchuk was his own worst enemy in a career marked by extreme peaks and valleys.

His glory days—and the ones which helped mold his image of immortality— were spent with the dynastic Detroit Red Wings of the early 1950s. He was named rookie of the year in 1951 and won the Vezina Trophy in 1952, 1953 and 1955. As a Toronto Maple Leaf he shared the Vezina honors with Johnny Bower and fully earned his half of the prize.

Creator of the crouch style of netminding, Sawchuk was named to the First All-Star Team in 1951, 1952 and 1953 and was a Second Team choice in 1954, 1955, 1959 and 1963. He played for four Stanley Cup winners and four first-place teams.

In Detroit, Sawchuk was fronted by an exceptionally gifted crew including Gordie Howe, Ted Lindsay, Red Kelly, Marcel Pronovost and Alex Delvecchio but he was as responsible as any for the club's success. He was an innovator and his ability to cope with screened shots by use of the crouch was considered a great advance in goaltending technique in its day.

Sawchuk was the product of the Red Wings' farm system, which developed a remarkable string of Hall of Famers, starting with Harry Lumley and also including Glenn Hall. Lumley had starred on the Detroit 1950 Stanley Cup winner while Sawchuk was in the wings, playing superbly on the Indianapolis farm team.

In a terrific gamble, Red Wings manager Jack Adams dealt Lumley to Chicago and elected Sawchuk as his number one netminder. The results were obvious from the start. Lumley was quickly forgotten and by springtime Sawchuk was the talk of the ice world. The Red Wings annexed the Stanley Cup in eight games during which Terry allowed but five goals for a 0.62 goals against average.

Nothing speaks more eloquently about Sawchuk's first five NHL seasons than his goals against average which never rose higher than 1.98. Yet, despite the triumphs there always was a shadow of gloom surrounding him. His right elbow, which had been dislocated in a childhood football accident, continued to bedevil him and he underwent operations in the summers of 1950 and 1951 for removal of pieces of bone that had chipped off in the elbow.

The operations were unsuccessful and surgery was ordered again in 1952, whereupon the surgeon removed 60 pieces of bone. Sawchuk believed his troubles were over; for the first time in ten years he had almost complete movement in his right arm.

But the cumulative effect of all the hospitalization seemed to have a boomerang effect on Sawchuk psychically, not to mention physically. His weight, which had consistently been around 205 pounds, dropped during the 1952–53 season, to 168. Sawchuk was given exhaustive medical tests.

Less than a month later he was hospitalized for an appendectomy. Even Terry himself found humor in his woes. When a reporter asked him what he did during the off-season, he chortled: "I spend my summers in the hospital."

He wasn't kidding. He returned to the hospital in 1954 after an auto accident resulted in severe chest injuries. Once again he recovered to play more than competently for the Red Wings but now—irony of ironies—Sawchuk's threat was the Detroit farm system. Jack Adams now had another whiz goalie in Indianapolis named Glenn Hall, who could not be kept in the minors.

Once again the Red Wings' boss packaged a major deal involving his goalkeeper, this time sending Sawchuk to the Boston Bruins. What few skeptics there were questioned Terry's ability to play superior goal for a relatively weak team such as the Bruins, but his high standard of performance delighted Boston Garden fans and, for one season at least, the deal looked good.

But his second year in Beantown was a disaster. He was stricken with infectious mononucleosis and spent twelve days in the hospital. When he returned to the ice —perhaps prematurely—he seemed almost skeletal and a shade of the Sawchuk who once had starred for Detroit.

He lost four of his next eight games and the Boston press turned on him. His weight was now 166 pounds and, at age twenty-seven, he felt he had had it. To the astonishment of teammates and foe alike, he announced that he was retiring. "I told them I thought it best to quit since my nerves were really shot."

It was suggested that much more was being concealed than reached print. Sawchuk, some noted, never did take to the Boston scene and yearned for his old digs in Detroit.

Sawchuk's "retirement" lasted until the beginning of the next season when Adams sweet-talked the Bruins into giving him the rights to Sawchuk "because he's too good a goalie to remain out of hockey." That done, Adams dealt Hall to Chicago and Sawchuk played seven more years for the Red Wings, often displaying the pre-illness form.

Following the 1963–64 season, the Red Wings high command figured that Terry was washed-up. Toronto Maple Leafs general manager Punch Imlach, always one to give a veteran a chance, signed Sawchuk and Terry demonstrated that, yes, there was still some good goaltending left in him. The Leafs won the Stanley Cup, defeating Chicago and Montreal, and Sawchuk won six of Toronto's eight victories.

While one might have expected Terry to be a joyful man in Toronto, where he was receiving unanimous raves, the fact remained that he seemed to be an unhappy man. "He reminded you of a prisoner in a wartime concentration camp," said Toronto journalist Jim Hunt.

Nevertheless, the Toronto experience was one that also provided some inner peace and satisfaction, particularly the Cup-winning effort. "I'd like to leave hockey like that," said Sawchuk. "In style."

He didn't, of course. When the NHL expanded from six to twelve teams in 1967, Terry was obtained by the new Los Angeles Kings, played one season on the West coast and then returned to the Red Wings in 1968–69. A year later he was signed by the Rangers, playing for Emile Francis, the man who had admired him so much.

It was clear that Sawchuk no longer considered the game anything more than a way of making a dollar but, every so often he would betray the beauty part of his game—the one that once moved Jack Adams to drop a superstar just to put Terry on his roster.

Terrance Gordon Sawchuk was born December 28, 1929, in Winnipeg, Manitoba, and, from all indications, was physically unfit to be a goaltender before he reached his teens.

An endless series of physical mishaps did not stop his climb to the top and one can only wonder what Sawchuk's fate might have been had he not reported to the Red Wings' camp one season weighing a roly-poly 229 pounds. Adams was furious and ordered Terry to go on a strict diet.

Week by week, Sawchuk's weight dropped until he had lost forty pounds. But now he couldn't stop the weight loss and management got worried. He was ordered to a doctor. The weight loss finally was stemmed but Terry never was able to put any of it back.

It has been theorized—and correctly so—that the pressure of his gruelling job had also gotten to him. From that point on his emotional graph described a downward turn that bottomed out in Boston. He had left his wife and children back home in Detroit and lived in a rooming house.

And while he did recover, it was always difficult for Terry to enjoy even the most intense moments of glee. One that should have brought him happiness was the Stanley Cup finale in 1967 when he and another veteran, Johnny Bower, guided the Leafs to the championship. While teammates exulted in the dressing room, sipping champagne, the goalies, as Jim Hunt observed, "sat in a corner by themselves, dragging deeply on cigarettes and grappling silently with the frayed nerves and many physical ailments that are an inescapable part of life for aging men."

He played his last professional game on April 9, 1970, against a mighty Boston Bruins team in the Stanley Cup playoffs. The Rangers were beaten 5–3 and soon were eliminated from the Cup round.

Conceivably, Emile Francis might have invited Sawchuk back to the Rangers for the 1970–71 season as a goaltending coach and possible second goaltender. But three weeks after the Rangers were eliminated Sawchuk, who shared a room in suburban Long Island with teammate Ron Stewart, had a row with his pal. The precise details never have been fully pieced together but Sawchuk was taken to the hospital for treatment of intestinal injuries.

At first it seemed just a matter of weeks until he would be released but Terry's condition worsened dramatically and, finally, he was moved to a more sophisticated Manhattan hospital where emergency surgery was performed.

It was all in vain. Sawchuk died of a pulmonary embolism on May 31, 1970. His was one of the most tragic of hockey careers but also one of the most glorious. He was a definitive goaltender—just short of being the greatest.

40 Ted Lindsay (1944–1960) (1964–1965)

Although he was one of the highest paid players of his time, Ted Lindsay often said that he would play the game for nothing. That is a measure of both his love for the game and the seething, combative spirit that he displayed every time he skated out onto the ice.

Lindsay was an intrinsic part of the intimidating Detroit Red Wings' dynasty of the early 1950s. It was Lindsay, Gordie Howe and Sid Abel who made up the famous "Production Line." During his thirteen seasons with the Red Wings, Ted played on eight first-place teams and skated on four Stanley Cup championship winners.

Lindsay's blazing competitive spirit made him one of the toughest and most feared skaters in the NHL. He was one of the best left wingers of his generation, and one of the meanest of all time.

More than that, Lindsay was a courageous rebel. He was one of the first organizers of the Player's Association. For this act, he was duly punished by the Lords of Hockey, and like fellow organizers—Jim Thomson and Doug Harvey—he was traded to a lower team, in Lindsay's case, the hapless Chicago Black Hawks.

To say that he was rowdy and rambunctious would be putting it mildly. Ted accumulated over 760 stitches on his person, all mementos from the various battles he waged on the ice. The stitches earned him the moniker "Scarface." He had many other nicknames that attested to his style of aggressive play—names such as "Terrible Ted" and "Tempestuous Ted."

Ted was a little guy (5'8", 163 pounds), and he resented players who thought they might take advantage of his small stature. He would not be intimidated. "Okay, so I was cocky," he admitted, reflecting back on his career, "I had the idea that I had to beat up everyone in the league, and I'm still not convinced it wasn't a good idea. Probably I'd do it the same way if I did it over again. That's the way I am."

Once during a game between the Red Wings and the Toronto Maple Leafs, Ted battled Gus Mortson all night. The peculiarity of this situation was that Gus had been Ted's friend since boyhood, a teammate of his at St. Michael's College, and also was in partnership with him in a gold mine they owned near Kirkland Lake. "I don't know anybody when a hockey game starts," Ted explained.

In Ted's seventeen-year career, he played in 1,068 games. Lindsay scored 379 goals, added 472 assists for a total of 851 points. He also had spent 1,808 minutes in the penalty box, ranking him fifth on the All-Time Penalty Leaders list.

In 133 playoff games Lindsay scored 47 goals and 49 assists for 96 points and spent 194 minutes in the penalty box.

Lindsay also made the First All-Star Team eight times, first making it during the 1947–48 season, and then from 1949–50 to 1953–54. He again made it during the 1955–56 and 1956–57 seasons. Ted made the Second All-Star Team in 1948–49.

In 1949–50, while playing in sixty-nine games, Ted scored 23 goals and had 55 assists for 78 points. It was this year that he won the Art Ross Trophy, emblematic of the player who leads the league in scoring points at the end of the regular season.

As was typical of his aggressive style of play, while playing for the Black Hawks in 1958–59, Ted led the league in penalties, spending 184 minutes in the penalty box.

Robert Blake Theodore Lindsay was born in Renfrew, Ontario, on July 29, 1925. Ted was the youngest of six brothers, coming from a large family that also included three daughters. His dad Bert was also a fine hockey player, being the star goalie for the Renfrew Millionaires in the early 1900s.

He tried goaltending in an attempt to follow in his dad's footsteps, "But I soon discovered I'd rather shoot than be shot at, so I gave up goaltending," he remarked.

The war had broken out, and in 1940, the five older Lindsay boys joined the armed forces. With no more family practices to participate in, Ted tried out—and made—the Holy Name Juveniles. He played with them four years, during which time they won the Ontario championship.

By the 1943–44 season, Ted was considered an up-and-coming player. He had accepted an invitation to join St. Michael's College. He played well the second half of the season, after a poor start. The St. Mikes were eliminated that year, but while on a trip to Hamilton in the spring of 1944, Carson Cooper, the chief scout for the Detroit Red Wings, spotted him.

The Red Wings' general manager Jack Adams signed him at once. Lindsay was drafted as a wartime replacement by the Oshawa Generals to help them win the Memorial Cup. With Ted scoring several goals, Oshawa did win the Cup.

It was in the fall of 1944–45 that Ted was invited to Detroit's training camp. Lindsay was only nineteen years old. Sixty-three rookies tried out—only two of them made the club. Ted was one of them.

Lindsay appeared in forty-five games for the Red Wings and had 17 goals and 6 assists. The next season was disappointing—only 7 goals and 10 assists.

In 1946 Jack Adams decided to take a risk with the young man from Renfrew. With only one year of junior hockey behind Ted, Adams placed him on the line with a farm boy from Saskatchewan—Gordie Howe, and the veteran center Sid Abel. That was the start of Detroit's immortal "Production Line," which became one of the greatest lines in hockey history.

To illustrate how powerful a team they were, Detroit won the Prince of Wales Trophy from 1948–49 to 1954–55, and again in 1956–57. At that time the trophy was presented each year to the team finishing with the most points (the league championship) at the end of the regular season.

That superior Detroit Red Wing team is also in the record books for having the longest winning record, including playoff games. They won fifteen straight games from February 27, 1955, to April 5, 1955, which included nine regular season games and six playoff games.

In 1948–49 the Red Wings finished in first place for the first of seven straight years on top (spanning from 1948–49 to 1954–55). During this incredible dynasty, they won the Stanley Cup four times, in 1949–50, 1951–52, 1953–54 and 1954–55.

The Red Wings again finished first in 1956–57. Ted had produced his greatest season—85 points on 30 goals and 55 assists—but it was also the season that Adams decided to break up the Red Wings' famous line. He traded Ted, along with goaltender Glenn Hall, to the Chicago Black Hawks for four players and cash.

Lindsay was now reunited with Tommy Ivan, who had coached him ten out of his thirteen seasons with the Red Wings. But the Black Hawks were a pathetic team; they had finished last in each of the previous four years.

Ted scored 15 goals in his first season with the Black Hawks. He scored 22 goals the next season, and in his third season with Chicago, only 7. Then he retired at the age of thirty-four in 1960. "I guess my heart wasn't in it at Chicago," Ted revealed. "They treated me well, but my home and business was in Detroit. I'm a Detroit guy."

For the next four years, Lindsay spent most of his time tending to his automotive plastics firm in Detroit. He would occasionally engage in workouts with the Red Wings.

In 1964 Ted applied for the job as color commentator for the Detroit Red Wings. Sid Abel, then the Wings' general manager, asked Ted if he would like to join Detroit again. After careful thought, Ted decided to report to training camp to give it a shot. He made the team, and when the Red Wings opened their 1964–65 season (ironically against Ted's most hated adversary, Toronto), Ted was playing left wing. The Olympia fans gave him a standing ovation. It marked his 1000th NHL game.

Reunited with Howe, the Wings finished in first place (after finishing fourth the previous year). Ted scored 14 goals, had 14 assists and, proving that nothing had changed since he left hockey, Ted spent 173 minutes in the penalty box. Even his long-time foe, Clarence Campbell, had to admit that the comeback after four years away from the game was ". . . one of the most amazing feats in professional sport."

Ted retired after that one season to the broadcast booth. When asked why he chose to play one final season, he answered, "I thought it would be nice to finish my career as a Red Wing."

In 1966, in honor of his illustrious career, Ted Lindsay was elected to hockey's Hall of Fame.

Ted was named general manager of the ailing Detroit Red Wings in 1977, and had a controversial reign until he was fired.

Today, Ted and his wife own and operate a 240-acre farm in Metamota, Michigan, where they raise horses. They also are involved with an energy conservation company. Ted, a physical fitness nutrition buff, also has a vitamin business.

His aggressive style has not eroded with time. Just as recently as the 1981 old-timers game in which he participated, he was so aggressive that some players urged that he not be invited back again.

"Old Scarface" had as many detractors as boosters. Some intimates swear by him, and others cursed him to the core. But there was no disputing his essential talent and the contributions he made to the superior Red Wings club. Like him or not, you can't keep Ted Lindsay off of *Hockey's 100*.

41 Phil Esposito
(1963–1981)

Who was the highest paid garbage collector in the United States? Well, you wouldn't have him working for any sanitation department, but during the last two decades he did his fair share of cleaning up—in the National Hockey League, that is. Phil Esposito, one of the finest scorers ever to lace up a pair of skates, was not particularly artistic. But when you shovel in 700 NHL goals, you don't have to be.

With his Northland magic wand in hand, Esposito kindled more goal lamps than all but one of his competitors—that being the incomparable Gordie Howe. Espo swept 717 pucks behind the men in the cages during his eighteen-and-a-half-year career. He turned goaltender's garbage into his G-O-A-L-S, and the Midas touch of his quick wrists has earned him one MVP award, four scoring titles, two Stanley Cup championships and a sea of ink in the NHL record books.

Throughout his career, Esposito was overshadowed by his teammates—the Golden namesakes of ice hockey: in Chicago it was the Golden Jet, Bobby Hull, and in Boston, the Golden Boy, Bobby Orr. As a result, people were skeptical about Espo's true ability. He was accused of being a selfish glory seeker who scored goals by hanging out in front of the net and depositing rebounds. But Esposito counters his critics saying, "Then why don't others do the same?"

Phil admits that he would have loved to score classic goals with the finesse of Orr or the power of Hull, "But I didn't have that hard of a shot," he said. "I could shoot from sixty feet out all season and not get a goal. A player must do what he does best." Thus, Phil did it his way.

What way was that? Chip Magnus, a reporter for the Chicago *Sun-Times* captured it best when he wrote, "We see Phil move into the slot, waiting, just off the right corner of the net. Keith Magnuson belts him back into the net post and Phil recovers. Jerry Korab traps Esposito's stick with his own, digs with an elbow, spins Phil around.

"Stan Mikita moves in and rocks Phil with a hip check as he swings past. Magnuson returns, sending a shoulder into Esposito's spine . . . Phil is once more bounced by Magnuson, but he regains his balance, gets the puck and scores."

Esposito began his NHL career in 1963 with the Chicago Black Hawks. Following a quiet rookie season, he returned to the Hawks as the center for Chico Maki and Bobby Hull. He averaged 23 goals per season over the next three years, but more importantly, Espo helped Bobby Hull lead the league in goals scored over this duration.

Esposito, however, was not to remain a permanent fixture in Chicago. Coach Billy Reay and Manager Tommy Ivan were disenchanted with Espo's playoff performance and decided to trade him. In May 1967, the Black Hawks and Bruins concluded a six-player deal. Esposito, center Fred Stanfield and winger Ken Hodge were sent to Beantown in return for defenseman Gille Marotte, crafty center Pit Martin and goalie Jack Norris. Hockey columnists regarded this deal as the "most one-sided trade in modern hockey history." Time would prove them prophetic.

The trade didn't surprise Esposito but the thought of joining a team full of guys that he'd grown to hate bothered him. Espo said, "to me, guys like Ted Green and Bobby Orr have been the villains. I don't know how I'll adjust to playing alongside of them." But the Bruins were understanding. They gave Espo the confidence he needed by immediately naming him the team's alternate captain.

Phil led the NHL with 43 assists in his first season with Boston and, by adding 35 goals to his totals, emerged as a substantial offensive threat.

Bobby Hull commented on the progress of his former linemate by saying, "The difference is that when Phil was with the Black Hawks he had to give me the puck all the time. Now, he can keep it for himself. He's gone from being the little toad in the big pond, to being the big toad in the little pond that turned out to be the big pond. Boston thought that Bobby Orr would lead them out of the wilderness. But Bobby couldn't do it alone. Orr and Esposito; they complemented each other."

The following season Coach Harry Sinden placed Espo and Ken Hodge on the same line and finished off the trio by adding Ron Murphy. The threesome decimated opposing defenses and established a line-scoring record of 263 points. Phil was TNT offensively, feeding his teammates for an NHL record 77 assists and 126 points, also a record. Never before had a player topped the 100-point plateau; Espo accomplished it with plenty of points to spare.

Judging by Esposito's accomplishments a case could be made for him as one of the finest centers of all time. He was a First Team All-Star in 1969, 1970, 1971, 1972, 1973, 1974 and 1975. Both in 1969 annd 1974 he was voted the Hart Trophy as the NHL's most valuable player. He led the league in scoring in 1969, 1971, 1972, 1973 and 1974. He wears a pair of Bruins' Stanley Cup rings—from 1970 and 1972. In addition, Esposito was considered the pivotal factor for Team Canada in its four-games-to three (one tie) victory over the Soviet National Team in September 1972.

Yet, there were those who found a flaw in Esposito's armament. His critics charged that he was a selfish hockey player, who lacked the ability to combine defensive aspects with his offensive game. Despite his many accomplishments, Esposito was traded—along with Carol Vadnais—from the Bruins to the New York Rangers on November 7, 1975, for Brad Park, Jean Ratelle and Joe Zanussi.

The adjustment was extremely difficult for Phil, who at first complained about conditions in Manhattan. But he gradually came around and, although he never regained his Stanley Cup form of the early 1970s, he won the hearts of New York fans.

In the midst of the 1980–81 season Phil startled the hockey world by announcing his retirement—then and there—and moving behind the bench as an assistant coach.

Philip Anthony Esposito was born February 20, 1942, in Sault Ste. Marie, Ontario. He was not very highly regarded as a youthful skater but the Chicago Black Hawks thought enough of him to place him with their St. Louis farm team in the early 1960s. It was there that he learned to employ his size and quick shot to advantage.

The season following his retirement Esposito was named "color" commentator for the New York Rangers. He soon organized the Phil Esposito Foundation, which became a force in the hockey world assisting retired players in career planning and other aspects of their post-hockey lives. The point was underlined in 1984 when Esposito was named to the Hockey Hall of Fame.

42 Doug Bentley (1939–1954)

When Doug Bentley arrived at the Chicago Black Hawks' training camp in the fall of 1939 coach Paul Thompson introduced him to club president Bill Tobin. Tobin courteously shook hands with the recruit and wished him luck. Later Tobin said to Thompson: "Is *he* one of our new prospects?"

Thompson nodded, while the players skated at the Hibbing, Minnesota, base.

Tobin shook his head, "I didn't know things were *that* tough," he sighed. "What did you say his name was?"

"Doug Bentley," Thompson replied.

"Doug Bentley, eh?" Tobin mused. "He's the first walking ghost I've ever seen."

Tobin returned to Chicago and a few days later Thompson contacted his boss. "He's not a walking ghost," said Thompson, "he's a skating ghost. The kid's terrific!"

Bentley was signed to a major league contract that included a minor league clause. It was a clause that in fifteen years neither the Black Hawks nor the New York Rangers had an occasion to utilize. Doug Bentley, for all his apparent fragility, was a big-leaguer through and through.

He led the National Hockey League in scoring once and was a First Team All-Star left wing twice and once a Second Team All-Star. More than that Bentley was the essential fibre of the Black Hawks through both good and bad years, although his younger brother, Max, reaped more of the headlines.

Doug had already established himself as a Black Hawk when he was summoned to Tobin's office and given a bonus. "Gee, Mr. Tobin," said Doug, "that's wonderful and I really appreciate it. But if you think I'm good, you should see my brother, Max. He's twice as good."

Unaware that there was still another Bentley with a surplus of hockey gifts, Tobin looked quizzically at Doug. "Is that so?" said the Black Hawks boss. "Well, in that case, maybe we'd better grab him, too."

Max Bentley became a Black Hawks regular a year after Doug. Max was the more sensational of the two and tended to obscure his older brother but those who knew the nuances of the game realized that Doug, in his own unobtrusive way, was a splendid stickhandler in his own right and, of course, proved it in years to come.

Playing alongside Max, Doug was able to engineer the give-and-take plays that the brothers learned on the outdoor rinks of their native Saskatchewan. They took Chicago by storm and seemed an inseparable team until Max was to join the Canadian army during World War II. This would be a particularly severe test for Doug since there were some who believed that he couldn't play capably without Max at center. But Doug was better than ever. With 38 goals and 39 assists for 77 points in fifty games he finished runner-up to scoring leader Herbie Cain of the Boston Bruins during the 1943–44 season. In the playoffs he was no less superb with 8 goals and 4 assists in nine playoff games.

When Max returned to the Black Hawks for the 1945–46 campaign he was aligned again with Doug on left wing and another smallish but speedy player on the right side, Bill Mosienko. Rarely have three skaters better complemented each other than the Bentleys and Mosienko. The trio was appropriately christened "The Pony Line" and added a dimension of vitality to attack that rarely has been seen in the National Hockey League.

Sadly, however, there was little else on the Chicago roster beyond the Bentleys and Mosienko. Because the Black Hawks were so shockingly bereft of depth, the enemy was able to zero in on The Pony Line and often battered them without retaliation.

Despite the endless assaults, the Bentleys and Mosienko scored plentifully, but one line simply could not carry a club that was woefully deficient on defense, in goal and on its second and third lines. The Black Hawks missed the playoffs in 1947 and were struggling again during the early part of the 1947–48 season when Bill Tobin decided that the only move—drastic as it was—had to be a trade and his most tradeable commodity was Max Bentley.

Curiously, when Tobin broached the subject of a *possible* deal involving Max, Doug, crushed as he was, suggested that it might be better for all concerned. "It might be the best thing for the two of us," said Doug.

Max was traded to the Maple Leafs and played brilliantly for one of the strongest sextets the league has known. Doug was not as fortunate. Despite Doug's game efforts along with those of Mosienko, the Chicago club remained essentially inept and Doug was never to skate for another playoff team.

Douglas Wagner Bentley was born September 3, 1916, in Delisle, Saskatchewan. Before reaching the NHL, he played on a team with four other Bentley brothers in Drumheller, Alberta. There were thirteen Bentley kids in all and their dad, Bill, had bought them all skates. They would skate on a backyard rink that Bill Bentley flooded behind the family farm.

The deal that sent Max to the Maple Leafs broke Bill Bentley's heart and both brothers wondered if they would ever skate together on the same team. It seemed unlikely, especially after Doug retired in 1952. But a miracle of sorts happened during the 1953–54 season when New York Rangers manager Frank Boucher persuaded the brothers to come out of retirement and skate for the Broadway Blueshirts. Boucher made his pitch to them during the summer of 1953.

The Bentleys were a sensation at their reunion. Before a crowd of more than 13,000 at Madison Square Garden, they teamed with Edgar Laprade to defeat the Boston Bruins and thrust the Rangers right into the playoff race. They continued to play well together down the homestretch but the Rangers, like Black Hawks teams of the past, were simply too weak and faltered at the end, missing the playoffs by a scant margin.

That season marked finis for both Bentleys in the NHL, although they continued to play organized hockey. Doug went back to coaching Saskatoon the next year and Max joined him in 1954. Incredibly, Doug made a brief comeback in 1962 with the Los Angeles Blades of the Western Hockey League and then retired for good. He returned to his native Saskatchewan and died on November 24, 1972. He had been elected to the Hockey Hall of Fame in 1964.

43 Frank Frederickson (1926–1931)

Frank Frederickson's glorious hockey career nearly ended in the Mediterranean Sea.

Frederickson was being transferred from Egypt to Italy during World War I when the transport on which he was a passenger was hit by a German torpedo. Frederickson, who was a member of the Royal Flying Corps (later the Royal Air Force), searched for an empty lifeboat but found none.

"Suddenly, I realized that I had left my violin in my bunk," Frederickson remembered. "My violin was very important to me. So, I ran back, got hold of it and gave it to one of the captains of another lifeboat and told him to take good care of it."

Before the ship went down Frederickson found a space on another lifeboat and, ultimately, was carried to safety. In time he returned to Canada and resumed his hockey career.

Frank captained the Winnipeg Falcons' team that won the Gold Medal in the 1920 Winter Olympics at Antwerp and later enjoyed a short but illustrious career as a professional.

He was a stylish center who scored 41 goals in thirty games for Victoria during the 1922–23 season and helped that club win the Stanley Cup two years later. There have been better centers, to be sure, but not many with Frederickson's grace both on and off the ice.

Frank Frederickson was born in Winnipeg, Manitoba, in 1895. His parents came from Iceland and spoke only Icelandic in the house. Frank couldn't speak a word of English until he was six years old. Yet, when I interviewed him in 1968 his English was perfect.

At the time of Frederickson's youth, the Icelanders in Winnipeg were treated as a second-class minority group and Frank found himself the target of insults when he would return home from school. During our interview, he recalled how he was able to find a safety valve in sports.

"My best outlet was hockey. I got my first pair of skates when I was five and had a great time learning to play. School came easy for me. After finishing grade eight I decided I ought to earn a living and got a job as an office boy in a law firm. This turned out to be an excellent move since the firms all sponsored hockey teams then so naturally we had one too. It was a seven-man team because in those days a rover was the seventh player, in addition to three forwards, two defensemen, and a goalkeeper.

"I played well and captured the attention of two of our attorneys. They took a great deal of personal interest in me, not just as a hockey player, and urged me to go back to school. So in 1914 I enrolled at the University of Manitoba, took liberal arts courses, and a year later was named captain of the hockey team."

Not long after the outbreak of World War I Frank enlisted in the 223rd Scandinavian Battalion but when he got to England he switched to the Royal Flying Corps and remained an airman—miraculously surviving several close calls—until the end of the conflict.

Once, during an interview in his Vancouver living room, he told me this tale:

"It took a year from the time the war ended before I could get back to Winnipeg. When I returned in 1919, a bunch of us led by Mike Goodman, the speed-skating champion of North America, and Slim Halter, a great big, gangling six-footer who was a beautiful stickhandler, organized the Falcon hockey team and applied for admission to the senior league.

"The leaders of that league wouldn't let us in because they claimed we weren't good enough to compete with teams like the Monarchs and Winnipegs. So we did the next best thing and organized our own league composed of such teams as Selkirk that had 'Bullet' Joe Simpson as captain. We later found out the reason we couldn't get in the senior league was because the players there were from well-to-do families and wanted no part of us. But they couldn't quite get away from us that easily. We finished in first place, then played the winners of the big league in a two-game series. In a terrific upset, we beat them in two games straight, 14–2. We then defeated Lake-of-the-Woods, Head-of-the-Lakes, and Fort William, and went on to Toronto where we won the Allan Cup for the senior championship of Canada, beating the famed University of Toronto.

"That was quite a triumph because it qualified us to represent Canada in the 1920 Winter Olympics at Antwerp, Belgium—the first time ice hockey was ever included on the Olympics program.

"Winning the Olympic championship was quite a feather in our cap and gave us all a lot of publicity. I had the world at my feet but instead of returning immediately to Canada I was asked by the Icelandic government to go there to do some experimental flying. As it turned out, I became the first pilot of Icelandic extraction to fly in Iceland.

"I flew from May to September and had to give it up at that time because they couldn't get petrol supplies. Then I went to England to try and get some of the English concerns interested in flying to Iceland but I failed in that and returned to Canada, making a stop in Toronto.

"When I got there, Mayor Church entertained me and asked, 'Now that you're back, Frank, what do you want to do?' I told him I wanted to join the Canadian air force but didn't think I could get in because there were many senior officers ahead of me. Church was a wonderful guy and a very influential man; when I got home to Winnipeg there was a telegram advising me to report to camp for duty. So, in 1920 I joined the Canadian air force.

"For all intents and purposes it appeared that my career was set for years to come. Life is funny though and out of the blue I received a letter from Lester Patrick, the Old Silver Fox of hockey, who was in Victoria, British Columbia, where he had a team in the old Pacific Coast League. It was top-notch hockey and Lester offered me what was a substantial contract in those days—$2,500 for twenty-four games. I call it substantial because the rest of the boys were playing for $800 and $900. I couldn't resist the offer and so found myself right back in the middle of hockey again."

Although Frederickson did not play in the NHL as long as other members of the Hockey Hall of Fame he was an eminent center in the years he played for Detroit, Boston and Pittsburgh.

Following the conclusion of his playing career he coached and managed Pittsburgh in 1930–31 and later returned to his home in Vancouver.

"I learned one important thing from hockey," said Frank, "and that is from cooperation and joint effort you can do an awful lot more than when you're just by yourself."

Frank remained a vigorous citizen even in retirement and followed the modern game of hockey with great interest. He died on May 28, 1979, a splendid human being and a worthy member of *Hockey's 100*.

44 Bill Durnan
(1943–1950)

During the latter part of the World War II years, and through 1947, you could not find a hockey expert who believed there was a better goaltender playing than Bill Durnan.

Canadian sportswriter Vincent Lunny expressed the prevailing sentiment in 1948, when he wrote the following appraisal: "It would be superfluous to say that Bill Durnan is the greatest netminder of the last twenty years and probably the greatest of all time. We'll accept that as an established fact."

What prevents Durnan from attaining a higher listing in *Hockey's 100* is his relatively brief big-league career. He came up the hard way, and was discovered late. Durnan played for the superb Canadiens during the 1940s with Rocket Richard. He joined the Canadiens in 1943 and, stricken with a nervous ailment, tearfully retired in the spring of 1950, although he had again won the Vezina Trophy. But during his seven seasons with the Canadiens, he set new standards for goalkeeping excellence.

Guarding the Montreal net, Bill won the Vezina Trophy in 1944, 1945, 1946, 1947, 1949 and 1950. He was named to the First Team All-Star those same seasons.

During his tenure in Montreal, the Canadiens finished first four times and twice won the Stanley Cup, in the years 1943–44 and 1945–46.

The ability that made Durnan unique among goaltenders was the fact that he was ambidextrous. It was Steve Faulkner, who coached him at Westmoreland United, who taught Bill that trick, which helped him become the best goaltender in the league. Faulkner showed Bill how to use his hands instead of relying solely on his stick and pads to block shots. Bill's switch was so deceptively quick that it fooled the opposing forwards.

Durnan became known as hockey's greatest "holler guy." With his deep voice booming, he advised, urged, and roared whenever the play was torrid around the Canadien end of the rink.

Big Bill (6'2", 200 pounds) had big hands, and lightning reflexes. Few players scored hat tricks against Durnan. His keen analytical mind simply soaked up hockey intelligence, although he made no conscious effort to study the styles of opposing forwards.

Durnan was one of the most popular Canadiens among his teammates, as is evidenced by the fact that his forwards were often willing to sacrifice their opportunities to score to help him. His teammates often thought of him and his bids for records when they might not have given another goaltender a thought. If they were leading by three or four goals late in the third period, one of the players would often say to Coach Dick Irvin: "We've got enough goals to win now, Skipper. Is it all right if we just backcheck and help Bill with his shutout?"

Bill was also a great team player. Irvin gave him the responsibility very few goaltenders ever had, by naming him captain of the Montreal Canadiens.

Durnan broke into the NHL in 1943, and despite his short career, he established many records. He won the Vezina Trophy in 1944, becoming the first rookie ever to win it. In the process, he also became the first player to win it four consecutive years, spanning 1944–47.

Turk Broda of the Toronto Maple Leafs won it the following season in 1948, but Durnan again won it the next two seasons before his sudden retirement.

In 1944–45, the Montreal Canadiens placed five players on the First Team All-Stars. It was the first time that had ever happened. The team consisted of Emile Bouchard on defense; Elmer Lach, center; Maurice Richard, right wing; Toe Blake, left wing; and Bill Durnan as goaltender. Dick Irvin was named coach.

It was during the 1948–49 season that Bill set the NHL modern record for the longest shutout sequence by holding his opponents scoreless for 309 minutes and 21 seconds with four consecutive shutouts. That was the longest shutout sequence in eighteen years.

Durnan had 10 shutouts in the 1948–49 season in sixty games, and it was in 1949 that he was the runner-up to Sid Abel (Detroit Red Wings) in the voting for the Hart Trophy, awarded to the most valuable player in the league.

During his entire career, which spanned 383 regular season games, he registered 34 shutouts and had a 2.35 goals-against average. In forty-five playoff games he shut out the opposition in two games and his goals-against average was 2.20.

William Durnan was born opposite a city dump in Toronto on January 22, 1915, the younger of two brothers. Bill was nine when he tried out for a hockey team of the Westmoreland United Church. The boys were grouped according to weight. Bill was a big kid, and it was felt he was too heavy to compete with the fellows on the forward line, so he was moved into the nets. Westmoreland won five city championships in the six years that Durnan played in the nets for them.

In 1930–31, Bill joined the North Toronto Juniors, a farm club for the Junior Marlboros, which was a farm team for the Maple Leafs. Red Burnett, a hockey writer for the Toronto *Daily Star* recommended Bill to the coach of the Sudbury Ontario Junior team. They invited him to play on their team the following year.

Durnan was considered a hot prospect while he was playing in Sudbury, as he helped them win the Memorial Cup in 1931. The Leafs were impressed, and signed an agreement with him. He was only twenty years old.

Before the start of the 1932 season, Bill and a friend were wrestling on Wasaga Beach and Bill twisted a knee. This sidelined him for a season, and it was then the Leafs dropped him as a prospect. It was at this point that Bill vowed he'd play pro hockey.

His pride was really hurt by Toronto's treatment of him. "I was disillusioned and figured if that was the kind of treatment I was to get, then hell, I didn't want any part of it."

During the 1934–35 season Bill ended up playing in the T and Y Mercantile League in Toronto.

In 1936 Bill took a job as a millwright in a gold mining mill in Kirkland Lake in northern Ontario. Between shifts, he played with the Kirkland Lake Blue Devils. For four seasons Bill played for the Blue Devils. In 1940 the Blue Devils won the Allan Cup, emblematic of the Senior championship of Canada, with Bill as their goaltender.

After the success of the 1940 season, Bill moved to Montreal to tend goal for the Montreal Royals, the top amateur club in the Quebec Senior League, a Canadien farm operation. At this point he had no plans of becoming a professional hockey player, as he was still smarting from the snub he received from Toronto.

Bill was a man of few illusions, and he would have been satisfied if he spent the rest of his career with the Royals. He was earning a comfortable living with his part-time job in the accounting department of the Canadian Car and Foundry. However, his boss was Len Peto, who was also a director of the Montreal Canadiens.

Peto pressured him into turning professional. Durnan said no, the incident with Toronto still burned in his mind. He did not want to play pro hockey. Peto insisted. Bill asked for the then huge sum of $4200. Surprisingly enough to Bill, the Canadien management agreed.

Bill tried out for the Canadiens in the autumn of 1943. He was scheduled to be the goaltender in a preseason exhibition game. The average rookie would have been ecstatic to receive an opportunity such as this. However, Durnan was not your average rookie. He was twenty-nine years old, and it didn't matter to him whether or not he played pro hockey.

His Montreal team was in the provincial softball finals and Bill was their star pitcher. He turned down the net assignment, unconcerned that it might endanger his NHL career. At his own expense, Bill instead went back to Montreal and pitched his team to the Quebec championship.

Coach Irvin persuaded Durnan that his place was in goal. In 1943, his first season with the Flying Frenchmen, remembering the advice of Faulkner, he used his hands in his goaltending and seldom let a rebound escape. He emerged as the premier goaltender that year and won the Vezina Trophy. In the process he helped his team beat the Chicago Black Hawks in four straight games to win the Stanley Cup.

However, Bill had trouble with the fans in Montreal. The Canadiens were in a slump in 1947 and the Forum crowd began chanting: "We want Bibeault!" (Paul Bibeault, the Canadiens' goaltender before Durnan.) "They booed me and made me feel six inches high," he said. All this despite the fact that he had won the Vezina Trophy.

Hockey started to get rough for him toward the end of the 1940s. Durnan had broken his hand earlier, and even though it had mended, his entire arm would ache whenever he caught the puck. He was going to be thirty-five years old in an era where the goalie played the entire season without an alternate, and with no mask for protection.

The 1949–50 season was the turning point for Bill Durnan. It was the beginning of the end for him. There was little fun left for him in the game. A lot of his friends were leaving—or had already gone. The old camaraderie was missing.

In January of 1950 he told Dick Irvin he would be retiring at the end of the season. He felt that his reflexes were slow. Although he had won the Vezina Trophy five times, and heard countless writers proclaim him the best goaltender ever, the most he had ever made in a season was $10,500. He wasn't educated and he had two girls to raise. He began to worry.

The end came quickly. In March 1950, the Canadiens would be playing the Rangers in the first round of the playoffs. Montreal had finished second, and the Rangers had finished fourth. Naturally the Canadiens were favored. Quickly the Rangers won three games in a row from the Canadiens.

The nerves and pressures began building up. It was then he decided to retire.

Before the fourth game, Irvin asked him to go in and tell the players it was Bill's decision to quit, not Irvin's. In a poignant scene in the dressing room, a tearful Bill

Durnan handed young Gerry McNeil his stick. McNeil, the successor, took the stick from the master, crying also. It was a very emotional scene.

The Canadiens with Gerry McNeil in goal went out and won the fourth game. The Rangers won the fifth game and took the series. "A lot of people thought it was a nervous breakdown," Bill said, "but it wasn't. To this day, people won't believe me. What the hell, I'm quitting and this is as good a time as any. If the kid goes in and wins, well great, it's a terrific start for him."

Durnan ended his professional career in the middle of the 1950 playoffs, a victim of frayed nerves. Although he played but seven seasons, his outstanding play was remembered and rewarded, as he was inducted into the Hockey Hall of Fame in 1964.

On October 31, 1972, in Toronto at the age of fifty-seven, Bill Durnan died in North York General Hospital. He had been in ill health for some time, having been afflicted with arthritis for years. He left his wife, a son and two daughters.

Durnan could pass for the greatest goaltender of all time had he endured the test of time and played more seasons. Although he played only seven seasons he raised the art of goaltending to new heights and in doing so, he more than earned his berth in *Hockey's 100*.

45 Brad Park
(1968–   )

There has been only one missing link in Brad Park's glorious hockey necklace—a Stanley Cup ring.

The consummate contemporary defenseman, Park was the master of the hip check as well as an exceptionally accurate shooter who could develop an attack and then retreat in time to intercept an enemy counterthrust.

His game was embellished by a fluid skating style that often underplayed his speed, as well as a storehouse of power that proved deceptive because of his relatively modest size.

It was Park's misfortune never to have skated for a genuine powerhouse. He was the ice general and captain of a modestly successful New York Rangers team in the late 1960s and early 1970s but never tasted the Stanley Cup champagne. After his trade to the Boston Bruins, he played for a team already describing a descent but one which remained competitive because of Park's combative play.

Because he played in the shadow of some of the all-time great backliners, Park may not have received the media attention he merited but the experts took due note of his excellence. Brad was voted to the First All-Star Team in 1970, 1972, 1974, 1976 and 1978. He made the Second Team in 1971 and 1973.

More than anything, Park was a refreshing player to watch and, in some ways, a throwback to an earlier, more robust era of defense play.

"One of the glorious aspects of sports," said author Roger Kahn, "is having your spirits renewed by Brad Park."

Park's own spirits occasionally have been deflated by Bobby Orr's presence in the same league. A defenseman like Park, Orr was regarded by many as the most-holy-blessed-be-he in hockey since the inventor of the puck. Playing second-fiddle to a superstar like Orr can't be the easiest thing in the world, but Park made the adjustment.

"If I have to be number two," Brad once said, "I might as well be number two to a super player like Orr."

Park has been super, or close to it, ever since he became a Ranger in 1968–69. An instant regular, he learned the ropes, took punches in the chops and scored goals almost immediately. His career almost came to an end with similar suddenness.

The Rangers were playing the Red Wings, and dangerous Gordie Howe was still playing for the Detroit sextet. Park was guarding Howe, notorious for his great strength, durability and viciousness. "Watch Howe!" Brad was warned. "He likes to club you with his elbows."

Park remained vigilant and when Howe confronted him, the young Ranger body-checked the veteran cleanly, depositing him on the ice. But then Brad became less vigilant and a few minutes later Howe's stick flashed, cracking into Park's Adam's apple.

For an instant it appeared as if the blow might have ended his career. Brad fell,

unable to swallow, gasping for breath. Ranger trainer Frank Paice dashed across the ice and calmed the kid until he was fully revived and able to skate off the ice under his own steam.

As Brad passed Howe, he turned to his assailant and rasped, "You sonofagun. It could have been my eye. From now on, when you're skating around me, you damn well better keep your head up."

The flak was never heavier than in the spring of 1974 when the Rangers met Philadelphia's ferocious Flyers in the semifinal round of the playoffs. Dave Schultz, number one hitter on the Flyers, made a point of zeroing in on Park early in the third game of the Cup round. First, he bodied Brad heavily in the corner and then, as play swung up-ice, Schultz charged into Park a second time, and knocked him down, straddling the semidefenseless Ranger and pouring punches at his face.

The Flyers' theory was simplicity itself—beat up on the best Ranger (Park) and Philadelphia would grind out a series victory. "You can't be hitting a team sixty minutes a game," countered Park. "It's exhausting."

But it was just exhausting for Park, mostly because his Ranger teammates failed to generate as much zest as he did. As a result, the Flyers edged New York, four games to three, and advanced to the Stanley Cup finals.

Because the Rangers failed to win the Stanley Cup during Park's golden years in New York he became the target of the Madison Square Garden boo birds and eventually was part of one of the biggest trades in NHL history. On November 7, 1975, Park, who was then the Rangers' captain, and Jean Ratelle, the club's foremost playmaker, were traded to the Boston Bruins for Phil Esposito and Carol Vadnais.

Park, who had been openly critical of the Bruins while playing in New York, now found himself in the enemy camp. He made the adjustment with ease and, under coach Don Cherry's guidance, seemed to be a better defenseman in Boston than he had ever been with the Rangers.

Douglas Bradford Park was born July 6, 1948, in Toronto, and learned the game on the city rinks. For many years Brad's size was against him, but he was also tough, tough enough to land a spot on the Toronto Junior Marlboros, a club that normally fed gifted stickhandlers to the NHL.

Normally, Park would have been graduated to the Toronto Maple Leafs but the NHL had instituted a seventeen-year-old draft rule which enabled the Rangers to land Park. To say the least, Brad was stunned.

When Brad arrived at the Rangers' training camp in September 1968 he was not even remotely considered for a position on the New York varsity. The Rangers had a well-rounded defense and also had been grooming a tall, well-built prospect named Al Hamilton as the fifth defenseman. But with each scrimmage Park outplayed Hamilton and the Rangers' braintrust was faced with a dilemma. It was "solved" by sending Park to the minors and keeping Hamilton with the big club. But Brad played too well to be kept down and Hamilton couldn't cut it with the Rangers so the call went out to Park and he has never looked back.

In no time at all he was being compared favorably with the inimitable Orr. Some observers claimed that Park was better defensively than Orr.

Injuries severely braked the careers of both Park and Orr but it was the latter who was ultimately forced to retire prematurely while Park, although severely hobbled with knee problems, continued to play but at a more modest pace.

"In some ways," said Don Cherry, "Brad was a better player after all the injuries because he began to pace himself. He wouldn't take as many chances on offense and that meant he was in better position on defense so he was caught out of position much less.''

The pain had so troubled Brad that it was freely predicted that he would retire by 1980, but he kept coming back and when the 1981–82 campaign began he was back on the Bruins' blue line playing as smart a game as he ever had in his life. He remained a Bruin until 1983 when he was signed by the Detroit Red Wings as a free agent. His intelligent and experienced play paced a young Detroit squad to its first playoff berth in five years. Despite his 36 years, Park performed in 80 regular season games, tallying 58 points on five goals and 53 assists. Park was voted winner of the Bill Masterton Trophy for his sportsmanship, perseverance, and dedication to the game in the spring of 1984.

A year later (1982–83) the Bruins added an impressive rookie by the name of Gord Kluzak. Under Park's tutelage, Kluzak ripened into a first-rate player and the Bruins finished with the best regular season record in the league. General Manager Harry Sinden of the Bruins likened Park to some of the foremost defensemen in hockey history. ''He has been a very special player,'' said Sinden. ''He has demonstrated a blend of extraordinary ability with admirable courage.'' The accolades notwithstanding, Park never obtained the positive critical acclaim that he deserved.

Unfortunately for him a number of younger, flashier defensemen such as Denis Potvin of the New York Islanders and Paul Coffey of the Edmonton Oilers were scoring more than Park although not necessarily playing better defense. The high-scoring defensemen got the accolades and Brad, as he had been during the Orr era, was relegated to the shadows.

But the purists remained appreciative of his skills, particularly the ''submarine bodycheck,'' with which he'd thrust his hip into the path of onrushing attackers, catapulting them upside down to the ice. In 1977 and 1978 Park was among the primary reasons the Bruins reached the Stanley Cup finals.

It was a case of close, but no cigar—the story of Park's hockey playing life despite a remarkably efficient career. His teams weren't champions but Brad certainly was and merits forty-fifth place on *Hockey's 100*.

46 Turk Broda (1936–1952)

The Turk was fat and funny. And maybe that is the reason why he often was bypassed when the cream of the goalkeeping fraternity was discussed.

Had he been a tragic figure like Terry Sawchuk, a worrier like Glenn Hall or an eccentric such as Jacques Plante, Broda might receive more serious consideration but the image of Toronto's fabulous fat man always was light and upbeat—except when it came to the big games.

While he is fondly remembered for winning his "Battle of the Bulge" campaign against excess poundage, Broda also is revered by historians for his impeccable ability to excel in the most critical moments.

It, therefore, is not surprising that he twice won the Vezina Trophy for having the best goals-against average, was twice a First Team All-Star, once a Second Team All-Star and played for five Stanley Cup-winning teams.

Broda, along with center Syl Apps, formed the cornerstone of manager Conn Smythe's rebuilding effort when Toronto began their ascent to dizzying heights in the 1940s. Their Cup win in 1942 was the first for Broda. Following service in World War II he returned to help Toronto win an unprecedented three consecutive Cups (1947, 1948, 1949) and still another in 1951.

Turk had the ideal disposition for a goaltender and was a superb team player on a club sprinkled with scintillating characters.

It could be said that Bill Durnan, who starred in goal for Montreal during the same era, was a better textbook goalie than Broda and produced superior averages but Durnan couldn't match the Turk in Stanley Cups nor longevity. Broda became a big-leaguer before Durnan arrived and outlasted him by two seasons.

The records indicate that Broda's best season—statistically speaking—was 1940–41 when he rang up a 2.06 goals-against average. But the vintage Broda appeared during the 1942 playoffs when he starred in the seventh (Cup-winning) game of the finals and in 1947–48 when he powered the Leafs to a first-place finish, won the Vezina and then, surrounded by one of the most formidable teams in history, annexed the Stanley Cup.

Yet, many Torontonians prefer the memory of November 1949 when Smythe demanded that a number of his stars trim their waistlines in a hurry. The antifat edict made headlines throughout North America.

Although Smythe singled out defenseman Garth Boesch and forwards Howie Meeker, Harry Watson, Vic Lynn and Sid Smith for his blasts, the key target of Smythe's ire was his longtime goaltending stalwart, Broda.

Smythe's opening gun in the "Battle of the Bulge" was a demand that his players reduce their weight to specified limits. Broda, who weighed 197 pounds, was ordered to lose 7 pounds. To underline the seriousness of his offensive, Smythe promptly called up reserve goalie Gil Mayer from his Pittsburgh farm team. It was Tuesday and he was giving Turk until Saturday to fulfill the demand. "I'm taking Broda out of the nets," Smythe said, "and he's not going back until he shows some common sense."

Smythe's outburst reverberated across Canada and parts of the United States, and soon "The Battle of the Bulge" became a cause célèbre. Neutral observers regarded Turk's tussle with the scales as a huge joke, win or lose, but to the Toronto boss it was no joke. None of the Leafs were particularly amused, either.

After one day of severe dieting Turk trimmed his weight from 197 to 193, and all of Canada seemed to breathe easier. Smythe had set the final weigh-in for Saturday afternoon, just before the evening match against the New York Rangers at Maple Leaf Gardens. He refused to divulge what specific action he would take against Broda or the other Leafs if they did not pass muster, but he suggested that it would not be lenient. Turk moved forward and gingerly placed his feet on the platform. The numbers finally settled—just under 190 pounds. He had made it! Turk was delighted, and Smythe was doubly enthusiastic because he regarded his goaltender with paternal affection. "There may be better goalies around somewhere," said the manager, "but there's no greater sportsman than the Turkey. If the Rangers score on him tonight, I should walk out and hand him a malted milk, just to show I'm not trying to starve him to death."

That night Maple Leaf Gardens was packed with 13,359 Turk fans, and when Broda skated out for the opening face-off, the Gardens' regimental band swung into "Happy Days Are Here Again" and followed it with a chorus of "She's Too Fat for Me."

Referee George Gravel dropped the puck to start the game, and the Rangers immediately swarmed in on Broda. This time, however, he was the Turk of old. Broda's slimmer teammates couldn't beat goalie Chuck Rayner of the Rangers, however, and the first period ended with the teams tied 0–0. It was the same story in the second period, as each team desperately probed for an opening. The Rangers got their big break late in the middle period when Pentti Lund bisected the Toronto defense and moved within easy scoring distance of Broda. Lund found his opening and fired the puck mightily, but somehow Broda thrust his pad in the way and deflected the rubber out of danger. To a man, the fans rose and toasted Turk with a standing ovation, and when the second period ended, the contest remained a scoreless deadlock.

Early in the third period the Leafs were attempting a change in lines when Howie Meeker and Vic Lynn, two of the marked fat men, combined to feed a lead pass to Max Bentley, who normally wouldn't have been on the ice with them. Bentley moved through the Rangers checkers and unleashed a steaming shot that flew past Rayner. Later in the period another fat man, Harry Watson, skimmed a pass to Bill Ezinicki, who also beat Rayner.

Now all eyes were on the clock as it ticked toward the twenty-minute mark and the end of the game. With only a minute remaining, Broda still had a shutout. The countdown began: ten, nine, eight, seven, six, five . . . the crowd was roaring as if the Leafs had won the Stanley Cup . . . four, three, two, one. The game was over; Turk dove for the puck and gathered it in. It was his symbolic trophy for winning the Battle of the Bulge.

Walter Broda was born May 15, 1941, in the wheat country of western Canada. His home town, Brandon, sent many a young hockey player to the professionals but few appeared less likely to make it than the portly young netminder. Although his skating was poor and his reflexes lacked the spark of a thinner player, Broda earned a spot on the school team—by default. Luckily his principal began working privately with his student, teaching him the finer points of goaltending, until Broda's game began to improve. He soon caught on with a local club called Brandon North Stars and played goal for them in a one-game playoff with the Elmwood Millionaires. Broda's club lost 11–1! In 1930–31 he somehow managed to take over the goalkeeping for the Manitoba Hydros, in the Brandon Commercial League. He played so capably in an intermediate league during that time that he was named to its all-star team.

Broda got his break after trying out and failing his audition with the Brandon Native Sons, a top junior entry. Although the manager had rejected him, the Native Sons' boss remembered Turk. He called on Broda that spring when the regular Native Sons' goaltender was ruled overage in a last-minute discovery, and the junior club desperately needed a goaltender.

Amused rather than annoyed at the sudden turnabout by the Native Sons, Turk accepted their offer to take over the goaltending during the Memorial Cup playoffs for the junior championship of Canada.

Brandon swept the series and Broda was at his best, as always would be the case, in the most excruciating moments. It was only a matter of time before he would make his way up the ranks to the pros. Conn Smythe signed him in 1936 for what turned out to be one of the best moves ever made by one of hockey's most insightful entrepreneurs.

After his playing career Broda took a number of coaching jobs in both amateur and professional ranks, the last of which was with Quebec in the American Hockey League. He died on October 17, 1972, much too soon, at the age of fifty-eight.

The Turk will always be remembered as a happy performer but most of all a clutch champion.

47 Bryan Hextall
(1936–1948)

On the night of April 14, 1940, when Mackenzie King was prime minister of Canada and Franklin Delano Roosevelt president of the United States, a red light flashed behind goalie Turk Broda of the Toronto Maple Leafs at the Toronto rink.

The time was 2:07 of the first sudden-death overtime and the capacity crowd was virtually silent as right wing Bryan Hextall of the New York Rangers waved his stick in the air. He had scored the goal that won the Stanley Cup for the Broadway Blueshirts.

Hextall did not know it at the time but with each year the goal that gave his Rangers a 3–2 victory over the Maple Leafs would grow in stature until, today, it has become a veritable legend in Manhattan simply because the Rangers have not won another Stanley Cup since the man called Hex beat the pudgy Toronto goalie. For more than four decades Rangers fans have had to savor that night before Pearl Harbor Day, a night that still provides solace for a frustrated Ranger fan's heart.

But Hextall did more than just win a Stanley Cup for the New Yorkers. "He was," said Herb Goren, who covered the Rangers for *The New York Sun,* "the hardest bodychecking forward I had seen in more than forty years of watching hockey."

Hex could hit and he could score. He led the National Hockey League in scoring in 1942, was a First Team All-Star in 1940, 1941 and 1942, made the Second Team in 1943 and played on one first-place team.

The line of Hextall, completed by center Phil Watson and left wing Lynn Patrick was among the most formidable of its time and might have established itself among the NHL's greatest ever were it not for the outbreak of World War II, the enlistment of Patrick into the armed forces and the ultimate breakup of the unit.

Bryan Aldwyn Hextall was born July 31, 1913, in Grenfell, Saskatchewan. He originally commanded attention during the early 1930s while playing for the Vancouver Lions of the Western Hockey League. The Rangers noticed him after Bryan led the Lions to a first-place finish. Two years later he was on Broadway at a time when the Rangers' patriarch, Lester Patrick, was dismantling an aging club and rebuilding it with youth. Hextall would soon be teamed with such powerful skaters as Alf Pike, Babe Pratt, Art Coulter and Alex Shibicky.

When Frank Boucher took over as Rangers coach in 1940 the Hextall-Patrick-Watson line became the hottest unit in the league, and Hextall was regarded as the best all-around player of the trio.

Unquestionably, Hextall's career was braked by the intrusion of World War II. Many of his teammates returned to the Blueshirts following the cessation of hostilities and discovered that they had lost their touch. Yet, in 1946–47 Bryan managed to crack the then coveted twenty-goal circle. But the following season his production plummeted to only eight goals and he called it a career in the spring of 1948.

Hextall had accumulated 187 goals and 362 points in 449 games over eleven seasons with the Rangers. "I scored 20 goals for seven straight years," Hextall recalled proudly. "Twenty goals was a big thing then."

He won the NHL scoring title in 1941–42 with 24 goals and 56 points in forty-eight games. He was league scoring leader and among the top ten scorers on four occasions. And he remembers his Stanley Cup-winning score as if it happened ten minutes ago.

"I took a pass from Dutch Hiller and Phil Watson," Hextall remembered. "The puck came out from behind the net and I took a backhand shot to put it past Broda."

After his retirement Bryan started a lumberyard and hardware business but his love for hunting inspired him to open a commercial shooting lodge in the fall near his home in Poplar Point, Manitoba.

He proudly watched his sons, Bryan, Jr., and Dennis, make their way up to the NHL. Each of them had a stint, albeit brief, with the Rangers. Then, hard luck took its toll on the old warrior.

Poor circulation forced doctors to amputate his legs below the knees in 1978. More surgery was required late in 1981 but Hextall's enthusiasm for life was not dampened. "I had artificial legs made," he said. "I could still walk a short distance."

The spirit that enabled Bryan Hextall to survive and excel in the NHL is what has carried him through his crises. He is a battler who belongs among *Hockey's 100*.

48 Tim Horton
(1952–1974)

Tim Horton had amazing strength. He was a compactly built 5'10", 180-pound man —one of the strongest players in the NHL. In spite of the fact that he was one of the most feared men in the game, his penalties averaged to only one minor penalty in every two games.

Tim was not a dirty player. Horton could hand out thumping bodychecks if the need called for it, but he preferred his own method of leaning on the opposition and steering him (along with the puck) into the closest corner. He would get a stranglehold on a player, and they'd end up on the ice, their breath squeezed out of them. "I tried him once," Derek Sanderson said, "and he just put the bearhug on me. After awhile I heard a cracking noise, and figured it was my ribs going, one by one. Never again." "What Tim was especially good at was breaking up fights," said Bob Haggert, the Toronto Maple Leafs' trainer during the 1960s where, with Horton on the rearguard, they won the Stanley Cup four times in six seasons. Horton had only one weakness, according to Punch Imlach (Buffalo general manager), "He hasn't got a mean bone in his body. If he had, they'd have to make a rule against him."

Number 7 of Toronto was a professional. He did not attempt to be sensational. He was so effective because he was taken for granted. He played with no con or showmanship that less talented players must resort to in order to win over fans. He had few peers who possessed his all-around ability. Horton was a superb skater, an adept playmaker with a deadly slapshot, and few players could match him when it came to lugging the puck out of his own territory to ease the pressure.

Swift skater that he was, along with his slapshot, he was awesome at the point. He had, in fact, been a pioneer in utilizing the slapshot in hockey. The coach of the Soviet National Hockey Team saw Horton in 1964 and felt that Tim was the most outstanding player he saw.

In 1965 King Clancy (who coached him at Pittsburgh, and later in Toronto) had this to say about Tim: "We were going nowhere fast. Then Punch Imlach moved Horton from defense to right wing—and the team started to move. I think Horton is as powerful or maybe stronger than Chicago's Bobby Hull."

Horton's accomplishments were many. At the time of his tragic death, he had played in 1,446 games (behind only Gordie Howe with 1,687 and Alex Delvecchio with 1,549). He had scored 115 goals and accumulated 403 assists for 518 total points. He played on four Stanley Cup championship teams, all with Toronto, in '62, '63, '64 and '67. His totals for 16 Stanley Cup playoffs (encompassing 126 games) were 11 goals and 39 assists for a total of 50 points. Tim was elected to a First Team All-Star three times (63–64, 67–68, 68–69) and was an alternate three times (53–54, 62–63, 66–67).

In the playoffs in 61–62, he set two records with 3 goals and 13 assists vs. the Rangers and Chicago. In 1964 he was runner-up to Pierre Pilote for the Norris Trophy.

It was in 1968–69, however, that Horton had his finest season. He scored 11 goals and had 29 assists, and again made the First Team All-Star. He also won the J. P. Bickell Memorial Cup as the Most Valuable Maple Leaf, and again finished second in balloting for the Norris Trophy, this time to Bobby Orr.

Norton also holds the all-time NHL regular season penalty-minute record, having played in 1,446 games (twenty-four seasons), with 1,611 penalty minutes, averaging to only 1.11 minutes penalty time per game. He also holds the club record with Toronto for the longest consecutive game streak spanning from February 11, 1961, to February 4, 1968.

Before the arrival of the great Bobby Orr, Tim was on center stage alone among all of the NHL defensemen. Even at the age of forty-three, while he was a Sabre, he was the only defenseman currently playing (besides Orr) to have scored more than 100 goals. He was also the only other defenseman (besides Orr) to be named to six All-Star teams.

Myles Gilbert Horton was born in Cochrane, Ontario, on January 12, 1930, the older of two brothers. He played his early hockey there. In 1945 his family moved to Sudbury. It was there he won a hockey scholarship to St. Michaels in Toronto because of his outstanding play during his high school career. He was a junior "A" player beginning in 1947 for two years while being coached by Joe Primeau (who later became his mentor with Toronto). Tim was a fierce competitor while a teenager playing in the Junior A division of the Ontario Hockey Association, where he oddly enough received 137 minutes in penalties in his first season while also making the All-Star team.

Undecided if he would turn pro, he made the decision in 1949 to sign a contract with Pittsburgh. At that time, Pittsburgh was a Toronto farm club. During his three seasons with the club, he helped Pittsburgh win one Calder Cup victory, and in the process, earned a berth for himself on the AHL All-Star team. In 192 games, he had 358 minutes in penalties. Tim spent three seasons with Pittsburgh, and was then called up to Toronto.

Towards the end of 1954–55, the Maple Leafs were convinced they had found a superstar in Tim Horton. All that changed one night in the Garden, when Bill Gadsby of the New York Rangers bodychecked Tim and dumped him to the ice. The end result was a broken tibia and fibula of Tim's right leg, and a fractured jaw. The cast wasn't removed until July, and from then until the 1955–56 training camp, he concerned himself with the recuperation process. When Horton finally got back into action, he was not the same player as before. He had no zip or swerve. Horton played in only thirty-five games. The following season he played in sixty-seven games. The next year held promise again, but he suffered a groin injury that cut down on his effectiveness. King Clancy felt that subconsciously Tim was protecting that leg.

It was in 1964, after Horton had been a pro for fourteen seasons, that his star began to rise. After years of injuries and warming the bench, being overshadowed by names such as Bob Goldham and Red Kelly, he began to emerge as the leader of the Maple Leafs. Slowly, but surely, Horton became the backbone of the team.

Tim was also involved in many business ventures, including "Tim Horton's Drive-In," and a car business in North Bay that his brother Jerry ran. Tim also saw his doughnut chain grow to thirty-three stores. Because of his success with that franchise, he announced in 1970 that he would be retiring from professional hockey to devote himself full-time to his thriving doughnut business.

There was also the matter of money. Tim wanted $85,000. The Leafs felt that they needed him for their chance to make the playoffs, but did not want to pay him that amount. They talked him out of that demand for a reported $80,000, and a chunk of money for "certain considerations." However, it was clear that Tim would not figure into the Maple Leafs' long-range plans, which included rebuilding with younger players.

However, the New York Rangers needed someone like Tim Horton. Brad Park and Jim Neilson were injured. A player like Horton could make the difference between winning the Stanley Cup or another year of frustration for the Rangers.

On March 4, 1970, Tim Horton was traded to the Rangers in exchange for "players to be named later." After eighteen years and 1,185 games with Toronto, Tim was no longer a Maple Leaf. However, his statistics spoke for themselves. He had scored 106 goals, 348 assists and missed only seven games with them in his last eight seasons. He made the All-Star team six times. Tim joined the Rangers on March 4, 1970, against Detroit.

After his departure from the Rangers in 1971, Tim was drafted by the Pittsburgh Penguins, now under his old friend and ex-teammate, Red Kelly. After suffering a broken ankle and separated shoulder in 1972, Tim announced again he would retire, and when Pittsburgh left him off of their protected list, the Buffalo Sabres and Imlach purchased him for $40,000. It was Imlach who made the sales pitch that Tim couldn't refuse. The money was right, and Tim felt Imlach was right in feeling that he had one year left.

Tim Horton was one of the most popular of all hockey players. Unfortunately, his career was cut short by a tragic accident. On Thursday, February 21, 1974, Horton was on his way back to Buffalo from the Maple Leaf Gardens when he was involved in a one-car crash on the Queen Elizabeth Way at St. Catherine's. He died instantly. Tim Horton was only forty-four years old.

The hockey world was stunned. Frank Mahovlich, who played ten years with Horton said, "Steady. I never knew a player so steady. No flash, no polish, all hard work."

The Toronto president, Harold Ballard said, "There was never a stronger player in the league, although he never used it to great excess. Hockey has lost a great competitor. He lived as a star and died as a star."

Punch Imlach honored him by saying, "I think Horton, more than any other one player, was the key to those glory days," referring to the great Stanley Cup years of the Maple Leafs.

Every year the Buffalo Sabres Fan Club present an Unsung Hero Award to the Sabre player who worked the hardest without gaining the recognition of some of the more flamboyant stars. After Tim's death, in honor of his style, never flashy—just hard work, they renamed the award the "Tim Horton Award."

The Buffalo Sabres retired the number 2 sweater he wore.

One can only guess how much longer this remarkable, robust and intelligent defenseman might have played. But this much we know. In his twenty-four seasons with the NHL, he was a winner, who more than qualifies for *Hockey's 100*.

49 Art Coulter
(1931–1942)

The last New York Rangers' team to win the Stanley Cup was the 1939–40 edition and anyone who had the good fortune to watch those Broadway Blueshirts in action would concede that bustling, rawboned Art Coulter, captain of that gloriously gifted club, provided the essential glue that kept it together.

When Rangers manager Lester Patrick obtained the strapping defenseman from the Chicago Black Hawks in exchange for an established favorite, Earl Seibert, the deal surprised the press and dismayed a number of fans. In the months immediately following the deal it appeared as if Patrick had goofed. Coulter's play was average, at best, and quite often less than that. But Frank Boucher, the Rangers' popular center and Patrick's confidant, had an insight into Coulter's character and requested a meeting with Patrick.

"I asked Lester what was wrong between him and Art," Boucher recalled, "and he said he didn't seem to be able to get through to him. I suggested that Art, being a man of tall pride, should be made captain of the team. If Lester did this and took Art in his confidence I was convinced the change would benefit Coulter psychologically."

Patrick agreed and the move seemed to be a tonic to the new Ranger. In no time at all Coulter became a mountain of strength behind the New York blue line. He was a Second Team All-Star in 1938, 1939 and 1940. Coulter also was a force behind the Rangers first-place team in 1941–42, the last time the New Yorkers finished atop the National Hockey League.

Tall and muscular, without a trace of fat, Coulter was teamed on defense with Lester Patrick's bruising son, Murray, also known as Muzz. Any forward who attempted to bisect that defense was guaranteed a surplus of black-and-blue marks.

As tough as Coulter and Patrick were on the ice, they were sweethearts in civilian clothes. Both enjoyed the good life of Broadway and Art, in particular, had a reputation as a free spender.

In those days during the Great Depression it was a rule on the Rangers that players travelled in groups of four in taxis and one of them was named "cab captain," in charge of the fares. Coulter was one of those "cab captains."

One day, after the Rangers had completed a road trip, Patrick invited all his cab captains into his office so that he could review the various receipts that the players were required to obtain from the taxi drivers. Patrick was unmoved as he noted the receipts ranging from $6.00 to $8.00, but he did a double take when Coulter handed him a chit that totalled $12.75.

"Art," Patrick inquired, "why is your bill so much larger than the others?"

"Well, Lester," Coulter replied, "you've told us that we're in the big leagues now, so I tip like a big-leaguer."

Patrick didn't blink an eyelash. "That's very commendable, Art," he shot back, "but I don't know if the Rangers can afford big tippers like you."

Art chuckled. "Okay, Lester. You have nothing to worry about. I resign my captaincy."

According to journalist Eric Whitehead, who wrote *The Patricks, Hockey's Royal Family,* Coulter retained the captain's "C" on his jersey. This permitted Art to play a part in an extraordinary Rangers conference held the night before the Broadway skaters annexed the Stanley Cup at Maple Leaf Gardens in Toronto.

Whitehead described it thusly: "The Blues had finished three points behind Boston in the league race, had ousted the Bruins in the first playoff round, and now had the Toronto Maple Leafs down three games to two in the final round. The superb goaltending of veteran Davey Kerr and a strong defense anchored by Babe Pratt and Ott Heller had been the principal factors in getting the Blues this far, and now a win in the upcoming sixth game in Toronto with the Leafs would wrap it up."

Frank Boucher, who had become Rangers coach, invited his players to the beer parlor of the Ford Hotel. While this may have seemed an unusual place for a team meeting, the gregarious Boucher figured it would set a mellow tone during an anxious time.

"Captain Coulter opened with a toast," wrote Whitehead, "coach Boucher responded by raising his ale glass, there was a rousing 'hear . . . hear . . .' from the troops, then a reverent silence as the steins were drained. This, oft repeated, was the extent of the team-meeting agenda, laced, of course, with convivial conversation, the odd burst of ribald laughter, and even an occasional more or less scholarly reference to the upcoming game against the Leafs."

Clearly, the psychology worked. "It was," said Coulter, "a loosener. The team had been playing great hockey and wanted no part of a seventh game in Toronto. The only danger was that of getting a little uptight, and pressing too hard."

"The next evening," wrote Whitehead, "everybody was beautifully loose and relaxed as the game started. And at the end of the first period the Rangers were down 2–0 after fast goals by Syl Apps and Nick Metz. Lester came into the dressing room, sat down on a bench beside goalie Davey Kerr and said quietly, 'Well, boys, you've had your fun. Now let's get down to business. I've made arrangements for a victory party in the Tudor Room of the Royal York. I'll see you there. Don't let me down.' "

The Rangers rallied to tie the score at 2–2 and then won the deciding game on Bryan Hextall's shot in sudden-death overtime. Understandably, Hextall captured the attention at that stupendous moment in Rangers history but the bosses, Patrick and Boucher, understood that the New Yorkers would never have gotten that far without the leadership and skill displayed by Coulter.

Arthur Edmund (Art) Coulter was born May 31, 1909, in Winnipeg, Manitoba. Like so many Rangers, he honed his hockey skills to sharpness on Winnipeg's outdoor rinks before becoming a professional in 1929.

The Black Hawks signed him in 1931 and, ironically, he teamed with a onetime Rangers star, Taffy Abel, on the Windy City blue line. The pair starred on Chicago's first ever Stanley Cup championship team in 1934.

Upon joining the Rangers he was nicknamed "The Trapper" because he would talk fishing and hunting by the hour. When Boucher, as coach, introduced a revolutionary offensive penalty-killing team in 1939 Coulter was the anchor man with forwards Alex Shibicky and Neil and Mac Colville. So effective was the system that over the season the Rangers outscored their opponents almost two to one when they were shorthanded.

Following the Rangers' first-place finish in 1942 Coulter enlisted in the U.S.

Coast Guard at a time when that branch of the service had established a hockey team at its base in Curtis Bay (near Baltimore), Maryland. A number of experienced hockey professionals, including Frankie Brimsek of the Boston Bruins and Johnny Mariucci of the Chicago Black Hawks, also joined the Cutters sextet, which played in the Eastern Hockey League. Not surprisingly, Coulter once again was at the helm of a championship team; the Cutters finished atop the Eastern League and Art was in vintage form.

He retired as an active player at war's end and eventually moved to Florida where he still lives today. One of the game's genuinely overshadowed heroes, Coulter was elected to the Hockey Hall of Fame in 1974. There were few better at plying the defensive trade.

50 Guy Lafleur (1971–   )

"Hockey," said Guy Lafleur, "is like a drug for me. I am hooked. I can't do anything about it."

In fact Lafleur did a lot about his hockey. He was the predominant National Hockey League player in the 1970s, skating for no fewer than five Stanley Cup championship teams and, in that span, six first-place teams.

More than any other NHL player, Lafleur both looked like and performed as if he had been trained at the Bolshoi Ballet. If there can be but one descriptive adjective for Lafleur it is exquisite.

When he was in his prime, Guy skated with a blend of power and grace that was unmatched among his peers. Despite a seemingly frail—by hockey standards—physique, Lafleur was able to generate one of the most dynamically accurate shots in NHL history. A perfect example was an incident in the 1979 semifinals between his Canadiens and the Boston Bruins. With 1 minute and 14 seconds remaining in the decisive game, Lafleur raced along the boards at thirty miles per hour. Suddenly, just inside the blue line, he drew back his stick and drove the puck into the far left corner of the net. Bruin goalie Gilles Gilbert never moved. The goal tied the score. Montreal went on to win in sudden-death overtime and later, with Lafleur leading the way, the Canadiens took the National Hockey League championship for the fourth straight time.

During the period 1975–79 when the Canadiens thoroughly dominated the NHL while capturing four consecutive Stanley Cups, Lafleur was their ace in the hole. When the game hung in the balance, the Habs would call Lafleur's number and he would invariably deliver. Time after time, the fleet right-winger would rise to the occasion despite everyone in the house knowing that he would often be the target of the opposition's most intense defensive efforts. His ability to play his game in the face of even the most determined checking separates Lafleur from any and all of his competition.

As solid as the Montreal team was in the mid 1970s, if you could stop Lafleur, opponents would figure, you could shut down his team. Judged by the success of the Habs it is apparent how difficult this strategy was to implement.

Lafleur first established himself as an offensive force in the 1974–75 season when he potted 53 goals and added 66 assists. The following year marked the first of three consecutive scoring titles for Lafleur, the only Canadien in the history of the organization to accomplish such a feat. His 80 assists in 1976–77 and 60 goals in 1977–78 were league highs for each year and career bests for Lafleur in each category. In 728 NHL contests, Guy Lafleur has scored 432 goals and 579 assists, good for fourteenth place on the all-time NHL scoring list. In 104 playoff games Lafleur garnered 125 points, including 55 goals. He has led postseason competition in goal scoring twice, assists twice, and total points three times.

Listed at a lithe 6 feet, 175 pounds, the graceful Lafleur, or the "Flower" as his name translates, was subject to numerous tests of physical toughness in his early years in the league. But it was soon evident that roughing him up only served to have him come back twice as hard. Those who considered Lafleur a personification of his nickname were far from accurate. He would not be intimidated. But by the mid 1980's it was apparent that Guy had lost his old scoring touch. In 1983–1984 he tallied only 30 goals and 40 assists for 70 points in 80 games.

Lafleur was drafted as the first pick overall in the 1971 amateur draft and was immediately dubbed a ''can't miss'' prospect with Orr-like potential. Coming off a spectacular junior career with the Quebec Remparts, young Lafleur was envisioned as the heir to the throne of the recently retired Jean Beliveau as leader of the Canadiens. With the stage set for his entrance, Lafleur was expected to display an Oscar-winning performance, nothing less.

With his first three year's totals reading 64, 55 and 56 points, Lafleur was considered a colossal failure by his audience in Montreal. ''What happened was very simple,'' Lafleur remembers. ''After my 130-goal season with the Remparts, everybody and his brother took me for some kind of superman. They established Herculean goals for me. The tension wound up crushing me.'' The ordeal finally came to a head in 1974 when, with his Canadiens contract expired, Lafleur received an offer from the newly formed Quebec Nordiques of the World Hockey Association.

Returning to the friendly confines of Quebec's *Colisée,* the building which was his home with the Remparts, was an attractive offer indeed to Lafleur, whose flagging fortune in Montreal was taking its toll on his psyche. Later, after signing a new contract with the Canadiens, Lafleur appeared to shed the weight that had hindered his career to that point. With the grief of his first three years now behind him Lafleur proceeded to tear up the NHL. In the following six seasons he scored no fewer than 119 points per year, with a high of 136 points in 1976–77 when he captured the Hart Trophy (league MVP), Art Ross Trophy (scoring title) and Conn Smythe Trophy (playoff MVP). The Flower had finally bloomed.

Guy Damien Lafleur was born September 20, 1951, in the town of Thurso, Quebec. The only boy in a family of five children, his first involvement in the game that would eventually spread his name across the Canadian provinces came when his father joined forces with some neighbors and erected an ice skating rink. It was on that surface that Lafleur took his first strides toward the game he grew to love.

To Lafleur, hockey was more than lacing up his skates for a game. The smell, sounds and ambiance of the rink were addicting. Arriving early for games and staying late at practice became Lafleur's habits. He would prowl around the arena hours before a game, mingling with the maintenance men and attending to his equipment. On a practice day, he would linger on after his teammates, refining the slapshot that was his trademark.

Streaking down the ice, slicing in on goal and firing a dart behind the goaltender will be the eternal image of Lafleur's ice capades. He stands as one of the finest pure scorers the game has ever seen. But what put him above the one-dimensional scoring machine was his play in both zones. Along with being a capable defensive forward, Lafleur was a playmaker nonpareil. When carrying the puck into the offensive zone he could be chased, harassed and molested and still retain possession long enough to make a nifty pass to a teammate who would be in the clear because of the opposition's overconcentration on Lafleur. As was predicted in his junior years, he had the ability to dominate the ice and control the tempo of a game.

With his angular features and blond mane flying behind him, Montreal's number

10 has earned a permanent home in the hearts of his fans. For his dedication to the game and extraordinary performances on the ice, Guy Lafleur is deservingly awarded a permanent place among the rest of hockey's greats here among *Hockey's 100*.

51 Bill Cowley
(1934–1947)

The odds are one in a million that a prospective big-leaguer will be discovered while playing in Paris, France, but such was the good fortune of Bill Cowley, who would become the stickhandling master of the Boston Bruins.

In 1934 the twenty-one-year-old center was accompanying the Ottawa Shamrocks on an extended European tour. It was in Paris that he caught the eye of critics and ultimately came away with a professional contract. It didn't hurt that the Shamrocks, with Cowley leading the way, produced thirty-three wins, no losses and two ties.

Within a decade of that junket Cowley had accomplished everything a major-leaguer could hope for, and then some. He won the Hart Trophy as the National Hockey League's most valuable player in 1941 and 1943. He led the NHL in scoring in 1941 and was chosen to the First All-Star Team in 1938, 1941, 1943 and 1944. He made the Second All-Star Team in 1945, and was a member of the 1939 and 1941 Stanley Cup champion Bruins.

Cowley's problem—if it can be called a problem—was the fact that he played on the same team with the formidable and infinitely more colorful Kraut Line of Milt Schmidt, Bobby Bauer and Woody Dumart. The trio's exploits frequently overshadowed the effortless grace and subtlety of Cowley, who was every bit as good as his more illustrious mates.

During the 1938–39 season Cowley teamed with Charlie Sands, a smooth-skating wing, and Ray Getliffe, a hard worker who knew how to get the job done. The unit jelled neatly and soon was rated above the Krauts.

The Bruins finished first that year and by playoff time coach Art Ross had made some changes to thwart the New York Rangers, their first-round opponents. Cowley was switched to center for Roy Conacher and Mel Hill.

At the conclusion of regulation time in the opening game the teams were tied, 1–1. Ross divined the Rangers' strategy—stifle Cowley with blanket checking and do the same to Conacher—and summoned Cowley to his side. "We've got to fool them," he said. "They're watching Conacher so carefully it would be better to feed Hill."

Cowley could have been forgiven if he had raised an eyebrow. At that point in time Hill was regarded as a Grade B shooter, at best, who scored only 10 goals all season. Cowley listened to his boss and then decided that Hill would get that puck if he had to present it to him on a lazy Susan.

The sudden death had begun and the teams conducted a series of thrusts and counterthrusts with no result. That they were evenly matched was obvious and it was equally clear that only a very special play would decide the contest. The first twenty-minute sudden death ended without result, as did the second overtime period. It appeared that the third sudden death would conclude without result when Cowley took control of the puck with less than a minute remaining.

Cowley crossed into Rangers territory and lured the big New York defenseman, Murray Patrick, toward him. Patrick couldn't quite get to Cowley in time and the Bruin eluded him, skated into the corner and fed a perfect pass to Hill, who was camped in front of goalie Dave Kerr. Hill deposited the puck behind Kerr at 19:25 of the third overtime. When the red light flashed it was 1:10 a.m.

The second game was virtually a carbon copy of the first. It was 2–2 at the end of regulation time and, once again, Ross employed the same strategy with Cowley —feed Hill. With 8 minutes and 20 seconds gone in the first sudden-death period Cowley charged the Rangers' defense. As the New Yorkers braced for his shot, Bill deftly dropped the puck back to Hill, who fired a forty-footer into the twine. The time was 8:24 of the first overtime and the Cowley-Hill combine was the talk of the hockey world.

The Bruins took game three, 4–1, in more traditional form but then it was the Rangers' turn. They won the next three in a row and seemed destined for a major upset as the teams lined up for the seventh and deciding game at Boston Garden.

Again they were deadlocked, this time 1–1 at the end of three periods. Wearied from the heat of an April evening the teams slogged through one, then a second sudden-death period without producing a score and with more than seven minutes elapsed in the third sudden death the Bruins moved to the attack. Roy Conacher fired the puck at goalie Bert Gardiner, who earlier in the series had replaced Kerr. Gardiner nabbed the rubber in the webbing of his glove and flipped the puck into the corner of the rink, expecting one of his defensemen to retrieve it. But Cowley got there first.

The crafty Boston center continued behind the goal, using the cage as a blocker, viewing the goal area for a possible opportunity. There was Hill, somehow unguarded. Again, Cowley distributed the perfect pass and, before Gardiner could move, Hill sped it home at exactly eight minutes of the third overtime. The Bruins had won the series four games to three.

William Mailes Cowley was born June 12, 1912, in Bristol, Quebec. The youngest member of the Cowley clan of four boys and a girl, Bill received his first pair of skates at Christmas 1924, when he was twelve years old.

Bill launched his youthful playing career as a goalie, gave up a dozen goals in the first period and was forever a forward after that. He broke into the NHL with the St. Louis Eagles in 1934. When the Eagles folded at the close of the 1934–35 season Cowley signed with the Bruins under coach Frank Patrick.

Cowley played three games on the wing before the veteran defenseman Babe Siebert took Patrick aside. "That kid can fly," Siebert said. "Put him at center and he'll rattle in the goals."

In his fourth game with the Bruins—against the Canadiens at Montreal—Cowley was at center. The game was tied in the third period when Bill moved into high gear and sped off on a breakaway with Siebert right behind. As he passed Montreal's blue line, goalie Wilf Cude crouched into position.

"Beat him—it's your play, kid," came Siebert's yell.

Cowley moved right in on goal, wheeled across the goal mouth and seemed ready to swerve behind the net. Cude was duped by the maneuver and Cowley backhanded the puck into the net.

It was the start of a career that spanned eleven years in Boston. Cowley retired after the 1946–47 season having suffered a broken left hand, a jaw broken in five places, torn knee ligaments, a shoulder separation and assorted cuts and bruises.

Following his retirement, Cowley coached teams in Renfrew, Ontario, and Vancouver before settling in his native Ottawa. He was elected to the Hockey Hall of Fame in 1968. If there are any doubts that Bill belongs with *Hockey's 100*, just check with Mel (Sudden Death) Hill.

52 Ching Johnson (1926–1938)

If ever there was a swashbuckling defenseman whose robust play was a perfect metaphor for hard hockey it was Ching Johnson. And if ever there was a gregarious personality who helped sell the still foreign game of hockey to New Yorkers during the Roaring Twenties it was Ching.

Johnson was twenty-eight years old when he made his debut on Broadway with the Rangers. It also was the debut for the Blueshirts, who were launching their National Hockey League franchise in the 1926–27 season against the powerful Montreal Maroons.

Before the game Ching suffered doubts about the Rangers' ability to withstand the mighty men from the North. The game itself was billed as the best (Maroons) against the worst (Rangers). Johnson was teamed on the blue line with Taffy Abel. Their names—Taffy and Ching—would soon become bywords to New York sports fans.

Johnson was a big, rawboned hunk of man with a bald head and an extremely positive view of life. "He always wore a grin," said teammate Frank Boucher, "even when heaving some poor soul six feet in the air. He was one of those rare warm people who would break into a smile just saying hello or telling you the time."

Abel was heavier and rounder than Johnson. It was said that when Taffy hit a foe it felt more like being swatted with a fat pillow. When Ching connected it was like being hit by a train. Ching hit often but he also was the recipient of many hits, and that opening game against the Maroons was a good example of what was to come.

In the first period the Maroons chose to intimidate the Rangers and Nels Stewart of the visitors went after Johnson, hooking him over the eye with his stick when they clashed along the boards behind the Rangers' net. Although blood was pouring from the cut Ching nevertheless crashed Stewart to the ice. Referee Lou Marsh gave them both penalties and Ching went to the dressing room where five stitches were placed in the wound. He soon returned to the fray wearing a white patch over the eye. Ching played more effervescently than ever and the Rangers scored what was considered an upset victory over the Maroons.

Johnson gave New York fans a million bucks worth of entertainment during his career. He was a First All-Star in 1932 and 1933 and made the Second Team in 1931 and 1934. With Ching starring on defense the Rangers finished first in the American Division and a season later won their first Stanley Cup.

Johnson helped the Rangers to a second Stanley Cup in 1933. "Ching," said Boucher, "loved to deliver a good hoist early in a game because he knew his victim would likely retaliate, and Ching loved body contact. I remember once against the Maroons Ching caught Hooley Smith with a terrific check right at the start of the game. Hooley's stick flew from his hands and disappeared above the rink lights. He was lifted clean off the ice, and seemed to stay suspended five or six feet above the surface for seconds before finally crashing down on his back. No one could

accuse Hooley of lacking guts. From then on, whenever he got the puck, he drove straight for Ching, trying to outmatch him, but each time Ching flattened poor Hooley. Afterwards, grinning in the shower, Ching said he couldn't remember a game he'd enjoyed more.''

Ivan Wilfred Johnson was born December 7, 1897, in Winnipeg, Manitoba. He was nicknamed Ching because he wore a wide grin on his face whenever he body-checked the enemy and when he smiled his eyes gave him an Oriental look; therefore Chink or Ching as in Ching-a-ling-Chinaman.

Johnson was discovered by Conn Smythe, when the hockey entrepreneur was scouting for the Rangers prior to their entry into the NHL. Both Ching and his buddy, Taffy Abel, were playing semipro hockey in Minneapolis. Smythe liked them both but found Johnson a hard bargainer.

"I must have reached agreement with Ching forty times," Smythe recalled. "Each time when I gave him my pen to sign, he'd say, 'I just want to phone my wife.' Then there'd be a hitch and he wouldn't sign. In my final meeting with him I said before we started, 'Ching, I want you to promise that if we make a deal you will sign, and *then* you'll phone your wife.' He promised. We made a deal. He said, 'I've got to phone my wife.' I said, 'You promised!' He said, 'Okay, Connie,' and signed.''

Smythe was unloaded by the Rangers before the opening season had begun and was replaced by Lester Patrick.

Johnson played for the Rangers until 1937 and then was dealt to the New York Americans. He completed his NHL career in 1938 but coached briefly in the minors and then turned to officiating. While officiating a game in Washington, D.C., he committed a memorable gaffe.

"I was calling this game," Ching recalled, "when some young forward broke out and raced solo against the goalie. Instinctively, I took this player down with a jarring bodycheck. Following the game, I apologized to his team. I don't know what made me do it but I did it. I guess it was just the old defenseman's instinct.''

Johnson eventually went into the construction business and remained in Washington where he occasionally attended games played by the NHL's Washington Capitals. He was elected to the Hockey Hall of Fame in 1958. Johnson died on June 16, 1979.

53 Sweeney Schriner
(1934–1946)

"He was the best left-winger I ever saw. That includes everybody—Frank Mahovlich, Busher Jackson, Bobby Hull, everybody."

The speaker was Conn Smythe, who coached and managed and studied hockey from the early 1920s through the late 1970s. The subject was Dave (Sweeney) Schriner, who played for the New York Americans and later for Smythe's Toronto Maple Leafs.

They called Schriner "The Great Smoothie" although he could have been tagged "Old Reliable" as well, based upon his knack for producing meaningful goals and assists at critical moments.

Schriner, who melded perfectly on a line with right wing Lorne Carr and center Art Chapman, won the Calder Trophy as rookie of the year in 1935 and led the NHL in scoring in 1936 and 1937. He was First All-Star left wing in 1936 and 1941 and made the Second Team in 1937.

It was Schriner, more than anyone, who lent dignity to an Americans team that often was the butt of twitting sportswriters. Red Dutton, who managed the Amerks during the 1930s, would bust his vest talking about his Sweeney. "What made me so proud," said Dutton, "was that I signed Schriner to his first pro contract. I brought him in along with Art Chapman and Lorne Carr and together they made one of the greatest lines in hockey."

Tall and husky, Schriner had remarkably thin legs for his size. When he won his first scoring championship in 1935–36, goals and assists were at a premium, yet he totalled 19 red lights and 26 assists for a total of 45 points at a time when the NHL played a forty-eight-game schedule. A year later he topped the league with 21 goals and 25 assists for 46 points.

Although the Americans never won the Stanley Cup they did enjoy a brief moment of glory in the 1938 playoffs when they went up against their hated rivals, the New York Rangers. Schriner and Company, always disparaged by their cotenants in Madison Square Garden, split the first two games with the Blueshirts. The third and decisive match was won by the Amerks when Schriner's pal, Carr, scored at forty seconds of the third overtime period.

Unfortunately, the Great Depression was at its height and the Amerks were hurting like so many professional teams. A number of Dutton's older players were retiring and he had to wheel and deal to fill their sweaters. Against his will, Dutton traded Schriner to Toronto in one of the NHL's biggest deals. In return he received Busher Jackson, Murray Armstrong, Buzz Boll and Doc Romnes.

If Sweeney was superb as an Amerk he was even better as a Maple Leaf, and his finest hour occurred during the 1942 Stanley Cup finals between the Detroit Red Wings and the Maple Leafs.

The teams were deadlocked at three games apiece with the seventh and final game being played at Maple Leaf Gardens. After two periods Detroit held a 1–0 lead and appeared capable of nursing it through the final twenty minutes of play.

Schriner, who was playing on a line with his old buddy, Carr, and rookie Billy (The Kid) Taylor, sat on his dressing room bench when manager Conn Smythe entered and walked over to the trio. Smythe recalled:

"I walked over to the corner where they were and gave it to them hard, one at a time and then all three. I'll never forget Sweeney looking up at me with a grin. 'What ya worrying about, boss? We'll get you a couple of goals.' "

Sweeney then made good on his word, scoring with assists from Carr and Taylor. Pete Langelle put the Leafs ahead, 2–1, but the Red Wings pressed for the equalizer. Schriner came back on the ice, accepted passes from Carr and Taylor and pumped the insurance goal home. The Maple Leafs won the game, 3–1, and the Stanley Cup.

Three years later Schriner helped the Leafs to another Stanley Cup while playing on a line with Carr and Gus Bodnar. That season, his tenth in the NHL, Sweeney scored 22 goals.

It was a magnificent last hurrah for Schriner and Carr. Smythe, who was convinced that both warriors were on the verge of decline, hoped his two aces would retire. "I could see it," Smythe said, "yet my toughness never extended to giving the chop to men who had worked hard for me. I talked this over with Schriner and Carr and they decided to retire which I thought was a more honorable way for two great performers to go out, rather than being shipped to the minors."

David Schriner was born November 30, 1911, in Calgary, Alberta. He was discovered by Red Dutton, a fellow western Canadian, and wasted little time persuading enemy goaltenders that he was for real. Curiously, Sweeney was persuaded to make a comeback in the fall of 1948 with the highly rated Regina Caps, a professional team just a cut below major league level.

"SWEENEY IS FLYING AGAIN WITH REGINA" was the way one headline evaluated his play. Schriner's comeback was remarkable, considering that he had been away from competitive hockey for three years but he retired from Western Canada Senior League play at the end of the 1948–49 season and turned to coaching.

After trying his hand at coaching Sweeney eventually returned to his native Calgary, his love of hockey undiminished. He is a regular at Flames NHL games and has retained the classy aura that long ago inspired someone to dub him The Great Smoothie.

54 Stan Mikita
(1958–1980)

Some years ago, a group of veteran hockey men got together at a banquet and began reminiscing about the sport they had all been associated with for so long. What evolved from their attempts to name the single greatest hockey player was a composite drawn from some of the greats of the past decade or so. This player would have Rocket Richard's accuracy, Gordie Howe's defensive mastery, Bobby Hull's speed and shot, and Jean Beliveau's stickhandling. He would, they agreed, be virtually unstoppable. Listening closely, Chicago Black Hawks coach Billy Reay stood quietly in amusement. After hearing the selections, Reay suddenly spoke up.

"That's Stan Mikita you're talking about," he said with finality. "He's done more with what he's got than any other player I've ever seen." And nobody argued. While probably a shade behind those stars in their particular areas of specialty, it was hard to think of any one player who was able to combine all his skills and achieve such a level of proficiency as Mikita. He was the embodiment of the consummate hockey player.

While blessed with a wide assortment of technical skills, Mikita battled every inch of the way to establish himself amongst the National Hockey League's large, often hulking, players. And from the outset his foes sensed that the pestiferous fellow with the slicked-back black hair was not going to allow himself to be run out of the league by anyone.

During his first six seasons in the NHL, the 5' 9", 165-pound centerman was described by one journalist as a "snarling, belligerent, gutter-fighting scamp who thought nothing at all about taking on the whole league." Nicknamed "Le Petit Diable" (The Little Devil) by fans in Montreal, Mikita's truculence earned calls for his blood in rinks throughout the NHL. A fighter he was, but by almost always going up against a larger opponent, he rarely found himself on the long side of the decision. He was, however, fearless in his desire to establish his place in the NHL.

During those early years of Mikita's career, his penalty minute totals often were considerably higher than his scoring numbers, ranging in the low to mid-100s. But between stints in the penalty box, Mikita was still able to spend enough time on the ice in 1961 to help lead the Black Hawks to their first Stanley Cup in twenty-three years. He led all playoff scorers that spring with 21 points in twelve games. Where the Hawks had previously been a one-line team with Bobby Hull blazing the way, the development of Mikita and the "Scooter Line" of Mikita, flanked by Ab McDonald and Ken Wharram, gave the Hawks the depth and balance they needed to take the Cup. They were small but aggressive; a tough checking line that managed to get its share of goals also. And Mikita was fast becoming the most dangerous two-way threat in the league.

Mikita's point and penalty totals continued to climb to the 1964–65 season when he earned 154 minutes in penalties and led the league in scoring with 87 points. But

at the start of the 1965 season, a remarkable transformation took place: the prince of pugnacity had reformed.

It seems as though Mikita's daughter had viewed a Black Hawks game on television and afterwards wondered aloud why her dad was beating a path to the penalty box while everyone else was busy playing on the ice. Unable to answer such a simply logical question, Mikita decided it was time for a change.

Realizing how much more valuable he could be to his team if he spent more time on the ice than in the slammer, Mikita did an abrupt about face. As hell-bent as he had been in establishing his tough-guy image, he was equally as determined to clean up his act. With everyone around the league finding it unbelievable that this was the same little devil that used to terrorize his opponents, Mikita became the target of antagonists who wanted to see how much he had actually reformed. Everyone tried to goad him into a fight, but even the stepped-up abuse couldn't change his mind. He was tamer, but as effective; aggressive, but legal.

His penalty marks plummeted, finally hitting a low of twelve minutes in 1966–67. Aided by his new-found temper, Mikita walked away with the scoring championship, MVP and Lady Byng Trophy that year and repeated his triple crown performance in 1967–68, a feat not accomplished by any other player before or since.

Stan Mikita was born May 20, 1940, in Sokolce, Czechoslovakia, to Mr. and Mrs. Stanislas Gvoth. He found his home in St. Catherines, Ontario, through an unusual arrangement between his parents and his aunt and uncle, the Mikitas. Since the Mikitas could have no children of their own, an agreement was made between the two families that would entitle the Mikitas to adopt the Gvoth's second child. During a postwar visit to Czechoslovakia, the Mikitas exercised their option and, in 1948, returned to Canada with their new son, Stanley, eight years old.

As a youngster, Mikita excelled in every sport he played, finally devoting his energies to hockey. He broke in with the Black Hawks in 1958 and remained with them for the next twenty-two years, finally retiring in 1980. Although always playing in the shadow of Bobby Hull, Mikita himself enjoyed a hugely successful career in Chicago. But to Mikita, there was no second fiddle.

Before the start of the 1972–73 season, rumor flew through the Windy City that Mikita was considering an offer from the Chicago Cougars of the World Hockey Association. After losing Hull to Winnipeg the previous season, the Black Hawks now stood to lose their second superstar in as many years. But when all was said and done, Mikita listened more to his heart than his head. "I had to consider my family and my future," he said, "but when it came down to it, I just wanted to stay with the Black Hawks. Everything doesn't revolve around money. After you play twelve or thirteen years with that Indian head on your jersey, it means something."

And what a main course he was. In his career, Mikita played 1394 games for the Hawks, piling up 541 goals and 926 assists to rank third on the all-time list behind Gordie Howe and Phil Esposito. Those credentials earned him a First Team All-Star berth six times and Second Team honors twice. He was also the NHL scoring leader four times, two-time MVP and Lady Byng winner, and recipient of the Lester Patrick Trophy for "outstanding service to hockey in the United States" in 1976. In 1983 he was inducted into the Hockey Hall of Fame.

Mikita suffered a serious back injury in 1969 and wore a brace through most of his career. Though playing in constant pain, he never let his team down, a testimony to his grit and determination.

When Mikita finally hung up his skates, teammate and goaltender Tony Esposito called it "the end of an era. I always considered myself fortunate to be out there with Stan. I'll probably never play with a greater hockey player."

Agreed.

55 Bullet Joe Simpson (1925–1931)

No less an authority than Edouard (Newsy) Lalonde, himself a titan of the sport, rated Bullet Joe Simpson "the greatest living hockey player" when they skated against each other in the early part of the century.

Simpson's Mercury-like moves inspired a reporter to tag him with the sobriquet "Bullet Joe" and it stuck for life, although the nickname would have been appropriate for another reason: Simpson performed a number of heroic feats on the battle-scarred Belgian countryside during World War I. Twice wounded, he received the Military Medal as a member of the 43rd Cameron Highlanders.

At the conclusion of hostilities, Simpson returned to Canada and began what was to become a spirited climb to hockey's crest. It began in his home town, Selkirk, Manitoba, continued in Edmonton where he became a cornerstone of the Eskimos franchise in the Western Canada Hockey League and concluded in the National Hockey League with the New York Americans.

Organized by bootlegger Big Bill Dwyer in 1925, the Americans—alias the Amerks—moved in to Madison Square Garden a year ahead of the Rangers. Thus, it was the Amerks who would sell (or fail to sell) hockey to the New York public. As it happened, the Americans did a remarkable job of winning the hearts of New Yorkers and Simpson proved to be one of the club's outstanding gate attractions. Bullet Joe was rechristened by Bill McBeth, the Amerks' eager press agent, "The Blue Streak from Saskatoon."

Simpson and center Billy Burch were among the more galvanic Americans and attracted the most attention from the media. The more the press touted the pair, the more the fans focused on them and demanded more production.

As defensemen went in those days, Simpson was a lightweight at 155 pounds but he tore into the foe with the confidence of a 200-pounder. Bill Corum, a distinguished columnist of the *New York Journal-American,* described Bullet Joe as "a rollicking, rocking man, flashing down the rink with the puck on the end of his stick."

H. J. Simpson was born August 13, 1893, in Selkirk, Manitoba, and played amateur hockey with the Winnipeg Victorias. He joined Winnipeg's 61st Battalion team and helped them win the Allan Cup, emblematic of senior hockey supremacy in Canada. Following that, he went overseas and ducked bullets in some of the heaviest fighting of a particularly vicious war at the Somme, Passchendael and Amiens.

Simpson played for the Americans until 1931 and then managed the team until 1935. He became one of New York's most popular professional athletes and was a close friend of Damon Runyon, Dan Parker and others among the city's sporting set. Like many of his teammates, Bullet Joe enjoyed Broadway's night life and once was the butt of an amusing incident at the end of the 1925–26 season.

Those were the days when Big Bill Dwyer's bootleg hooch often would find its way into the Americans' dressing room, with zany results. One such incident took

place after an exhibition match with a touring team from Portland, Oregon. The game took place just prior to the arrival of the Ringling Brothers and Barnum and Bailey Circus at the Garden.

As was normally the case, circus officials moved their animals into the menagerie several days before the show opened and in this instance the floating zoo was located about a hundred feet from the teams' dressing room toward the rear of the arena.

Following the exhibition game with Portland, the Americans were greeted with a case of bootleg booze which Simpson eagerly poured. After a few hearty rounds, Bullet Joe left the dressing room and headed for Broadway. However, he made a wrong turn and walked straight into the menagerie where he was greeted by a trumpeting elephant and several boisterous lions. Incredulous, Simpson wheeled in his tracks and fled to the dressing room where he grabbed Percy Ryan, the Americans' trainer.

"Where in hell did that bad hooch come from?" Joe demanded. "Christ! I could swear I saw a herd of wild elephants out there!"

Simpson was elected to the Hockey Hall of Fame in 1962 long after he had retired to Florida. He suffered a heart attack in the late 1940s and was close to death when rival hockeyist Art Coulter, NHL President Clarence Campbell and Simpson's wife, Grace, helped rally him from the brink.

"I was laid up for two years," Simpson recalled. "I was really down when Art took me in. He gave me a job selling skates in his hardware store, four hours a day.

"It may sound funny, selling skates in Florida, but Coral Gables, at that time, had an arena."

Simpson remained a favorite of friend, foe and the media long after he retired. "Joe," Bill Corum once said, "was the first hockey player I ever knew and remained the favorite of all I have ever known."

Bullet Joe died in December 1973.

56 Marcel Dionne (1971–   )

It always will be the bane of Marcel Dionne's professional athletic life that he never will *really* know how good he could have been as a major-leaguer. From the very moment when he stepped on to National Hockey League rinks as a well-trumpeted rookie in 1971, Dionne has been burdened with mediocre teammates and subpar teams. This, however, has not prevented him from achieving bountiful goals and an assortment of prizes.

He twice won the Lady Byng Trophy for good sportsmanship and high-quality play. He twice was voted to the First All-Star Team at center, and twice was Second Team center. In 1980 he led the NHL in scoring.

Yet, Dionne's biggest challenge—lifting a team to a first-place finish or the Stanley Cup—eluded him in more than a decade of NHL play. Time and again, Marcel would fail in the playoffs and the Kings would make a hasty exit in postseason action. Nevertheless, until the advent of Wayne Gretzky at the start of the 1980s, Dionne was the single most productive center in the league and had been a luminary ever since he made his debut at the beginning of the 1970s.

Marcel completed his rookie season with 28 goals and 49 assists for 77 points, a new NHL record for points in a season by a rookie. Thus, it hardly was surprising that he received a veteran's responsibility.

For inexplicable reasons, Dionne finished a distant third in the voting for the Calder Trophy, given to the NHL's outstanding rookie. Marcel placed behind Buffalo's Richard Martin, who scored 44 goals, and Montreal's goalie-lawyer Ken Dryden. The rejection of Dionne inspired a hail of protest, especially in Detroit.

As a second-year man, Dionne enjoyed an outstanding offensive year, with 40 goals and 50 assists for 90 points. In Marcel's third season irascible Ted Garvin took over as head coach, and instantly there was a personality clash. Garvin accused the young center of loafing, and Dionne responded by demanding to be traded.

By now the troubles were having a telling effect. Dionne slumped off to a disappointing twenty-four-goal year.

The 1974–75 season, Dionne's fourth in the majors, brought yet another head coach, this time former Detroit superstar Alex Delvecchio. But more importantly, it was Marcel's option year—by not signing a new contract, Dionne would be free to go to the team of his choice at the end of the campaign. Knowing this, the Red Wings attempted to make Marcel happy by giving him more responsibility. In a shocking move, Dionne was named team captain.

Playing like the Dionne of old, Marcel had his finest season as a Red Wing, amassing 47 goals and 74 assists for 121 points, placing him behind only Phil Esposito and Bobby Orr in the NHL scoring race.

But the productive campaign failed to erase the scars of bygone years and, once the season ended, Eagleson informed Delvecchio that Dionne would be taking his services elsewhere.

"We offered him a four-year contract for a million—$250,000 per year," said Delvecchio. "But he thinks he can get more money somewhere else. He said he didn't want to play in Detroit anymore. He said 'the name of the game is money' and he thinks he can get more money somewhere else. Personally, I think Dionne is a pretty selfish individual. Now it looks as though what he did for the Red Wings last year was all for himself." And so the big question: who would sign Marcel for 1975–76?

Six teams were in the early running—the Montreal Canadiens, St. Louis Blues, Buffalo Sabres, Toronto Maple Leafs, Los Angeles Kings, and Edmonton Oilers (of the WHA). Dionne's demands were high, as were the Red Wings', who were entitled to compensation from the team that signed Marcel. Ultimately, the Kings, whose owner Jack Kent Cooke had just acquired Kareem Abdul-Jabbar for his basketball Lakers, offered the most money.

The Kings won the bidding war, and surrendered veteran defenseman Terry Harper and rugged forward Dan Maloney to Detroit. Cooke signed Marcel to a five-year, $1.5 million pact.

Although Dionne and Cooke danced cartwheels of joy, Kings Coach Bob Pulford unhappily muttered that the deal was not in the best interests of the club. Under Pulford's disciplined defensive style, the Kings previously had enjoyed an extremely successful season. Los Angeles had the fourth-best won-lost record in the league, and only the Stanley Cup champion Philadelphia Flyers allowed fewer goals. Terry Harper had been the captain of the squad and the leader on defense. Maloney, a muscular winger, could score goals and tend to checking. In Dionne, the Kings were adding a freewheeling player whose style appeared conspicuously out of place in the Kings' system. Coach Pulford worried that Dionne might disrupt his previously sound club, both on and off the ice.

Marcel Elphege Dionne was born August 3, 1951, in Drummondville, Quebec. He required only two years before he began skating on a makeshift rink in his backyard. His parents encouraged young Marcel to play hockey, aware that if he didn't make a career of hockey, he inevitably would spend his life working in the steel mills, like his father.

As a result, the Dionnes saw to it that their son's hockey thirst always was quenched.

When Marcel was fifteen, he had established himself as a professional prospect and he had outgrown Drummondville. It was time for him to move on to the big time and play for the Montreal Junior Canadiens, one of the strongest amateur teams in all Canada.

The move to Montreal also was part of the price of wanting to make it to the pros. Dionne played spectacularly for his new club, and after his rookie season he received an invitation to play for the St. Catherines Ontario Junior A team, a club that had developed and sent such stars as Bobby Hull and Stan Mikita to the majors. Dionne accepted the offer although St. Catherines was in Ontario, where only English was spoken. Since Marcel could only speak French, he had catapulted himself into a very awkward situation.

During his three-year pro apprenticeship at St. Catherines, Marcel established a career Ontario Hockey Association scoring record of 375 points. He attracted attention throughout Canada and NHL clubs scouted the mighty little scoring machine as if they had found a gold mine of goals. In fact, Dionne was so highly regarded that he was selected second in the 1971 NHL amateur draft by the Detroit

Red Wings; only Guy Lafleur of the Canadiens was chosen before Dionne. Desperate for help, the Red Wings expected instant miracles from Marcel. Detroit General Manager Ned Harkness sought a replacement for the legendary Gordie Howe, who had quit the Wings following the 1970–71 season. Dionne hired super-attorney Alan Eagleson to negotiate his contract, and the result was a pact that Eagleson labelled "the best I've ever negotiated for a rookie . . . better even than the original one I negotiated for Bobby Orr with the Boston Bruins."

Along with big money, Dionne received unprecedented attention from the Detroit press and the fans, who expected the kind of results that a six-figure contract suggests.

Consequently Dionne found himself in a pressure-cooker atmosphere before he even put on a Red Wings' uniform. He scored a paltry two goals, and the press promptly needled him.

"It was more difficult in the NHL than I imagined," Dionne says. "There was such a big difference in the style of play; it's so much faster in the majors. I had scoring chances as a rookie, but I just couldn't connect. My teammates told me not to miss on those kind of chances in this league. They are so much quicker and the checking is quicker, and then there is the pressure because here you are playing for money: big money."

Red Wings coach Doug Barkley defended and shielded his prize twenty-year-old rookie. "I'm not disappointed with Marcel," Barkley said at the time. "He's improving with each game. He can skate. He can shoot. He has all the moves. But he must learn the difference between the NHL and junior hockey. And, mark my words, he will!"

Marcel did. His arithmetic is among the best in all NHL history. Dionne had the fastest 500 goals and 1,000 points in league history. He has had six 50-goal seasons and five straight 100-point seasons. At the conclusion of the 1982–83 season he again led the Kings with 56 goals, 51 assists and 107 points. "It's very impressive," said an NHL scout who remembered Dionne as a rookie. "But it would have been even more impressive if he had managed to skate for a champion."

But it was not meant to be; the Kings continued to flounder, and in 1983–84, beset by injuries, Dionne's production "slumped" to 39 goals and 53 assists for 92 points in 66 games.

57 Yvan Cournoyer
(1963–1979)

Speed and guile always have been essential elements in the composition of Montreal Canadiens teams as far back as the early years of this century. Players like Howie Morenz, "The Stratford Flash," Maurice Richard, "The Rocket," and Henri Richard, "The Pocket Rocket," dazzled the foe with their footwork. So, it was not surprising that, when the Canadiens' fortunes were in decline in the early 1960s, the Habitants' high command once again turned to a skater with a special get up and go.

A right wing like Richard, Cournoyer proved to be just the catalyst required by Les Canadiens. During his sixteen-year career in the National Hockey League he played for no fewer than ten Stanley Cup champions and ten first-place teams. He won the Conn Smythe Trophy as the most valuable player in the 1973 playoffs, was a Second All-Star in 1969, 1971, 1972 and 1973 and played for Team Canada when it defeated the Soviet All-Stars during an eight-game tournament in 1972.

Nicknamed "The Roadrunner," Cournoyer offered an accurate shot to complement his speed. "He was a tremendous shooter," said Joe Daley, who played goal for the Pittsburgh Penguins when Cournoyer was terrorizing the opposition. "His slapshot was awfully hard and he had the ability to put the puck high or low with great accuracy."

A product of the Canadiens' farm system, Cournoyer was born in the French-speaking city of Drummondville, Quebec, on November 22, 1943. He played junior-level hockey in Montreal and graduated to full-time work in the National Hockey League after a successful tryout the previous year.

At first Cournoyer was burdened with the rap of being a one-way player and was frequently harangued by his martinet coach, Toe Blake. "I was disappointed," said Cournoyer. "At first, when I came into the league, I thought I'd score anywhere from 15 to 20 goals."

The Montreal brass had patience. They were willing to concede some of Yvan's defensive faults as long as he could develop as a power-play ace; and he did. "For a couple of years after Rocket Richard retired," said Sammy Pollock, then the Canadiens' general manager, "our power play wasn't too good. But Yvan worked well and he developed nicely on right wing."

Although Canadiens' captain Jean Beliveau was in the twilight of his career, Cournoyer provided a spiritual and artistic lift to the aging captain. Beliveau recalled a night in Chicago when Yvan faked a shot, noticed the goalie tense up for the drive, but then circled the defense before relaying the puck to Beliveau. By that time the goaltender was drawn so far out of position Beliveau had little trouble finding an opening.

During the 1968 Stanley Cup finals against the St. Louis Blues, Cournoyer put two enemy defensemen out of action with slapshots on the same shift. After both Al Arbour and Barclay Plager were felled by Yvan's bazooka shots, the puck came back to Cournoyer, who finally shot it past goalie Glenn Hall.

Yvan Serge Cournoyer was born November 22, 1943, in Drummondville, Quebec. When he was fourteen his family moved to Montreal and Yvan eventually won a spot on a team in the suburban community of Lachine. During a game between Lachine and Verdun scouts watched in awe as Yvan orchestrated a rink-length dash culminating in the tying goal with less than a minute remaining in regulation time. When the game went into sudden-death overtime it was Cournoyer who scored the winner.

Cournoyer soon moved up to the powerful Montreal Junior Canadiens where he was coached by Claude Ruel. "Yvan," said Ruel, "had a very special scoring knack. He reminded me in some ways of Maurice Richard, one of the greatest scorers of all time."

The resemblance to Richard was heightened when Cournoyer was promoted to the Canadiens in the 1963–64 season and he scored a goal in his first game. Lacking the physical stature of a Jean Beliveau or the leadership qualities of a Richard, Cournoyer nevertheless became an essential part of the Habs' attack because of his scoring prowess. In the 1973 Stanley Cup playoffs, for example, he scored 15 goals in seventeen playoff games and a total of 25 points, tops in that series.

As Cournoyer reached maturity as a big-leaguer he was labelled "hockey's most promising scoring superstar of the future." Yvan never quite fulfilled that promise. He never led the NHL in scoring but he amply demonstrated that a little man with many skills could play as long and as efficiently as the big men. The miniature Stanley Cups on his mantlepiece underline the Roadrunner's qualifications for *Hockey's 100*.

58 Sid Abel
(1938–1943) (1945–1953)

Sid Abel, the artful center of the Detroit Red Wings' famed "Production Line," along with Gordie Howe and Ted Lindsay, was reflecting back on his good fortune and longevity as a big-leaguer. "I kept telling Gloria to pinch me," he said, referring to what he told his wife during the 1948–49 season. "I felt sure that I was going to wake up someday and find that I had been having a wonderful dream." It was no dream; rather, it was the talent of Sid Abel that made everything happen.

He was as creative a center as he was abrasive. His passes were crisp and accurate and his bodychecks were lusty. His durability fooled those who thought he was over-the-hill.

In 1949 at the age of thirty-one, he blasted the winning goal past Turk Broda of the Toronto Maple Leafs one night. After the game, Broda met Abel in the corridor and shook his head. "What's got into you?" Broda asked, "You found the fountain of youth?"

"I don't know," Abel grinned, "But boy, this is living! Don't ask me what's happening. It just seems that everytime I shoot, I score. And I love it!"

The Abel-Lindsay-Howe line developed into one of the finest lines in hockey history. Abel had the savvy and Howe and Lindsay had a mixture of style and aggression that intimidated their opponents.

Sid was the backbone of the Red Wings. While he played for Detroit, the powerful team won the Prince of Wales Trophy in 1942–43, and then four straight years from 1948–49 to 1951–52. (The trophy is awarded to the team finishing with the most points in the Prince of Wales conference at the end of the regular schedule.)

In 1941–42, Sid was named to the Second Team All-Star at left wing. In 1948–49 and 1949–50 he was named to the First Team All-Star at center. Again in 1950–51 he was named to the Second Team All-Star at center, sharing the honor with Ted Kennedy of the Toronto Maple Leafs. He thusly became the first player ever to win All-Star rating in two different positions.

In 1948–49, while playing in sixty-nine games, Sid was the individual Goal-scoring leader, scoring 28 goals. Most of his goals that year were tying or winning goals, and it was in 1949 that he won the Hart Trophy—emblematic of the player judged to be the most valuable to his team. *Sport Magazine* also bestowed upon him the honor of "Hockey's Man of the Year."

With Sid playing for them, the Red Wings won the Stanley Cup in 1942–43, 1949–50 and 1951–52. They finished first five times, in 1942–43, 1948–49, 1949–50, 1950–51 and 1951–52.

In his thirteen seasons of professional hockey, Sid played in 612 games, scoring 189 goals and 283 assists for a total of 472 points. In ninety-seven playoff games his statistics were 28 goals and 30 assists for a total of 58 points.

The Red Wings' intimidating Production Line was acclaimed as one of the all-time great lines in hockey, and they had the statistics to prove it. In 1948–49 their goal total of 66 ranked as the high mark for any line in the league.

To illustrate how powerful a line they were, during the 1949–50 season, Abel scored 33 goals (finishing third to Rocket Richard with 43, and Howe with 34), and the Production Line swept to new heights as they finished 1-2-3 in the scoring race. Lindsay won the championship with 78 points, Abel had 69, and Gordie was third with 68.

Sid's career was filled with many highlights, including a game against the Boston Bruins. On November 2, 1949, Abel fired three pucks past goalie Jack Gelineau as the Wings beat the Bruins, 5–3. It was the first time he had ever scored a hat trick. "It took me ten years to do it," he cracked, "but is was sure worth the wait."

Sid realized another one of his lifelong ambitions in the 1948–49 season when he scored his 100th goal of his NHL career. It was his 18th goal that year, and the goalie was Turk Broda in a game at the Maple Leaf Gardens. Shortly afterwards, at the age of thirty-one, another one of Sid's dreams came true when he had his first 20-goal season, as he scored 28 goals. That same season he had a total of 54 points, ranking him third in the league.

In the 1949–50 playoffs, the Red Wings had to recover from a 5–0 beating in the first game against Toronto and the loss of the injured Gordie Howe. Sid's leadership finally helped the Red Wings end the Toronto jinx and eliminate the three-time Stanley Cup winners.

It would be Sid's indomitable play that would prove to be the turning point in the championship series with the New York Rangers.

Sidney Gerald Abel was born in Melville, Saskatchewan, on February 22, 1918. Like all of the other youngsters of that area, he played hockey every available moment, wherever there was ice to be found.

Fortunately for Sid, he became the "favorite son" of the postmaster, "Goldie" Smith. Smith was also a scout for the Detroit Red Wings, and had helped discover other great stars in the NHL, including the great Eddie Shore.

The quality that Abel possessed that caught Smith's eye was his earnest approach to the game. Just like Smith's other protégés before him, Sid had drive and tenacity of purpose, and this impressed Goldie so much that he invited Abel to visit the Red Wings' training camp in the fall of 1937.

Abel reported to manager Jack Adams. Adams took one look at this slim, 155 pound, 5'11" westerner and out at the intense practice session that was taking place out on the ice. Adams felt sure that this young man would never stand up under the battering of the pro game. Still, Adams was impressed with Sid. He suggested that Sid stay in Detroit and play in the Michigan-Ontario area. Abel gratefully declined the offer.

He told Adams that he would be going back to his home to play for the Flin Flon team and for Goldie Smith. With that, the young man turned, and went back home.

Sid Abel played left wing for the Flin Flon Bombers of Manitoba during the winter of 1937. They enjoyed a fine season, and ended up as finalists in the Western Canada playdowns for the Allan Cup. Abel was thought to have been one of the better players on the team, but he felt that his performance that year was only mediocre. Upon his return to Melville, he met a very excited Goldie Smith.

"We're in, Sid," Smith excitedly told Abel, "The Detroit Wings want to sign a contract with you!" Abel was stunned, as he felt that he had not had a good season. "Sign me—what for?" was his reply.

The two men excitedly examined the contract. Then on June 25, 1938, only a few short weeks later, Sid was stunned by the shocking news that his friend Goldie had died. With Goldie gone, Abel suddenly felt alone. Sadly, Sid reported to the Wings' training camp. Goldie had discovered his last star.

In 1938, the Red Wings' camp was in the process of rebuilding. There were almost sixty youngsters, all with hopes that they could make the team. Sid was nervous until he happened to overhear Adams say, "If he can stand up to the rugged going, young Abel is our best bet for the future."

Sid was sent down to the Pittsburgh Hornets that season. He played under Larry Aurie (former Red Wing star) and scored 21 goals, adding 24 assists for 45 points. Occasionally during the season he would be called up to join the Red Wings.

Sid played the next season with the Red Wings. However, he began to think Adams' initial fears might become reality. He was injured smashing into an opponent and broke his shoulder. When he recovered from that injury, he was sent down to the Indianapolis farm team.

But Abel's tenacity on the ice soon had him back on the parent club. It was from that point on that Sid improved his playing ability at left wing and at center ice.

In 1942–43 his natural ability for leadership saw him elected captain of the Red Wings, and Detroit went on to beat the Bruins in four straight games to win the Stanley Cup.

The war was on and Sid saw many of his friends leaving to join the armed forces. At the end of the 1943 season, Sid joined the Royal Canadian Air Force, and in doing so, left a void in the Red Wings' club.

In February 1946, Sid returned to hockey. He was twenty-eight years of age, and he found it was difficult picking up from where he left off. The younger players were fresher than ever, and the game was now so much faster due to the "red-line" pass, a wartime innovation.

In 1946–47, back at center ice, Sid was tried with many wing combinations, but mainly played with Lindsay and Pete Horeck. Abel had to force himself to keep up with the young men's pace. He practiced skating and strategy for long hours until he caught up with the new "modern" game.

Sid again became the spark plug for Detroit. "Old Bootnose" suddenly found himself scoring goals again. That year he scored 19 goals and had 29 assists for 48 points. The hours he had spent adjusting to the new style of hockey were well spent. What a comeback he had achieved!

The next season (1949–50), Old Bootnose again rose like the phoenix. Skating effortlessly, he swept between Ted and Gordie, passing and scoring as though he were a rookie. In one of the great thrills in sport, Captain Sid Abel helped the Red Wings beat the Rangers and brought the Stanley Cup back to the Olympia.

In 1952–53, Sid Abel was released from the Wings to become player-coach of the Chicago Black Hawks. The Black Hawks were a pathetic team, a team that had finished last in five out of six previous seasons. It was yet another challenge for Sid Abel to conquer.

Sid turned the club around. His spirited play at center, along with the incredible goaltending of Al Rollins, helped the Black Hawks into the playoffs. They almost beat the Canadiens in the semifinal, but lost the series in the seventh and final game.

Abel returned to Detroit, becoming the coach of the Red Wings in January 1958. He remained at that position until 1962–63 when he became the Red Wings' general manager. Despite the fact that Abel and Jack Adams were at odds with each other,

Sid remained with Detroit in one way or another through part of the 1970–71 season.

In 1971–72 Sid signed to coach the St. Louis Blues. That was a mistake from the beginning. He was named general manager of the Blues in October 1971, and stayed until April 17, 1973, when he was named general manager of the Kansas City Scouts. As a manager-coach, Sid never did enjoy the success he had achieved as a player. In 1976 he left hockey to become a broadcaster for Detroit.

Few centers have been more productive than Sid in the vital areas. He was a dogged and creative playmaker, the cog in the wheel with Howe and Lindsay. In 1969, Sid was elected to hockey's Hall of Fame in recognition of all he accomplished during his career.

"Sid," said hockey historian Ed Fitkin, "will go down in the Red Wings' history as the greatest competitor and inspirational force the Red Wings ever had."

59 Johnny Bower (1953–1970)

He had been called the "ageless wonder." Playing in the goal, the position that is generally thought to be the most dangerous and demanding job in all of sports, Johnny Bower of the Toronto Maple Leafs was well into his forties and was still a first-string goaltender, even though by athletic standards, he should have been well past his prime.

Playing in the nets has driven younger men into early retirement, the demands on their bodies are so great. Physical injuries notwithstanding, the goaltender must also carry the psychological burden of knowing that if he makes a mistake, it often shows up on the scoreboard. Still, Bower continued to play at an age when other men were entering their middle years.

Many felt that without Bower in the nets, the resurgence of the Leafs may never have taken place. He was the key to their success. He joined the club when they were in last place in 1958. Since he took over goalkeeping for them, Toronto was in the playoffs for nine straight years from 1958–1967, and again in 1968–69, and he led them to win four Stanley Cup championships.

Johnny played on a Toronto team with some fine players, including Red Kelly, Tim Horton, Carl Brewer and Frank Mahovlich, but he was the essential cog of their Cup-winning teams.

Bower claimed he was born November 8, 1924, but there has been a great deal of speculation on that. On three different occasions when he had been hospitalized due to hockey-related injuries, he gave three different birthdays. "I've lied about my age so often that I've forgotten how old I really am," he joked.

Regardless of how old he really was, Bower was a wonder in the world of hockey. He was still sprawling to stop shots, kicking deftly at pucks; he was alert and agile. Remarkably enough, he had the reflexes of a much younger man.

Bower would defend his goal with short, desperate moves from side to side, bent in his familiar crouch, bulky and alert. He played every workout, every game, like he was playing the seventh game of a Stanley Cup final.

When Bower joined the Leafs, they soared from last place to make the playoffs in 1958–59, only to lose in the finals to Montreal. In 1959–60 they again made the finals, again losing to the Flying Frenchmen. In 1961–62 they won the Cup for the first time in eleven years. In fact, while Bower guarded the net for the Leafs they won the Stanley Cup four times—in 1961–62, 1962–63 (finishing first), 1963–64 and 1966–67.

Bower was such a superb competitor that he never complained over the many injuries he suffered. Injuries would not stop him. He suffered broken ribs when he was shoved into the iron goalposts; a skate blade gashed against his jaw, ripping out a tooth and requiring thirty-two stitches; all of his teeth had been knocked out, and once, while diving for a puck, a stick wedged under his tongue.

Standing 5'9" and weighing 188 pounds, Johnny's face is carved with lines—some curved, some jagged—all healed scars from cuts inflicted by skates, sticks, and pucks. He estimates that he has had over 200 stitches on his face alone just to close the facial cuts he has received.

He enjoyed a fine career, both in the minor leagues and the NHL. At Providence, Johnny's club won the Calder Cup and he was chosen for the AHL's All-Star Team. He was also named Athlete of the Year, which he considered to be one of the highlights of his career. In fact, he won the AHL's Most Valuable Player Award three times, and the Outstanding Goalie Award. He was also named best goalie the one season he played in the WHL.

In 1960–61 he played in fifty-eight games, had two shutouts for a 2.50 average. He was elected to the First Team All-Stars that year and subsequently won the Vezina Trophy.

Bower continued his fine playing in the 1964–65 season when he played in thirty-four games and had three shutouts for a 2.38 average. That year he also won the Vezina Trophy, this time sharing it with his teammate Terry Sawchuk.

Johnny Bower played thirteen seasons in which he played in 552 games and had thirty-seven shutouts for a 2.52 average. His playoff statistics included seventy-four games (five shutouts), for a 2.54 average.

John William Bower was born in Prince Albert, Saskatchewan, on November 8, 1924. Growing up in the middle of the Depression, Johnny knew what it meant to be poor. His first pair of goalie pads were fashioned from an old mattress, and his stick was cut from a branch with a suitable bend.

Bower received his first pair of skates from a player from a senior team. He was ten years old at the time and the skates were much too big for him. Glad to even have a pair of skates, he said, "I worshipped those skates even if I couldn't get used to them." Bower ended up playing in the nets because it was the one position in hockey where you didn't have to have skates.

Bower spent two years with the Canadian army during World War II. Receiving a medical discharge in 1943, he returned to Canada. He was still eligible for junior hockey. He played for Prince Albert that season. Other teams in the league questioned how a man who served two years overseas could still be of junior age. But his birth certificate could not be found (and still hasn't been found to this day), and he was allowed to finish the season.

Bower turned pro in 1945, signing with the Cleveland Barons of the American Hockey League. He played well for eight seasons, but in relative obscurity. At that time there were only six goalie jobs in the NHL, and it was difficult to rise quickly from the minors.

In 1953 Johnny Bower got his chance, as the New York Rangers obtained him. Gump Worsley, then the Rangers' goalie said, "We thought he was an old man then, and that was nearly fifteen years ago." Worsley had been rookie of the year the season before, but Bower won the job away from him.

The Rangers failed to make the playoffs that year, through no fault of Bower. He gave up only 2.60 goals a game and had five shutouts. Still, the next season Bower was replaced by Worsley and he was shipped off to Vancouver of the Western Hockey League. From there he was sent off to Providence of the American League, and finally wound up back in Cleveland in 1957.

Bower might have remained in the minors had it not been for Lady Luck. The Maple Leafs had finished in last place during the 1957–58 season for the first time in the history of the club. Billy Reay, who was the coach at that time, was searching for a new goalkeeper. He was going to sign Al Rollins (who was playing for Calgary in the WHL), but on the night that he was scouting Rollins, Al had an off-night. Reay then decided to sign Bower, who was his second choice. Reay bought Johnny for $10,000 and a junior player.

However, Bower was undecided as to whether or not he wanted to go to Toronto. He was very happy in Cleveland, and he didn't think he could help the Maple Leafs. However, the Leafs offered him a large, two-year contract, and he was persuaded to sign.

Johnny Bower was almost thirty-four years old when he was rescued from the obscurity of the minor leagues. He battled goalie Ed Chadwick for the job for a few months, and then Chadwick was sent to the minors.

Unfortunately, Reay never saw the benefits of his move of signing Bower, as he was fired midway through the season and Punch Imlach took over. Reay's signing of Bower ended up making Imlach look like a genius.

In 1964 Bower once again led the Leafs to championship heights. He had the lowest goals-against average in the league (2.12). Bower was unbeatable when tension was at its highest, and he finished up an incredible season by shutting out the Detroit Red Wings, 4–0, in the seventh and deciding game of the Stanley Cup finals.

In 1964, Johnny won the J. P. Bickell Memorial Cup, emblematic of the Maple Leaf's most valuable player. It was the second time he received that honor, having won it in 1960.

In 1964–65, the Maple Leafs obtained Terry Sawchuk from the Detroit Red Wings to share the goaltending chores with Johnny. Most athletes, with their enormous egos, would have been devastated if their team picked up a player of Sawchuk's ability. Johnny Bower didn't resent it. "I just can't play seventy games," he said at the time. "We need two goalies, and Terry is a great one. I'm glad he's with us."

In 1966, Bower played in only twenty-seven games due to injuries, caused mainly by pulled muscles. In 1967, when he was forty-five years old, Bower was still doing workouts every day. "Of course, I get tired in those two-a-day workouts," he admitted, "but I know if I'm tired then I've been working hard. That's how I stay in shape."

After the 1966–67 season, Bower had to face the threat of expansion and the fact that Toronto might not protect him. But he was not yet ready to retire. The Leafs in fact did keep him, instead letting Sawchuk go to the Los Angeles Kings.

"When hockey's no longer fun, it's time to quit," Bower once remarked. The fun went out of it for Johnny Bower when constant injuries made him feel "painful muscles I didn't know I had." In 1970 Johnny Bower retired from hockey.

He would join the Leafs' scouting staff as their chief eastern scout and would also coach their goaltenders. Johnny was also a partner in ownership of a resort hotel in Prince Albert, having bought it with the money he had made from his thriving hamburger business.

In 1976, this remarkable goaltender was elected to hockey's Hall of Fame. King Clancy remarked, "Of all the people who are in the Hall of Fame, there is none more worthy than Johnny Bower. He is one of the most honest and conscientious hockey players I've ever met. He is in a class by himself as a person. During my fifty-four years of association with the game, I have seen few better hockey players."

Johnny Bower was a fiercely competitive man who often played wracked with pain. He went all-out whether it was workouts, games, or Stanley Cup competition. Bower was agile and ageless and he enjoyed a career of incredible accomplishments. Whether he was forty-six or fifty when he retired, it did not matter. He belongs in *Hockey's 100*.

60 Ken Dryden
(1971-1973) (1974-1979)

The pose was the person.

More than any of his many dazzling moves in the nets for the Montreal Canadiens, goaltender Ken Dryden will be vividly remembered most for his posture in the crease when the hail of enemy shots had desisted. Big number 29 would dig the tip of his stick into the ice and fold his arms across the knob, coolly relaxing until the action resumed. Uncharacteristic of the nervous and beleaguered sort that is the stereotypical goalie, Dryden was as cool and confident inside as he appeared on the outside.

In the late 1960s and early 70s, Montreal was far from a likely setting for a rookie goaltender to make a spectacular entrance; the Canadiens were stockpiled with talent to the envy of the rest of the NHL. It was standard operating procedure with the Habs for freshmen to serve a lengthy apprenticeship on the bench before being thrown into the fray. But after being called up from the Montreal Voyageurs of the American Hockey League in the spring of 1971, Ken Dryden made proponents of the "sit before you skate" theory blush.

After watching his first game from the press box, Dryden played six regular-season games and was impressive in allowing only nine goals. But many hockey people thought the Canadiens were merely throwing Dryden a bone—a couple of games of NHL experience—as they ran through the end of their schedule. The playoffs lurked just around the bend and veteran Rogie Vachon was expected to tend the twines in the postseason. No one thought they would ever go with a rookie at such a crucial point. No one, that is, except Voyageurs coach Floyd Curry. He recalled: "I told Sammy Pollock when he took Dryden from us that he had just assured himself of the Stanley Cup. He was that good."

Coach Curry's praises notwithstanding, the Habs' choice to go with their rookie in the opening round of the playoffs against the defending Cup champion Boston Bruins rocked the hockey world. Throwing a twenty-four-year-old rookie against the Orr- and Esposito-led Bruins was likened to sending David with one arm tied behind his back against Goliath. It was not long, however, before it became obvious that this rookie played with the composure and guile of a hardened veteran.

In the see-saw, seven-game series, the Montrealers prevailed, led by Dryden's one spectacular save after another. His performance left the Bruins slamming their sticks against the boards and glancing toward the heavens in hope of some sort of divine intervention.

Propelled by their mammoth upset of the Beantowners, the Canadiens dispatched the Minnesota North Stars in six and the Chicago Black Hawks in seven games to annex the Cup. And it is hard to believe any of it could have been possible without the standout performance of Dryden. Through twenty playoff games, he compiled a 3.00 goals-against average and was awarded the Conn Smythe Trophy as the most valuable player of the playoffs. This, with merely six games of NHL experience under his pads.

Instantly, experts began comparing Dryden to past goaltending greats. At 6'4", Dryden reminded observers of another tall Canadien goalie of the 1940s—the expertly ambidextrous Bill Durnan. "The way Ken gets in front of shots to make impossible saves," said Habs captain Henri Richard, "he's a lot like Durnan used to be. Dryden murders you with surprise moves from seemingly impossible positions. It's great for a defenseman or a forward to know he's behind you."

As impressive as Dryden's playoff record was in 1971, his 3.00 goals-against average was to be the most permissive digit of his career, regular season or playoffs. In 1971–72, the big fellow became the workhorse in the Montreal nets by playing sixty-four games with a 2.24 goals-against, good enough to earn him the Calder Trophy as outstanding rookie of the year. Dryden thus became the first player to ever be named the MVP of the playoffs before proving himself the best rookie in the league.

Dryden became the model of consistency the following season by working fifty-four games between the pipes, compiling a 2.25 goals-against average and walking away with his third major award in less than three seasons, this time the Vezina Trophy for the best goals-against average.

Although performing at the top of his sport, Ken Dryden was never mistaken for a one-dimensional jock type. Wire-rimmed spectacles, long hair and mod style of dress separated the young star from his peers almost as much as his semiintellectual personality. A graduate of Cornell University and McGill Law School, Dryden was as unpredictable in his career decisions as he was consistent in the nets for the Canadiens.

By 1973 it appeared as though the sky would be the limit for the young netminder. He had reached the peak of his game and seemed a fixture at the Forum. But then he dropped his bombshell. Prior to the 1973–74 season, Dryden announced that, at the age of twenty-six, he was retiring from hockey to accept a job "articling" for the Toronto law firm of Osler, Hoskin and Harcourt for the sniveling salary of $7,500 a year. At this, the collective jaw of Montreal dropped in amazement.

Dryden had never been secretive of his desires to pursue a career in law and if worse came to worst, would be prepared to sacrific hockey for the rigors of the courtroom. With the Canadiens, Dryden had been earning a modest salary despite enormous appeal and proven ability. He believed he deserved more money, a salary equal to his standing as one of the best goaltenders in the NHL.

The Canadiens, however, would not budge and Dryden departed. For that season the Habs struggled with three goaltenders to no avail, being bounced from playoff competition in the first round by the Rangers. A few hundred miles west of the Forum, Dryden worked diligently at his profession and enrolled with an industrial league team where he played defense.

After considerable haggling and finally give and take by both parties, Dryden and the Canadiens came to terms. He rejoined the team for the 1974–75 campaign and found that kicking around the industrial league had done little to keep him on top of his game. He struggled some and wound up with what would be his highest regular season goals-against average of his career, 2.69. The Canadiens again did not reach the Cup finals and the masses buzzed with speculation over the future of their once-prized goaltender.

From the 1975–76 season until his retirement in 1979 Ken Dryden was absolutely outstanding, a goaltender nonpareil in the NHL. His personal statistics, in addition to the fact that the Canadiens earned four consecutive Stanley Cups during that period, is testament to the excellence of both the team and its goaltender.

In the four years of Dryden's dominance, his GA average climbed never higher than 2.30 in 1978–79 and reached its miniscule low of 2.03 in 1975–76. Between those years he enjoyed his finest season in 1976–77; fifty-six games, 10 shutouts, 2.14 GA average for the regular season. In the playoffs, fourteen games, 4 shutouts and an invisible 1.56 GA average.

Kenneth Wayne Dryden was born August 8, 1947, in Hamilton, Ontario. During his career, in addition to the Calder and Smythe Trophies, he received the Vezina one time himself and shared it with Michel Larocque three other times; he was named First Team All-Star five times and Second Team All-Star on one occasion. As an example of Dryden's exceptional ability to handle the puck after making the save, he accumulated nineteen regular season and four playoff assists.

Apparently at the top of his game, Dryden suddenly called it quits—for good this time—after the 1979 season. Just four years later, he was named to the Hockey Hall of Fame.

In a brief career Dryden helped the Canadiens to six Stanley Cups and it is not a coincidence that Montreal has been Cup-less since their last Dryden-led team won it in 1979. His mettle in the clutch separated Ken Dryden from his peers more than his exceptional size and personality. The combination of all his abilities made him distinctive enough to be ranked here among *Hockey's 100* as one of the finest goaltenders ever to roam a crease in the NHL.

61 Jack Adams
(1917–1927)

Because he is best remembered as a dynasty-builder with the Detroit Red Wings of the 1940s and 1950s, Jack Adams is not known as the superlative player he was. In fact, Adams was inducted into the Hockey Hall of Fame as a player in 1959. So diverse were his talents that Adams was one of the few men to savor Stanley Cup triumph as player, coach and general manager.

"Adams' name," wrote columnist Red Smith, "was the greatest in hockey in the United States."

His name also was one of the greatest in his native Canada as well. Adams helped the Toronto Arenas down the Vancouver Millionaires for the Stanley Cup in 1918 and then left when he was twenty to play for Frank Patrick's Vancouver club.

Between scoring goals for Patrick, Adams watched and listened carefully as his boss would explain the operation of a hockey club. More than four decades later, Adams would say: "Managing a hockey club is easy, if you've been properly educated. I had the best teacher in the world: Frank Patrick."

Conversely, in Adams Patrick had one of the best centers in the world. After joining Patrick's Millionaires, Adams won the scoring title with 24 goals and 18 assists in twenty-four games. Adams soon was joined by another brilliant youngster, Frank Boucher, and together they made the Vancouver club the envy of their eastern rivals. Adams was lured back to Toronto in 1922, playing for the St. Pats. He moved on to the Ottawa Senators in 1926 and became part of an NHL powerhouse.

His teammates included King Clancy, Frank Nighbor, George Boucher, Cy Denneny, Frank Finnegan and Alex Connell. Adams regarded that season as the apex of his playing career as the Senators won the Stanley Cup.

John J. Adams was born June 14, 1895, in Fort William, Ontario, a hockey hotbed. The son of a locomotive engineer, Adams earned a dollar here and a dollar there until he had enough cash to buy a pair of skates. With his new blades, he became a "rink rat" scraping the ice to get free skating time. At fifteen, he left high school to work in the grain elevators.

"I was a skinny kid," said Adams, "and I worked ten hours a day for twenty-two cents an hour. But that wasn't for me. I wanted to see the world. I moved to Calumet, Michigan, to play in the Northern Michigan Senior Hockey League—a real blood-and-thunder deal."

He was a mere 166-pound sixteen-year-old, playing against husky adults who had no pity on the kid. One bruiser laid Jack out so viciously that he was carted off to the hospital for repairs. By sheer coincidence his sister was on duty at the time and, at first, did not recognize her battered brother. She later offered him some kernels of advice: "Jack, hockey will kill you if you don't quit—and it's changing you."

Jack learned to fight back and never had to worry about being intimidated. His loathing of losing eventually became legendary, first as a player, then as a coach and finally as a manager. He once said he was the hardest loser ever born.

After starring for Ottawa's Stanley Cup winners, Adams seized the opportunity to become coach and manager of Detroit's year-old team. In time he would become an institution in the Motor City. As coach he got his name on three Stanley Cups. After turning over the coaching job to Tommy Ivan in 1947, he produced four more championship teams.

Adams was responsible for many a superstar making it to the majors but his most significant discovery was Gordie Howe, who previously had been rejected by the New York Rangers. "Y'know," Adams recalled, "I almost missed the bus on Howe. He said to me one day 'Mister Adams, I'd like one of those windbreakers the Red Wings wear.' I said 'Okay, son. I'll get you one.' Then it promptly slipped my mind. Next fall at training camp I decided I wanted him to turn pro and I offered him a contract. He looked at it but he didn't sign it. So I asked him what was wrong, wasn't it enough money? He just looked at me and said 'I'm not sure I want to sign with your organization, Mister Adams. You don't keep your word.'

"Naturally, I was flabbergasted, and I asked him what he meant. 'Well,' he said, 'you promised me a windbreaker and you never gave it to me.' You can imagine how quickly I apologized . . . and how quickly I got that windbreaker. But that's how close I came to losing him."

With Howe leading the way, the Red Wings ripened into one of the National Hockey League's most powerful units. The 1951–52 club, which became the first team to win the Stanley Cup in eight straight games, was regarded by Adams as his greatest machine.

By the start of the 1960s Adams's dynasty began crumbling and he was finally retired on full salary in 1962, a move that he bitterly contested. But he stayed close to the game he loved and was named president of the Central Professional Hockey League, a job he retained until he collapsed at his desk and died of a heart attack on May 1, 1968.

When news of his death reached the hockey world his longtime foe, Frank Selke, Sr., noted: "Jack was a tough competitor. He was everyone's enemy during a game and a good friend after it was over. He helped build hockey to what it is from the horse-and-buggy days."

He was a winner on the ice, behind the bench and in the front office. As such, he belongs among *Hockey's 100*.

62 Dit Clapper
(1927–1947)

Bobby Orr, Eddie Shore and Milt Schmidt rank among the most revered of the Boston Bruins but close behind in the hearts of Hub hockey fans who remember the team prior to World War II is the elegant and versatile Dit Clapper.

Clapper left his imprint in many ways. He was the first National Hockey League player to last in the majors for twenty full seasons—*and all of them with the same team*. He starred as a right wing for the first nine years of his career and then reverted to defense where he proved no less adept with the puck.

As a forward he was a Second Team All-Star in 1931 and 1935. As a defenseman he was a First All-Star in 1939, 1940 and 1941 and a Second All-Star in 1944. His championship dossier includes three Stanley Cups and six first-place teams.

Although Clapper preferred the role of pacifist his temper occasionally boiled out of proportion to his character. His most notorious eruption took place during a game with the Montreal Maroons. An opponent named Dave Trottier jammed the butt end of his stick into Clapper's face. Normally this would have resulted in a penalty but referee Clarence Campbell (who eventually became president of the National Hockey League) failed to detect the foul play.

Clapper took the law into his own hands and jumped Trottier, whereupon Campbell skated to the scene of the crime. "Clapper," said the referee, "you're a dirty sonofabitch!"

The accusation was doubly surprising to Clapper because everyone in the NHL realized that the distinguished Campbell was a Rhodes Scholar and not given to profanity.

"What did you say?" demanded Clapper.

"I said you're a dirty sonofabitch," he repeated. Instead of leaving bad enough alone, Clapper followed up his tirade with a right cross to Campbell's head, sending the referee staggering back into the arms of the pleased players.

The act of punching out a referee was considered severe enough to warrant a long-term suspension. Instead, NHL President Frank Calder slapped a $100 fine on Clapper and a mild tongue-lashing.

Pressed as to why the punishment was so light, Calder revealed that he had received a report from referee Campbell which tended to shift the blame away from Clapper.

"I was talking loud," Campbell admitted, "when I should have been throwing them into the penalty box."

Clapper is best remembered for his gallant efforts as a forward and a defenseman, not to mention his Beau Brummel appearance. With his hair impeccably parted down the middle, Dit dressed meticulously and exuded class. He was the same way on the ice. *The Canadian Press* in describing Clapper noted that he was "the Jean Beliveau of his day," a reference to the classic Montreal Canadiens center of the 1950s, 1960s and early 1970s. Today, Clapper would be compared to Wayne Gretzky.

Aubrey Victor Clapper was born February 9, 1907, at Newmarket, Ontario. After playing amateur hockey in the communities surrounding his home, he showed enough promise to earn a contract with the Bruins in 1927 when Art (Uncle Arthur) Ross was constructing one of the strongest teams to grace NHL ice.

Within two years of his debut, Clapper had outshown virtually every forward in the league. During the 1929–30 campaign—his most productive—Clapper totalled 41 goals and 20 assists for 61 points in a forty-four game schedule. (That was the one season in which the league allowed forward passing from zone to zone.)

Dit, of course, did not work alone. He was fortunate to be aligned with the gifted center Cooney Weiland and left wing Norman (Dutch) Gainor to form what was to become "The Dynamite Trio," a gallant and effective scoring unit.

Clapper once recalled that his 1st goal—scored but ten seconds into his first shift —and his 200th goal, which was the winner in a game against Toronto at Maple Leaf Gardens in 1942, were his most memorable.

Many hockey critics regard the 1941 Bruins team, on which Clapper was a defenseman, as one of the most powerful in history. That Boston club won the Stanley Cup with Frankie (Mister Zero) Brimsek in goal and The Kraut Line of Milt Schmidt, Woody Dumart and Bobby Bauer spearheading the attack.

During Clapper's final seasons with the Bruins he assisted Ross with the coaching chores and then took over as the full-time coach after retiring in 1947. He gave up coaching after two seasons and retired to Peterborough, Ontario, where he made an unsuccessful run as a Liberal candidate in a federal election.

Although he was away from the NHL scene in retirement, Clapper continued to follow the professional game. When Bobby Orr began starring for the Bruins in the late 1960s comparisons were made by the experts who rated the stars of different eras. When Orr surpassed Clapper's lifetime mark of 228 goals and 248 assists Dit never pouted but, rather, toasted the lad from Parry Sound, Ontario.

Dit was so enthralled with Orr's Bruins that, in April 1970, he returned to Boston at his own expense to see if the Bruins could win their first Stanley Cup in twenty-nine years.

"I'm looking forward to drinking champagne out of that Cup," Clapper enthused. "It's been such a long time."

The Bruins obliged by winning the Cup and Dit returned to his home a happy man. The Boston club retired his number 5 jersey along with his shoulder pads and, to this day, his name remains one of the most revered in Boston sports. He died January 20, 1978, long after being inducted into the Hockey Hall of Fame.

At the time of Clapper's death *The Canadian Press,* in a long and glowing obituary, stated that Dit was "one of the NHL's all-time greats." And that he was, on the attack as well as on defense: a worthy member of *Hockey's 100.*

63 Eddie Gerard
(1914–1923)

In the spring of 1922 the Toronto St. Patricks and Vancouver Maroons met in the Stanley Cup finals. Under professional hockey's loosely interpreted rules of the day it was possible for an undermanned team to "borrow" a player from a club which had been eliminated from contention.

Harry Cameron, a stalwart on the St. Pats defense, had taken sick and Toronto replaced him with Eddie Gerard of the Ottawa Senators. Gerard already had played for the Senators' Stanley Cup winners in 1920 and 1921.

Gerard performed so nobly and was so instrumental in providing Toronto with two victories in a best-of-five series that was tied at two apiece that Frank Patrick, boss of the Maroons, refused to permit Gerard to play in the fifth and final game. Nevertheless, the St. Pats won the game and the Cup.

During the postgame festivities Charlie Querrie, who operated the St. Pats, shook Gerard's hand. "You were great, just great," said Querrie. "What do you think I should pay you for playing for us?"

Gerard looked up at the Toronto manager and smiled. "Forget it," said Gerard, ever the sportsman. "I don't want a penny. This was as much fun as I've had all year."

Fun was an intrinsic element in Gerard's game, ever since he was discovered by Frank Shaughnessy, manager and coach of the Ottawa Senators, just before the outbreak of World War I.

As a member of the Senators, Gerard blossomed into one of the outstanding defensemen in the game. "He was the greatest defenseman I ever played with or against," said Hall of Famer Sprague Cleghorn.

Gerard and Cleghorn provided Ottawa with a formidable defense combination. "The two of them," Montreal *Star* columnist Baz O'Meara once said, "may have been the greatest defense formation of all time."

Difficult as it may be to imagine, Cleghorn and Gerard, though they worked regularly in tandem night in and night out, rarely spoke to each other. "Gerard," O'Meara once revealed, "didn't always like Sprague's freewheeling way. It was long after they were through with their playing days that Sprague rushed up to Gerard one day on a golf course, offered his hand and said, 'Eddie, let's not be foolish any longer. You were the greatest player on defense I ever played with.'"

Gerard took Cleghorn's proffered hand, and returned, "You were pretty good, too."

Edward Gerard was born February 22, 1890, in Ottawa, and as a teenager was equally brilliant at hockey, football, baseball, cricket and aquatics. He played hockey for the Ottawa New Edinburghs. It was then that Shaughnessy discovered him and decided to approach him with a big-league hockey contract.

Shaughnessy found Gerard difficult to sign and, finally, enlisted the aid of Frank Ahearn, an up-and-coming sports tycoon. Ahearn sorted out fifteen crisp $100 bills and suggested that Shaughnessy try that out on Gerard when next they spoke.

After nine extraordinary years in the majors Gerard hung up his skates, but not before he played for four Stanley Cup winners. In 1925 he became manager of the newly organized Montreal Maroons, and a year later led them to the Stanley Cup as coach and manager.

Gerard left the Maroons to become general manager of the New York Americans in 1929. One of his first—and most important—moves was acquiring defenseman Red Dutton. He dealt Lionel Conacher to Montreal for the redhead who emerged as a vital leader needed by the Amerks, and also obtained Hap Emms in the deal.

The Americans were owned by bootlegger Big Bill Dwyer at the time and thought nothing of partaking of the boss's product. In Gerard's first year with the Americans his club was struggling for a playoff berth when Dwyer invited several players to his horse farm in New Jersey. Not surprisingly, the players soon were more enthralled with the booze than the thoroughbreds. After downing considerable Jersey Lightning—the Amerks' name for Dwyer's product—they thought it would be a good idea to race some of his steeds. George Patterson, a first-rate forward, took his jockey act too far, fell off the horse and broke an arm. Gerard learned that Patterson was lost for the season.

Gerard returned to the Maroons in 1932 and two years later moved to the St. Louis Eagles but had to forsake the job because of illness. He died on December 8, 1937, of a throat ailment, at the age of forty-seven. "He was," said Baz O'Meara, who knew him well, "a natural athlete."

64 Bill Mosienko
(1941–1955)

It has been mistakenly assumed that a truly unique performance on one night in the fourteen-year major league career of Bill Mosienko assured his entrance into the Hockey Hall of Fame.

On the night of March 23, 1952, the man they called Wee Willie *singlehandedly scored three goals within a space of twenty-one seconds.* Nobody is expected to duplicate the feat as long as professional hockey is played.

Yet, Mosienko had more than that one-night stand. He was a remarkably agile right wing who played all his hockey for the Chicago Black Hawks and, often, was the sole redeeming feature on an otherwise awful Windy City franchise.

For better or worse, though, all of Mosienko's accomplishments—including his Lady Byng Trophy win in 1945—have been overshadowed by the game, as Mosienko put it, "when I caught lightning in a beer bottle."

Mosienko had 28 goals prior to the final game of the 1951–52 season against the New York Rangers at Madison Square Garden. In those days, reaching the 30-goal mark was the equivalent of batting .325 in baseball.

The Black Hawks, who were locked into last place, had little motivation other than professional pride. The Rangers, who were guaranteed a fifth-place finish, simply wanted to end the campaign with a win before the few thousand fans sprinkled throughout the Garden for the finale.

Since the Rangers' regular goalie, Chuck Rayner, had been bedeviled with injuries and New York's backup netminder, Emile Francis, also was sidelined, the Black Hawks found themselves up against a virtual unknown guarding the home team's goal.

Crew-cut Lorne Anderson had been a varsity netminder for the New York Rovers, the Rangers' farm team in the Eastern League. He had played only two games in the NHL but was young and promising enough to be given another examination by the Rangers' brass. What better time than the final game—against the subterranean Chicago sextet. "We scored the first goal off him in forty-four seconds but after that for two periods he looked good," said Mosienko.

Mosienko, who was thirty at the time, still had good feet and was skating on a line with two of the few other competents on the team—Gus Bodnar, the center, and George Gee, the left wing. After five minutes of the third period the Hawks were floundering.

"It looked like we were headed for a beating when our coach, Ebbie Goodfellow, sent our line back on the ice," said Mosienko. "There was a face-off and Bodnar won the draw. He got me the puck in center ice."

The Rangers had Hy Buller on defense. He was a Second Team All-Star, the best the New Yorkers had at the time but he apparently had concealed an injury in order to play that night.

"When Bodnar got me the puck," said Mosienko, "I took off and went in around Buller. That left me one on one with the goalie. I got off a low wrist shot, along the ice, and it went in on the right side."

As soon as the puck bulged the white twine behind Anderson the elated Mosienko practically dove into the net after the rubber. The slim crowd was unsure why the visiting player was so anxious to retrieve the puck.

"It was my 29th goal," Mosienko explained, "and I didn't expect to get another. I figured that since I was so close to a milestone—30 goals—I might as well save the puck. I skated back to the bench and handed it to the coach. The time was 6:09 of the third period."

Goodfellow decided to keep his big line on the ice. It was now 6–3 Rangers and, who knew, maybe his Hawks would get hot. "Bodnar won the draw again," said Goodfellow, "and sent the puck to Mosie at the blue line. He was really flying."

For the zephyrlike Black Hawk it was like déjà-vu. Once again he was confronted by defenseman Buller and he outflanked the Ranger as easily as he had the first time, and zeroed in on the suddenly beleaguered Anderson.

"I had him all to myself," said Mosienko, "and I figured since I'd been able to beat him on the right side, his glove hand, I'd try it again. So, just like the first time, I slid the puck along the ice. I don't think Anderson was ready for the quick shot and it got by him. The time was 6:20, just eleven seconds after the first goal. Now I had number 30, so I rushed to retrieve that one, too."

"Anderson was naturally unhappy about what had happened and I'll never forget the look he gave me as I reached into the net for the puck. I took it over to the bench and gave it to Goodfellow."

Neither the coach nor Mosienko even dreamed about his scoring a third goal, nor were they aware of the NHL record of fastest three goals (one minute, 52 seconds) set by Carl Liscombe of the Detroit Red Wings in 1938.

"It's funny," said Goodfellow, "but I was thinking of pulling Mosie off the ice after his second goal but I decided to let him stay on for another minute."

This time the scenario differed somewhat. Bodnar won the face-off again, to be sure, but this time the center ladled a pass to the left wing, Gee, rather than Mosienko on the right. The score was now 6–4 and the Black Hawks were hoping to rally for a tie.

"Naturally," said Mosienko, "I was thinking about the hat trick although I wasn't prepared for what actually happened. After all there were more than thirteen minutes left in the game and the Rangers, now only leading by two, figured to tighten their defense."

When Gee got the puck he moved toward the Rangers' blue line on the left side while Mosienko kept pace along the right alley. As Gee crossed the line into the New York defensive zone Mosienko streaked goalward from the right.

"George saw me cutting over the line and laid a perfect pass on my stick. Buller was waiting for me, but like the first two times I cut around him and went in on Anderson. He'd been burned twice on the right side and this time he moved to the right, figuring I'd try it again."

Mosienko decided to alter his strategy but led Anderson to believe that he was going to shoot the puck along the ice on the right. "Instead," Mosienko recalled, "I pulled him out of the net to the left, then put one over him high into the top right hand corner."

The time was 6:30. Mosienko had scored three goals within twenty-one seconds. It was a new NHL record but nobody really knew it at that moment. In fact, Mosienko didn't even attempt to obtain the puck a third time around, until Jimmy Peters, one of his teammates, decided Bill should have it. "He had played with the guy who set the old record so he went and got the puck for me and now it's in the Hockey Hall of Fame.''

With a break Mosienko could have made it four goals in sixty-six seconds. Goodfellow kept him out on the ice and, sure enough, the line soon moved into attacking formation, with Mosienko in possession of the puck.

''I was in alone again,'' said Mosienko, ''and faked Anderson out of position. I actually had an open net to hit but I missed the far post by a matter of inches.''

The exhausted right wing finally skated past the bench where his coach was waving him off the ice. ''When he was in earshot,'' said Goodfellow, ''I said, 'Bill, get off the ice, you're in a slump!' ''

Mosienko's three goals reduced the Black Hawks' deficit to 5–6. They scored two more and won the game, 7–6. ''It was the last game I coached,'' said Goodfellow, ''and one I'll never forget because that's one record that'll never be broken.''

William Mosienko was born in hockey-mad Winnipeg, Manitoba, on November 2, 1921. The son of poor parents, Mosienko, growing up during the Great Depression, was delighted when the Black Hawks showed interest in him at the age of eighteen.

When he was nineteen, the Hawks farmed him to Providence and then Kansas City but his speed was such that the Chicago club finally brought him up to stay and put him on a line with center Max Bentley and left wing Doug Bentley. Thus, one of the NHL's most glittering units, The Pony Line, was formed.

''The Black Hawks publicity man, Joe Farrell, came up with the name,'' said Mosienko. ''It was because of our size. The three of us were so small and every time we'd go for the puck we'd give it a little bounce.''

The tragedy of Mosienko's fourteen-year NHL career is that despite his 258 goals and 282 assists in 711 games he never sipped champagne from the Stanley Cup, although The Pony Line gave the Black Hawks the nucleus of a championship team.

Wee Willie's exceptional speed and guile did not immunize him from injury. He twice tore ligaments in his knees, fractured his toes, suffered a broken collarbone and broke his nose three times.

Psychologically speaking, Mosienko's worst injury occurred on October 13, 1947, during the first official NHL all-star game. Early in the second period Wee Willie was checked into the boards by Toronto Maple Leafs defenseman Jim Thomson and was carried off the ice on a stretcher with a fractured left ankle.

The player-short Black Hawks were panicked into a trade, dealing Max Bentley to Toronto for five regulars. Superficially, it appeared to be a good deal for the Hawks but it irrevocably broke up The Pony Line and Chicago remained a noncontender for years after.

Mosienko retired from the NHL in 1955 and, with ex-Ranger Alf Pike, helped launch pro hockey in Winnipeg. Their Warriors won the Edinburgh Trophy in their first year and helped lay the groundwork for what eventually would be Winnipeg's entry into the NHL.

Wee Willie eventually gave up coaching the Warriors to operate a twenty-lane bowling alley in Winnipeg. He still appears in old-timers games, and inevitably is reminded of that night when he ''caught lightning in a beer bottle'' with three goals in twenty-one seconds.

''It's a wonderful thing that so many people remember it,'' said Mosienko. ''I'm very proud of what I did.''

65 Larry Robinson
(1972–   )

Until the 1974–75 season the only fame defenseman Larry Robinson attained was from an incident on February 17, 1974. That was when he clipped the wings—and the ego—of Philadelphia Flyers' brawler Dave Schultz before a delighted Montreal Forum crowd and a national television audience. Most Canadiens' fans who had witnessed the fight came away convinced that head-knocking was Larry Robinson's destiny—being a policeman on the ice. But what was not as obvious at the time was that this big fellow was quite a talented as well as rugged defenseman and would soon become the cornerstone of the impenetrable defense of the Canadiens' teams that captured five Stanley Cups in the 1970s.

Robinson, at 6'3", 210 pounds, was exactly what the stylistic Canadiens' team needed. With the majority of their personnel being more artistic than overtly physical, the Habs needed a tough, no-nonsense type of rearguard, someone who could force the opposition to think twice before trying any intimidation tactics on their mitelike forwards and keep the Canadiens' crease clear of belligerent types who might make life a bit too difficult for Kenny Dryden. After the Schultz incident, Robinson's reputation had been established. He would no longer have to drop his gloves to prove his point. He could now concentrate on the physical but clean game that was his natural style and spend more time on the ice than in the sin bin, thus helping his team's cause to the maximum.

Though not the prolific scorer that some of his contemporaries were, Robinson established his ability as a strong, rushing puck carrier. And his ability to lug the rubber and engineer the offense in clutch situations made his offensive contributions most timely. "He's taken quite a few games I've seen and broken them open with an end-to-end rush," said Bruins defenseman Mike Milbury. "That's his biggest asset. As far as I'm concerned, Larry's far and away the Canadiens' MVP."

The tall, gangly Robinson was drafted as Montreal's fourth choice, twentieth overall, in the 1971 amateur draft. At the time, it was hard to understand what the Canadiens' management saw in the kid. Storklike with a head of wild red hair, Robinson was easily underestimated. The fact that he was picked in the first round was deceiving. The Canadiens had tapped three players ahead of him and the other clubs had already chosen a handful of supposed "quality" defensemen. But the big guy was not surprised. Rather, he was more baffled that he was picked anywhere near the top. "I didn't have an outstanding year in juniors (with Kitchener of the OHA) by any means," he remembers. "I was married, and was working at the Pepsi-Cola plant to make a living. I was just worn down."

The day Larry Robinson became a Montreal Canadien, the world did not stop. But it did pause just long enough to surprise the dickens out of young Larry. "I never knew much about the draft, so I went to Montreal after the 1971 season and went to see what happened. When I heard them say 'the Montreal Canadiens pick Larry Robinson,' my mouth dropped to my knees."

From that point on, the surprise was on the rest of the NHL.

Larry Clark Robinson was born June 2, 1951, in Winchester, Ontario. He had not planned on a career in pro hockey, necessarily. In his neighborhood, the business was dairy farming and hockey was something that came after chores.

He arrived in Montreal, permanently, after two years of seasoning with the Nova Scotia Voyageurs. At the time, ironically, it was the physical side of the game that worried him. He was still a young man filling out the bulk of his frame. Robinson emerged as the most forceful defenseman on the Canadiens in the late 1970's and was as important as any member of the team during the Habs four year Stanley Cup reign from 1976 through 1979.

With 17 assists and 21 points. Robinson led all playoff competition in each category in 1977–78, and thus was awarded the Conn Smythe Trophy as playoff MVP. His 69 playoff points, good for eleventh place on the Canadiens' all-time list and the highest ranking defenseman in team history, is evidence that postseason play has been Robinson's forte. Robinson's effectiveness diminished by the 1980's. However, he returned to form late in the 1983–84 season especially when he led his Habs past Boston and Quebec in early playoff rounds, thus earning Les Canadiens a berth in the Prince of Wales Conference championship against the four-time champion Islanders. Robinson performed nobly although the Canadiens were defeated, four games to two.

The Big Man, both literally and figuratively, has been the stalwart of some of the best teams the Canadiens have ever iced, and for those and his numerous other contributions to the NHL (two-time Norris Trophy recipient, for example), Larry Robinson has earned a berth among *Hockey's 100.*

66 Hobey Baker (1910–1918)

When the Washington Capitals signed eighteen-year-old Bobby Carpenter to a six-figure contract in September 1981 it was freely predicted by many sportswriters that Carpenter could be the first American-born forward to become a superstar in the Canadian-dominated National Hockey League.

While there have been Americans who have excelled at goaltending (Frankie Brimsek) and defense (Johnny Mariucci) few attackers have been able to attain the level of a Wayne Gretzky, Guy Lafleur or Bryan Trottier. There was, however, one of Uncle Sam's skaters who was so accomplished that, had he played today, there is little question that he would have been an ace in the Gretzky manner.

His name is Hobey Baker and the tragedy of it all is that this Pennsylvanian, who might have been the greatest hockey scorer of all time, died the year that the National Hockey League was just getting off the ground.

Like Gretzky, Baker was a natural, a genius at manipulating the puck almost from the very moment he laced on a pair of skates and grasped a hockey stick. His skills as a shooter gained national prominence while Hobey was a student at Princeton University. Incredibly good-looking, Baker captained the Princeton skaters to a pair of intercollegiate championships and immediately captured the attention of professional scouts who sought his services. Baker repeatedly rejected the offers but that just whet the appetites of the pros even more.

Skating for New York's St. Nicholas hockey club, Baker was the star of an upset victory over a strong Montreal sextet in the Ross Cup series. The fact that an American player could reach Baker's level of proficiency astounded the Canadian critics. One Montreal reporter noted: "Uncle Sam has the cheek to develop a first-class hockey player—who wasn't born in Montreal."

Princetonians were not the least surprised. In a game against Williams College, Baker shredded the enemy defense and scored six goals and three assists. Similar performances against other opponents inevitably resulted in a Hobey Baker mystique and attempts by the enemy to cut down Baker at all costs. During one game Hobey was slashed across the face but refused to yield.

Hobey gave up hockey after the outbreak of World War I and, typically, enlisted in the most daring fighting group, America's air arm which had been embraced by the French and called the Lafayette Escadrille. Apparently, air combat offered Baker the same thrills, suspense and, ultimately, triumph which he found on the ice. According to reports, Baker piloted his aircraft with sheer dedication and skill. He downed three German planes and was well decorated for his bravery under fire. The French army awarded Hobey its highest military honor, the Croix de Guerre, for exceptional valor.

Having nobly served the Allies' cause in victory, Hobey prepared to return to the United States and continue his enormously promising hockey career. On December 21, 1918, the very day he was to return home, Baker told his comrades that he wanted to take one last flight. His crew tried to talk him out of it, fearful of the last-flight superstition. Hobey nonchalantly dismissed their protests and took off in a recently repaired aircraft. Once aloft, the plane stalled and Baker was unable to re-start the motor. The disabled aircraft plummeted to earth, carrying Hobey to his death.

Hobart Baker was born on January 15, 1892, of wealthy parents at Wissahickon, Pennsylvania. Although he was a product of a genteel suburban Philadelphia up-bringing, Hobie liked his sports rough and seemed to thrive on the violence of hockey. But, most of all, he was a craftsman with the puck, his ability the result of endless hours of practice.

He began playing organized hockey at St. Paul's School in Concord, New Hampshire, from where he graduated to Princeton. His feats as a varsity member of Princeton's hockey team turned him into a living legend. Baker's mastery of the puck—and the opposition—was reinforced during his play with the St. Nicholas club.

The tragedy of Hobey Baker is twofold: his death at age twenty-six when he was approaching the prime of life and the fact that he never fulfilled his hockey destiny in the NHL. Based on the reports of those who viewed stars such as Bill Cook, Frank Nighbor and Bullet Joe Simpson, Hobey Baker would have been every bit as good as they. Unfortunately, we'll never know for sure.

67 Black Jack Stewart (1938–1952)

"He wasn't dirty," Hall of Famer King Clancy said, "but he was the roughest sonofagun you ever would want to meet."

The subject was Jack Stewart, a defenseman first with the Detroit Red Wings in the late 1930s and 1940s and later with the Chicago Black Hawks, with whom he concluded his career.

Any forward who attempted to penetrate the Detroit defense of Stewart and his sidekick Jimmy Orlando took his life in his hands. Red Wings manager Jack Adams, who paired them, boasted one of the most muscular one-two combinations on any blue line.

Apart from being a rough hombre, Stewart (unlike Orlando) was a highly polished defenseman who was named to the First All-Star Team in 1943, 1948 and 1949. He made the Second Team in 1947.

A stickler for conditioning, Stewart would spend the summer on his farm in Manitoba and then report to training camp ready for the season to start. "He would be tougher than a pine knot," recalled Toronto *Star* columnist Milt Dunnell, "dour, dedicated and full of pride. He was fast for a defenseman. In the routine practice races around the rink, few of the forwards could outskate him."

Because of his swarthy appearance he was nicknamed "Black Jack." He played on two Stanley Cup winners and three first-place clubs.

John Sherratt Stewart was born May 6, 1917, in Pilot Mound, Manitoba. He was discovered by a chap named Gene Houghton, who worked in the grain exchange at Winnipeg and was friendly with Red Wings owner Jim Norris, Sr., who happened to be a grain tycoon as well.

Stewart was as fine a sportsman as he was a hockey player. Toronto hockey historian Ed Fitkin, who once was publicist for the Toronto Maple Leafs, recalled how Stewart could perceive the worth of the opposition even in defeat.

"Jack was always one of the first to congratulate the victors after the Wings participated in a lost cause. Once, when Turk Broda of Toronto won the Vezina Trophy in the last game of the schedule at Olympia Stadium in Detroit, Jack heartily threw his arms around the Turk.

"The two game veterans skated off the ice arm in arm. Thousands in Detroit Olympia stood up to give them thunderous tribute."

Although Stewart's checks have been described as thunderous, Black Jack, the man, was quiet to a fault, except on special occasions. One such occasion was the seventh game of the 1950 Stanley Cup finals against the New York Rangers.

"At our pregame meeting," said Jack Adams, "I warned our forwards they weren't hitting anybody. Rangers had been making them look silly. I tried to tell them they should do some bumping.

"Suddenly, Black Jack jumped up. I don't think he ever opened his mouth at a club meeting before—unless he was asked a question. This time, he said: 'You bums get out there and hit somebody. If you don't, I'll be hitting you.' That night we got some bodychecking."

And with Stewart providing airtight defense the Red Wings won the Cup in the second sudden-death overtime on Pete Babando's screened shot.

As much as he revered Stewart, Adams realized that his thumping warrior was approaching the end of his career. Fewer than five months after the defeat of the Rangers, Adams included Stewart along with goalie Harry Lumley, defenseman Al Dewsbury and forwards Pete Babando and Don Morrison in a blockbuster deal with the Chicago Black Hawks. The Red Wings received goalie Jim Henry, forwards Metro Prystai and Gaye Stewart and defenseman Bob Goldham in return.

Black Jack was playing capably for Chicago when he suffered a ruptured spinal disc. Doctors wrote him off as a hockey player. He was thirty-four and they said he should be grateful if he could walk again, without a cane or crutch.

Stewart accepted their advice, applied some of his own willpower and returned to the Black Hawks' lineup. He did, after all, have a job to do. Unfortunately, the fickle finger of fate was working against him. During a game against the Rangers, Stewart and Clare Martin were paired on defense. They liked to line up an onrushing forward and put him in a human vise as the enemy tried to split their defense. On this night, the eellike Edgar Laprade moved into the Black Hawks' zone. Stewart and Martin figured Laprade was coming through and closed the trap. But the little Ranger fooled them and Martin rammed his partner to the ice, as one observer noted, "colder than a mackerel."

Black Jack was hospitalized and required twenty-one stitches to close his wounds. After spending two weeks in the hospital, he announced his retirement. Then, to the amazement of all, he returned to the ice and played two more games for Chicago.

He concluded his career after the 1951–52 season and 566 regular-season games. He then went into coaching, starting with Chatham in the Ontario Hockey Association's Senior League. He then coached two years on the junior level with Kitchener before moving up to the high pro ranks with Pittsburgh of the American League. He gave up coaching for good in 1963 but remained active as a horse racing steward. His love for racing began in his native Pilot Mound, Manitoba, where his father staged race meetings.

Black Jack was as pure as any bodychecking defenseman could be, respected by friend and foe alike, a natural for *Hockey's 100*.

68 Cooney Weiland (1928–1939)

Any discussion of the golden age of hockey in Boston would have to include the name of Cooney Weiland. He launched his career in Beantown in 1928 and played for the Bruins until 1932, returning again in 1935. He concluded his National Hockey League career as a Bruin in 1939.

By any standard of comparison, Weiland was a superlative center. He was the balance wheel on Boston's "Dynamite Trio," playing between Dit Clapper and Dutch Gainor when the Bruins won their first Stanley Cup in 1929. He scored 43 goals in forty-four games that year.

Cooney led the National Hockey League in scoring in 1930 with the Bruins but two years later he was dealt to the Ottawa Senators and then the Detroit Red Wings.

"Weiland," said former goalie and author S. Kip Farrington, Jr., "was a great face-off man, one of the best I've ever seen. He also was—like Hooley Smith and Frank Nighbor—an excellent three-way stick checker. He was a master of the poke, sweep and hook checks."

He played well for Detroit but the feeling was that Weiland would be at his best back in Boston. One night, in 1935, the Bruins' manager Frank Patrick met with his Detroit counterpart, Jack Adams.

"If I had Cooney Weiland," Patrick said, "Boston would be able to make the finals."

"If I had Marty Barry," Adams retorted in reference to Boston's big, dour center, "Detroit would win the Stanley Cup."

That did it, and a trade was made that, literally, helped both teams. Cooney moved between Gainor and Clapper while Barry was inserted between Larry Aurie and Herbie Lewis to form the set of forwards chiefly responsible for Detroit's first Stanley Cup triumph in 1935–36. Weiland guided the Bruins to a pair of first-place finishes and another Stanley Cup in 1939.

Ralph Weiland was born November 5, 1904, in Seaforth, Ontario. He turned pro with the Minneapolis Millers and then graduated to the Bruins. In his book, *Skates, Sticks and Men,* Farrington noted that Weiland had a vast repertoire of ice skills.

"Cooney was outstanding at breaking up power plays and getting the puck in breakaways out of the end zone when the Bruins were playing shorthanded," wrote Farrington. "I believe his greatest night was January 1, 1931, in Madison Square Garden in a game against the Rangers. The Bruins and the Rangers were tied 3–3 in the third period, with about ten minutes to play, when Cooney was tripped from behind while he was going in alone to shoot against John Roach.

"Cooney slid headfirst into the boards and was knocked cold. By the time he was revived, the game was eight minutes into overtime and the Bruins were playing not one but two men short. Cooney returned to the ice and a minute later broke away and started in toward the goal in a duplication of his play in the third period.

Only this time he scored the winning goal *before* he fell and slid into the boards again. Momentarily, Cooney was out again, but he had won the game, 4–3.''

Weiland produced a 100 percent effort whether he was with a winner or loser. During his one full season with the Ottawa Senators he was the leading scorer for the last-place club. Yet, it was his precision in handling the subtle skills of the game that caught the attention of experts.

''The finest individual face-off that I can recall, and the most important in a terrible spot, occurred in the Stanley Cup semifinals between Boston and Toronto in April 1939,'' said Farrington.

''There was a rule that year that if anyone other than the goalie fell on the puck in his defensive zone, there was a face-off directly in front of the crease. Cooney was called off the bench for the face-off with Bingo Kampman, the tough defenseman and the Maple Leafs' best face-off man. The puck was square in front of the net, the Bruins were leading by one goal, and there were about five minutes to play. The referee blew his whistle, the puck dropped—away it went, and wound up across the Toronto blue line into their zone. Nobody was able to touch it on the way back. I will never forget it.''

Following the Bruins' 1939 Stanley Cup victory, Weiland retired to become coach of the Boston sextet. They finished first in 1939–40 and 1940–41 and also won the Stanley Cup in the latter season. Surprisingly, Weiland achieved even more acclaim as a collegiate coach than he did in the majors. He was recommended for the Harvard coaching job in 1950 by Farrington and turned the Crimson team into an Ivy League power. Between 1950 and his retirement in 1971 Weiland was named the New England Coach of the Year in 1955, 1957, 1961 and 1962—and the American Hockey Coaches Association Coach of the Year in 1957 and 1971. He retired as Harvard hockey coach in 1971 and that same year was voted into the Hockey Hall of Fame. A year later he received the Lester Patrick Trophy for his outstanding service to amateur hockey in the United States.

69 Mike Bossy
(1977–)

They come once in a decade; sometimes not even that often. They are so superior in their craftsmanship that it is not at all unreasonable to call them inimitable.

In the 1930s it was Howie Morenz, "The Stratford Streak." In the 1940s, Maurice Richard, "The Rocket." In the 1950s, Gordie Howe, "Mister Hockey." In the 1960s, Bobby Hull, "The Golden Jet." In the 1970s, Bobby Orr. And now Mike Bossy, "The Goal Machine."

The genius of Bossy was evident before the 1980–81 season but it was somewhat muted by other events and performances of import. In 1980–81, however, the twenty-four-year-old native of Montreal told the world that he would like to equal the Rocket's accomplishment of scoring 50 goals in fifty games.

Tradition demanded that Bossy keep his intentions to himself. But Mike is not a traditionalist. "Nobody sets out to break records," said Bossy. "You just play, you score, and they happen. But the 50-in-fifty, that's one I want. Having my name next to Richard would not be too shabby."

The Bossy-Richard connection was not a figment of the author's imagination. Often without Bossy's knowledge, the legendary Richard watched young Mike mature as a kid player on assorted Montreal rinks. In 1968 Bossy was the proud recipient of an award from the Rocket himself. The Richard-Bossy link was forged early.

Early in 1980–81 it had become apparent that Bossy was carrying an unusually hot stick. This had happened to extraordinary athletes before, and inevitably, they would be struck down by injury or slump. Bossy just kept scoring until the Richardian mark suddenly became a possibility and Mike underlined the point by stating that obtaining 50-in-fifty would be his dearest personal achievement. That done, the media responded to his clarion call.

Occasionally, Bossy broke stride and fell behind the goal-a-game pace but in mid-January he came on strong, scoring seven goals in two games. After his forty-seventh game Bossy had 48 goals!

The Calgary Flames, Detroit Red Wings and Quebec Nordiques would form the final blockade in games forty-eight, forty-nine and fifty.

"It's a challenge," said Bossy before game forty-eight (vs. Calgary at Nassau Coliseum). "I think I owe it to everybody to get the record now because I sort of announced it and I owe it to myself, too."

The Flames' blockade was flawless. They double- and sometimes triple-teamed the Isles' gifted right wing. New York was able to score (the final was 5–0 Isles) but Bossy was manacled at every turn, especially when tenacious Eric Vail shadowed him.

Two nights later Bossy took the ice at Joe Louis Arena against the Red Wings. "We're going to do everything we can to see that Mike gets it," said Potvin, "and he's going to get it. I'll be surprised if he doesn't do it against Detroit. But I'll guarantee he'll get it."

The captain's guarantee looked fragile after the Detroit match. Once again Bossy had been stymied. The final score of game forty-nine was 3–0. Mike had zip.

"If I didn't get the record," Bossy allowed, "it would have been embarrassing because I had made it such a big thing."

Game fifty was at Nassau Coliseum. Now he needed not one but two goals to tie the mark yet he had been unable to scrape up even one goal in the past two games.

Nordiques coach Michel Bergeron knew Bossy from junior hockey days. He did not subdue his admiration for the Islanders' ace and said straight out that he would not try any dirty tricks.

"Calgary and Detroit both lost their games by zeroing in on Mike," said Bergeron. "I'd rather win our game and see him score a pair of goals. He'll get no special attention."

Bergeron's words had a hollow ring once the puck was dropped. Although the Nordiques did not assign one special shadow to follow Bossy, they were no less attentive than the Flames or Red Wings; and for most of the game Mike was no more productive than he had been in the two previous games.

After two periods of play in which Bossy seemed almost invisible he had nothing to show for it but the look of an anxious young man. "I had never been so frustrated in all my hockey career," he admitted later. "I couldn't do anything right. I felt as if my hands were bound with tape and my stomach was tied in knots."

Still, there were twenty minutes of hockey left on his itinerary so he took the ice and gave it a good Bossy try. At first he seemed to be on a treadmill to nowhere but by mid-period some of Mike's magic became evident although he still had a goose egg for his efforts.

More than anything Mike needed a break and then, almost miraculously, it happened. With a little more than five minutes left in the game Quebec was hit with a minor penalty. Bossy was dispatched to the scene for the Islanders' power play.

For forty seconds the pattern of futility continued. The clock relentlessly ticked away "4:15 . . . 4:14 . . . 4:13 . . . " Suddenly, the puck was cradled on Bossy's stick. "4:12 . . . 4:11." He released a backhander in the direction of the crouched goalie Ron Grahame. "4:10." The red light flashed behind the Nordiques' net.

With a little more than four minutes remaining, Bossy was now back in the chase. Could he translate 49 into 50? If cheers could help, the 15,000 faithful supported Mike with lung power, but with three minutes remaining and then two he was still stuck at 49 goals.

Early that afternoon Charlie Simmer of the Los Angeles Kings also had taken aim at the 50-in-fifty mark. Simmer came up short by one although he had scored a hat trick against the Boston Bruins. Unlike Bossy, Simmer had a minimum of pressure. He never was as candid as Mike about his desire to equal the Rocket's record.

"The pressure Mike put on himself to score amazes me," Simmer had said.

That pressure had never been more intense than in the final minute-and-a-half of the Quebec game. Once again coach Al Arbour signalled Mike to the ice.

The Bossy-watchers wondered what Mike would do if he got the puck in scoring position. Some recalled what he had said about his shot: "About 90 percent of the time I don't aim: I just try to get my shot away as quick as possible as a surprise element. I just try to get the puck on the net."

Again the clock was working against him. "1:36 . . . 1:35 . . . 1:34 . . . 1:33 . . . 1:32 . . . 1:31." The puck came to Bossy. He was camped near the left face-off circle. Goalie Grahame prepared for the shot. Mike cracked his wrist and the puck arched goalward. Grahame never touched the rubber. It hit the twine with 1:29 remaining and the Coliseum reverberated with a noise rarely heard in an arena.

Mike Bossy had challenged himself and triumphed.

Nobody said it better than *Newsday's* Joe Gergen about Mike Bossy, his accomplishment and his future.

"This particular challenge is ended. There will be others. For Mike Bossy, it is not enough to play the game; he must excel."

Michael Bossy was born in Montreal, Quebec, on January 22, 1957. The streets of the Canadiens' home town were the early stages for young Bossy's hockey antics. And with the legend of the Rocket everywhere around the Forum, it is easy to understand Bossy's obsession with the 50-in-fifty record. His reaching that plateau might go some distance towards fulfilling every Montreal boy's dream, growing up to be a Canadien. While Bossy did not accomplish that, he did at least as well by sharing an honorable line in the record books with one of the best players ever to grace the Forum ice.

Mike's stature grew even more during the 1981–82 campaign. He led the champion Islanders in scoring with 64 goals, 83 assists and 147 points. Despite a debilitating leg injury that clearly cramped his style, he choreographed the Islanders to their third consecutive Stanley Cup championship in May 1982 and was awarded the Conn Smythe Trophy as the most valuable player in the playoffs. He also was voted to the First All-Star Team at right wing, garnering 309 points out of a possible 315.

Bossy maintained his standard of excellence during the 1982–83 season. He scored 60 goals, 58 assists and 118 points. It marked the third consecutive season that he reached the 60-goal plateau. Bossy had proven an able successor to Howie Morenz, Rocket Richard, and Bobby Hull.

He didn't win the Conn Smythe Trophy in 1983 but Bossy was an invaluable member of the Islanders attack as the team from Nassau Coliseum won its fourth consecutive Stanley Cup defeating the Edmonton Oilers in four straight games.

During the 1983–84 season Bossy scored 51 goals, extending his consecutive 50-plus-per-year mark to a record-breaking seven seasons. He added 67 assists for a total of 118 points. And his eight minutes in penalties enabled him to capture the Lady Byng Memorial Trophy as the most gentlemanly player. Bossy also was voted to the first All-Star team for the fourth successive year.

70 Dave Keon
(1960–1982)

When Lou Fontinato cruised and bruised his way around Madison Square Garden for the Rangers in the late 1950s, he abided by a simple personal philosophy: "*You gotta hit first, or they'll run you out of the league.*" That line of reasoning remains the rule more than the exception as much today as twenty years ago. But there is, and has been since 1960, one small (5' 9", 167 pound) nonobserver of that rule who outlasted Fontinato and the rest of his ilk: a speedy little center named Dave Keon.

"It's a good theory," Keon once said of Fontinato's rule of the ice. "Good in the sense that there's some truth to it. But it doesn't apply to *everybody*. I know I don't have to go around hitting to stay up here."

The only thing Keon needed to hit was the enemy net, which he did well enough to keep him around the NHL for the better part of two decades. But Keon was more than a goal scorer. He always has been respected as a tenacious checker and a leader.

In his own way, Keon was as tough and aggressive as his larger opponents. The difference was Dave's preference for playing within the rules. It would have been easier for Keon to compensate for his lack of size with an illegal stick here or a grab there, but that was not Dave Keon. Between 1960 and 1981, he served a total of 111 minutes in penalties, a figure many players eclipse in a year. But for Dave it was easy since he had been Mister Clean since his early amateur hockey days in Canada.

Keon attended St. Michael's College in Toronto on a scholarship from the Maple Leafs, who then sponsored the school's hockey program. It was there that Keon developed his inimitable style while under the guidance of Father David Bauer, his coach.

When Keon left St. Michael's and jumped directly to the Leafs without wasting a minute in the minors, he found himself playing for Punch Imlach, who endorsed the hockey maxim, "If you can't beat 'em in the alley, you can't beat 'em on the ice." A happy marriage between the impudent Imlach and choirboy Keon seemed unlikely, to say the least.

So when Keon hit the ice in 1960 all eyes focused on the lithe youngster to see if he could handle the rough going in the pros. In his third game, Keon pumped in his first NHL goal and by season's end he had scored 20, which, in those days, was the equivalent of a .300 batting average in baseball. Keon's play earned him the Calder Trophy as rookie of the year and prompted Imlach to concede that "in time, Keon may be as good as Henri Richard of Montreal." That was high praise indeed.

As Keon's career in Toronto progressed, it became obvious that comparisons were irrelevant. He distinguished himself among his teammates as a leader, a catalyst. He didn't wait for things to happen, he made them happen. The ultimate team player, Keon was the spark that ignited the Maple Leafs' diverse mixture of talent. In his second season with the club, Keon helped lead the Leafs to their first Stanley Cup in eleven years, totalling 26 goals and 35 assists during the regular season and 8 points in twelve contests in postseason play.

Toronto went on to annex the Cup the following two years as well and then again in 1966–67, when Keon was voted the most valuable playoff performer. Keon, while establishing himself as one of the most dangerous two-way players in the league, played on four Cup-winning teams in his first seven seasons in the NHL, a feat rarely accomplished by many professionals in their entire careers.

David Michael Keon was born March 22, 1940, in the mining village of Noranda, in northwestern Quebec. As a means of avoiding the lifetime in the copper mines that was the destiny of most youngsters in his home town, Keon turned to hockey. Laboring in obscurity both on the ice and under the ground, at the age of fifteen, opportunity approached Dave Keon.

Vince Thompson, geologist and part-time Maple Leafs scout, happened to see the young lad playing a hockey game in Noranda. After watching him play, Thompson composed a short but urgent letter to Maple Leaf Gardens. "Come get this boy," implored Thompson. "If you don't, another team will hurt you with him some day." With that, Leafs' scout Bob Davidson was immediately dispatched to the scene and Keon's career was under way.

In addition to the Calder Trophy in 1960–61, Keon also captured the Lady Byng Trophy in 1961–62 and 1962–63, along with the Conn Smythe Trophy as the most valuable player in the playoffs of 1966–67. A two-time Second Team All-Star at center, Keon toiled fifteen seasons for the blue and white, scoring 365 goals and 493 assists. And, remarkably, he never received more than 12 penalty minutes in any season.

In 1975, Keon signed a contract worth approximately $300,000 with the Minnesota Fighting Saints of the newly formed World Hockey Association. The Leafs' captain at the time, Keon was not anxious to abandon his old club and there was more than money behind his motivation. The Leafs, undergoing one of their many housecleaning periods, had let it be known that veterans such as Keon and Norm Ullman were expendable. It was Keon's feeling that had he signed anew with the Maple Leafs, he would have been traded. He did not foresee himself a Leaf in the future and by accepting the Saints' offer, simply wished to control his future. And, as Minnesota's coach Harry Neale so aptly put it, "Dave's strength has always been the things he can do when he *doesn't* have the puck."

Keon played with the Fighting Saints, Indianapolis Racers and New England Whalers of the WHA before finally returning to the NHL when the New England entry was absorbed as the Hartford Whalers in the league's expansion movement in 1979–80. During his WHA career, Keon netted 102 goals to go along with 189 assists.

In the fall of 1981, at the ripe old age of forty-one, Keon opened yet another NHL season as captain of the Whalers, finally retiring at the end of the 1981–82 campaign.

Keon's career is summed up best by his former teammate and Hall of Fame goaltender, Jacques Plante: "Keon is proof that it's not the size of the body but the size of the heart that counts in this game." He retired in the summer of 1982.

The Davey among the Goliaths of the NHL, he is honorably awarded his hard-earned place here among *Hockey's 100*.

71 Babe Pratt
(1935–1947)

Babe Pratt had a certain joie de vivre that reminded old-timers of another Babe from a different sport and an earlier era, that being Babe Ruth. Both indulged in the good life, often to excess yet they were capable of extraordinary accomplishments.

Pratt was a defenseman who could rush the puck and score goals in the manner of latter-day blueliners such as Bobby Orr and Denis Potvin. He had a flair for the dramatic and the ability to satisfactorily conclude a project he had begun. The Babe was architect of one of the most dramatic winning goals in Stanley Cup history. This was in the seventh game of the 1945 Stanley Cup finals against the Red Wings. With the score tied 1–1, late in the game Pratt fired the puck behind goalie Harry Lumley and the Leafs triumphed, 2–1.

By all rights, Pratt should have been a New York Ranger at the time. He had come up through the Ranger system and was a star playing for Lester Patrick's team but Patrick must have had second thoughts about Babe's off-ice deportment. Conn Smythe, the Toronto manager, had been watching Pratt for years and dealt for him when he got the chance.

"I remember once," said Smythe, "when Pratt was with the Rangers and we were tied late in the game. A good Ranger forward got hurt and Pratt was moved up to a wing. I thought, 'Aha, here's our chance to win.' Who got the winning goal? Pratt, playing forward."

The Babe won the Hart Trophy as the National Hockey League's most valuable player in 1944 and was a First All-Star that same year. A season later he was voted to the Second All-Star Team.

"If he'd looked after himself he could have played until he was fifty," said Conn Smythe in his memoirs, *If You Can't Beat 'em In The Alley.* "But he was as big a drinker and all-around playboy as he was a hockey player."

Walter Pratt was born January 7, 1916, in Stony Mountain, Manitoba, but grew up in the metropolis of Winnipeg. His hero was National Hockey League star, Frank Frederickson, who lived near the Pratt home.

Babe played his early hockey on Winnipeg's numerous outdoor rinks in temperatures as low as forty degrees below zero Fahrenheit. When he was fifteen he moved up to the junior level and began demonstrating the moves that soon would attract the attention of major league scouts. Al Ritchie, a New York Rangers bird dog, took a look at Pratt and reported back favorably to Rangers manager Lester Patrick. The Babe was invited to the Rangers' camp in 1934 and played well enough to win a professional offer but he chose to return to the amateur ranks for another year.

A year later he returned to the Rangers' base and was signed to a contract. Babe was farmed out to Philadelphia at first but soon was recalled by Patrick as part of a dynasty-in-the-making. Here is what Pratt told me about the club in an interview:

"By the end of the thirties Patrick had really developed a powerful hockey club;

we could play terrifically, offensively as well as defensively. Conn Smythe, who was then running the Toronto Maple Leafs, said that the 1940 Rangers were the greatest hockey club he'd ever seen. In those days, whenever we came to Toronto, Smythe would advertise us as 'The Broadway Blues, Hockey's Classiest Team.'

"Our club was so well-balanced that our first line scored 38 goals, the second, 37, and the third line, 36, over the season.

"On that Ranger team we had three great centermen—Clint Smith, Phil Watson, and Neil Colville—plus so many good wingmen that we were able to put the pressure on the other team when we were a man short. Our power play was so strong that once the Toronto Maple Leafs took a penalty we kept the puck in their end of the rink for the entire two minutes—and scored two goals.

"It was a different kind of game then. Today, they stress boardchecking and checking from behind, both unheard of when we played. We'd hit a man standing right up and now the players don't seem to want to take that kind of check. The only check they want is on the first and fifteenth of the month."

"Sure, we played a tough game but we also had a million laughs. There was a newspaperman from *The New York World-Telegram* named Jim Burchard who liked to drink, tell stories, and do wild things like swim across the Hudson River. Once, we had Ukulele Ike travelling with us and, naturally, Burchard had his own ukulele which he played every night we were in a Stanley Cup round. We also had quite a few jokers on the team. Ching Johnson was one; he was also one of the finest players when it came to working with rookies. Ching was from Winnipeg too, and he sort of took me under his wing."

It also probably helped speed Pratt's exit from New York. When the Rangers traded the Babe, they accepted an untried rookie, Red Garrett (who was killed during World War II) and a mediocre forward, Hank Goldup, for Pratt. Babe stabilized the Toronto backline and personally delivered a Stanley Cup in 1945. But the Maple Leafs floundered the following year and Smythe decided to go with youth.

Pratt was traded to the Boston Bruins, played one season with them and then was sent to the minors. Instead of quitting, he played for the Hershey Bears, Cleveland Barons and New Westminster Royals before calling it a career in 1952 after skating for the Tacoma Rockets.

Those who knew and loved the Babe were delighted when the Vancouver Canucks signed him as a goodwill ambassador when they entered the NHL in 1970. There were few big-leaguers with as much goodwill as Pratt and even fewer with his talent.

72 Charlie Gardiner
(1927–1934)

Only his relatively brief career prevented Charlie (Chuck) Gardiner from receiving a higher place among *Hockey's 100*. Certainly, there have been few better goal-tenders during any of the game's epochs.

Before illness cut short his career Gardiner played seven years with the Chicago Black Hawks and produced 42 shutouts and a remarkable 2.13 goals-against average. He won the Vezina (best goalie) Trophy in 1932 and repeated in 1934. Thrice (1931, 1932, 1934) he was voted to the First All-Star Team and in 1933 made the Second Team.

The Black Hawks had never won a Stanley Cup championship until 1934 and it was then, thanks to Gardiner's efforts, that they prevailed. He permitted only 12 goals in eight playoff games for a 1.50 average.

Gardiner was one of the first of a legion of Windy City hockey heroes and Chuck, few could dispute, helped plant the seed of hockey interest in that city. A cocky Scotsman, he nevertheless distracted fans from an abysmally weak Black Hawks team.

Charles Robert Gardiner was born December 31, 1904, in Edinburgh, Scotland, and arrived in Canada with his family in 1911. He grew up in hockey-mad Winnipeg during the 1920s and was discovered in 1925 while playing for a team in Selkirk, Manitoba.

Signed by the Winnipeg Maroons, he played through the 1926–27 season unaware that the Black Hawks were scouting him. He was signed by Chicago owner Major Frederick McLaughlin and played poorly in his first four games with the Black Hawks. Shortly thereafter he turned it around and was en route to permanent stardom.

One could fill a volume detailing Gardiner's exploits. A game against the powerful Boston Bruins is a case in point. Eddie Shore, the premier defenseman of the Bruins, was zooming in on Gardiner for a shot when the Black Hawk goalie edged out of his crease to meet him. In this way, Gardiner trimmed down the shooter's angle and forced Shore to shoot wide of the target. Undaunted, Shore pursued the puck behind the net, but Gardiner wheeled around and tripped the big Bruin.

In those days the NHL awarded one-minute penalties to goalies, and Gardiner was ordered off the ice. While he sat out his foul, teammate Cy Wentworth moved into the nets without the benefit of goaltender's equipment and managed to blunt the Bruins' attack.

Meanwhile, the impatient Gardiner was leaning on the boards awaiting the moment when he would finally spring from the penalty box. When his sentence expired, he leaped over the wooden boards and dashed headlong for the goal.

At the moment Gardiner was released, Boston defenseman George Owen captured the puck. He carefully aimed for the four-by-six-foot opening and drilled the rubber for what appeared to be a goal. But it never went in.

By 1929, Gardiner had improved so much that he finished second to the immortal

George Hainsworth of the Montreal Canadiens in the race for the Vezina Trophy. In 1932, he would finally win the coveted prize and be named to the All-Star Team. Charlie was the one piece of pure gold on the roster and the lever that could catapult the Hawks to the heights of greatness.

In 1932–33, the Black Hawks finished fourth—out of the playoffs. The following year they rallied and launched their most serious assault on first place. That they failed by seven points and finished second to Detroit was no fault of Gardiner's. His goaltending reached new degrees of perfection. He allowed only 83 goals in forty-eight games and registered 10 shutouts. In fourteen other games he permitted just one goal.

But astute Gardiner watchers perceived that there was something unusual about the goalie's deportment and they couldn't figure out just what it was. Gardiner had lost his jovial manner and appeared to be melancholy.

Unknown to everyone, Gardiner was suffering from a chronic tonsil infection. The disease had spread and had begun to cause uremic convulsions. However, the goaltender pressed on. Winning the Stanley Cup became an obsession with him, and the Black Hawks responded by defeating first the Canadiens and then the Montreal Maroons. This put them in the Cup finals against the awesome Detroit Red Wings.

The best-of-five series opened in Detroit and the Black Hawks won the first game, 2–1, in double overtime. In the second, also at Detroit's Olympia Stadium, he Hawks ran away with the game, 4–1. When the teams returned to Chicago for the third, and what appeared to be the final game, all hands were ready to concede the Stanley Cup to the Black Hawks.

But it was not to be Charlie Gardiner's night. His body was wracked with pain and he prayed that he might recapture his physical condition of seasons past. Charlie moved between the pipes for two periods but the relentless Detroit attack overcame him in the third. Detroit won the game, 5–2.

Gardiner collapsed on a bench in the dressing room minutes after the final buzzer, but recovered quickly enough to realize that, psychologically, the Black Hawks were collapsing with him. Summoning all the strength at his command, Charlie peered across the room and said: "Look, all I want is one goal next game. Just one goal and I'll take care of the other guys."

On April 10, 1934, Gardiner returned to the crease, hunched his shoulders, tapped his pads and prepared for battle. His body was numb from fatigue but he was determined to overcome the pain and play his game.

For two periods Gardiner was never better. He held the Detroiters scoreless but the Black Hawks were also unable to score. Even as it drained him of energy, Gardiner screamed encouragement to his players but it was to no avail. The red-shirted Detroiters counterattack developed new intensity and Charlie had all to do to keep them at bay, but he did and the game went into sudden-death overtime.

There were those who doubted that Gardiner could sustain both the physical and mental strain much longer, yet when the overtime began he was smiling and even waved his stick to the crowd. For another twenty minutes he blunted the best shots the enemy could hurl at him but his mates could do no better and a second sudden-death period was required.

Charlie could no longer smile. Flames of pain burned his insides as he tried to concentrate on the black rubber disk. The overtime had begun again and for ten minutes there was no resolution. Suddenly, little Mush March of the Black Hawks took command, skating into Detroit ice. He cracked his wrist and the puck took off and sailed past Wilf Cude and into the net. The time was 10:05 when the Black Hawks had annexed their first Stanley Cup.

Gardiner hurled his stick in the air and then just barely made it back to the dressing room under the backslaps of his mates.

The roar of the crowd had hardly subsided when Charlie was taken to the hospital. He underwent brain surgery and following the operation died on June 13, 1934.

Those who watched Gardiner in action on a regular basis suggest that he was the greatest of all time. Certainly, in the seven years of NHL play he demonstrated an uncanny puck-stopping ability. However, his career was too short to permit inclusion on a higher plane although this, in no way, diminishes from Gardiner's accomplishments.

73 Syd Howe
(1929-1946)

Midway in the 1981–82 season, when Wayne Gretzky began dominating the hockey scene at the tender age of twenty, someone asked Hall of Famer Gordie Howe whether he got as much acclaim at age twenty as Gretzky was obtaining.

"Hell," said Gordie, "the only thing people ever asked me when I was twenty was whether I was related to *Syd Howe*."

In the 1940s it was considered an honor to be related to Syd Howe. He wasn't the greatest of the Detroit Red Wings but he ranked among the most versatile shooters ever to torment an enemy goaltender. Syd could play virtually any position but was used mostly as a left wing and center.

He was named to the Second All-Star Team as a left wing in 1945 but, by far, his most notable accomplishment took place a year earlier, on the night of February 3, 1944, to be exact. The Red Wings were at home to the New York Rangers on that night and at 11:27 of the first period Howe launched what was to become known as one of the most impressive individual performances in history.

Taking a pass from Don (The Count) Grosso, he beat Ken (Tubby) McAuley in the Rangers' net. Just eighteen seconds later, Howe scored again. The score was 3–0 for Detroit late in the second period when defenseman Cully Simon delivered a pass to Howe and he beat goalie McAuley at 17:52, giving him a hat-trick. Exactly sixty-two seconds later Grosso spotted a free Howe, dispatched the pass and still another red light went on for Syd. It was 5–0 for the Red Wings and Howe already had four goals.

For eight minutes of the third period the Rangers stymied him but then his linemates Grosso and Modere (Mud) Bruneteau moved rapidly into the Rangers' zone. Howe was in position and whipped the rubber home at 8:17.

By now Detroit coach Jack Adams knew he had the game in the bag—it was 8–0 for the Red Wings—so he gave his top line as much ice as possible and, sure enough, less than a minute later Bruneteau and Grosso collaborated once more, fed Howe and just like that he had *his sixth goal of the game*.

"They left me out there on the ice to try and get more goals," Howe remembered. "I had a good chance to break the all-time record (Joe Malone scored seven goals for the Quebec Bulldogs in 1920) but I couldn't do it."

Over the years Howe has played down the importance of the six-goal game. "I got a lot more satisfaction out of two other nights," he said.

In one of them he set a league record for the fastest overtime playoff goal, twenty-five seconds after the start of the extra period. It happened on March 19, 1940, against the New York Americans.

"The score was 0–0," Syd recalled, "and I was playing on a line with Bruneteau and (Carl) Liscombe. I went down the left side and sent a low shot into the corner. The other time I'll never forget is the 'night' Detroit fans gave me toward the end of my career. I got a lot of gifts, including a piano.

"You know how it is when they give you a 'night.' It usually turns out that the

team gets beat and you can't come close to scoring. I was a lot luckier. We beat the Black Hawks, 2–0, and I scored both goals.''

Sydney Harris Howe was born September 18, 1911, in Ottawa, Ontario. He broke into the National Hockey League with his hometown team, the Senators, during the 1929–30 season and a year later was with the Philadelphia Quakers before returning to the Senators in 1932. He was transferred to the St. Louis Eagles in 1934 and came to Detroit in 1935 along with defenseman Ralph (Scotty) Bowman in a deal said to involve $50,000, which was big money in those days of the Great Depression. It was one of Detroit's best deals, for Howe emerged as a versatile forward who could play virtually any position, and play it well.

Point-wise, Syd's best season was 1943–44 when he scored 32 goals and 28 assists for 60 points in forty games. He played for three Stanley Cup winners and three first-place teams.

It is noteworthy that Howe pinpointed the turnabout in hockey's attacking style as taking place during the 1942 Stanley Cup finals between the Red Wings and Toronto Maple Leafs "Up until that time," Syd explained, "the attacks and counterattacks were more or less straight up and down, with the puck either carried or passed back and forth into the enemy zone. But in the 1942 series Detroit started the 'new' way of *shooting* the puck into the opposition's zone and *chasing* after it.''

Syd remained a Red Wing through the 1945–46 season and then retired just before Gordie Howe came on to the scene. After retirement Syd Howe returned to his native Ottawa and would be reminded of his six-goal accomplishment whenever another NHLer came close to matching his feat. In the early 1960s he was attending a gathering at the home of friends in Ottawa. On that night, word got around that Bobby Rousseau had scored five goals. "The people at the party," said Howe, "were more worried than I was about Rousseau breaking the record.''

In time Red Berenson of the St. Louis Blues would equal Howe's modern mark but nobody has ever surpassed it. Howe was elected to the Hockey Hall of Fame in 1965. In a sense it is unfortunate that his skill has been overshadowed by the *other* Howe, the greatest player of all time.

74 Dick Irvin
(1915–1929)

Were it not for a fractured skull suffered while he was playing for the Chicago Black Hawks, Dick Irvin very likely would have written an even more glorious chapter in National Hockey League history than already has been transcribed. But when Red Dutton of the Montreal Maroons flattened Irvin, Dutton inadvertently launched one of the most accomplished of NHL coaching careers. As time unfolded, Irvin's name became synonymous with coaching excellence while his extraordinary feats as a player faded from memory.

Those who remember Irvin as a young professional in western Canada invariably mention his prowess as a scorer and his courage under the cruelest conditions. Once, while playing for Regina, Irvin was deliberately hooked under the chin by a notorious foe named Spunk Sparrow.

Irvin had a habit of playing with his tongue between his teeth and the blow of Sparrow's stick was so severe that Dick bit right through his tongue. Instead of heading to the infirmary for repairs, Irvin insisted upon continuing. He won the face-off, wheeled past the penalty bench where Sparrow was incarcerated and walloped his adversary so hard that Sparrow required sixteen stitches to close the wound. Only *then* did Irvin head for the dressing room, where the doctor sewed up his tongue, which was hanging by a shred.

Throughout most of his playing career Irvin was eclipsed by only the very best. While playing for the Portland Rosebuds, for example, Irvin finished second in scoring to Bill Cook of Saskatoon, who was regarded as the finest right wing of his time.

Coincidentally, in Irvin's rookie year in the National Hockey League he finished runner-up to the scoring champion—Bill Cook.

James Dickenson Irvin was born July 19, 1892, in Limestone Ridge, Ontario, just outside the city of Hamilton. His family moved to Winnipeg in 1899 and it was while living there that Dick learned to skate on the Red River.

In time he became well known throughout Winnipeg amateur hockey circles. One night, while watching a game at the Winnipeg Amphitheater, Dick was a witness while Dolly Gray of the Winnipeg Monarchs broke his shoulder. Irvin was asked to replace the injured Gray and obliged by scoring five goals in an 8–3 win over Winnipeg Varsity. From that point on Dick never looked back.

Playing for the Monarchs against the Toronto Rugby and Athletic Association team in 1914, Irvin scored *all* of his team's goals in a 9–1 victory. The nine-goal effort earned Dick a place in Robert Ripley's "Believe It or Not" syndicated newspaper feature.

Irvin turned pro with Portland in 1914 and played one full season before enlisting in the Canadian army. He served for three years, returning to Canada where he resumed his hockey career with Regina. Following two years with Regina, Irvin moved west to Portland during the golden era of western hockey.

Irvin was an instant hit skating for the Rosebuds in Portland and undoubtedly would have remained there for several seasons were it not for the fact that the Western League could not weather its financial crisis and finally packed it in. The NHL, meanwhile, was expanding throughout the United States, and Chicago, among other cities, obtained a franchise.

The Chicago Black Hawks' owner, Major Frederick McLaughlin, decided to purchase the entire Portland Rosebud hockey club and in 1926 Irvin made his debut in the Windy City. Coach Pete Muldoon named Dick captain of the new entry and Irvin responded by leading the Black Hawks in scoring.

It was early in his second year as a Black Hawk when Irvin was flattened by Red Dutton and hospitalized with a fractured skull. After his release from the hospital, Dick was refused permission to play for the remainder of the season. He returned the following year, played a few games and then was appointed coach of the Chicago sextet.

The conclusion of Irvin's playing career marked the start of a twenty-six-year career as an NHL coach. He remained behind the Black Hawks' bench until 1931, when he switched to the Toronto Maple Leafs. He stayed in Toronto, working under manager Conn Smythe, until 1940.

He led the Maple Leafs to their first Stanley Cup championship in 1932, but his halcyon years as a coach were spent in Montreal during the 1940s and early 1950s. He won Stanley Cups with Les Canadiens in 1944, 1946 and 1953.

As a coach, he became increasingly truculent behind the bench as he aged. Irvin was considered a terrific stimulant for Canadiens super-scorer Maurice (The Rocket) Richard during The Rocket's early years but in the early 1950s, some critics believed that Irvin prodded Richard into tempestuous combat too often and this, in turn, led to innumerable penalties for Richard. Frank Selke, Sr., a great friend and booster of Irvin, was managing director of the Canadiens at the time, and finally decided that Irvin was having a negative effect on Richard. Irvin resigned from the Canadiens in 1955 and took the job as head coach of the Chicago Black Hawks for the 1955–56 season.

Those close to Irvin realized that he already was suffering from a terminal ailment and, as the season progressed, Dick's condition worsened. Gamecock that he was, Irvin remained at the helm until the end of the campaign and even considered a return for the 1956–57 season. He finally acknowledged the depth of his illness and retired at the start of the new campaign. The NHL immediately named him to the position of goodwill ambassador and Dick worked when he could. He died in May 1957 and was elected to the Hockey Hall of Fame a year later.

75 Duke Keats
(1916–1929)

For sheer smarts as a hockey player few could equal and nobody could top Duke Keats. Frank Patrick, a Hall of Famer and himself one of the most astute judges of hockey talent, once observed of Keats:

"Duke is the possessor of more hockey grey matter than any man who ever played the game. He is the most unselfish superstar in hockey. I have watched him innumerable times. In one game, I specially checked up on his play. He gave his wingmen thirty chances to score by perfectly placed passes. He's the brainiest pivot that ever pulled on a skate, because he can organize plays and make passes every time he starts."

Keats originally made his mark with the Toronto Arenas in 1916, then the Edmonton Eskimos of the Western Canada Hockey League, operated by Frank and Lester Patrick. It was a splendid league, the equal of the National Hockey League. Keats' Edmonton teammates included aces such as Barney Stanley and Bullet Joe Simpson, each of whom is in the Hockey Hall of Fame.

By the early 1920s The Duke reigned as one of the most popular and accomplished players in western Canada. "He was the hero of Edmonton," wrote Canadian journalist Ken McConnell, "and undoubtedly one of the greatest center-ice men who ever laced up a skate."

Gordon Keats was born March 1, 1895, in Montreal, but learned his hockey in North Bay, Ontario. He joined the McKinlay-Darragh mine team in the old Cobalt Mining League when he was fourteen. Two years later, when he was only sixteen, he joined the Toronto Arenas.

One night in 1916 Keats scored two goals in twenty seconds for the Toronto club against Quebec City. "He is the one hockey player who will always remain my superstar," said McConnell.

While playing for the Arenas—also known as the Blue Shirts—Duke enlisted in the 228th Sportsmen's Battalion of Toronto, which entered a team in the NHA for the 1916–1917 season, when wartime spirit was reaching its peak.

From time to time the schedule called for the Arenas to play the Battalion sextet. By no small coincidence Duke's sergeants made a point of assigning him to guard duty on those occasions. This piqued several Blue Shirts fans, who were worried that the Duke would be absent from the match between the 228th and Toronto on January 20, 1917.

Word of Keats' impending guard duty was leaked to the Toronto newspapers, and public sentiment was militantly against the sergeant's shenanigans. "Keats," said reporter Ken McConnell, "was thrown into the guardhouse but was released the day of the game after every newspaper in Toronto had printed the story. He was allowed to play against his battalion mates."

For some time the army regretted its decision. Early in the third period Toronto's goaltender, Billy Nicholson, was penalized. In that era goaltenders had to serve their penalties in the penalty box, so a replacement for Nicholson was needed. The

Duke himself strapped on the goalie pads and took his position in front of the nets. "He played the remaining twenty minutes," according to the NHL history, "without allowing a goal."

Further controversy about Keats' right to play for Toronto was ended on February 10, 1917, when the 228th Battalion received orders to go overseas. Duke, of course, was with them. When he returned from active duty, Keats signed with Edmonton, of the Western Canada Hockey League. According to Babe Donnelly, he was a better hockey player than ever.

Keats led the Western Canada Hockey League in scoring in 1922–23 and steered Edmonton to the league championship and a match-up against the Ottawa Senators in a battle for the Stanley Cup. But the easterners prevailed although Duke had made a very favorable impression on NHL types. This was significant because the WCHL was in the process of disintegrating and the Patricks, Frank and Lester, had decided to sell their best players to the expanding National Hockey League.

The Duke was plucked by manager Art Ross of the Boston Bruins who, in turn, dealt him to the Detroit Cougars during the 1926–27 season. The following season the Cougars dispatched Duke to the Chicago Black Hawks. He concluded his big-league career in 1928–29, returned to western Canada but remained close to the hockey scene.

He was elected to the Hockey Hall of Fame in 1958 and died January 16, 1972.

"In all sports," wrote Ken McConnell, "there is an outstanding figure and Duke Keats, the grand old center-ice man of the West, was just such an individual."

76 Frank Brimsek (1938–1950)

"Mr. Zero."

There was never one before, and there will never be one again. Frank Brimsek was the original, and after him they threw away the mold. One would be hard pressed to find an American-born player who made a more emphatic impact on "The Game." And were it not for a World War II stint in the United States Coast Guard—which significantly disturbed his future—Brimsek might well have emerged as the greatest exponent of goaltending we have ever known.

As it was, his career featured a number of truly sensational chapters from the moment it was announced that he would depose the remarkable Tiny Thompson in the Boston Bruins net.

In Frankie's rookie season of 1939, he won both the Calder Trophy as the best newcomer in the league, and the Vezina Trophy for his outstanding play in the nets, the only American player ever to accomplish that achievement. That year Frankie was voted to the First All-Star team. He repeated as the Vezina winner in 1942, and was the First All-Star Team goalie that year. Six times Brimsek was named to the Second All-Star Team during his Boston career. With Frankie in the nets, the Bruins won the Stanley Cup twice, and three times finished first.

He was an American legend in hockey. In 1966, Frankie Brimsek, born and raised in Eveleth, Minnesota, became the first United States player of professional hockey elected to the Hockey Hall of Fame. He was also inducted into the U.S. Hockey Hall of Fame.

Brimsek had quite a sensational break into the majors. In 1937 he had been assigned to Boston's American League farm club, the Providence Reds. Boston's goaltender was none other than Tiny Thompson, known to the hockey world as "the goalie without a weakness." Thompson was the best in the business, a four-time Vezina Trophy winner. Prospects didn't look good for the American kid buried in the minors.

It was quite by accident that Brimsek got his first chance to play in a big-league game. Thompson developed an eye infection, and Art Ross, the general manager and coach of Boston, sent for Brimsek. Frank was nervous. It was tough enough to fill in for any goalie, but the pressure was colossal considering the kid was being asked to fill the nets for the great Tiny Thompson.

Frank's jitters vanished once the game started. Frankie, then only twenty-three years old, won his NHL debut by a score of 3–2. Three nights later, with Brimsek in the nets, the Bruins beat the Detroit Red Wings.

Thompson recovered, and Frankie was sent back to Providence. But Ross had liked what he had seen. He now had a dilemma on his hands. Popular with the fans, Thompson was great, and had been Boston's solid rock for ten years. At thirty-three he would have several more outstanding seasons.

Trading Thompson would not go over well with the multitude of Bruin supporters, especially if Tiny's replacement failed. Ross journeyed to Providence to take another look at Frankie, who turned in a couple of shutouts while Ross scouted him. On November 28, 1938, Tiny Thompson was dealt to the Red Wings for $15,000.

On December 1, 1938, in a game against the Montreal Canadiens, Frankie Brimsek went into the nets not as the replacement for an injured Thompson, but as the regular goalie for the Bruins. Although the game was played at the Montreal Forum, Brimsek was aware there were critical eyes watching his every move.

The evening turned into a disaster. Montreal, who had won only once in their eight previous contests, beat Boston 2–0. In Detroit, the exiled Thompson beat Chicago 4–1. It left little reason to doubt that Ross had made a mistake.

Frankie Brimsek was down, but not out. It took only the next seven games for him to become a hockey legend. Playing the next game against the Chicago Black Hawks, Brimsek recorded his first ever NHL shutout, as Boston beat Chicago by a score of 5–0.

However, the fans were not yet warming to him, and Frankie did little to improve his image. He had an idiosyncrasy of wearing red hockey pants instead of the team's then gold, brown and white colors, and his footwork left much to be desired. But his glove was quick and his confidence was enormous. The Boston fans would be in for a surprise.

Two nights later, the same teams met in Boston. It was Frankie's first appearance before the hostile Bruins fans. Brimsek scored a 2–0 shut out.

Frankie's next game was against the New York Rangers. Although the Rangers belted him with thirty-three shots on goal, Frankie stopped them all, as he earned his third straight shutout by a score of 3–0. By now he had 192 minutes and 40 seconds of scoreless goaltending. Thompson's modern record of 224 minutes and 47 seconds was in reach.

By now even the Boston fans were wildly supporting Brimsek. The Bruins were so confident of Frankie's ability that they often sent five men into enemy territory, leaving Brimsek to fend for himself. The next game was against Montreal at the Boston Garden. Boston jumped to a 2–0 lead in the first period, while Frank held Montreal scoreless. The amazing string of scoreless goaltending ran to 212 minutes and 40 seconds.

At the 12:00 minute mark of the second period, the tension in the Garden grew. At 12:08 the arena went wild! Brimsek, in only his fifth game as the Bruins' regular goalie, had erased Tiny Thompson's scoreless record. However, with less than a minute to go in the second period, four Bruins were caught down ice, and Herb Cain took a pass from George Brown and dumped the puck in the Boston goal. Brimsek's marvelous streak had ended at 231 minutes and 54 seconds. Boston went on to win the game 3–2.

Thanks largely to the talents of the young American goalie, Boston was now in first place. Brimsek next shut out Montreal 1–0. Next were the Detroit Red Wings, and the first face-to-face meeting with Thompson. Both goalies played well, but Boston won 2–0. Frankie cut down the New York Americans next, by a score of 3–0. It was his third straight shutout, and his sixth in seven games.

Brimsek went after his own record in the next game against the Rangers. He held New York scoreless during the first period. During the second period, Phil Watson put the puck in the net for the first goal on Brimsek in 220 minutes and 24 seconds of hockey. When Frankie reached down to retrieve the puck, the fans gave him a standing ovation. Frankie Brimsek had done the impossible—he had won over the Boston fans, and made them forget Tiny Thompson.

Francis Charles Brimsek was born on September 26, 1915, in Eveleth, Minnesota. His interest in hockey, oddly enough, was accidental. His older brother John was the second-string goaltender on the Eveleth High School team, but what he really wanted to be was a defenseman. John moved up to the blue line, and brother Frank took over in the nets.

After playing at Eveleth High, he goaltended for a short time at St. Cloud Teachers College. He decided to give the pros a shot, and in 1935 Frankie traveled to Baltimore for a tryout with Baltimore of the Eastern Amateur Hockey League. He gambled everything he had, including his savings, on making the club. He failed.

Hitchhiking back home to Minnesota, depressed and disappointed, Frank was about to land in hockey by accident once more. Running out of cash while he was in Pittsburgh, Frankie stopped off at the old Duquesne Arena to see if he could borrow money for food. Lady Luck shined again on the Minnesota native, as the Pittsburgh team in the Eastern League, the Yellow Jackets, needed a goaltender. Frankie got the job. For two years Brimsek was that club's goalie.

In the fall of 1937, Ross signed Brimsek to a pro contract. He had never even seen the young man play. Assigned to the Providence Reds, Boston's American League farm club, Frankie waited in the minors. In 1938, Brimsek, barely one year out of the amateurs, was Boston's goalie.

Looking back on that rookie season, Frankie said, "Tiny was such a great goaltender, I had to be good or they would have chased me right out of Boston."

During that spectacular rookie season, Brimsek finished with a brilliant 1.59 average, and had 10 shutouts. He had given up only 70 goals in forty-four games. Rightfully, he was awarded both the Calder Trophy and the Vezina Trophy.

Frankie played for Boston for five sparkling seasons, winning the Vezina Trophy again in 1942. At the end of the 1942–43 season, he enlisted in the United States Coast Guard, and for the next two years he served aboard a patrol craft in the Pacific.

After the war, Frankie gave the National Hockey League another try. He returned to Boston for four seasons, but his comeback was a great disappointment. He had lost his edge. The Bruins kept waiting and hoping for the magic to come back. It never did. Boston traded Frankie to the dismal Chicago Black Hawks in 1949. There, Brimsek bombed terribly, and he retired after one season.

Frank had retired at the relatively young age of thirty-four. He had been the best, and he had been unique, an American-born, American-developed goaltender excelling at his skill. He had played on Stanley Cup winners. He had stood alone on the mountaintop, the finest at his profession. The war had caused him to lose his skill. Brimsek had little choice but to retire.

After he retired, Frankie settled in Virginia, Minnesota, a small town only five miles from Eveleth. He became an engineer for the Canadian National Railroad, guiding freight trains between the various cities in Canada.

His goaltending for the prewar Boston Bruins will forever be cited by hockey's *cognoscenti* as the definitive work of its time. Frankie Brimsek proved beyond a doubt that an American could make it in the Canadian-laden National Hockey League.

77 Babe Dye
(1919-1929)

Long before the slapshot or curved stick made its debut in National Hockey League rinks, the powerful drives of Babe Dye were giving goaltenders ulcers throughout the NHL.

Dye's mighty and accurate shot won him scoring championships in 1923 and 1925, and the right wing's name became a household word in Toronto, Hamilton, Chicago and New York during his hockey career in the NHL.

Playing ten seasons of hockey, Dye had a great career in the game. Thanks largely to their high-scoring right wing, the Toronto St. Pats finished in first at the end of the 1920–21 season. In the 1921–22 season, the St. Pats won the Stanley Cup. At the top of his game in 1923 and 1925, the Babe was well deserving as he led the league in scoring points. In 1923 he had 26 goals and 11 assists for 37 points, and in 1925 he did even better, with 38 goals and 6 assists for 44 points.

Among players with 200 or more goals, Dye is third on the all-time list of the highest goals-per-game average, as he scored 200 goals in 271 games, for an outstanding average of .738. In 1921, the Babe's goals-per-game average was an amazing 1.46, good enough for sixth on the all-time list. He was honored for his outstanding play in 1970, when he was inducted into the Hockey Hall of Fame.

"Babe could shoot the puck from any length or from any spot on the rink," said Canadian author Ron McAllister. "He could score with his back turned, or from any side at all." As a testimony to Dye's scoring ability, twice in his career with Toronto he scored five goals in a single game.

Dye was a small but strong right wing with limitless potential. He was unique among the long list of athletes who had learned their sport in the famous Jesse Ketchum School playground in Toronto. For unlike the others, Dye had lost his father only a year after he was born, and it had been his mother, Esther Dye, who had vowed her son would have an athletic background. Essie proceeded to instruct him herself.

Cecil Henry "Babe" Dye was born in Hamilton, Ontario, on May 13, 1898. An all-around athlete, Babe played all sports. He eventually joined the Hillcrest Seniors in the Toronto Senior Hockey League, starting as a right-winger.

In 1917, Babe joined the De La Salle Hockey Club, and that year the team won the championship. At nineteen Dye joined the artillery, and soon found himself playing on the hockey and baseball teams. Victory was near, and soon the army hockey players were in civilian clothes. In 1918, Charlie Querrie, manager of the Toronto St. Pats of the Senior League, contacted the players of the army squad.

Babe made himself a household word, as he played brilliantly. Dye scored 30 goals in twenty-four games to tie for the league lead with Harry Broadbent of Ottawa. Unfortunately, Toronto finished second behind their archrivals, but the St. Pats were to get another shot at them on March 11, 1922, before 8,000 screaming fans in Mutual Street Arena.

Rookie goaltender John Ross Roach complemented the Babe's offensive artistry. A nervous goalie, Roach held the Senators to four goals while Toronto scored five to take a surprising one-game lead. The two-game total-goals series moved to Ottawa, and all the home team needed was a two-goal lead to beat the upstart Toronto team.

The defending champs could not get one past Roach, although his defenses were crumbling around him. Roach held tight, and Toronto managed to hold the powerful Senators to a 0–0 tie, good for a 5–4 total goals advantage, and the right to meet Vancouver for the Stanley Cup.

In the playoffs, Babe did not fully assert himself until the Stanley Cup finals reached the second game. Vancouver, with Lester Patrick behind the bench, edged the St. Pats 4–3 in the first contest. The Babe scored a goal at 4:40 in the sudden-death overtime to give Toronto a 2–1 win in the second game. Vancouver went ahead for the last time in the series with a 3–0 win in the third game.

Now on the brink of elimination, the St. Pats showed their mettle in the fourth game, beating Vancouver by a score of 6–0. Dye was impressive, as he led the rout with a pair of goals.

The fifth and final game took place on March 28, 1922, at Mutual Street Arena. Hockey critics agreed that for two periods the final game between Vancouver and Toronto was a Stanley Cup classic. With the St. Pats holding a 2–1 lead in the third period, Babe scored his memorable ''mystery goal.'' Dye's blast, hit with such ease and speed, made the flight from stick to cage so quickly that Lehman, the goalie, waited crouching for it—long after it had left Dye's stick.

No one but Dye knew where the puck was. McAllister said, ''The crowd finally roared and pointed to the Vancouver net. There was the puck! Then, the light was flashed on and the goal registered.'' Totally blown away, Vancouver gave up two more goals. Toronto won 5–1, and became the Stanley Cup champions.

Dye's sparkling hockey play continued as he starred in Toronto's colors. Scoring 17 goals in nineteen games in the 1923–24 season, the Babe had not even reached his athletic peak.

In the 1924–25 year, Toronto finished a close second to Hamilton, thanks to their offensive weapon, Babe Dye. He had scored 38 goals in twenty-nine games. League arrangements dictated that second place Toronto would meet the third place Canadiens for the right to play Hamilton in the NHL finals. Demanding more money, the Hamilton players staged a surprise strike. League President Frank Calder angrily rejected the demands, and ordered the winner of the Toronto-Montreal series to be the league champions.

Dye was overshadowed by a new star on the NHL horizon—Howie Morenz—a spectacularly speedy center who overwhelmed every skater on Toronto. He led Montreal to a 3–2 win, and then a 2–0 victory. The Babe was held scoreless in the series, and Toronto lost possession of the Stanley Cup.

Dye played one more season for the St. Pats. Although he scored 18 goals in the 1925–26 year, the team slipped to sixth place in a seven-team league. He was traded to the Chicago Black Hawks the following season, where he scored 25 goals.

In a preseason practice with Chicago in 1927, Dye broke his leg. The injury hastened the end of his career. His swan song came one year later, during the 1928–29 season, as Babe played briefly and ingloriously for the New York Americans. It was the end of Babe Dye's illustrious hockey career.

After his retirement from the sport he loved so much, Dye lived in Chicago where he worked for a large construction company. Cecil Henry ''Babe'' Dye passed away January 3, 1962. Hockey had lost one of its most spectacular players.

78 Frank Nighbor (1913–1930)

The very model of a gentlemanly hockey player who also fused durability and craftsmanship into his game, Frank Nighbor was a center after whom many future Hall of Famers modelled their game. It is not, in fact, too farfetched to suggest that Wayne Gretzky is the Frank Nighbor of the contemporary game.

Nighbor not only was good, but he was a winner—a big winner. In his third year of professional hockey, skating for the Vancouver Millionaires, Nighbor tasted the Stanley Cup champagne. Already he was a star among the greats and, not insignificantly, every skater on the 1915 Vancouver club is now enshrined in the Hockey Hall of Fame. The aces included goalie Hugh Lehman, defensemen Frank Patrick and Si Griffis, rover Fred Taylor, center Mickey Mackay, with Nighbor and Barney Stanley on the wings.

He soon moved to the Ottawa Senators where he began a long and industrious career, spanning thirteen years and including four Stanley Cup winners. He was the first to win the Hart Trophy as the National Hockey League's most valuable player, which he annexed in 1924. He won the Lady Byng Trophy for good sportsmanship combined with competence in 1925 and 1926. Which is not to suggest that Nighbor was flawless as a person or a player. He had his weak moments and he was given to needling the enemy and the referee of the moment. One of his targets was Cooper Smeaton, a distinguished arbiter who himself is a member of the Hall of Fame.

"One night," Smeaton recalled, "Nighbor really gave me trouble. Every time a pass was made by the other team he'd yell 'Offside, offside!' That irked me and I skated over to the Ottawa bench and told him, 'Nighbor, if you yell 'offside' once more I'm going to let it go.'

"Sure enough, on the next rush Nighbor yelled 'offside' and even though it was about ten feet offside I ignored the whistle and the other team nearly scored. After that Nighbor stopped screaming."

Nighbor's admirers would be quick to dismiss such an incident as an aberration. Hall of Famer Joe Primeau, who starred at center for the Toronto Maple Leafs in the 1930s, regarded Nighbor as his super-hero. "He was my inspiration," said Primeau. "As a kid, I'd get on the ice and say 'I'm going to be Frank Nighbor.' I never dreamed that, someday, he'd actually be a teammate of mine, but that's what happened."

Another future Hall of Famer who revered Nighbor was Frank Boucher. In his memoirs, *When The Rangers Were Young,* Boucher provided a vivid word picture of Nighbor:

"He was a great checker, either poking the puck from an opponent's stick as he came head-on, or hooking it from him as he attempted to go by. I learned that Nighbor had spliced an additional eight inches to the handle of his stick, and it was perfectly legal because the rules specified only that sticks must not exceed three inches in width at any point, making no reference to the length. Eventually, with the arrival of such great checkers as Hooley Smith, Pit Lepine, Cooney Weiland and many more in the NHL, the rulemakers restricted the length to fifty-three inches in an effort to open up the game.

''Nighbor was quite tall, and he skated in an upright position. Of all the hockey players I've seen, no one was more scarred about the face than Frank. I've watched the famed Newsy Lalonde give it to Frank in the face-offs, deliberately ripping his stick straight up into Frank's face. He'd have to go in and get stitched, then he'd come back for more. And this was a common occurrence, yet I can honestly say I don't recall him ever hitting back. My brother George used to fight a lot of Frank's battles when they were with the Senators. Buck couldn't stand Frank's taking this abuse and he'd sail in and help out, knocking the other guys cockeyed. If they retaliated, there'd be a hell of a fight. If they didn't, that was the end of it. Buck would snarl at them, 'Goddamn you, you lay off Nighbor.' But I really admired how Frank refused to play the other fellow's game. He knew he was taking his beating because his checking was so effective, and he just went right ahead demoralizing the other team's offense.''

Nighbor played his last NHL game, teaming up with Joe Primeau of the Toronto Maple Leafs in 1930. He was elected to the Hockey Hall Of Fame in 1945 and died of cancer in his native Pembroke, Ontario, on April 13, 1966.

79 Red Dutton
(1926–1936)

By all odds Red Dutton did not figure to enjoy a decade-long National Hockey League career and then further honors as a club owner and president of the NHL. The hard-bitten son of a wealthy Canadian, Dutton had fought with Canada's legendary Princess Pats regiment in World War I and nearly lost both legs when an artillery shell exploded a few feet away from him.

At first doctors were prepared to amputate but decided against such a measure. Dutton recovered sufficiently to be shipped back to Canada and, despite the early medical report to the contrary, was eventually back on skates. By the early 1920s he was playing for the Calgary Tigers in the old (but top-grade) Western Canada Hockey League alongside such high-quality players as Eddie Shore, Bill and Bun Cook and Frank Boucher.

A defenseman with flaming red hair, Dutton teamed with Herb Gardiner and had become so proficient that the leg wounds suffered in the battle of Vimy Ridge were forgotten as was the seven-hours-a-day training regimen that enabled Dutton to achieve big-league condition. When the WCHL went under, Red was signed by the Montreal Maroons of the NHL and played four seasons with them until he was obtained by the New York Americans, who sought him mostly for his combative nature.

Above all, Dutton was renowned as a scrapper. Playing for Calgary, he originally made his mark during the 1924 Stanley Cup finals against the Montreal Canadiens. The Habitants had a defenseman named Sprague Cleghorn, whose vicious play had earned him a reputation as the scourge of big-league hockey.

Dutton was unimpressed. When Cleghorn butt-ended him with a stick, Red turned around and belted the Canadien in kind. "Cleghorn is remembered to this day as one of the meanest men who ever played the game," said Toronto *Sun* columnist Trent Frayne, "but there was nothing surreptitious about Dutton's responses; he simply threw down his stick, tossed off his gloves and sailed into Cleghorn. Blood flowed like wine."

Red was no less courageous as a Maroon. He teamed up with Reg Noble, and the way Dutton would tell it, just sitting next to Noble in the dressing room should have qualified him for the Victoria Cross. "Reg," said Dutton, "would drink a case of beer the day of a game. His breath would knock you down."

An incident that best symbolizes Dutton's approach to hockey took place at the Forum in Montreal. The Maroons and Canadiens had become archrivals and they were lined up, on this night, preparing for the opening face-off. For some reason the referee was unable to find a puck with which to launch the game. The official skated over to the timekeeper's table but there was none there so he asked someone to obtain a puck from the dressing room. Dutton was so frustrated, and so anxious to get the fray going that he shouted: *"Never mind the damn puck. Let's start the game!"*

Dutton's truculence was translated into penalty minutes that usually reached

three figures. Although the NHL only played a forty-four-game schedule at the time Red then set what was a record of 139 minutes for a season. His coach Eddie Gerard eventually tired of Dutton's excessive penalties and finally benched him for three games.

Gerard actually admired Dutton. When the former was named general manager of the New York Americans he went out of his way to deal for Red. It was a fortuitous move. Long after Gerard departed the Manhattan scene, Dutton had established himself as one of the city's most popular sports figures.

Red played splendidly on defense for the Amerks who, unfortunately, were suffering financial woes. At one point Dutton loaned owner Big Bill Dwyer (New York's most notorious bootlegger) $20,000. When Dwyer's fortunes collapsed, the NHL took over the Americans and placed Dutton in charge. He played through the 1935–36 season and then became owner-coach.

Dutton was as crafty on the bench and in the front office as he had been on the ice. Lacking a farm team, he still managed to ice a respectable and, occasionally, a contending team. His finest hour as a coach came in the spring of 1938. The Amerks finished second in the NHL's Canadian Division and then whipped the Rangers in the opening playoff round. They came within a whisker of beating the Chicago Black Hawks in the next playdown before being eliminated.

Mervyn A. Dutton was born July 23, 1898, in Russell, Manitoba. His father had a construction business and, before he entered pro hockey, Red worked on one of his dad's railway construction projects.

He enlisted in the Canadian army at the outbreak of World War I and was in the midst of the action when a hunk of high explosive nearly killed him. The shrapnel hit him in the buttocks and ripped open his thigh and calf. He was only eighteen when it happened, having lied about his age to get into the service to begin with. This was his twentieth month at the front line when he was felled. When he got back to Canada in 1919 he was determined to play hockey.

And he did. Not with the dexterity of an Eddie Shore but with a verve that endeared him to all but his victims.

After retirement, he carried the Americans, financially and otherwise, until the 1942 season when the decimation of the lineup caused by World War II forced abandonment of the team. When NHL President Frank Calder died Dutton was asked to replace him. He remained president until 1946 when he opted for the construction business and turned the gavel over to Clarence Campbell. Now retired and living near Calgary, Dutton was asked to drop the first puck at the Stampede Corral in 1980 when the Calgary Flames made their NHL debut. He was one of a kind—a man you would want on *your* hockey team.

80 Chuck Rayner (1940–1953)

It is mind-boggling to imagine what dizzying heights Chuck Rayner might have reached if he had enjoyed the luxury of playing for a genuinely powerful hockey team. But such was not "Bonnie Prince Charlie's" good fortune. The bushy-browed goaltender made his debut with the subterranean New York (Brooklyn) Americans and finished his valorous puck-blocking career with a rather pathetic New York Rangers aggregation.

In between he demonstrated that he was either the very best or certainly among the top three goalies in the world, despite the fact that he never had a first-place team or a Stanley Cup championship to show for it, but his hard-fought reputation spoke for itself.

Rayner nonetheless made a permanent impression on the NHL and earned his way into the Hockey Hall of Fame. He is the only goaltender ever to have scored a goal by skating the length of the rink in an organized hockey game (although not in the NHL).

He was also amongst the very first to participate in what was then a revolutionary two-goalie experiment, along with his long-time sidekick and pal, James (Sugar Jim) Henry.

The 1949–50 season was in many ways the high point of Rayner's career, as he singlehandedly led the Rangers to the Stanley Cup finals.

It is a measure of Rayner's ability that he won the Hart Trophy—only the second goaltender in history at that time—as the NHL's most valuable player in the 1949–50 season.

Playing for a mediocre Ranger team that never finished higher than fourth, Bonnie Prince Charlie led the Rangers to upset the Canadiens in the 1950 play-offs. They went on to the final round against the Detroit Red Wings. Playing not one home game, they surprised the entire NHL with their strong bid, only to lose the seventh game in dramatic fashion—in an electrifying, double-overtime affair.

Rayner became the first goaltender ever to score a goal. During World War II, while he was playing for the all-star Royal Canadian Army team, Chuck was guarding the goal when a ten-man scramble occurred behind his net. He saw the puck squirt free, with no one between him and it. The temptation was too much for him to resist.

He left his net and charged down the ice. His opponents were so surprised that they simply stopped in their tracks. Rayner skated within a few feet of the goal and shot. The opposing goaltender was dumbfounded and lunged, but the puck sailed right into the net.

When he won the Hart Trophy in 1950, it was one of the most popular announcements in the annals of the game, as he was one of the nicest guys in the sport. Oddly enough, the year he won the Hart Trophy he placed only fourth in the race for the Vezina Trophy.

It was his remarkable and sensational performance in the 1950 playoffs that compensated for this. He was incredible during the series, as he stopped virtually impossible shots. Although the Rangers' quest for the Stanley Cup was stopped, the results of the voting for the Hart Trophy were a credit to the sportsmanship of hockey when the tall goaltender's name was announced.

He was only the second goaltender at that time to win the Hart Trophy. Rayner received thirty-six out of a possible fifty-four points for a thirteen-point lead over Ted Kennedy of the Toronto Maple Leafs. The great Maurice Richard of the Montreal Canadiens finished third in the balloting with eighteen points.

Chuck made the Second Team All-Stars three times, in 1948–49, 1949–50 and 1950–51. In his eight seasons with the New York Rangers, encompassing 424 games, he had 24 shutouts, plus 1 shutout in the playoffs.

Rayner won the West Side Association Trophy as the Rangers' most valuable player during the years 1945=46 and 1946–47, and shared it in 1948–49 with Edgar Laprade.

In August of 1973, Bonnie Prince Charlie was inducted into hockey's Hall of Fame, in honor of his contributions to his sport.

Claude Earl Rayner was born in the small town of Sutherland, Saskatchewan, on August 11, 1920. Like all of the youngsters of that locale, he went down to the local skating rinks to play the national pastime. Chuck always wanted to be a goaltender. In 1936 when Chuck was sixteen years old, he played goal when the Saskatoon Wesleys reached the junior playoffs against the Winnipeg Monarchs. He then went into the goal for the Kenora Thistles in 1936.

At the end of the 1939–40 season, Chuck went down to the New York Americans farm club, the Springfield Indians. Rayner had only played seven games for the Indians when Earl Robertson of the Americans suffered a head injury, leaving open a berth in the nets.

Rayner was called up to take over Robertson's place and so, in 1940, the young man from Sutherland was playing in the NHL.

Rayner played in the goal for the Americans throughout the 1942 season. He then went home and joined the Royal Canadian Armed Forces. Discharged from the service in 1945, Chuck returned to hockey to discover that the New York Americans had disbanded, and that all members of the team were to be part of a raffle for the other NHL teams.

Chuck Rayner's name was pulled out by Lester Patrick of the New York Rangers. And thus began one of the oddest stories in sport. Patrick had already hired a goalie, Sugar Jim Henry. Chuck finally won the Ranger goalkeeping job permanently.

Rayner had to retire after the 1952–53 season. He had damaged the cartilage in his knee. An operation temporarily held the knee up, but again, the knee weakened to the point where he felt he couldn't do the job anymore.

Chuck suffered through many injuries, and there's no telling how long he could have played if he had a mask and an alternate goaltender.

After his retirement as a player, Chuck returned to western Canada where he coached the Nelson Leafs. After two years there he went to Alberta and coached the Edmonton Flyers. He then did some work for the Rangers, and then for the Detroit Red Wing organization with his friend Sid Abel.

By the mid-sixties he had been coaching nine years, but he didn't enjoy it. Chuck didn't like having to tell a kid that he was traded.

Bonnie Prince Charlie left the sport completely. By 1979 he had been away from hockey for almost ten years.

Chuck was a courageous man who often played black-and-blue. He was the kind of man who played when a lesser man would have sat out. It was tragic that such a nice guy with his capabilities never played on a Stanley Cup championship winner. However, no one will ever forget the heroics that Rayner accomplished during the exciting 1950 playoffs with the Cinderella Rangers, and he is well-deserving of his spot in *Hockey's 100*.

81 Tom Johnson
(1947–1965)

There were few more durable or intelligent defensemen in the National Hockey League than Tom Johnson. Although he played in the shadow of the great Doug Harvey during much of his NHL career, Johnson proved as capable at his profession as any defenseman. Playing on the dynastic Montreal Canadiens for thirteen seasons, he played on six Stanley Cup championship teams, and six first-place clubs, which merely serves to emphasize the point.

Johnson was indefatigable, durable, playing in 978 games, and might have played a full twenty years of big-league hockey, had he not been felled by a serious leg injury. He finished first in the balloting for the Norris Trophy as the National Hockey League's best defenseman in 1959, and was named to the First All-Star Team that year. In 1956 he had been a Second All-Star Team member.

During the 1958–59 season, when Harvey was injured, Tom became the new team leader. He baffled the opposition with his inimitable but unheralded double-back play. As an opponent would speed in, Tom would lunge at the puck.

Lynn Patrick, Boston Bruins general manager, said, "I'd always been a great admirer of Tom Johnson. I'll never forget the year we were leading Montreal in the playoffs while he was out with an injury. Well . . . he returned to the lineup and that was the end of us. He was one of the game's outstanding competitors for a long time."

That was the kind of athlete Tom Johnson was—talented, hard-working and unrecognized. Playing next to Harvey, the best defenseman of his time, and perhaps the greatest ever, Johnson's hockey contributions went unnoticed. "It's simple," Emile Francis, then the general manager of the New York Rangers, said, "Johnson's trouble was playing on the most colorful team in hockey history. With guys like Maurice Richard, Boom Boom Geoffrion, Jacques Plante and Jean Beliveau in the lineup, nobody ever noticed Johnson. But he was the *real* worker on the team."

When Johnson won the Norris Trophy in 1959, he interrupted what would have been an eight-year ownership of that award by Harvey. "That was the year Doug was hurt," Tom good-naturedly said. "The Norris Trophy and the time the Canadiens won their fourth straight Stanley Cup championship were the biggest satisfactions for me," Tom stated.

Much to his own amazement, Tom Johnson was elected to hockey's Hall of Fame in 1970. If Johnson was surprised, then Hall of Famer Eddie Shore was outraged. So upset with Johnson's entry into the Hall was Shore that he offered to buy back his own induction.

Johnson looked back at his banner year of 1959 with pride, but he put it in perspective. "I didn't really consider it my best year. It just happened that year I got a lot of scoring points (10 goals, 29 assists). It seems that's what a lot of the voters look for, even in defensemen. I thought any year between 1955 and 1960 I played the game about the same."

Although Tom returned to hockey following a serious eye injury, the Montreal brass later questioned the quality of the vision in his right eye. Johnson never again reached his former level of play, and when he continued to miss his checks and began to cost the Canadiens' goals, the Forum fans turned on him. Eventually Montreal left Tom unprotected in the draft, and the Bruins claimed him for $30,000 in 1963.

Thomas Christian Johnson was born February 18, 1928, in Baldur, Manitoba. Young Johnson knew early on what he wanted to be. "When I was in the third grade," Tom said, "the teacher asked us to write down what we wanted to do when we grew up. I wrote 'professional hockey player.' That was the first time I'd ever thought about it."

When Johnson was seventeen, he tried out for the Winnipeg Monarchs. "I wasn't much of a skater, and I didn't think I'd make the team." When the coach went over to Tom, he prepared for the worst, and expected to take his skates packing. Instead, the coach said, "Johnson, where do you want to play, forward or defense?"

After training with Winnipeg, the Montreal Royals, and the Buffalo Bisons for a few seasons, Johnson, a gawky but determined youngster, moved up to Montreal in 1950. Teammate Ken Mosdell recalled, "Everybody said Tom was a bad skater, and that might have been. But, dammit, nobody could catch him. He could move."

Tom also gained the reputation that he could hit. In his first game at Detroit, Johnson banged with notable toughs Gordie Howe and Ted Lindsay. "He's a villain," accused former goalie John Ross Roach, "one of the cruder woodchoppers to appear here in some time." Not an all-time dirty player, Johnson nevertheless was well known for his physical style of play. Stan Mikita, the Chicago Black Hawks all-star center, once said, "Johnson's on my black list. He liked to hit you from behind. When he got into a fight he never dropped his stick. Instead of using his fists, he used his stick for protection."

Andy Bathgate, then the New York Rangers' leading scorer, believed Johnson was one of the five most notorious spearing specialists in the NHL. "Spearing is the most savage, sneaky trick in hockey," he said, "and the most lethal. It's going to kill somebody."

Johnson felt Bathgate was being unfair in his criticism. "When Bathgate made that crack about my spearing, I didn't have a *single* spearing penalty in my entire career. His remarks were in poor taste. Not so much for me, but for hockey in general. I don't like to see people knock the game." However, the underrated defenseman never apologized for his fighting. "Fighting is a necessary part of the game. If you're challenged, you've got to stand up to the guy and fight. But on skates, and with all the equipment, fighting takes a lot out of you. After one or two minutes, you're exhausted." Tom, muscular and strong at 5'11" and 190 pounds, could certainly hold his tough ice attitude responsible for getting him into fights, although he admitted he'd lost more fights than he'd won.

While most hockey players married early, saved their dollars, and led simple lives, Tom Johnson proved to be the exception. The flashy, well-dressed Johnson remained single, spent freely, owned race horses, and indulged in the finer things of life. While his teammates dined at club quarters in Manhattan's Picadilly Hotel, Tom dined at the Americana Hotel. "Tom's first class all the way," Harvey said. "I can remember Tom cracking up a Thunderbird after he had only seventy miles on it. The old boy didn't blink an eye. Just went out and bought another. He's more conservative now—he only buys one new convertible a year."

Playing for Boston during the 1964–65 season in a game against Chicago, forward Chico Maki's skate slashed the motor nerve in Johnson's left leg, ending his playing career. He had played in fifteen big-league seasons, and probably would have played in five more if not for the crippling injury. There was an emergency 3½ hour operation to patch Johnson's leg back together, but he would never again play in the National Hockey League.

"Nobody—nobody—tried harder to make it back as a player than Tom Johnson," said Bruins boss Weston Adams. "He worked like mad, but he just couldn't make it."

Following the leg injury which ended his playing career and gave him a permanent limp, Johnson remained with Boston and briefly became head coach. His club won the Stanley Cup in 1972, and he remained behind the bench one more season. He then became assistant to general manager Harry Sinden. Johnson has remained Sinden's first lieutenant and troubleshooter to this day. His affable, cigar-plugged-in-mouth appearance has cheered all twenty-one press rooms around the NHL. The unsung player of the dynastic Canadiens still remains in the background, but, as always, he gets the job done. On artistry and longevity, Tom Johnson is a deserved member of *Hockey's 100*.

82 Gerry Cheevers (1961–1980)

An interesting blend of healthy truculence, daring inventiveness, superior intelligence and amazing agility (even when he appeared overweight in his declining years) made Gerry Cheevers unusual and several cuts above most of his goaltending peers.

Pugnacious almost to a fault, Cheevers more than anything was a winner. He shared the goaltending—with Eddie Johnston—on the Boston Bruins' last two Stanley Cup championship teams in 1970 and 1972. In 1973 he was voted the best goaltender in the World Hockey Association. He was the number one goalie for Team Canada in 1974 during the series against the Soviet All-Stars and was durable enough to span two decades as a professional.

Few could match Cheevers's competitive zeal. His policy was strict and honest: when you lose it's like being shot on the battlefield and don't go shaking the hand of the enemy for that! Such was the case in 1971 when goalie Ken Dryden and the Montreal Canadiens upset Cheevers's Bruins. At game's end the teams lined up for the traditional handshaking ceremonies but Cheevers already had made a quick exit to his dressing room.

"I wanted to tell Dryden when it was all over that he'd done a big, big job, but I didn't," said Cheevers. "When the teams met in a straggly line at center and shook hands, I wasn't among those present. I've never congratulated a guy for beating me. I sure as hell didn't feel like gripping Mahovlich's paw, and Harper's and Lemaire's. They put lumps on me and took my money; why should I applaud them?"

Later, Cheevers called over Jacques Beauchamp, a Montreal journalist who was heading back to the plane that would carry the victorious Canadiens—and Dryden —back to Montreal. "Jacques," he said, "when you get on the plane, tell that giraffe (Dryden) he had one hell of a series. Tell him congratulations for me, Jacques."

The congratulations had enveloped Cheevers many times during a career that included 418 regular season National Hockey League games and 88 playoff matches. His goals-against average was 2.89 for the regular campaigns and 2.69 for the playoffs.

In a sense, the figures were deceptive because Gerry goaled for a Bruins club that invariably accented offense—Phil Esposito, Bobby Orr, Ken Hodge were the big guns—and ignored defense. Which meant that Cheevers was pretty much on his own.

Nicknamed "Chessie," Cheevers set an NHL record during the 1971–72 season when he played goal through thirty-two unbeaten games. "He was one of the all-time greats when it came to money games," said Phil Esposito, a long-time teammate.

Gerald Michael Cheevers was born December 7, 1940, in St. Catherines, Ontario, and seemed destined for a career with the Toronto Maple Leafs, which owned his rights during the early 1960s. He was obtained by the Bruins in 1965 and, after a few trips to the minors, made it to stay in the NHL in 1967, at a time when Boston's fortunes were on the rise.

In time fans were hanging banners over the Boston Garden balcony: "WE'RE BELIEVERS IN GERRY CHEEVERS."

After the Bruins won the Stanley Cup in 1972 Cheevers jumped to the Cleveland Crusaders of the World Hockey Association and remained in the WHA until 1976 when he returned to the Hub sextet. It was no coincidence that Cheevers's return marked another upturn in the Bruins' fortunes. His habit of pursuing and stickhandling the puck delighted Boston Garden fans and his goaltending still had a snap of sharpness.

Gerry remained a Bruins goalie until his retirement after the 1979–80 campaign when he was named Boston coach. The transition from the nets to the bench was not an easy one. "It was," said Cheevers, "a tremendous learning experience."

Bruins General Manager Harry Sinden nevertheless expressed confidence in Cheevers. "He has acquired an excellent grasp of the coaching technique," said Sinden, who retained Gerry as head coach through the 1981–82 season, in which the Bruins displayed a marked improvement. With Cheevers behind the bench the Bruins remained the class of the Adams Division, finishing first in the 1982–83 and 1983–84 seasons.

However, as one press box critic noted, Cheevers the coach will always be at a disadvantage, "because he doesn't have Gerry Cheevers in the net!"

83 Bill Quackenbush
(1942–1956)

One of the ironies of major-league hockey is that some of the toughest, most bloodthirsty teams down through the years also have been graced with calm, cerebral, discreet players who have been the antithesis of their team's image.

Bill Quackenbush, a defenseman with both the Detroit Red Wings and Boston Bruins, was just such a gentleman. Like Red Kelly, another decorous Red Wings defenseman, Quackenbush was clean enough and competent enough to win the Lady Byng Trophy in 1949 while playing for a Detroit club notorious for such sluggers as Terrible Ted Lindsay and Black Jack Stewart.

Although the temptation to join the brawlers always was quite apparent, Quackenbush resisted the lure and played a pure defense. In so doing, he made a greater impact on the game than some of his more violent teammates.

More than anything, Quackenbush was an extraordinary practitioner of his art. He was named to the National Hockey League's First All-Star Team in 1948, 1949 and 1951 during an era when the NHL was oozing with top-notch backliners. Bill made the Second Team in 1947 and 1953.

It is a measure of the influence of Quackenbush that some hockey writers have suggested that the NHL name a trophy in his honor to be given to the league's best defensive defenseman.

Along with winning the Lady Byng trophy in 1949, quite an accomplishment for a defenseman, he once went a span of 137 games (over three different seasons) without taking a penalty.

Bill Quackenbush played with some of the all-time greats of the sport, and was a regular when a kid by the name of Gordie Howe came to Detroit.

"He came in when he was seventeen and anyone looking at him could tell he had talent. It was just a matter of time before he became the kind of hockey player he was. He's one of the best all-around hockey players I've ever played with."

Hubert George Quackenbush was born March 2, 1922, in Toronto, Ontario. He played his hockey on the city's innumerable outdoor rinks during the Great Depression and was ready for the big time shortly after the outbreak of World War II.

Quackenbush played on the Red Wings' 1943 Stanley Cup-winning team and played on two first-place teams. When the Red Wings finished first at the conclusion of the 1948–49 season there was no hint that Bill would be traded but Jack Adams stunned the hockey world by dealing Bill to the Boston Bruins.

For Quackenbush, it was a comedown in more ways than one. Not that life in Detroit was all glamour. Adams ran a spartan ship at Olympia Stadium but conditions in Boston Garden were even worse.

In the spring of 1952, the Boston Bruins took on the powerhouse Montreal Canadiens in the Stanley Cup semifinals. Bill Quackenbush, normally known for his sturdy, inconspicuous, mistake-free play, was involved in one of the most famous hockey episodes in Stanley Cup history. The series had gone seven games with Montreal winning the first three games and Boston winning the next three.

Early in the seventh game, Maurice "The Rocket" Richard was knocked flying by a vicious check from burly Leo Labine. As the Rocket lay on the ice, motionless, speculation was that he was through for the series, if not longer.

The game was tied late in the third period, 1–1. The Bruins, with steady Bill Quackenbush on his right-defense position, had just killed off four minutes of penalties.

All of a sudden the Rocket was on the ice and the puck was on his stick. With a quick motion he dug his blades into the ice and turned toward Quackenbush's side of the ice. Quackenbush remembered:

"I was on the left side just then, normally I played the right side, when the Rocket started coming down towards me. I chased him into the corner, and I thought I'd closed him off, but he made a quick turn and was moving out in front of our net. My partner on defense was a rookie and from lack of experience he neglected to come out and cut off the Rocket, who swiftly put the puck behind Sugar Jim Henry. That made it 2–1, and eventually we lost 3–1 on an open-net goal.

greatest goal-scorer ever to play the game."

The play is one of the all-time greats in hockey lore, and though Quackenbush boasts, "It's the only time in fourteen years the Rocket beat me," Richard made this type of play a common element in his arsenal against rival teams and shell-shocked goalies.

At the conclusion of the 1955–56 season Bill Quackenbush hung up his skates for good, opting to return to school. For seven years he attended Northeastern University in Massachusetts at night while working as a manufacturer's agent during the day. He also raised three sons after retiring from the NHL, while at the same time earning an associate's degree in engineering.

"After about twelve years out of hockey I decided I'd like to get back into it, so I talked to Herb Gallager at Northeastern, and went to work there as assistant coach," he said.

In the mid-sixties Princeton was looking for a quality coach for their men's ice hockey team. Bill Quackenbush applied and was accepted. For six years he coached the team, lending his vast knowledge and great understanding of the game to the young men of the Princeton University hockey team. When, after his sixth year, the team began failing to win, Quackenbush stepped down as coach, but was soon back coaching a different kind of ice hockey.

"Eventually they got a girl's team here and they needed a coach. They asked me to volunteer. I felt that anything I can do to help them learn the game would be a pleasure for me. The girls were very receptive, they really wanted to learn. When I tell them things, even now, they thank me. It's a lot of fun."

Aside from coaching the women's hockey team, Quackenbush also coached the varsity golf team. Always, he remained the same gentleman and scholar he was when he originally signed a contract with crusty Jack Adams in 1942.

There have been better defensemen than Bill Quackenbush but none who was classier, on or off the ice. His career proves that there *is* credibility to the line that nice guys can survive in the war games on ice.

84 Clint Benedict
(1913–1930)

Jacques Plante has received the lion's share of the credit for introducing the face mask as a regular piece of a goaltender's armor but Plante was not the first goalie to wear a facial protector. That distinction belongs to Clint Benedict.

Playing for the Montreal Maroons against Howie Morenz and the Montreal Canadiens, Benedict suffered a broken nose when his proboscis stopped a Morenz shot. Rather than risk missing any games, Benedict returned to the ice for the next game wearing a leather contraption that was designed to protect his nose from high-flying pucks.

While the mask certainly made news it didn't provide Benedict with much comfort. He disposed of it after a 2–1 loss to Chicago, complaining that it limited his vision. Under normal conditions, Benedict's vision was rarely limited, and his overall goals-against average—better than the legendary Georges Vezina's—attests to that.

Clint was an innovator. He was responsible for the practice of goalies flopping to the ice to stop a shot. Prior to 1918 a penalty was called if a goalie left his feet to block the puck. But Benedict, who insisted on flopping when necessary, helped alter the obsolete rule.

He played on four Stanley Cup winners in an eighteen-year career, thrice with the Ottawa Senators and once with the Montreal Maroons. In the opinion of some, Benedict was the best goalie of all time.

Clinton Benedict was born in Ottawa, Ontario, in 1894 and was playing professionally in his hometown before he reached the age of twenty.

For some goaltenders, the physical punishment can inspire them to bury their pads. One of the first of the really great ones to experience this was Benedict, who broke in as a pro way back in 1913 with the Ottawa Senators. "After the first couple of seasons," said Benedict, "I lost count of the stitches they put in my head. They didn't have a goal crease in those days and the forwards would come roaring right in and bang you as hard as they could. If they knocked you down you were supposed to get back on your feet before you could stop the puck—those were the rules.

A strapping six-footer, Benedict absorbed such punishment for eighteen years. Obviously, his sturdy physique was an asset to his playing longevity. "I remember," he once said, "at least four times being carried into the dressing room to get all stitched up and then going back in to play. There were some other times, too, but I don't remember them."

Benedict ranked with Georges Vezina, George Hainsworth and other of the early great goaltenders. He played in 32 Stanley Cup games. But one of his signal contributions to the art of goaltending was his innovative decision to fall to the ice in order to block a shot.

"It actually was against the rules to fall to the ice," Benny explained. "But if you made it look like an accident you could get away without a penalty. I got pretty good at it and soon all the other goalies were doing the same thing. I guess you could say we all got pretty good at it about 1914 and the next season the league had to change the rule.''

Benedict's revolutionary maneuver was greeted with the same hostility as Jacques Plante's decision to wander out of his net when he joined the Montreal Canadiens in the fifties. The first time Benedict displayed his flopping style in Toronto, the fans shouted, ''Bring your bed, Benny!''

Clint scored another triumph when he became one of the first goaltenders to be hailed in the press for a losing performance. That was in 1924 after the Montreal Canadiens routed the Maroons, 5–0. ''They took more than sixty shots at me,'' said Benedict. ''At least twenty-eight in the second period alone.''

There are those who say that Benedict single-handedly won the 1923 edition of the Stanley Cup for Ottawa. The Senators were playing Vancouver for the title and in the final game of the series Ottawa nursed a 2–1 lead with only three minutes remaining in the contest.

At this point the Senators were penalized twice in succession and had to defend against the determined Vancouver club with only three skaters to the home team's five. It was Benedict who rose to the challenge at this point and blunted every one of the enemy's dangerous thrusts. ''We were out on our feet at the end,'' Clint said, ''but we won.''

Benedict was elected to the Hockey Hall of Fame in 1965 and died on November 13, 1976. His name does not have the same ring to it as Vezina but Benedict belongs in the select circle of all-time puck-stoppers.

85 Roy Worters
(1926–1937)

The dream of every hockey scout in search of a goaltender is to find a man who is agile, but tall and wide so that he can fill as much of the six-feet-wide by four-feet-high entrance to the net. Some of the greatest of netminders, from Georges Vezina to Ken Dryden, were big men who filled much of the air space leading to the net. All of which helps explain why Roy Worters was such a marvel at his profession.

Worters was a goalie who measured only 5'3" and 130 pounds, yet his stature compared to other notables who guarded the twine remains immense to this day. And the fact that he generally played for inferior clubs such as the New York Americans merely adds to his glitter.

His drawbacks notwithstanding, Roy was the Hart Trophy winner in 1929 as the National Hockey League's most valuable player, the Vezina (best goalie) Trophy winner in 1931 and was twice voted to the Second All-Star Team (1932, 1934).

Worters is best remembered for his heroic performances with the Americans but he actually broke into the majors as a member of the Pittsburgh Pirates, which joined the NHL in the fall of 1925. After a salary dispute with the Pirates, Worters was traded to the Amerks for the then unheard of sum of $25,000 plus two players.

At first the deal was the bane of Worters' hockey life. Hard-nosed galleryites at Madison Square Garden taunted him with catcalls. "So, you're worth twenty-five grand, eh? Worters, you're not worth twenty-five cents!"

At first the goalie, who, inevitably, had become known as "Shrimp," was distressed by the insults but gradually he pulled his game together and captured the imagination of Madison Square Garden spectators. After one match he received a standing ovation.

Shortly thereafter Worters had the distinction of losing a game to the Montreal Canadiens *without a goal being scored against him*. It was a 0–0 tie late in the match when Howie Morenz of the Canadiens broke into the clear for a shot at Worters. Roy stopped the blistering drive, deflecting it into the corner. But, as Morenz unleashed his shot, Bullet Joe Simpson of the Americans tossed his stick at Morenz. In those days the stick-throwing foul was punishable with an automatic goal. Montreal won the game, 1–0.

"Although Roy never saw the Stanley Cup awarded to his team," said Ron McAllister, "he won every individual honor that a goalkeeper could possibly earn, and more. The thought of what he might have achieved with a winning team before him makes him a man of mystery in the record books."

Worters could have gained entrance to the Hockey Hall of Fame on guts alone. He suffered 216 stitches *in his face alone* and continued playing despite the pain of cracked ribs, a broken kneecap, three broken toes and countless lesser injuries, including the loss of eight teeth.

Roy Worters was born October 19, 1900, in Toronto, Ontario, the son of a trolley car motorman. When he was old enough to carry a load, Roy began delivering milk

for his uncle's dairy. In return Roy received free milk. "The future goalkeeper knew the lesson of work before he learned the meaning of life," said a friend.

He began his hockey career as a forward and remained up front until he was seventeen when the goal-weak Toronto Riverdales searched for someone to tend the twine. Roy volunteered and the Riverdales suddenly began winning games. Eventually, he moved up the junior ranks to the Toronto Canoe Club.

The Canoe Club, with Worters performing uncanny feats in goal, marched to the Memorial Cup, symbol of junior hockey supremacy in Canada. One of Roy's most formidable opponents was a young whiz named Howie Morenz who later would ripen as a superstar with the Montreal Canadiens. "Morenz," Worters once said, "is some wild wind, that number 7 of Canadiens. To me, he's just a blur—77777!"

To Morenz, Worters was like a wall in front of the uprights, despite his miniscule size. Over a span of 488 games, Worters' goals-allowed average was 2.36; uncanny considering the feeble defense in front of him.

Worters also was an innovator. He was the first netminder to direct rebounds into the corners of the rink with the back of his gloves and, needless to say, demonstrated that a smallish goalie could be as good as a big man with the pads.

At the age of thirty-seven he was still blocking shots for the Amerks when he suffered a hernia and was hospitalized. Red Dutton, who had become manager of the team, believed that Roy was capable of a comeback and offered Worters a sizeable sum to return to the wars but the goalie declined and returned to his native Toronto.

"When Roy quit the game," said Ron McAllister, "few players or fans remained untouched by his tremendous contribution to the game."

A foe, who had been frustrated by Worters for several seasons, said later: "For years after Roy left the game it was hard to realize that he had been gone from the NHL for good."

He stayed close to the sport he loved so well and worked with the NHL Old-timers Association as well as local charities. He was inducted into the Hockey Hall of Fame in 1969, twelve years after he had died of throat cancer. He was a David among Goliaths.

86 Roger Crozier
(1963–1977)

Roger Crozier was one of the great stylists of goaltending. Small for a goalie, he nevertheless played fourteen seasons in the National Hockey League. Unfortunately for Roger, he played most of his hockey career on mediocre teams, playing for the Detroit Red Wings, the Buffalo Sabres, and later the Washington Capitals. Equally unfortunate were the stomach and pancreas problems that plagued Roger throughout his career.

A compulsive worrier, Crozier developed an ulcer at age seventeen. Many times he could not eat before a game, or afterwards. Despite the many troubles that faced Roger—the illness, the nerves, or the mediocre clubs that he played on—he was an outstanding goaltender during his long career.

Roger followed a line of great Detroit goaltenders, beginning with Johnny Mowers, Harry Lumley, and Terry Sawchuk, and he was more than capable of continuing the tradition. Crozier broke into the National Hockey League in the 1964–65 season, when he was only twenty-two years old. "The Dodger" played extremely well, and won the Calder Trophy as the best newcomer in the league. Detroit finished in first that year with him in the nets.

Crozier was the goalie for the First All-Star Team in 1965, an honor he richly deserved. In the 1966 Stanley Cup finals, Roger won the Conn Smythe Trophy as the MVP for his team in the playoffs, even though Detroit lost the final to the Montreal Canadiens, after a two-games-to-zero Red Wing lead in the series.

Hockey critics weren't fans of Crozier, who was small at 5'8" and 155 pounds, and they doubted that his sprawling style would succeed in the NHL. Crozier had spent his 1963–64 season in Pittsburgh, but Detroit coach Sid Abel had faith in him.

During the 1966 playoffs Roger shined so brightly he was awarded the Conn Smythe Trophy, even though Detroit had lost the dramatic final to Montreal. Losing the first two games to the Red Wings on Detroit's home ice, Montreal was being beaten by Crozier. Jacques Laperriere, the fine Canadien defenseman, remembered it like this. "We were just as good, maybe better. What won those first two games for them was their goaler, Roger Crozier. He was making all the saves, and it looked like we could never get the puck past him."

Montreal took the next two games from Detroit on the Red Wings' home ice, and then took the fifth game at Montreal. Leading three games to two in the series, Montreal went back to Detroit to try and wrap it up.

The Canadiens got started when Jean Beliveau scored a goal in the first period. In the second, Montreal's Leon Rochefort put the puck past Roger, and Norm Ullman scored for Detroit to make it 2–1. Floyd Smith tied it in the third period, and the game went into overtime.

With two minutes into the overtime, a rush was mounted toward the Detroit goal, with Henri Richard heading for the slot. Just as Henri tried to get his stick on the puck, Detroit defenseman Gary Bergman knocked him to the ice.

Laperriere said, "Richard fell to the ice on his stomach and I remember him sliding. I don't know how many feet, toward the goal, the puck against his arm or his body. Crozier was hugging the post as Richard slid toward him. It looked like he had it covered. But somehow the puck slid with Richard and as he went past the post the puck slid past Crozier—there couldn't have been more than four inches of opening—and across the goal line. There it stopped.''

An unusual ending, and Montreal had won the Stanley Cup. The most valuable player? Roger Crozier, whose play had been sparkling as he held off the Chicago Black Hawks, and played so well against Montreal.

Roger got his ulcer when he was seventeen, playing junior hockey in St. Catherines, and he was never again 100 percent healthy. The years of pro hockey only made him more nervous and neurotic. However, nerves were not his only ailment. One morning Roger woke up with a massive pain in his stomach. He was rushed to the hospital, where doctors diagnosed his condition as pancreatitis. The infection of the pancreas gave him only a 50–50 chance for survival. For four days Roger hovered near death as he was treated with drugs and fed intravenously. Roger recovered, but when he reported to training camp for the 1965–66 season, his weight had dropped twenty pounds, and his skin coloring had a yellowish hue.

Traded to Buffalo in 1970, Roger played several seasons, but missed many games due to his illness. He had five pancreas attacks that put him in the hospital for over nine months. When Crozier came back to Buffalo after almost a year of illness, he was scheduled to start against Toronto. During the warm-ups, he was hit on the right side of his neck, just above the collarbone by a drive off the stick of defenseman Jerry Korab. That area is just about the only spot on a goaltender's body that is not protected by a pad or a mask. Roger was knocked unconscious by the powerful shot.

Because of his constant illness, even when Roger returned to action, he was still not in the best of health. On a bad day he felt weak and nauseated. And even on the good days he wasn't feeling well. Roger said, ''I never feel one hundred percent, and I never will again. I just have to accept it.''

Roger Allan Crozier was born March 16, 1942, in Bracebridge, Ontario. Born to a family of fourteen children, Roger began playing goaltender at six years of age. When he was fourteen, he was still in the nets; by this time he was playing goal on an intermediate team with men twice his age. It was then that Bob Wilson, the scout who discovered Bobby Hull, spotted Roger. The only difference was that Wilson knew immediately that Hull would be a star, and with Crozier he figured he was too small to ever make it to the National Hockey League. But the Black Hawks were in desperate need of a goalie for their junior team in St. Catherines, so Wilson signed Crozier.

Crozier's next step up was to the St. Louis squad of the Central Pro League for the 1962–63 season. Roger figured that was as high as he could ever hope to aspire. ''I never even thought about the NHL then,'' he said later.

Little did Roger Crozier know what would lie in his hockey future. The antics of defenseman Howie Young had been grating to the Detroit Red Wings, and they decided to unload him—for any offer. They sent Young to Chicago for Crozier and a minor league defenseman. Roger then spent the 1963–64 season playing for Pittsburgh, and doing such a good job that Abel decided he belonged in the NHL.

Crozier made good on Abel's faith with his outstanding play in his rookie season. He was the only goaltender in the NHL to play all of his team's games, playing in seventy, and allowing an average of just 2.42 goals per game. Roger led the NHL in shutouts that year with 6. The Detroit Red Wings finished in first place, and the excellent goaltending by Crozier was largely responsible for it. He made the First All-Star Team, and won the Calder Trophy for the best rookie of the year. He lost the battle for the Vezina Trophy on the final day of the season to the Toronto duo of Terry Sawchuk and Johnny Bower.

Roger went home that year with $9,000 of bonus money, and the proof that he belonged in the National Hockey League. Although by now his self-confidence should have been growing, he worried more than ever. "The only time I really forget about my problems is after a game when we've won," Roger said. "But by the next morning I'll be worrying again."

Roger was one of the first modern goalies—he perfected the butterfly style. He was a great stylist, and was an interesting goalie to watch. To think that his minor-league coaches had tried to "cure him" of his habit of sprawling! Had they been successful, it would surely have been hockey's loss.

Roger Crozier, all-star fretter, recollected on life as a National Hockey League goaltender. "I like everything about hockey, the travelling, the friends I've met, the interviews. Everything but the games. They're pure torture."

In 1974, when Roger was with Buffalo, he demanded his release from the club. He had a three-year $250,000 contract, but he had been shipped to the minors after his continuous illness. In 1977, he was sent to the Washington Capitals. After his retirement, Roger remained with the Capitals' organization as the assistant general manager until he was relieved of his duties in a club shakeup.

Roger Crozier, worrier *extraordinaire,* was a fine goaltender who finished his career with a respectable goals-against average of 3.04, and had a lifetime 30 shutouts. He was a gutsy man who was plagued by nerves, stomach problems, and a pancreas infection, but Crozier never let those handicaps stand in his way of competing. Despite his recurring illness, Roger played in 518 pro games. One of his finest assets was that Crozier had the ability to keep his wits when the going was the toughest. Even if Roger Crozier sometimes let his own worrying create problems, he was always a more than capable goaltender in the nets.

87 Carl Brewer
(1967–1980)

In a sport that treats iconoclasts like lepers, Carl Brewer was regarded by some hockey conservatives as an unmanageable kook who would have been better suited for the ministry or lighthouse work.

His clashes with Toronto Maple Leafs general manager-coach Punch Imlach became legend and set the tone for Brewer's later challenges to the hockey establishment. It was Carl, as much as any other player, who was responsible for the ascendancy of the NHL's first and only union leader, Alan Eagleson.

None of this would have been possible unless Brewer had been one of the best players of his era; and that he was. Carl played defense for three Stanley Cup-winning Toronto sextets and one first-place team. He was a First Team All-Star in 1963 and made the Second Team in 1962, 1965 and 1970.

A lyrical skater who obtained the most out of every stride, Brewer possessed an excellent poke check and was as capable of organizing a rush as he was in clearing his defensive area of attackers. In some quarters he was considered a "bad man" but this was more a function of Brewer's bluster than an actual mean streak.

Brewer epitomized the thinking man's hockey player. Teamed with rugged Bob Baun on the Toronto backline, Carl worked splendidly with his hard-hitting buddy. Together, they formed one of the best defensive duets the NHL has ever known.

For a time it seemed that Brewer and Baun would go on indefinitely, keeping the Maple Leafs in contention for the Stanley Cup. But suddenly, at the end of the 1964–65 season, during which he led the NHL in penalties, Brewer announced that he was quitting professional hockey to study at the University of Toronto.

From then on his career took one bizarre turn after another. Although he was in the prime of his playing life, Brewer chose to (a) coach in the grade B International Hockey League; (b) play hockey in Finland; (c) skate for the Canadian National Team and (d) return to the NHL—first with the Detroit Red Wings, then the St. Louis Blues and, finally, the Maple Leafs.

Carl Thomas Brewer was born October 21, 1938, in Toronto, Ontario. Like so many of his teammates on the championship Maple Leafs' teams, Brewer made his way to the top through the labyrinth of Toronto amateur leagues until he finally won a tryout with the Maple Leafs in the 1957–58 season.

A year later he was a Maple Leaf regular and, along with Baun, helped execute one of the most amazing comebacks in hockey. The Toronto club trailed the New York Rangers by nine points with only two weeks remaining in the season. With Brewer playing like a ten-year veteran, the Leafs caught the Rangers on the final day of the season and, ultimately, beat them out for a playoff berth.

At the time Carl was a happy-go-lucky kid, quite willing to accommodate the martinet Punch Imlach. But as the years progressed Brewer became increasingly disenchanted and more the rebel.

The Brewer-Imlach controversy had widespread implications in terms of management-player relations. Those in the pro-Imlach camp charged that Brewer was disturbing the status quo that had worked so well. They also emphasized that

Brewer was challenging one of hockey's most successful men, based on the number of Stanley Cups Imlach had won.

A major cause of Brewer's problems with Imlach was Carl's liaison with Eagleson. "There was no doubt in my mind at the time that Eagleson was destined for big things in many areas. He was the type of person who made things fall into place. Thanks to the Eagle, I believe I was the first hockey player to earn a six-figure salary, and take satisfaction in that. Today people wonder whether the kids coming to the NHL are worth the kind of big money they are being paid. My answer is that the hockey establishment has dictated that the kids are worth six figures. The media plays a part in it, too. Someone else, not the kids, created this situation. I also think it came about because such stars as Ted Lindsay and Doug Harvey—the original players who tried to organize a union—had been underpaid and they made so much of what eventually happened with the Players' Association possible."

Although the Brewer-Eagleson liaison could have proven destructive to both player and attorney it proved just the opposite. Eagleson's power increased by the season until it reached a point where he dealt with the NHL power structure on an equal footing.

Brewer, although he had made several enemies around the league, established himself in business and made a number of friends in Europe, especially with those connected with the Finnish hockey leagues.

What puzzled those who knew the man was whether or not his thirst for competition would be satisfied by playing—or coaching, for that matter—on a level below that of his innate talents.

For several years he seemed capable of rationalizing his moves but, by the end of the 1960s, he appeared to be in need of major league action once more.

His problem was his difficulties with Imlach. The Maple Leafs' boss, who could be vindictive at times, was in a position to blacklist Brewer. Instead, he included Carl in a trade with the Detroit Red Wings.

After being away from the NHL scene for five years, Brewer returned—as a member of the Detroit Red Wings—in 1969–70 and was a major reason why the Red Wings enjoyed a renaissance. "In seventy-six games we had 40 wins, 21 losses and 15 ties. For me it was a fascinating experience because this had been a team that was down; yet it had a lot of poised veterans like Gordie Howe and, to my way of thinking, was the best team in the NHL."

For Brewer, skating as a teammate of the inimitable Gordie Howe was an experience that produced mixed emotions. As a kid growing up in Toronto, he had admired Howe as a superstar. As an opponent of Howe when Carl was with the Maple Leafs, Brewer deplored what he considered Howe's indiscriminate use of his hockey stick to injure opponents. Now he was viewing Gordie from still another perspective. "As a person, I considered him an ordinary guy. As a superstar, he was extraordinary. He could change the complexion of the game with just his presence on the ice. His opponents, many of whom were kids when he was already a star, were awed by Howe. They would play ten minutes and then spend the rest of the game watching him.

After only a season in the Motor City, Brewer was dispatched to St. Louis where he was signed by the Blues' owners, Sid Salomon, Jr., and his son, Sid Salomon III. It had been said that the Salomons were too involved with their hockey club, and that they did not allow the hockey men to run the operation. Whatever the case, Brewer seemed pleased to be a member of the Blues.

When Brewer left the Blues following the 1971–72 season it was believed to be his NHL swan song. He disappeared from the big-league scene and concentrated on a number of business ventures. But during the 1979–80 campaign, when the Maple Leafs were undergoing a rejuvenation—under Imlach, of all people— Brewer asked his old adversary for permission to attempt a comeback. Imlach agreed and Carl played twenty games for his alma mater. He collected five assists.

That, however, was enough and when the 1979–80 season had ended, Brewer called it quits—for good. He was a rare individual, kept the pot boiling at all times and, most of all, was a superb defenseman. That, unfortunately, was overlooked in all the turmoil he created.

88 Guy Lapointe
(1968–   )

Virtually lost in the crowd during an era when Bobby Orr, Brad Park, Denis Potvin and Larry Robinson were the predominant defensemen, sloe-eyed Guy Lapointe nevertheless was consistently among the best.

"He's such a nice guy," former Boston Bruins coach Don Cherry once said of him, "that I can't get mad at Lapointe even when he is killing my team."

Compared to other aces, Lapointe always has been a Mister Inbetween. He lacked the élan of an Orr, the stickhandling skills of a Park or the muscle of a Potvin yet he invariably got the job done for the Montreal Canadiens.

Lapointe was named to the First All-Star Team in 1973 and the Second Team in 1975, 1976 and 1977. During a seven-season period, from 1973 through 1979, he skated for five Stanley Cup winners and played on a total of seven first-place teams.

As calm and deliberate off ice as he is on, Lapointe was able to adjust to a variety of coaches, from Claude Ruel to Scotty Bowman to Bob Berry, and maintained a high standard of excellence into the 1980s, while never dominating in the manner of an Orr or Potvin.

Guy Gerard Lapointe was born March 18, 1948, in Montreal. His father was a captain in the Montreal fire department and his older brother, André, was a Montreal cop. At age eighteen, Guy seriously considered following in the family tradition of public service, and filled out an application with the Montreal police department. However, some splendid play for the Montreal Junior Canadiens attracted the eyes of the parent club and Lapointe was dissuaded from pounding a beat. Instead, he began pounding opponents on the Canadiens' blue line. By the early 1970s he had become a regular and emerged as one of the league's best backliners.

It was in the spring of 1973 that Guy was named to the NHL's First All-Star Team and not coincidentally the Canadiens won their eighteenth Stanley Cup championship. Combining bruising bodychecks with nimble puck-carrying, Guy quarterbacked the Canadiens' attack. In a typical attack Guy would circle the net driving his legs like pistons en route to the enemy goal. The opposing team was confounded by Lapointe's versatile activities, particularly his hard shot from the point or his radar-sharp passes that bear the Canadiens' "Head-Man-The-Puck" trademark.

Until the 1972–73 season, Lapointe had been known as a defenseman with modest offensive abilities. He scored 15 and 11 goals in the 1970–71 and 1971–72 seasons, respectively, before bursting out with 19 goals in 1972–1973. It was then that coach Scotty Bowman decided to place Guy on the potent Montreal power play. The result—the Canadiens improved their scoring on the man-advantage situation.

Early in his career, the Canadiens had dispatched the youngster to their Houston farm club in the Central League. Lapointe, who had never lived any place other than the province of Quebec and spoke only French, had difficulty stickhandling the English language.

Mastering English was only one of many problems for Guy in Houston. An attack of viral pneumonia threatened to end his career before it had peaked. But he licked the ailment and, a season later, skated for the Canadiens' Montreal Voyageurs farm club. That was a time he savored.

Guy scored eight goals from his defense position and displayed enough talent to win a spot on the parent club during the last, hectic, unfortunate days of the 1969–70 season. On the season's final night Montreal was eliminated from a playoff berth and the Forum was shrouded in gloom. It was the first time in thirty years that the proud Habitants had failed to make the playoffs!

Although the team was down, Lapointe was on the way up and nobody could stop him. On the ice the Canadiens looked like a brand-new team as the ebullient Lapointe orchestrated defense and offense en route to the 1971 Stanley Cup championship. Lapointe's 107 penalty minutes indicated that the Canadiens had a stick-handler who wasn't afraid to battle yet was prudent enough not to fight at the drop of a puck.

A fractured cheekbone ruined the 1971–72 season for Lapointe. Even after it had healed, Guy appeared hesitant and hardly the musketeer of old.

But by 1972–73 his health was A-1 again and so were the Canadiens. The point was demonstrated most vividly in the third game of the Stanley Cup quarterfinal series with the pesky Buffalo Sabres. Trailing 2–0, the Frenchmen appeared grounded after one period of action. Guy, who had developed into a formidable leader, tongue-lashed his teammates during the intermission. The Canadiens responded to Lapointe's bilingual blast and went from a collection of Clark Kents to Supermen. They disposed of Buffalo, then Philadelphia and Chicago en route to their eighteenth Stanley Cup triumph.

Lapointe, thus, followed a long and distinguished tradition set by Montreal all-star defensemen Doug Harvey, Tom Johnson, Butch Bouchard and Lapointe's older teammate Jacques Laperriere.

None of those, however, combined the strongest elements of offense with defense in the manner of Guy Lapointe, the total fireman-cop-on-ice! However, at the start of the 1980s Lapointe's craftsmanship began to suffer. He played only thirty-three games during the 1980–81 season, appearing in but one playoff game, for him an all-time low. At first, under new coach Bob Berry, Guy appeared to be springier and infinitely more effective during the early part of the 1981–82 competition and indicated that he was not quite ready for the scrap heap. But the Canadiens disagreed and dealt him to the St. Louis Blues late in the season. Lapointe performed well in his year and month with the Blues, but the team was committed to youth. The then 35-year-old defenseman signed as a free agent with the Boston Bruins for the 1983–84 season, playing in 45 games. He totaled two goals, 16 assists for 18 points. He retired in 1984 to become an assistant coach with the Quebec Nordiques.

Lapointe's star began falling during the 1982–83 campaign when he suffered along with the insufferable St. Louis Blues. Unfortunately for the gallant backliner, his best days were past him and it appeared that retirement was just around the corner.

Lapointe can rest assured that he will be long remembered for his solid, if unspectacular, contributions to one of the most glorious periods in the Canadiens' long and rich history.

89 Didier Pitre
(1904–1923)

"One of my toughest tasks," Hall of Famer Cy Denneny once said, "was trying to cover Didier Pitre. He was one of the fastest skaters of all time."

Pitre, who played right wing for the Montreal Canadiens, among other clubs, was nicknamed "Cannonball" but not for his flashing skates. He owned a dynamic wrist shot that enabled him to prevail in an assortment of professional leagues just after the turn of the century.

He started out as a rover—rovers alternated between offense and defense—when hockey was a seven-man game, and then moved to right wing. Pitre broke in with the Ottawa Nationals in 1904, then skated for the Montreal Shamrocks, the Canadiens (when they were members of the National Hockey Association), Vancouver Millionaires and finally the Canadiens who, by then, were members of the National Hockey League.

Denneny, who played for the Ottawa Senators, frequently waxed lyrical over his peripatetic foe. "We were playing at Montreal," said Denneny, "and I was on left wing. Eddie Gerard, our captain, soon realized what a chore I had on my hands. Pitre was repeatedly breaking away from me and giving our defensemen a hectic night. So, Gerard gave me some fresh instructions about covering the great winger.

"Gerard told me, without hurting my feelings, that I just couldn't hope to skate with Pitre. I was to check him hard over the feet, give him plenty of wood in a legal way, and try to get the speedster's temper up.

"I did just that. But it seemed that the more I worked on Pitre's feet and shins, the faster he travelled. At the end of the first period, I discussed the problem with Gerard in the dressing room. 'What'll I do next?' I asked.

"He suggested that I attempt to needle Pitre by constantly talking to him in a near-insulting manner. In concluding his plan of desperation strategy, Eddie added, 'and call him plenty of names.' "

Denneny obliged by delivering every cuss word he knew but Pitre ignored the tirade, skating with more vigor than before. Frustrated beyond words, Denneny retreated to the dressing room after the game, wondering why he couldn't rile Pitre.

"Then," said the Ottawa ace, "I found out the reason; Pitre didn't understand a word of English!"

But Pitre understood the hockey puck and how to manipulate same. In his time he was the most sought after stickhandler in Canada and on January 5, 1910, the Montreal *Star* emphasized the point with an eight-column headline which read: $2,000 FINE AND SIXTY DAYS JAIL FOR PITRE IF HE PLAYS.

Pitre, who had been playing for the Ottawa Nationals, had jumped to the upstart Canadiens who were making their debut in the NHA. Pitre, whom the author Andy O'Brien likened to an angry buffalo with a charging shot, was set to play for Montreal when the Ottawa club threatened to sue and suggested that Pitre could be fined $2,000 and given six months in jail.

The legal tangle was soon unsnarled and Pitre remained with Les Canadiens. In 1916 he helped them win their first in a long line of Stanley Cup championships.

Didier Pitre was born in 1884 in Sault Ste. Marie, Ontario. Although he broke in with the Ottawa Nationals, Pitre, like so many players in frontier hockey, would think nothing of joining a team for a game—or playoff—or two. Thus, in December 1907 when Edmonton challenged the Montreal Wanderers for the Stanley Cup, a hefty number of ringers were added to the western club's roster. These included Lester Patrick, Bert Lindsay (father of Ted Lindsay) and Pitre, who last had been playing for the Kenora (Ontario) Thistles.

"It was the all-time high for ringers on a challenge team," wrote *Vancouver Province* columnist Eric Whitehead.

Pitre's club lost, 7–3 and 7–6, but his excellence could not be dimmed by defeat. It was merely confirmed when he became a Canadien. He survived the legal battle but came perilously close to succumbing to influenza during the 1919 Stanley Cup series with the Seattle Metropolitans.

During the fifth game of the series, which ended in a bitterly fought 3–3 tie, a number of players including Bad Joe Hall of the Canadiens were hospitalized. Pitre and others ultimately were released but Hall died ten days after he was admitted.

Pitre's classy play graced Montreal until his retirement in 1923. He was one of the first of the grand Flying Frenchmen, later to be followed by the likes of Maurice Richard, Jean Beliveau and Yvan Cournoyer. Pitre died on July 29, 1934, and was elected to the Hockey Hall of Fame in 1962.

90 Sylvio Mantha (1923–1937)

Apart from being a remarkable hockey player, Sylvio Mantha was involved in two of the game's most bizarre episodes; one being the loss of the Stanley Cup and the other being the breaking of a distinguished referee's ribs.

Mantha was a defenseman on the Montreal Canadiens when the Flying Frenchmen defeated Ottawa, Vancouver and Calgary in 1924 to win the Stanley Cup.

The champions were hailed at a public reception near the National Monument in Montreal and were honored by the University of Montreal. (It was the only time in history that a professional hockey team was honored by a major seat of learning.)

Following the reception, Mantha and some teammates headed for owner Leo Dandurand's home to hoist a few while reviewing their noble effort. The Model T Ford in which Sylvio and his fellow Canadiens were riding stalled on its way up Cote St. Antoine Road and all hands climbed out to give it a push.

The Stanley Cup, which had been taken aboard, was placed at the curb by the roadside until the car could be started. The Ford was finally revived and the players jumped in—but forgot the Cup. It wasn't until they arrived at Dandurand's house that they realized the silverware was missing. The boys had given it up for lost but an expeditionary force of Canadiens sped back to Cote St. Antoine and reclaimed the trophy in all its shining majesty.

The case of the battered referee took place in 1933 when Mantha came to the aid of his tiny teammate Johnny (Black Cat) Gagnon during a game with the Boston Bruins. Eddie Shore, the bruising Boston defenseman, had crosschecked Gagnon across the bridge of his nose with his stick. Mantha waited a few minutes and then clashed with Shore. It was a bloody battle which referee Cooper Smeaton attempted to mediate but the combatants continued swinging and Smeaton took three of Shore's hardest blows before falling to the ice with two broken ribs.

Sylvio Mantha was born April 14, 1902, in Montreal, and became a Canadien at the age of twenty-one. His effectiveness as a defenseman is reflected by the fact that he played for nine first-place teams and three Stanley Cup winners. He was voted to the Second All-Star Team in 1931 and 1932.

He was named player-coach of the Canadiens in 1935–36 but was dealt to Boston. He concluded his career with the Bruins in 1937.

Mantha's affiliation with the professional game continued for a number of years. He became a linesman in the National Hockey League and, later, a referee in the American Hockey League. He was elected to the Hockey Hall of Fame in 1960 and died in August 1974.

91 Gordie Drillon
(1936–1943)

It was Gordie Drillon's misfortune in life to be known as the man who was benched in 1942 thereby enabling his Toronto Maple Leafs to win the Stanley Cup. It was, unfortunately for this commendable right wing, a bum rap but nonetheless it has stuck through the years.

The big right wing's contribution was not entirely overlooked. He was voted into the Hockey Hall of Fame in 1975 and is remembered as the National Hockey League scoring champion in 1938 as well as a First All-Star in 1938 and 1939 and also as a Second Team All-Star in 1942.

Another dilemma which Drillon never thoroughly solved was how to win the hearts of Toronto hockey fans. He was designated to replace Charlie Conacher, one of the most popular players ever to wear the royal blue and white of Toronto. It is doubtful if anyone could have fulfilled that challenge and, Lord knows, Gordie tried.

At first he was placed on a line with another promising youngster, center Syl Apps, and aging veteran Harvey (Busher) Jackson. A season later Bob Davidson replaced Jackson and the Maple Leafs had one of the best lines ever to enter the portals on Carlton and Church Streets.

With Apps feeding him computerized passes, Drillon became the nemesis of enemy goaltenders and soon word passed up and down the NHL grapevine that Gordie was scoring "mystery" goals while stationed in front of the net.

Bill Roche, who covered the Maple Leafs for *The Toronto Globe and Mail* at the time, told a story about the Apps-Drillon tandem and the "mystery" goals. The scene was Maple Leaf Gardens during a practice session. Only Drillon, Apps and goalie Turk Broda were on the ice.

"The only sound," said Roche, "at rinkside as they settled down to work that afternoon was the ringing of Apps' skates and the sharp click of his passes against Drillon's stick—a stick that was being pressed to the ice with all the right-winger's power. Broda was kept jumping from one goalpost to the other as the puck bounced sharply off Drillon's blade.

"They were testing the speed, strength, length and angle of Apps' passes on this play, a play that often looked like a fluke when it was performed at high speed in a game. Actually, it was the result of alert perception and long, hard practice periods. Months before, Apps and Drillon had found that some passes would deflect with considerable accuracy from a stick held solidly in a certain way."

While Drillon and Apps were in the midst of their "private" workout, manager Red Dutton of the New York Americans and his players walked into the arena. "Stand still, all of you!" he ordered his Amerks. "Take a good look at what's happening on that ice. Maybe we weren't supposed to see this, but I want you to look hard at it. Do you see what Drillon is doing? He's working *overtime*. And his coach isn't standing along the boards to see that he does it."

The Americans watched as Drillon bent over in front of the net, his stick held rigidly to the ice. Apps delivered a fast pass, which ricocheted off Drillon's stick and past Broda. The Americans jeered but Drillon did it again, beating Broda no matter how hard the goalie tried to cope with the inventive drives.

"Drillon," said Dutton, "knows what he's doing."

In fact, Gordie was a capable playoff performer and did exceptionally well in both the 1938 and 1939 Stanley Cup rounds. In the 1939 semifinal match-up against the Red Wings he was at the top of his game.

Toronto won the first game, 4–1, thanks to Gordie's pair of goals. Drillon's performance was rather ironic since Maple Leaf Gardens fans had begun to display a great deal of antagonism for the high-scoring forward.

Detroit won the second game 3–1 (Drillon got the lone Toronto goal) at the Olympia, sending the teams back to Maple Leaf Gardens on April 1, 1939, for the last match of the semifinals. The Red Wings hurled their best shots at Broda and got past him four times, but Toronto matched that. The teams were to settle the round in sudden-death overtime.

With the overhead timer ticking into the fifth minute of the game, the chronically unpopular Drillon eased the puck onto his stick deep in his own territory. The Red Wing backcheckers tried to zero in on Gordie as he accelerated at the Leaf blue line, but his fierce strides carried him past one red shirt after another. By the time he had zoomed over the Detroit line, Drillon was skating like a man possessed, determined to erase the criticism once and for all. His shot was flawless, hitting the twine at 5:42, and the crowd in Maple Leaf Gardens roared their approval. Drillon had carried the Leafs into the finals.

Gordon Arthur Drillon was born October 23, 1914, in Moncton, New Brunswick. He captured the attention of Maple Leafs boss Conn Smythe while playing for Syracuse, a minor league affiliate, during the mid-1930s.

Smythe signed him for the 1936–37 season and Drillon responded with 16 goals and 17 assists for 33 points in forty-one games, a healthy amount for a rookie in those days. As an NHL sophomore he produced 26 goals and 26 assists for 52 points, enough to lead the league.

Drillon remained productive through the 1941–42 season but was dealt to the Montreal Canadiens the following year and played capably for them both during the regular season and the playoffs before calling it a career.

Like many of his peers, Drillon is seen from time to time at the NHL Hall of Fame banquets, a hefty, hearty fellow who is remembered as a superstar with a bum rap.

92 Hap Day
(1924–1938)

Hap Day was a player of whom it could legitimately be said that he was as effective a coach as he was a player—and was very good at both occupations.

An aspiring pharmacist, Day wound up starring for the Toronto Maple Leafs' 1932 Stanley Cup-winning team. Exactly ten years later he coached the Maple Leafs to another Cup triumph and followed that with an unprecedented run of three consecutive Stanley Cups in 1947, 1948 and 1949.

Throughout his career Day was closely linked with Maple Leafs founder, Conn Smythe, both as a business partner—Smythe had a very successful sand and gravel company in Toronto—player and coach. Smythe admired Day's durability and dedication as a defenseman and his insights and iron-fisted rule as a coach.

"When I named Hap coach in 1940," Smythe once recalled, "he was everything I wanted. He could do things I couldn't: fire people; bench them; live always on what a man could do today, not what he had done a few years ago."

Day's dependability as a player was never more evident than on the night of April 2, 1932, at Maple Leaf Gardens when the Leafs faced-off against the Montreal Maroons. This was the second of a two-game total-goals series. The first game had ended in a 1–1 tie.

In game two the Maroons built up a 2–1 lead on goals by Hooley Smith and Jimmy Ward while Red Horner scored Toronto's lone goal. The third period was nearing conclusion, and Maroons goalie James (Flat) Walsh was repelling the Maple Leafs' most dangerous thrusts. It remained for Day, who was team captain, to deliver his finest moment as a player.

He gathered the puck on his stick deep in Toronto territory and proceeded to pick his way through the Montreal defense like a pinball making its way down the machine. He outfeinted Nels Stewart and decked first Lionel Conacher and then Archie Wilcox, until he was face to face with goalie Walsh.

Day's shot was described by one reporter as "whizzing and bounding," but whatever it did, it slithered past Walsh to tie the game and force a sudden-death overtime. Late in the first overtime period Bob Gracie scored for the Maple Leafs, who advanced to the Stanley Cup finals whereupon they routed the Rangers.

Clarence Henry Day was born June 14, 1901, in Owen Sound, Ontario. Like so many stars of the 1920s and 1930s, Day learned his hockey under severe conditions. At times he would plod miles through the snow to find a place to play hockey and he eventually became a leader with the Midland Juniors.

Hap's courage and ability enabled him to climb the long, hard hockey ladder in Ontario. He moved from the Midland Juniors to the intermediate sextet and then to Hamilton's Tigers. Hockey was not the only subject on his mind: Day wanted very much to be a pharmacist, and he enrolled at the University of Toronto, from which he eventually obtained a degree. While attending the university he played for the varsity hockey club, was discovered by Toronto hockey entrepreneur Charlie Querrie and was persuaded to turn pro.

At the time Toronto's major league team was known as the St. Pats. The name was changed to Maple Leafs when Smythe bought the team and obtained all the former St. Pats players. "Day and Ace Bailey," Smythe remembered, "were about the only two real hockey players we got in the deal."

Apart from his significant contributions to the Maple Leafs on the ice Day was a marvelous team player and one who infused considerable humor into the team's dressing room. The Toronto club of the early 1930s was known as "The Gashouse Gang of Hockey" because of the joie de vivre exuded by Day and his cohorts.

Day was strong and fearless. He could bodycheck with the best of them but he was not averse to using his arms to envelop the foe. "Some other teams didn't like him being such a heavy lover on the ice," said Smythe. "He'd have those arms around a guy and never let go. He was a 'what we have, we hold' man, all the way."

Smythe released Day after the 1936–37 season whereupon he signed for one more year with the New York Americans, and then retired. He returned to Toronto and was hired by Smythe to coach the Maple Leafs in 1940.

Day was at the helm in the spring of 1942 when the Maple Leafs authored the most extraordinary comeback in the history of any major sports world championship. Down three games to none in the Stanley Cup finals with the Detroit Red Wings, *the Maple Leafs then won the next four straight games and the Stanley Cup*.

In 1945 the same teams met in the finals. This time the Maple Leafs won three in a row. Detroit rebounded to take games four, five and six, setting the stage for the pulsating seventh match. Again, Day's strategy prevailed and Toronto triumphed.

Never was a coach more exceptional than in the late 1940s when Day engineered the first ever three-year parlay. Toronto annexed the Cups in 1947, 1948 and 1949.

Following the 1949–50 season Day retired as coach. He liked to tell the story about how fame is fleeting although he was regarded as one of the greatest coaches of all time. "It was 1951 and I was on a scouting trip out west for the Leafs. I was in a rail seat in the Edmonton rink when the Edmonton and Saskatoon teams came on the ice.

"One of the Saskatoon players was leaning on the boards near me, and I recognized him as Reg Bentley, brother of Max and Doug. I had known Reg from a few years before when the Chicago Black Hawks gave him an NHL tryout.

"So I called, 'Hi, Reg!' He looked so puzzled that I decided to help him out. I leaned forward and said, 'Happy Day.'

" 'Thanks, and the same to you,' answered Reg, as he smiled politely and skated away."

After coaching, Day was promoted to manager of the Maple Leafs but the club faltered—through no fault of his—and Day ultimately became embroiled in a dispute with Stafford Smythe, Conn's son, who was taking over the operation of Maple Leaf Gardens.

Bitter about the manner in which he was being treated, Day resigned and returned to private business. His relationship with Conn Smythe was injured but eventually repaired and the pair remained friends until Smythe's death in 1980.

They were a grand duet and Day, almost as much as Smythe, helped develop the Maple Leafs into one of the most formidable teams in professional sports.

93 Bobby Baun (1956–1971)

At a time when the emphatic stand-up bodycheck was going out of style, a compact yet robust Toronto Maple Leafs defenseman was proving that there still was room for the clean, solid use of the shoulder, chest or hip with which to stop an opponent. Bobby Baun was that man. He was tough in the very best sense of the word and surely one of the most courageous players of any era.

While Baun lacked the fluidity of his long-time defense partner, Carl Brewer, he more than compensated for any deficiencies with his unquenchable zest for battle and a desire to play when virtually all others would have called it quits. *This* was a competitor.

Some of Baun's one-on-one battles—particularly with the equally clean and competitive Andy Bathgate of the New York Rangers—were a delight to behold. Baun didn't win them all but he never failed to give a good account of himself.

Anyone familiar with the Punch Imlach-orchestrated Maple Leafs of the 1960s would agree that the turbulent Toronto sextet never would have won four Stanley Cups in a span of six years without Baun on the blue line. "He came as close to being indestructible as anyone in his era," said former NHLer Aldo Guidolin.

Some purists might argue that since Baun never placed on an all-star team he, therefore, has no business being placed among *Hockey's 100*. Such criticism lacks validity when one takes into account the fact that the writers who vote for the all-star teams invariably consult a defenseman's scoring statistics before marking their ballots. *Offensive* defensemen traditionally have been the big winners in all-star voting. Nuts and bolts backliners such as Baun, invariably, have been the losers.

But Baun's role never was overlooked by Imlach, who employed him in the most critical situations and, invariably, obtained the best results.

Because of his robust play, Baun would, from time to time, become embroiled in a fight. In the eyes of some, he was invincible, although Bobby himself never accepted that view of himself. "There are some awfully tough players in the NHL," Baun once observed. "And there are some guys who look like they can never be knocked down. But, I'll tell you this, the man hasn't been born who can go through his entire career without losing a fight."

Robert Baun was born September 9, 1936, in Lanigan, Saskatchewan. When he decided to make professional hockey a career the acceptable procedure was to line up with a strong Junior A (amateur) club and, from there, climb to the pros. Baun won a place on the Toronto Marlboros of the Ontario Hockey Association's Junior A division and played alongside some of the most gifted teenagers in Canada. It was there that he teamed with Carl Brewer, Bob Pulford and other Maple Leaf farmhands who, eventually, would make their way to the National Hockey League.

Throughout his career, which began in Toronto in 1956 and lasted (in the NHL) until 1971, Baun's name became synonymous with courage and hard hitting. Billy Harris, who was his teammate on Toronto's Stanley Cup winners, once recalled how Baun seemed to duplicate the immovable object in relation to Bobby Hull as the irresistible force. "His duels with Hull were legendary," said Harris. "The respect they showed each other was evident every time they collided. You seldom saw an elbow or a raised stick. Just a brutal test of strength between two athletes."

Baun collided with the best of them—Gordie Howe, Andy Bathgate, Jean Beliveau—during his commendable career but, for some reason, the vision of Hull bearing down on Bobby has remained the most vivid to railbirds, and to Hull as well. "I remember," Hull once said, "a night Baun missed a game when I was in Chicago with the Black Hawks. That night we started taking liberties. We realized that Baun wasn't in town, so we could get away with a lot more. When Bobby was around the right side was like an obstacle course."

When the National Hockey League expanded from six to twelve teams in 1967, Baun was drafted by the Oakland Seals. A year later the Detroit Red Wings dealt for him and he finished his career in the Motor City at the conclusion of the 1970–71 season.

Apart from his bruising play, Baun was renowned as one the most sophisticated NHL personalities. Reporters wrote about his taste for gourmet cooking and his love of the good life. One newspaperman recalled how Baun dazzled the Toronto training camp at Peterborough, Ontario, by driving up in a spanking new Toronado before any of that make car appeared on the road. It was a far cry from Baun's days as a kid growing up in the eastern part of Toronto.

Baun, and his Marlboro teammate, Carl Brewer, helped develop the Toronto defense into a formidable bulwark that would become the base of the Maple Leafs' Stanley Cup foundation. Punch Imlach was the creator of the Toronto dynasty and frequently feuded with his young defenseman. "I considered Punch one of the two toughest coaches I ever worked under," said Baun, "the other being Bert Olmstead. But I have to give Punch credit; he always seemed to get the most out of his players. And even though I had a falling out with him when I was playing, I've come to appreciate him more now, in retirement, than I did when I played for Toronto."

Had he been more of a sycophant and less forthright, Baun no doubt could have played out his entire career with the Maple Leafs. But he ran afoul of Imlach, who then held the Field Marshall's baton in Toronto, and was drafted by the Oakland Seals in 1967. That Baun was even allowed to be placed in the draft pool was the height of insult.

Undaunted, Bobby played his usual vigorous game for the Seals—one of the NHL's six expansion franchises at the time—until he was traded to the Detroit Red Wings in 1968. He finished his major league career in the Motor City in 1971 but did not give up pro hockey altogether. In 1975 he was signed as coach of the Toronto Toros of the World Hockey Association.

Coaching proved to be a disillusioning experience for so hard-nosed a competitor as Baun. He couldn't understand why players who were earning six-figure salaries simply would not generate the kind of effort he himself had put into the game. He gave up coaching the following year and returned to business in the Toronto area.

Bob Baun may never make the Hockey Hall of Fame. But if that is the case it will be an egregious oversight. "Any team that wants to build a winner," said Aldo Guidolin, "has to start with a player of Baun's fibre."

He was pure bedrock—a defenseman's defenseman.

94 Andy Bathgate
(1953–1971)

For about five years in the late 1950s and early 1960s there existed in New York City a cult of hockey fans the members of which were quite content to do very little else but visit Madison Square Garden simply to see Andy Bathgate in action on right wing for the Rangers.

"Watching Andy play a good game," said Joseph Breu, who then covered the NHL for *United Press International,* "was no less enjoyable than watching Jason Robards starring in *Long Day's Journey Into Night* down the block on Broadway."

Like Robards, Bathgate was the consummate performer. He combined the art of stickhandling and shooting to near perfection. His shot, which he endlessly practiced, became so devastating that it was favorably compared with the mighty blasts of Bobby Hull and Bernie (Boom Boom) Geoffrion, both of whom were his contemporaries.

Bathgate wasn't quite as flashy as Hull nor as blessed with all-star teammates as Geoffrion but he was good enough to win the Hart Trophy as the NHL's most valuable player in 1959 and was voted to the First All-Star Team at right wing in 1959 and 1962 as well as the Second Team in 1958 and 1963.

The Bathgate bloc could recite a litany of beauteous plays executed by their hero. One that qualifies among his best was a one-on-one play—Bathgate vs. the goaltender.

Perhaps his most difficult move was executed against Glenn Hall of the Chicago Black Hawks. At the time, Hall, alias "Mister Goalie," was the best netminder in the business. On this occasion Bathgate received the pass directly in front of Hall but more to the right of the net. Rather than simply shoot the puck, Andy performed a 180-degree pirouette, culminating with the puck on his stick at the left side of the cage. Hall remained with Bathgate until Andy then completely reversed the move with another pirouette, this time winding up precisely where he had begun. By this time Hall's body was so contorted he was literally unable to move whereupon Bathgate deposited the rubber in the empty right corner for a goal. It was vintage Bathgate and a play that few, if any, could duplicate.

Andy had been tabbed a future big-leaguer when he was still a teenager playing for the Guelph (Ontario) Biltmores in the Ontario Hockey Association's Junior A division. When Guelph won the Memorial Cup, emblematic of junior hockey supremacy in Canada, a number of the Biltmores were earmarked for the Rangers.

Under Phil Watson' coaching, the Rangers made the playoffs three straight years (1955–56, 1956–57, 1957–58). In March 1958, the club finished second, the highest for a New York club since 1942.

Bathgate earned acclaim as one of the most threatening shooters in the game. "I worked on my shooting at least fifteen minutes every single day. To my mind shooting practice is one of the most overlooked aspects of the game. I see coaches emphasizing skating all the time but, to me, the most important thing is shooting the puck. When you shoot the puck it's not how straight it is that counts, it's

the quickness of the release, and that's what I kept working on when I was a Ranger.''

Unlike many of his contemporaries, Bathgate was extremely scrupulous about conditioning. ''In my entire life I've never had a drink or a cigarette and it made me feel good as a player. Some nights I'd go out on the ice and I'd know just by looking at the opposition that I was in much better shape than him and it was to my advantage, both physically and mentally.''

Bathgate was also a cut above the average player in terms of his intellect. He was thoughtful and sensitive to the needs of his teammates. When a core of NHL players began laying the groundwork of a union Bathgate was one of the organizers. He believes that his participation in developing a players' association inspired the Rangers to deal him to Toronto at the very apex of his popularity as a Ranger.

It was no secret that Bathgate's success in Toronto would vitally hinge on his relationship with the boss, Punch Imlach. At first, all went well. Imlach was more than pleased with Bathgate's efforts in February, March and April 1964. ''Andy did,'' said Imlach, ''exactly what I'd had in mind when I made the deal.''

The 1964 Cup win marked the high-water level of the Bathgate-Imlach relationship. From then on it was all a *decrescendo,* marked by bitterness and an eventual trade. The feud came to a head in the spring of 1965 when Montreal eliminated the Maple Leafs in six games of the Stanley Cup semifinals. ''He was a different Bathgate from the guy who had said being traded to Toronto was the biggest break of his life,'' charged Imlach.

In no time at all, Imlach traded Bathgate, Billy Harris and Gary Jarrett to the Red Wings for Marcel Pronovost, Ed Joyal, Larry Jeffrey, Lowell MacDonald and Autry Erickson. ''Frankly,'' Bathgate explained, ''I didn't enjoy Punch's methods of training. By my second season in Toronto I just wasn't enjoying playing so I spoke to Punch and I had to give him a reason to get me out of Toronto. So, I said something to one of the reporters; Punch overemphasized it and I wound up in Detroit.''

Andrew James Bathgate was born August 28, 1932, in Winnipeg, Manitoba. He followed his older brother, Frank, east to play first-class amateur hockey in Ontario.

As much as anyone, Andy helped develop the hockey renaissance in New York City during the 1950s, and it seemed almost heretical for the Rangers to trade him to Toronto. After his feuds with Imlach, Andy began to lose his touch. He was drafted by the Pittsburgh Penguins when the Steel City sextet entered the NHL in 1967.

While still displaying flashes of the old brilliance, Andy no longer had the legs to enable him to keep up with the play. He later quit the NHL and played briefly in Switzerland. When the World Hockey Association planted a franchise in Vancouver he returned to the ice wars as coach, although an eye injury suffered in a home accident in 1973 limited his vision by 80 percent in his right eye.

Nevertheless, Andy returned to action once more in 1974 with the Vancouver Blazers and actually was a dominant factor for the seven games in which he played, but a contract dispute with management finally inspired him to pack it in once and for all.

Bathgate returned to Toronto where he went into the golf business and also became involved with agricultural investments. He never did get completely away from the rinks. He soon joined the Toronto edition of the NHL Old-timers. Late in the summer of 1981 Andy took part in a hockey tourney with members of the original six NHL teams. "He looked like he could have stepped right back into the NHL today," said tourney director Gerry Patterson, "and been a superstar." He was voted into the Hockey Hall of Fame in 1978.

Class was Andy Bathgate's hallmark—as a teenager, as a big-leaguer and as an NHL old-timer. If ever a man was a credit to the game Bathgate was it.

95 Alex Connell
(1924–1937)

Ottawa, the capital of Canada, spawned many an exceptional hockey player but few were better than Alex Connell, who tended goal for the Ottawa Senators, Detroit Falcons and, finally, the Montreal Canadiens in a National Hockey League career spanning thirteen years.

Playing for Ottawa in 1927–28 he set a league record of *six consecutive shutouts.* Like his Ottawa neighbor, Clint Benedict, he played on Stanley Cup-winning teams in two different cities—for the Ottawa Senators and the Montreal Maroons.

Connell's career record, 1.99 goals-against average, is astonishing under any set of circumstances. After helping the Senators win the Stanley Cup in 1927 he amassed 15 shutouts the following season as well as a remarkable goals-against average of 1.30. Connell had permitted but 57 goals in forty-four games. His record-breaking shutout run spanned 446 minutes and 9 seconds.

Alex Connell was born February 8, 1902, in Ottawa, and seemed destined for a career as either a lacrosse or baseball player. He turned to professional hockey with the Senators in 1924 and played for Ottawa until 1932 when he had a brief fling with the Detroit Falcons. It was during that stint that he became famous for yet another reason. "Alec," said Bill Roche, "was the only hockey player to cause the police riot squad to be called out in New York City."

The episode took place in 1932 at the old Madison Square Garden on Eighth Avenue and Fiftieth Street in New York when the Americans were hosting the Detroit Falcons in a game that would decide whether or not the Amerks would go into the playoffs later that spring. At the time, the Amerks were owned by the infamous Bill Dwyer, reputed mob boss, and undisputed King of the Bootleggers in New York as well as several other states.

The game was tied at the end of regulation time, 1–1, and the two teams went into a ten-minute overtime period. With about five minutes left in the period, Detroit received a penalty, giving the Amerks the much-needed advantage in man-power. New York players realized it was their opportunity to take initiative and win the game. It was a must situation.

The red-, white- and blue-clad Americans bore down and administered intense pressure on the Falcons. Red Dutton, then a battling defenseman for New York, took a blistering shot that, according to the goal judge, eluded Connell and rico-cheted in and—just as quickly—out of the net. The red light went on and the Amerks celebrated their "win." But trouble was brewing: the referee, George Mallinson, disallowed the goal. He claimed he had perfect view of the play and the puck never went in. Connell agreed.

During the melee that ensued, the goal judge berated the shocked goaltender with a string of the vilest profanities Connell had ever heard. Connell was not about to stand for any more of that kind of abuse. He skated around back of the net and, taking advantage of the man's nose which was sticking through the mesh, bopped the goal judge directly and resoundingly on his protruding proboscis. This sent the

surprised and infuriated goal judge reeling in his own blood, and started a panic among the security force at the Garden who knew the man to be a "high official in Bill Dwyer's mob."

Alex Connell had unknowingly put his own life in grave danger with one well-placed, ill-timed punch. But Connell was more concerned with the game, and after play was resumed (the goal was not allowed) he held the Americans scoreless and the game ended in a 1–1 deadlock.

As Alex Connell left the ice he noticed for the first time that there were policemen lining the walkway. Everywhere he looked he saw the boys in blue in great force blocking the spectators from approaching the players. When he got into the dressing room and began peeling off his sweaty uniform, two plainclothes detectives walked up, identified themselves to him, and then stood on either side of him, with their guns drawn. It was explained to him that the man he had punched out was Dwyer's right-hand man, and that there might be some serious ramifications if proper precautions were not taken.

Quickly, after he had finished dressing, Connell was shuffled into a waiting taxi and driven, along with his police escort, to the hotel where the team was staying. The cops combed the lobby for suspicious looking characters before bringing in the befuddled Alex Connell. He was then given strict instructions not to leave his room for the remainder of the evening.

Connell recalls how the rest of the evening went: "An old friend was visiting with me that night and after we had talked about the strange goings-on, we decided to leave the hotel to get some sandwiches before I went to bed.

"We went out the front door and had only walked about ten feet when I remembered the cop's warning. Then I noticed there were some people standing around us, one big mean-looking guy looked right at me and came toward us. We ducked into a diner and seated ourselves at separate counters. The large man came in and ordered me to go over to him for questioning. I paid no attention to him, so he repeated his order, adding that if I knew what was good for me I'd do what I was told.

"Then I walked over to him. He demanded, "Aren't you Alex Connell, goalkeeper with the Detroit Falcons?" I replied that I not only did not know who Alex Connell was, but that I'd never heard of any Detroit Falcons.

"After a couple of minutes of him repeating the question and me repeating my answer, he apologized for bothering me and left."

When the cops heard about the incident from the hotel night manager, they decided to stand guard outside Connell's room for the rest of the night.

The next day Connell learned that his quick thinking and fast talking had probably saved him from a one way "ride" with the gunslinging hoodlums.

Connell finished his career in 1937 with the Maroons. Even then, at the age of thirty-six, he was able to produce a nifty 2.37 goals-against average. He then retired, and died May 10, 1958.

96 Allan Stanley
(1948–1969)

Allan Herbert Stanley holds the dubious distinction of being booed out of his NHL home in New York not once but *twice*. No other member of hockey's Hall of Fame can make that statement.

Few who applauded the debonair defenseman in September 1981 at the induction ceremonies in Toronto recalled that Stanley holds the world's record for villification by a professional athlete. Nor did they realize that his ascent to stardom despite such adversity is as much a reason for his induction as was Stanley's pure defensive ability.

If "Big Allan," as we knew him, had told anyone in 1954 that someday he would make it to the Hall of Fame, New York City's Tactical Patrol Force would have rushed him to the Bellevue Hospital psychiatric ward in a straightjacket.

At the time Stanley was a member of the New York Rangers and happened to be the unwilling recipient of the biggest buildup of any hockey player in the Blueshirts' history.

The men responsible for the torrent of ink were Frank Boucher, general manager of the Rangers, and Stan Saplin, the club's creative press agent. Together in the fall of 1948, they created the myth of Stanley's invincibility.

"One night," said Saplin, "Allan was a minor-leaguer in Providence, enjoying a postgame glass of beer with a few teammates at midnight. The next noon he was in Leone's restaurant and being acclaimed, in effect, as the savior of the downtrodden Rangers."

Rangers fans, who had savored the luxury of but one playoff team in seven years, delighted in Stanley's buildup but could not tolerate the letdown that followed. They had expected a combination of Superman and the Incredible Hulk. Instead, they got a defenseman who played D-E-F-E-N-S-E.

To obtain Stanley, the Rangers dispatched three pro players, cash and the rights held by the Rangers to the services of an amateur. The value was estimated at the time to be about $70,000. By today's fiscal standards it would be close to $1,000,000.

In no time at all the "70,000 Rookie" was being chided as the "70,000 Beauty" and then the "70,000 Lemon." None of this would have happened had the Blueshirts been winners, but they hovered between mediocrity and melancholy.

Boucher, who had brought Stanley to New York, appreciated Allan's talents more than most and was upset by the fans' reaction. He decided to spare Stanley any more hurt by playing him only in away games, but that just left the Rangers with a rusty defenseman, and further increased the fans' hostility.

"They'd boo every time I touched the puck. Then they began to boo every time I got on the ice. Why, even the few games when I sat on the bench, they'd yell at me."

The agony endured for six years, with one brief break when the Blueshirts took the Detroit Red Wings to the seventh game of the 1950 Stanley Cup finals before losing. Lynn Patrick was the New York coach at the time and called Stanley his most valuable Ranger.

"Every summer," Stanley once recalled, "I'd think about improving my play the next year and winning the fans over to my side. I was always in hopes that I'd play like Superman."

And so Stanley's agony went on, seemingly interminable, until a cool Wednesday in 1954, when Allan's agony was stilled.

Boucher raced into the Ranger press office and announced with a mixture of anger and relief that he had traded Stanley and forward Nick Mickoski to the Chicago Black Hawks for Bill Gadsby, a high-quality defenseman, and Pete Conacher, a forward.

The trade was as sensational as the original deal for Stanley since Gadsby also was considered a potential star. (As it happened, Gadsby played twenty years in the NHL, never skated for a Cup winner, and was named to the Hall of Fame in 1970.)

Big Allan played two seasons in Chicago with little hint of martyrdom. In the fall of 1956 the Black Hawks gave up and GM Tommy Ivan prepared to send him to the Hawks' minor league affiliate in Buffalo.

Lynn Patrick, who had moved on to Boston, quickly grabbed the "70,000 Beauty" for less than $15,000 and the Bruins were off and running.

Needless to say, Stanley played some of his best games against the Rangers at Madison Square Garden. He played two seasons in Boston and when the Bruins figured Big Allan had had it, Punch Imlach gladly interceded and signed the old geezer for his Toronto Maple Leafs. It was the kind of move that helped brand Imlach a genius.

Stanley skated just as deliberately in Toronto as he had with the Rangers. The difference was that he was now playing before a sophisticated Maple Leaf Gardens audience who appreciated his defensive gifts as much as his boss, Imlach.

It was no coincidence that the Leafs annexed four Stanley Cups with the big guy snowshoeing behind the blue line. Stanley's play had a blend of majesty and intelligence that was both hard and clean. Textbook defense, you might say, the kind that is as rare today as a nickel cup of coffee.

Could Big Allan have achieved the same distinction as a Ranger? Under the circumstances, it would have been a 50–1 shot.

The inescapable problem in New York was frustrated fans who would not—or could not—get off his back.

"There is always a nucleus of fans," said Saplin, "who pay their way in whether their team is a winner or not. They need an outlet, though, for the bitterness that grows within them as failure piles upon failure."

In the eyes of the Ranger faithful, Stanley was an abject failure, a skater who never fulfilled his notices, who would never cut it on Broadway and, needless to say, would never make it to hockey's Hall of Fame.

Welcome, now, to the distinguished company among *Hockey's 100*, Big Allan. Nobody ever beat bigger odds than you.

97 Gump Worsley
(1952–1974)

He looked more like a beer salesman—who enjoyed tasting his product—than a hockey goaltender. His potbelly made it seem like a Herculean task for him to even wave at, let alone nab, the swiftly flying rubber puck. His lack of height gave one the impression that he never could see the shooters what with the bigger men blocking the view in front of him. Nevertheless, Gump Worsley proved to be one of the best at his trade—blocking pucks—and one of the most courageous as well as one of the most unorthodox.

Nothing says it more for Worsley's courage than the fact that he was the very last of quality goalies to play between the pipes without a protective face mask. Nothing says it more for his ability than the fact that he was winner of the Calder Trophy as rookie of the year in 1953 and the Vezina Trophy as top goaltender in 1966 and 1968 (the latter of which was shared with Charlie Hodge). He was named to the First All-Star Team in 1968 and the Second Team in 1966. Gump was formally inducted into the Hockey Hall of Fame in September 1980.

There have been few first-rate netminders more durable than Worsley. He turned pro in 1952 when the National Hockey League embraced but six teams and retired more than two decades later when there were more than twice that number. He was goalie on four Stanley Cup-winning Montreal Canadiens' sextets yet he is best known for his escapades as a member of the New York Rangers between 1952 and 1963.

The Rangers often seemed mired in a subterranean section of the NHL, yet Worsley always seemed to be performing like Horatio at the bridge. New York fans appreciated the roly-poly goalie but his coach, the volatile Phil Watson, was less enthused. Watson constantly singled out Worsley for criticism in one form or another. Despite Watson's harangues, Worsley played splendid goal for the Rangers in the late 1950s, but then the team began to decline.

In his autobiography, *They Call Me Gump*, Worsley admitted that he turned to the bottle to ease the anguish. "I was using the bottle to chase all of those bad games and bad goals. I used to feel like a duck in a shooting gallery."

Worsley's Manhattan miseries ended on June 4, 1963, when he was traded to the Montreal Canadiens. As Gump succinctly put it, "That was the day I got out of the Ranger jailhouse."

Playing for the Canadiens was not exactly utopia for Worsley, at least not at first, but there was no question that he would be an asset. He proved it in the spring of 1965 during the Stanley Cup finals against the Chicago Black Hawks.

After playing the first two games of the series Gump tore a thigh muscle in game three and had to be replaced. The series went down to a seventh and final game with the teams tied at three wins apiece. Gump had been taking injections for his injury and was improving but doubted that he would play in the seventh match.

Prior to the game Worsley was sitting in the Forum lounge when Larry Aubout, the Canadiens' trainer, walked in and told him he *was* playing. "I glanced at my

wife, Doreen, as she ordered a rye and ginger ale—for herself. I could have used one, too, but instead I headed for our dressing room to get ready for the game. Was I nervous? Here I'd been playing pro hockey for fifteen years and finally was getting the big opportunity. This was it. The final game for the Stanley Cup championship. You bet your ass I was nervous.''

Almost immediately, Camille Henry of the Black Hawks skated in alone on Worsley. ''My legs were knocking,'' Worsley admitted. But he made the save and went on to blank the Black Hawks, 4–0.

''Nothing,'' said Worsley, ''has ever matched that thrill. The first Cup victory is always the biggest moment in a hockey player's life. I was the luckiest guy in the world.''

Lorne Worsley was born May 14, 1929, in Montreal. As a kid, Worsley liked Davey Kerr, hero of the Rangers' 1940 Stanley Cup championship team. He got his first break after winning a tryout with the Verdun Cyclones, a junior team from a Montreal suburb, while playing for a second commercial-league club.

In 1949 Worsley was invited to the Rangers' training camp and was assigned to the Rangers' farm team, the New York Rovers of the old Eastern League. He played well and drank well. ''We ran from bar to bar in those days,'' Worsley confessed, ''and you know how many bars there are in New York. About 10,000. After most games we'd go out drinking and stay out until the joints closed at four in the morning. We were always there for the last call.''

Nevertheless, Worsley continued the upward climb: from the Rovers to the New Haven Ramblers of the American League, with stopovers at St. Paul and Saskatoon, before reaching the Rangers.

Although Worsley won the rookie of the year prize in 1953 the Rangers had bought Johnny Bower, a highly regarded minor-leaguer, and installed him in the net the following season ahead of Gump. But Worsley returned to stay the following year and remained a New Yorker until he was dealt to the Canadiens. After a squabble with the Canadiens in 1970 he was picked up by the Minnesota North Stars and concluded his career in April 1974.

Nicknamed Gump because, as a kid, he resembled the cartoon character Andy Gump, Worsley played his 860th regular-season NHL game against the Philadelphia Flyers on April 2, 1974. The final goal—he allowed 2,432 in his NHL career—was scored by Dave Schultz, who was born the year Worsley played his first pro game in 1949.

''That made me feel old,'' said Worsley. ''Too old to consider another comeback.''

He retired and became a scout for the Minnesota North Stars, a position he retained through the mid 1980s. Never did The Gump look like much, but he did know how to stop the puck and his longevity and championship rings attest to the fact that he did his job better than most.

98 Murray Murdoch
(1926–1937)

If ever the Hockey Hall of Fame selection committee was guilty of a miscarriage of justice it was in its failure to nominate Murray Murdoch to its ice pantheon. If for no other reason than the fact that Murdoch was the National Hockey League's first iron-man, he rated entry. But he was more than that. As a New York Rangers left wing, he epitomized the work ethic, was a guiding force on Stanley Cup-winning teams in 1928 and 1933, and later became one of the most respected collegiate coaches in North America.

"Murdoch gave his all to the game," wrote S. Kip Farrington, Jr., in his book *Skates, Sticks and Men.* "He literally ate, slept and breathed hockey. He gave the sport all he had, but he would be the first to admit that hockey has given him a multitude of satisfying rewards in return."

One of those, quite naturally, was his iron-man mark. *Murray never missed a Ranger game for eleven successive seasons,* which amounted to 508 NHL regular-season games and 55 Stanley Cup playoff matches.

When the original Rangers' team was being organized by Conn Smythe in 1926 —Smythe was fired before the season started and replaced by Lester Patrick— Murdoch had just graduated from the University of Manitoba. Smythe liked what he saw of the lad although he couldn't have imagined how durable he would be. Murdoch was in Winnipeg when Smythe was signing other would-be Rangers in Duluth.

Murdoch, who was a newlywed, received a telegram from Smythe. MEET ME HERE IN DULUTH STOP ALL EXPENSES PAID.

To that, Murdoch wired back: IF YOU WANT TO SEE ME COME TO WINNIPEG.

Decades later, Murdoch recalled the fateful rendezvous. "Smythe came to Winnipeg, we talked and he offered me a $1,500 signing bonus and a $5,000 salary. I remember sitting in the lobby of the Fort Garry Hotel, thinking it over, and I was just about to say no when Conn leaned over a coffee table and slowly counted out $1,500 in $100 bills. That clinched it. For a young guy just married and with a summer job selling insurance, that looked like an awful lot of money."

Despite the agreement with Smythe, Murdoch was less than enamoured of the man who was designated to lead the New York sextet. But when Lester Patrick took over as manager and coach, Murdoch became one of the most valuable Rangers. Patrick played him on a line with Billy Boyd and Paul Thompson. It was the New Yorkers' checking line and one of the best there was.

"Murray didn't get the buildup that the modern players receive, but he was a superstar in his own right," said Kip Farrington. "His iron-man record stood as a tribute to his durability and desire."

John Murray Murdoch was born May 19, 1904, in Lucknow, Ontario, and was skating shortly after he learned to walk. He made his first name in the sport while attending the University of Manitoba.

Following the Rangers' 1933 Stanley Cup championship—their second in seven years—Murdoch and other members of the old guard began to falter, although Murray played capably through the 1936–37 season, the last for himself and defenseman Ching Johnson. Shortly thereafter General John Reed Kilpatrick, himself an alumnus of Yale, recommended Murdoch for the job of head coach of the Eli hockey team.

From that point on Murdoch became something of a hockey legend on the collegiate coaching level. "Murray brought to Yale a quiet dignity and professionalism," said Farrington. "The ruddy-faced Canadian, once a handsome, blond-haired centerman, helped popularize the sport at Yale."

Murdoch coached at Yale for twenty-eight years before retiring in 1966. One of Murray's players, Bill Hildebrand, captain of the 1963 squad, said this of his coach: "Murray was one of the greatest college coaches who ever lived, if just from the standpoint of his knowledge of hockey. He knows the game inside out but, most of all, the players respect him because he's a real man in every way."

In 1974 Murdoch was awarded the Lester Patrick Trophy for service to hockey in the United States. He deserved it as much as he deserves to be in the Hockey Hall of Fame.

99 Alex Delvecchio (1950–1974)

When the Detroit Red Wings' "Production Line" is mentioned as one of the most accomplished offensive trios of all time, Sid Abel is invariably noted as the center between Gordie Howe on right wing and Ted Lindsay on the left. And while this was true for a significant period of time, the fact remains that Alex (Fats) Delvecchio was as relevant, if not more so, than his predecessor.

Less abrasive than Abel, Delvecchio nevertheless was a stylist in the clean, competent manner of such respected centermen as Syl Apps and Jean Beliveau.

Delvecchio was a three-time winner of the Lady Byng Trophy (1959, 1966, and 1969) and was voted to the Second All-Star team in 1953. He was also one of the few players to gain All-Star acclaim at two different positions, being named to the All-Star squad as a left wing in 1959.

There was good reason why Fats never made the First Team—during his 23-year National Hockey League career he played mostly in the shadow of such classic centers as Beliveau, Stan Mikita and Henri Richard. Nevertheless, Delvecchio's credentials are evident. He played on three Stanley Cup championship teams and seven first-place clubs. He became captain of the Red Wings in 1961, and scored 20 or more goals in 13 of his seasons.

Delvecchio was polished, both on and off the ice. "Respect, that's the word," said Canadian journalist Earl McRae. "It's not hard to respect Fats Delvecchio." In his 23 seasons with the Wings, Delvecchio was widely known as one of the classiest players around.

He also had durability, missing only 43 games in 22 full seasons. And from 1957 to 1964, Fats played in 490 consecutive games.

Bruce MacGregor, Delvecchio's Red Wings teammate during the late 1960s, also remembers big-number-10's easy and graceful approach to the game. "Alex was a natural athlete," MacGregor said. "His biggest assets were his skating and passing, a fluid skater with an effortless style. I remember him centering for big Frank Mahovlich. Frank had that big, sweeping stride, and it was tough for centers to judge where he'd be for a pass. But Alex would hit him almost every time, right on the money."

Born December 4, 1931, in Fort William, Ontario, Peter Alexander Delvecchio broke onto the Red Wings squad at the tender age of 19 and contributed 15 goals in his rookie campaign as the Wings swept to the Stanley Cup championship. Alex went on to roll up some very impressive statistics in his career, placing himself second to Gordie Howe on all-time NHL lists for seasons, games (1,549), points (1,281), and assists (825). Potting 456 goals as well, Fats currently sits ninth on the all-time scoring list.

His calm but firm demeanor eventually made Fats one of the most suitable candidates to take over the chores behind the bench of a struggling Red Wings team in 1973, and in November of that year, Alex Delvecchio was officially named coach of the 2-9-1 club. His controlled discipline, laced with a healthy respect for

his players as individuals, made Fats successful at his new craft, raising the coma-
tose Detroiters to a level of respectability, and at the same time making life plea-
surable for his troops. He was not averse to picking up some cold cuts and beer
after a game, or taking the team out to dinner after a practice. But rather than being
taken advantage of because of his good naturedness, Delvecchio gained the respect
of his entire team, allowing them to simply go out and do what they were paid to
do: play hockey.

A man of skill, honor and respect, Alex Delvecchio was a realist as well. A poem
that hung on the wall of his office during his term as Red Wings' coach summarized
the precarious nature of the NHL coach and player:

The Indispensable Man

Sometimes when you're feeling important
Sometimes when your ego's in bloom
Sometimes when you take it for granted
You're the best qualified in the room
Take a bucket and fill it with water
Put your hand in it up to the wrist
Pull it out and the hole that's remaining
Is a measure of how much you'll be missed.

Although as dispensable as any other mortal, Alex Delvecchio, and the greatness
that earned him his rank in *Hockey's 100,* is remembered as a pure center and
diligent coach, although he no longer is behind the Red Wings' bench.

100 Pierre Pilote (1955–1969)

One of the most deceptively effective defensemen of modern hockey, Pierre Pilote hardly looked imposing yet managed to deliver many a thumping bodycheck behind the Chicago Black Hawks' blue line. Others have described Pilote's style as elegant and smooth skating. The three Norris Trophys he won (1963, 1964, 1965) as the National Hockey League's best defenseman solidify his claim to fame along with five selections to the First All-Star Team, three to the Second Team and election to the Hockey Hall of Fame in 1975.

He captained the Black Hawks to their last Stanley Cup championship (1961). Pilote played in a total of 890 games, during which he scored 80 goals and 418 assists. He was remarkably rough for a fellow who measured 5'10" and 178 pounds. In 1961 he was the NHL's penalty leader with 165 minutes.

Unlike many of his superior defensive counterparts, Pilote never exuded the brand of confidence that was the hallmark of an all-star. When he came to training camp, no matter how superlative his play had been the previous season, Pilote questioned his ability to make the big club. His return to the Black Hawks for thirteen years confirmed their faith in him.

Pierre Paul Pilote was born December 11, 1931, in Kenogami, Quebec. Considering his background, it is even more remarkable that he developed into so effective a skater. Because a fire had destroyed the local rink, Pilote was unable to find a place to skate between the formative years of fourteen and seventeen when he played his first game of organized hockey.

Pierre polished his game enough to draw the attention of Rudy Pilous, then manager of the St. Catherines Teepees, a Chicago affiliate. The Teepees had plenty of talent then and only Pilous paid much attention to Pierre. "He was little more than a tough kid when I brought him up," says Pilous. "But he worked hard, improved his skating and stickhandling and every phase of his game." Chicago's Buffalo farm club called him up for a two-game trial during the 1951–52 season and he turned pro the next year. When Pierre was recalled for the last nineteen games of the season, he showed enough stability to win an invitation to Chicago's training camp the following fall. He never saw the minors again, a fact that startled most hockey men.

Sometimes Pilote's desire betrayed a mean streak. At least one of these traits was once evident during a Hawks' exhibition game in Baltimore. Dave Richardson, an innocent Baltimore rookie, committed the unpardonable sin of trying to check Pierre during a scrimmage around the Chicago net. Pilote wrapped his arms around the youngster's neck and flung him to the ice. In case Richardson cared to debate the issue, Pierre cruised around him for a few seconds daring a reprisal. When none came, he triumphantly skated back to the play.

A New York fan who was watching the game turned to a friend and summed up the majority opinion on Pierre Pilote.

"That guy is a dirty, filthy hockey player," the fan said furiously. "But brother, I wish he was on our team."

One of Pilote's problems was that the Black Hawks never repeated a Stanley Cup victory after the 1961 triumph although the Chicago club was sprinkled with stars. During the 1967–68 season he collected 1 goal and 36 assists and then was traded to the Toronto Maple Leafs. He played one season for the Maple Leafs and then packed it in, although he had been drafted by the Buffalo Bisons of the American League. He realized that he didn't have it and chose not to embarrass himself for a minor league paycheck.

Following his retirement from the NHL, Pilote became involved in a number of businesses including a car dealership, a laundry and ultimately luggage manufacturing.

In retrospect, he said his selection to the Hockey Hall of Fame was "the biggest hockey thrill" and, of course, the Stanley Cup win was fun. But he retained the anger over the fact that he couldn't finish his career in Chicago. He once told Toronto author Rick Boulton:

"Loyalty in hockey doesn't mean a thing but I don't carry a grudge. It was a fair exchange. I gave everything I had to the game and it gave me everything. Hockey owes me nothing. I owe it nothing."

Pilote is owed something—a position among *Hockey's 100*.

Honor Roll

George Armstrong
Irvin "Ace" Bailey
Donald "Dan" Bain
Marty Barry
Red Berenson
Dickie Boon
Emile "Butch" Bouchard
George "Buck" Boucher
Russell Bowie
Harry "Punch" Broadbent
John Bucyk
Billy Burch
Harry Cameron
Neil Colville
Samuel "Rusty" Crawford
Jack Darragh
Allan "Scotty" Davidson
Cy Denneny
Charles Drinkwater
Thomas Dunderdale
Tony Esposito
Arthur Farrell
Frank Foyston
Herb Gardiner
Jimmy Gardner
Rod Gilbert
Hamilton "Billy" Gilmour
Frank "Moose" Goheen
Mike Grant
Wilfred "Shorty" Green
Silas Griffis
George Hainsworth
Joseph Hall
George Hay
William "Riley" Hern
Hap Holmes
George "Tom" Hooper
George "Red" Horner
Henry "Harry" Howell
John "Bouse" Hutton
Harry Hyland
Ernest "Moose" Jackson
Harvey "Busher" Jackson
Elmer Lach
Jacques Laperriere
Jean "Jack" Laviolette

Hugh Lehman
Jacques Lemaire
Percy LeSueur
Harry Lumley
Jack Marshall
Frank McGee
Billy McGimsie
Duncan "Mickey" McKay
George McNamara
Patrick "Paddy" Moran
Edward "Reg" Noble
Harry Oliver
Bernie Parent
Joseph Lynn Patrick
Tommy Phillips
Harvey Pulford
Frank Rankin
Jean Ratelle
Ken Reardon
George Richardson
Gordon Roberts
Arthur Ross
Blair Russell
Ernest Russell
J. D. "Jack" Ruttan
Serge Savard
Fred Scanlan
Earl Seibert
Oliver Seibert
Albert "Babe" Siebert
Darryl Sittler
Alfred Smith
Reginald "Hooley" Smith
Thomas Smith
Russell "Barney" Stanley
Bruce Stuart
Anatoli Tarasov
Cecil "Tiny" Thompson
Vladislav Tretiak
Norm Ullman
Jack Walker
Marty Walsh
Harry Watson
Harry Westwick
Fred Whitcroft
Gordon "Phat" Wilson

Ten Best Playoff Performers

1. *Maurice Richard:* The Rocket's red glare was invariably more evident in the playoffs than at any time during the season.
2. *Gordie Howe:* Some have disparaged Howe for his failure to score big goals during the Stanley Cup rounds but Gordie was the leading playoff scorer *no fewer than six times in his career.*
3. *Dickie Moore:* Twice the leading playoff scorer, Moore had his last hurrah with the St. Louis Blues after twice retiring and, despite gimpy legs, still produced an astonishing 7 goals and 7 assists in eighteen games.
4. *Billy Smith:* The best clutch playoff goaltender of all time, Smith has been a major reason why the New York Islanders won four consecutive Stanley Cup championships between 1980 and 1983. Smith won the Conn Smythe Trophy as the most valuable player of the 1983 playoff round. His performance in defeating the Edmonton Oilers, 2-0, in the first game of the 1983 finals is regarded as a Stanley Cup classic. Smith shut out Wayne Gretzky in the four straight games of the 1983 finals.
5. *Bobby Orr:* The Bruins' extraordinary defenseman scored the Cup-winning goal in the 1970 clincher against St. Louis and was equally dominating for Boston when the Bruins won the Cup again in 1972.
6. *Ted Kennedy:* When the Maple Leafs were in a jam during the halcyon years of the late 1940s, Kennedy could be counted upon to produce the big play. He played on five Stanley Cup winners.
7. *Nels Stewart:* When the Montreal Maroons won the Stanley Cup in 1926, Stewart scored 6 goals. *No other player scored more than one.* Ole Poison always was a threat in the postseason tourney.
8. *Syl Apps:* The stalwart Maple Leafs captain was chiefly responsible for the ultimate playoff comeback—Toronto won four straight from Detroit after being down three games to none—in 1942, and led the Leafs to Cup wins in 1947 and 1948.
9. *Bill Smith:* Chiefly responsible for the Islanders' four straight Stanley Cup championships (1980–1984), Smith holds records for most games played (123), most wins (85), and most minutes (7,176) of playoff competition.
10. *Jacques Plante:* There never would have been a Canadiens' playoff dynasty without the peerless goalkeeping of Plante. He produced the best goals-against average from the 1956 playoff through the 1960 round.

Ten Best Clutch Scorers

1. *Maurice Richard:* The one shooter any coach would ever want on the ice in sudden-death overtime would be The Rocket. His flair for the dramatic has never been matched.
2. *Mel "Sudden Death" Hill:* A modest scorer for the Boston Bruins during the 1938–39 season, Hill scored a pair of sudden-death goals against the Rangers early in the playoff series and was the overtime winner in the seventh game.
3. *Modere "Mud" Bruneteau:* The Detroit Red Wings and Montreal Canadiens played the longest game ever on March 24, 1936. Bruneteau scored the winner for Detroit four minutes and forty-six seconds after the ninth period began.
4. *Ken Doraty:* Prior to Bruneteau's classic, Toronto Maple Leafs forward Ken Doraty settled what then was the longest game (April 3, 1933) with a goal against Boston at four minutes and forty-six seconds of the sixth overtime.
5. *Howie Morenz:* The Stratford Streak was the Maurice Richard of his era and generally conceded to be the hardest player in the league to stop.
6. *Frank Boucher:* Ever reliable, Boucher paced the New York Rangers to their first Stanley Cup in 1928 with the only goals in a 2–0 win over the Montreal Maroons in the decisive game.
7. *Nels Stewart:* Ole Poison was *the* man for the Montreal Maroons, a shooter of consummate accuracy and one whose clutch skills were underestimated.
8. *Max Bentley:* The manifold skills of The Dipsy Doodle Dandy were amply demonstrated in 1947, 1948, 1949, 1950 and 1951 when the Toronto Maple Leafs were the class of the NHL.
9. *Bryan Hextall:* The foremost Rangers' shooter in the late 1930s and early 1940s, Hextall won the last Stanley Cup for the Blueshirts with a sudden-death goal against the Maple Leafs in April 1940.
10. *Leo Reise, Jr.:* Basically a defensive defenseman with limited scoring talents, Reise emerged as an incredible clutch shooter in the bitter and bloody 1950 Stanley Cup semifinal between the Red Wings and Maple Leafs. With Detroit trailing two games to one, Reise scored a sudden-death goal in the second overtime of game three. He won the series with another overtime goal in the seventh match.

Ten Best Defensive Forwards

1. *Claude Provost:* The eminently clean guardian of the likes of Bobby Hull and other big guns, Provost played on *nine* Montreal Canadiens Stanley Cup winners. They couldn't have done it without him.
2. *Joe Klukay:* Known as "The Duke of Paducah," Klukay labored on the Toronto Maple Leafs late 1940s' Cup winners in the shadow of Syl Apps, et al., but his defensive work and penalty-killing was flawless.
3. *Ed Westfall:* When Bobby Orr and the Big Bad Bruins were winning Stanley Cups in 1970 and 1972, Westfall was neutralizing the enemy aces with magnificent aplomb while managing to score a few himself.
4. *Marty Pavelich:* Complementing the Production Line on the awesome Detroit Red Wings of the 1950s was this slithering center who tormented the foe with his tenacious checking.
5. *Bob Gainey:* The NHL struck the Frank J. Selke Trophy for the best defensive forward in 1978 and Bob Gainey of the Montreal Canadiens won it for the next four consecutive seasons. 'Nuff said.
6. *Bob Nevin:* During the Toronto Maple Leafs' playoff-winning reign of the early 1960s, Bob Nevin's work on right wing went unheralded by the masses but not unnoticed by general manager-coach Punch Imlach.
7. *Nick Metz:* Joe Klukay's alter ego for several years in Toronto, Metz preceded the Duke, playing on Cup winners in 1942 and 1945 before the late 1940s' dynasty gave him a smidgen of prominence.
8. *Tony Leswick:* So effective was Leswick, the New York Ranger, against Gordie Howe that the Detroit Red Wings dealt for him to get him off Howe's back. With Tony on their side, the Wings won three Stanley Cups.
9. *Red Kelly:* Having been an all-star defenseman, Kelly was superbly equipped to play defensive center as he did after being dealt from the Red Wings to the Maple Leafs.
10. *Bryan Trottier:* A latter-day Gordie Howe, Trottier has been the hardest-checking forward of the 1980's. No offensive ace in history has ever been called on to do as many defensive chores, particularly face-offs. Result, among other things, was four straight Stanley Cups for the Islanders from 1980–84.

Ten Best General Managers

1. *Frank Selke, Sr.:* At the close of World War II Selke moved from the Toronto Maple Leafs to the Montreal Canadiens and constructed the foremost dynasty the sport has known.
2. *Conn Smythe:* Selke's mentor, Smythe organized the original New York Rangers and then built the Maple Leafs into a winner. His signal accomplishment was the design of the Stanley Cup winners in 1947, 1948 and 1949.
3. *Bill Torrey:* At a time when the World Hockey Association had decimated NHL rosters in 1972, the New York Islanders were born. Torrey patiently designed the club around brilliant draft choices such as Denis Potvin and Bryan Trottier and produced the fastest dynasty in the history of sports—four straight Stanley Cup championships in 1980, 1981, 1982, and 1983.
4. *Tommy Gorman:* Never has a general manager been successful with more different teams than Gorman. He managed three different Stanley Cup winners (Ottawa Senators, Chicago Black Hawks, Montreal Canadiens) and also provided the New York Americans with a few moments of glory.
5. *Lester Patrick:* Having proven his managerial ability on the west coast, Patrick then took over the Rangers from Conn Smythe and provided New Yorkers with a magnificent team for more than a decade.
6. *Jack Adams:* The Detroit Red Wings during the 1930s and 1940s were among the NHL's most consistently dominating teams. Adams created the farm system that delivered Gordie Howe, et al., to Detroit.
7. *Sam Pollock:* Although the Canadiens' machine might have faltered after Selke's retirement, Pollock redesigned it, assuring that Montreal would remain a major contender throughout the 1970s.
8. *Art Ross:* One of the most creative hockey thinkers, Ross developed an endless series of aces, starting with Eddie Shore and culminating with the Boston Bruins' renowned Kraut Line.
9. *Tommy Ivan:* A crumbling Chicago Black Hawks' franchise was saved from complete destruction by Ivan, who rebuilt a farm system that led to the Windy City's last Stanley Cup in 1961.
10. *Punch Imlach:* The retirement of Conn Smythe left the Maple Leafs aimlessly fluttering in the 1950s. Imlach resurrected the club and produced four Stanley Cup winners in the 1960s.

Ten Best Coaches

1. *Al Arbour:* When Arbour took control of the New York Islanders they were at a subterranean level. He patiently guided them to a position of eminence and respect while winning three consecutive Stanley Cups in the process. Seasoned critics assert that Arbour's generalship of an injury-riddled team in the 1983 playoffs—especially in the finals against the Edmonton Oilers—was one of the best coaching jobs ever.

2. *Scotty Bowman:* Arbour's mentor when the two were with the St. Louis Blues, Bowman won four consecutive Stanley Cups for the Montreal Canadiens (from 1976 through 1979). More recently, he demonstrated his ability by creating a renaissance with the Buffalo Sabres. He was an effective martinet.

3. *Hector "Toe" Blake:* It is enough to say that Blake guided the Montreal Canadiens to *eight* Stanley Cup championships, including a run of five straight from 1956 through 1960.

4. *Hap Day:* The man who engineered the greatest comeback in Cup history (1942 vs. the Detroit Red Wings), Day coached five Stanley Cup winners, including a then unprecedented run of three in a row in the late 1940s.

5. *Lester Patrick:* Patrick's name is etched on three Stanley Cups, once with the Victoria Cougars and twice with the New York Rangers. He was innovative and inspiring.

6. *Dick Irvin:* After coaching the Maple Leafs to a Stanley Cup in 1932, Irvin later won three Cups for the Canadiens. He harnessed Maurice Richard and produced magnificently exciting "firewagon-style" teams.

7. *Jack Adams:* Sometimes too volatile for his own good, Adams nevertheless produced a number of winners, including three Stanley Cup champions for the Detroit Red Wings.

8. *Tommy Ivan:* When Jack Adams molded the Red Wings into a contender in the early 1950s it was Ivan who masterminded Stanley Cup wins in 1950, 1952 and 1954.

9. *Punch Imlach:* Carrying the dual title of general manager and coach never bothered Imlach. Apart from his four Stanley Cups, he demonstrated that older skaters could be resurrected and turned into big winners.

10. *Anatoli Tarasov:* The "father of Soviet hockey," Tarasov demonstrated to the North Americans that European creativity could be used to advantage in the NHL. His teams were among the first to persuade both Canadian and American fans that the best hockey was not necessarily played on this side of the Atlantic.

Ten Best Defensive Defensemen

1. *Doug Harvey:* Best known for his total ice generalship, Harvey was the centerpiece of the successful Montreal Canadiens' club in the 1950s because of his defensive excellence.
2. *Tim Horton:* Somewhat less creative than Harvey, Horton nevertheless patrolled his side with diligence and power during the Toronto Maple Leafs' golden era of the early 1960s.
3. *Eddie Shore:* Shore's versatility as a rushing defenseman with the Boston Bruins has beclouded his crunching play behind the blue line.
4. *Ching Johnson:* The towering New York Ranger spent little time rushing when there was so much bodychecking to be done. He was the best Manhattan has ever seen.
5. *Hap Day:* A vastly superior intelligence (in relation to most other defensemen) gave Day an advantage which he exploited to the full on the Maple Leafs of the early 1930s.
6. *Emile Bouchard:* Overshadowed by the Punch Line, "Butch" Bouchard was the first of the grand post-World War II Canadiens' defensemen who made life infinitely easier for Vezina-winner Bill Durnan.
7. *Jack Stewart:* There were few stronger men, or more emphatic hitters or diligent defense players than "Black Jack." The Detroit Red Wings would have been impotent without him.
8. *Dit Clapper:* The Bruins' defense centered around this stately and thoughtful athlete who was quite willing to use his body as well as his head.
9. *Jim Thomson:* When the Toronto Maple Leafs won three straight Stanley Cups (1947, 1948, 1949), the defense of Thomson and Gus Mortson was impenetrable. Mortson rushed more often. Thomson quietly did the defensive work.
10. *Ken Morrow:* The quintessential defensive defenseman, Morrow not only helped the United States team win a gold medal at the 1980 Olympics but he moved right up to the New York Islanders and helped the National Hockey League club to four straight Stanley Cup championships.

Ten Best Little Men

1. *King Clancy:* There never was a more resilient defenseman who managed to distill humor and courage with his artistry. The fact that he never won a fight during his lengthy NHL career never tempered his pugnacity.
2. *Roy "Shrimp" Worters:* Although the goaltending theory has always been "the more net filled the better," Worters amply demonstrated that a tiny man with catlike moves could play as well—or better—than the best of the big ones. Worters was the best of the little men and, in the opinion of some, the best of them all.
3. *Ted Lindsay:* Notorious for his vicious use of the stick, Lindsay nevertheless could handle his dukes and was one of the most dangerous offensive left wings in the game. "Old Scarface" was never hampered by his size.
4. *Henri Richard:* A French-Canadian version of Lindsay, the "Pocket Rocket" was every inch as tough as his brother Maurice and a remarkable playmaker to boot. The mind boggles at the thought of Henri Richard's ability inside Jean Beliveau's body.
5. *Yvan Cournoyer:* Never one to raise a fist in anger, the "Roadrunner" exploited speed above all. His pacifism never proved to be a deterrent.
6. *Denis Savard:* This slippery little Chicago Black Hawks' centerman effectively dodged all determined efforts by opposing checkers, to tally 87 assists and 119 points in the 1981–82 season, his second in the NHL. Savard proved sufficiently quick and tough to become the mainstay of the Black Hawks' attack through the 1983–84 campaign.
7. *Pat "Whitey" Stapleton:* Remarkably agile, this Chicago Black Hawks defenseman pressed plenty of muscle into his miniframe. He was an unsung hero during Chicago's golden hockey era of the early 1960s.
8. *Aurel Joliat:* A ferocious five-feet-six and 135 pounds, Joliat earned the nickname "Mighty Mite" with his amazingly tough, physical style. A marvelous stickhandler and passer, as well as a lethal shot, Aurel combined finesse and feistiness to become one of the most respected players of his time.
9. *Buddy O'Connor:* The one-time member of the Montreal Canadiens' "Razzle-Dazzle" line, this slightly built center became an NHL hero after being traded to the New York Rangers. He went on to miss the scoring title by a single point, but captured both the Hart and Lady Byng trophies during the 1947–48 campaign.
10. *Harold "Mush" March:* A fifteen-year veteran of the Chicago Black Hawks, March is best remembered for a shot he fired at Detroit goalkeeper Wilf Cude on April 10, 1934. The score was tied at the time when Marsh dented the twine at 10:05 of the second overtime period to give the Black Hawks their first Stanley Cup championship.

Ten Best Hockey Arenas

1. *Boston Garden:* Reeking with nostalgia and never modernized in the manner of the Montreal Forum or Maple Leaf Gardens, the Bruins' home is the Ebbets Field of the NHL and, hopefully, will remain that way.
2. *Maple Leaf Gardens:* The jewel of Canadian arenas, "The House That Conn Smythe Built" has retained much of the flavor of opening night in 1931. Introduction of organ music has diminished its appeal.
3. *Montreal Forum:* Like its Toronto counterpart, the Forum remains a shrine. Its lobby is graced with bronze castings of the Canadiens' top heroes. Post-World War II improvements have embellished the aura.
4. *Chicago Stadium:* Despite its location in a seedy part of town, the Stadium—like Boston Garden—oozes with history. The cavernous interior still echoes with cheers for the Bentleys and Bobby Hull.
5. *Detroit Olympia:* Gone but not forgotten, the showcase "theater" for Gordie Howe, Ted Lindsay and Sid Abel, Olympia also is remembered for Pete Cusimano, the octopus-thrower at Red Wing games.
6. *Old Madison Square Garden:* Located at Forty-ninth Street and Eighth Avenue, a block from Times Square, the old Garden had terrible sight lines from the side balcony, but a magnificent ambiance that made one love New York.
7. *Quebec Colisée:* "The House That Jean Beliveau Built" has been enlarged since "Le Gros Bill" played for the Quebec (Junior) Citadelles. The 100 percent Gallic crowd is unmatched throughout the league.
8. *The Checkerdome:* Although it has been completely refurbished, the Checkerdome (originally, the St. Louis Arena) dates back to 1929. Its loaf-of-bread center and two adjacent towers mark it unique in its field.
9. *The Spectrum:* One of the least flawed hockey rinks, the Spectrum is equally appreciated by fans and media alike. There is good seating for all, and rooters, they say, will boo the loser of a wheelchair race.
10. *Nassau Coliseum:* Not only are even the cheapest seats obstruction-free but the sky boxes and press areas provide the best views possible. While relatively new, the Coliseum has the good feel of a venerable arena.

Ten Best Referees of All-time

1. *John Ashley:* Invariably calm and always in complete command of the ice, Ashley was both distinguished in appearance and performance. The fact that he had been a professional defenseman for many years added to his insights.
2. *Mickey Ion:* When this man told a colleague, in a rink jammed with 15,000 frenzied fans, "There are only two sane people here—you and me," he was betraying the good sense that made him a superior whistle-blower.
3. *Bill Chadwick:* Although sightless in one eye, this courageous New York-born official saw more than most refs. He backed down from no one and made some of the most difficult calls in critical situations of any of his ilk. When Detroit owner Jim Norris tried to have him fired, it proved he was a winner.
4. *King Clancy:* Like Ashley, Clancy had been a defenseman who could translate his playing experience to hockey's penal system. His ebullience and humor gave him an edge over his more serious brethren.
5. *Bobby Hewitson:* Remarkably, this gentle, perceptive fellow was the sports editor of the *Toronto Telegram* while a full-time NHL referee. He handled a whistle as well as he did an editorial pencil.
6. *Red Storey:* A flame-haired, towering referee, Storey imparted his knowledge as both a football and hockey star to the rinks. Controversial to a fault, Storey cut short his own career, resigning in protest over an "off the record" critique made by NHL president Clarence Campbell.
7. *Jack Mehlenbacher:* "The Sleeper" of referees, Mehlenbacher did his job so quietly, effectively, and efficiently, that no one ever bothered to acknowledge his superiority, other than the players, who respected his work.
8. *Mike Rodden:* It is no accident that this referee from hockey's earlier era is in the Hall of Fame. Curiously, Rodden, like Bobby Hewitson, also was a sports editor for a Canadian daily.
9. *Cooper Smeaton:* An official who saw things clearly and saw them whole, Smeaton was so distinguished a referee that he was later named a trustee of the Stanley Cup.
10. *Frank Udvari:* An absolutely abysmal (even he'd admit that) whistle-blower in his early years, Udvari eventually ripened into one of the very best. Long after his retirement, he was summoned from the stands at Nassau Coliseum to pinch-hit for an injured referee. Although wearing his suit pants and borrowed skates, Udvari proceeded to officiate one of the best games ever handled in the building by any referee before or since.

6839